AFTER HITCHCOCK

Edited by David Boyd and R. Barton Palmer

AFTeR HiTCHCOCK

INFLUENCE, IMITATION, AND INTERTEXTUALITY

University of Texas Press ◆ Austin

Unless otherwise credited, the photographs in this volume are courtesy of the Academy of Motion Picture Arts and Sciences.

A portion of Chapter 2 appears in *Crowds, Power, and Transformation in Cinema* (2006), by Lesley Brill. Courtesy of Wayne State University Press.

"For Ever Hitchcock: Psycho and Its Remakes" by Constantine Verevis appears in altered form in the "Authors" chapter of Film Remakes, by Constantine Verevis, courtesy of Edinburgh University Press (*www.eup.ed.ac.uk*).

Requests for permission to reproduce material from this work should be sent to:
> *Permissions*
> University of Texas Press
> P.O. Box 7819
> Austin, TX 78713-7819
> www.utexas.edu/utpress/about/bpermission.html

♾ The paper used in this book meets the minimum requirements of ANSI/NISO Z39.48-1992 (R1997) (Permanence of Paper).

Library of Congress Cataloging-in-Publication

After Hitchcock : influence, imitation, and intertextuality / edited by David Boyd and R. Barton Palmer. — 1st ed.
    p.   cm.
  Includes bibliographical references and index.
  ISBN-13: 978-0-292-71337-6 (cl. : alk. paper)
  ISBN-10: 0-292-71337-1
  ISBN-13: 978-0-292-71338-3 (pbk. : alk. paper)
  ISBN-10: 0-292-71338-X
  1. Hitchcock, Alfred, 1899—Criticism and interpretation. 2. Hitchcock, Alfred, 1899—Influence. 3. Thrillers (Motion pictures, television, etc.)—History and criticism. I. Boyd, David, 1944– II. Palmer, R. Barton, 1946–
  PN1998.3.H58A68 2006
  791.43'0233092—dc22   2006001351

Contents

AFTER HITCHCOCK

Introduction

David Boyd and R. Barton Palmer

Hitchcock . . .

The half century or so of Alfred Hitchcock's career spanned crucial eras in the history of world and, especially, Hollywood cinema: from the refinement of the silents' ability to tell feature-length stories with images in the years before the coming of sound; to the reconfiguring of film style necessitated by the conversion to "talking pictures" a few years later; to the refinements, both narrative and visual, made in the so-called Classic Hollywood text during the 1930s and 40s; to the advent in the next decade of wide-screen cinematography (which required further adjustments to "corporate" techniques); to the industry's accommodation with its erstwhile rival, television; to the changes in the marketplace that followed in the wake of the weakening and eventual abandonment of the Production Code in 1966.

Perhaps most important, however, Hitchcock's impressive oeuvre of more than fifty feature films reflects the constant (and often unexpected) evolution of cinematic subject matter and treatment, broadly conceived—both the kind of stories the cinema chose to tell and also the manner of their telling. The conventions of Victorian melodrama that held sway in his youth made way for a succession of modern forms and practices of storytelling to which Hitchcock responded in a strongly individualistic fashion. Thus Hitchcock's continually evolving approach to filmmaking, strongly influenced at the outset by German Expressionism, came to reflect not only several subsequent and distinct waves of realism, but also modernist and even postmodernist styles (the influence of the latter being quite evident in his last two projects). From his first silent features made in late-1920s Britain to his last post-studio production (1976)

made in the United States, however, Hitchcock not only exemplified and reacted to changes in the cinema; he also affected the course these were to take.
Of course, he was born too late (and arguably in the wrong country) to be an
innovating pioneer on the model of a D. W. Griffith or Sergei Eisenstein. Yet
like them, his film practice may be conceived as a dialectic that yokes entertainment and expressive forms of authorship. This instability of purpose and
resulting rhetoric heavily marks his body of work and career. Specifically, any
fair account of the medium's first century must acknowledge the many ways
in which Hitchcock helped sustain and further filmmaking as a commercial
enterprise—and as a respected art form as well.

It is thus hardly surprising that many aspects of Hitchcock's accomplishments have received a good deal of attention in recent years, as film scholars
have focused their attention less on the idealism and master schemes of subject
positioning theory and more on delimited historical questions. Chief among
such developing historicisms have been more nuanced forms of auteurist inquiry that, avoiding the distorting excesses of neoromanticism, have attained
a substantial popularity on the current critical scene, as accounts of the careers
of well-known directors have proliferated. The occasion of Hitchcock's birth
centenary in 1999 saw the publication of many important works, recalling the
flurry of discussion his films received from the *Cahiers* and *Movie* critics nearly
a half century earlier. Of course, the films, especially those made in Hollywood, have now been the subject of a constant stream of close theoretical and
textual analysis for more than three decades. Scholarly interest in Hitchcock,
we can affirm, is hardly slackening. In fact, his may well constitute the most
discussed body of films ever made.

Because it has focused on him for the most part, however, this valuable
criticism has generally acknowledged only in passing his impact on other filmmakers, on genres and fashions, even on the field of cinema studies as an academic discipline. It is an often acknowledged, but as yet largely unexamined,
fact that Hitchcock's films have exerted, and continue to exert, a wider and
more profound influence than those of any other director. One obvious sign
of this has been that the term "Hitchcockian" has entered the international
language of academicians and film publicists alike as a common way of referring to a certain kind of cinematic narrative characterized by heightened effects of "suspense," the much-debated concept that Hitchcock co-opted to
describe both his designs on the spectator's emotions and his peculiar talent
for engaging them. No other director has been accorded a similar linguistic
honor.

How did Hitchcock come to wield the influence that he now does? The short answer to this difficult question is that Hitchcock had achieved a position of hitherto unparalleled preeminence for a director who was not also his own main performer (as in the case of Charles Chaplin). Hitchcock's prominence, at least in part, resulted for reasons beyond his control. Most importantly, changing critical fashions made his work more highly valued, often through the unsolicited sponsorship of strategically placed critics. But much of the credit for this achievement must go to Hitchcock himself.

The director-star who ceaselessly promotes himself as a brand name in order to market his films and solidify his place within the industry is a common figure on the contemporary movie scene. The prominence achieved today by many who remain behind the camera is arguably the most obvious sign of how moviemaking has changed its public face since the studio period, when directors, by and large, were more or less invisible craftsmen. Today, the director-star, above all else, plays an important role in the marketing of films, as the sophisticated are regularly guided in their viewing by the director's name above (or immediately below) the title. Associated with the New Hollywood of the post-studio era, such imprints of authorship are often (or often thought to be) reliable guides to subject matter, visual style, and themes. In any event, directors such as Steven Spielberg, Martin Scorsese, Spike Lee, and Quentin Tarantino have become as well known and as familiar as the biggest screen stars of the current era.

Self-promoting directors, however, were also a discernible, if rarer and more problematic, presence during the Classic Hollywood period—from the beginnings of the studio system in the early 1920s through to its decisive transformation (some would say collapse) by the beginning of the 1970s. D. W. Griffith, Cecil B. DeMille, Ernst Lubitsch, and Frank Capra (just to take some of the most obvious examples) campaigned, with varying results, to make sure that their films were considered, within Hollywood and by its eager public, as decisively marked by their creative, personal touch. However, one director proved phenomenally successful in shaping his public image to commercial and critical advantage. That was Alfred Hitchcock, the British expatriate and renowned "master of suspense" (a title he may not have created, but whose use he certainly encouraged).

In his *Alfred Hitchcock: The Making of a Reputation,* Robert E. Kapsis demonstrates that a full-length book could indeed be devoted to Hitchcock's efforts at various forms of self-fashioning (efforts which were substantially aided, of course, at different times by well-placed others).[1] As a mature artist in the 1950s and 60s, Hitchcock strove to cultivate his image with both paying customers and critics, particularly those in New York and Paris, who then had the power to take his reputation within the film culture of his era to a higher level. From the very beginning of his career in Britain some three decades earlier, however, Hitchcock aimed to establish himself as a commercially successful director in a national film industry subject, because of unstable market conditions and unsustained attempts at government support, to unpredictable oscillations between boom and bust. During his collaboration with producer Michael Balcon at the Gaumont British Picture Corporation, for example, Hitchcock began to specialize in the film genre that would become most associated with his career: the suspense thriller.

This genre offered him a number of advantages, and seizing upon it as a base of practice must be counted a wise and well-considered career move. Hitchcock certainly recognized that value of this early decision, for he sought to reestablish himself in this genre after the perhaps inevitable move to Hollywood. On the one hand, the thriller's literary connections might be seen as a direct appeal to middlebrow viewers, a reflection of the director's artistic interests. In the hands of Hitchcock and Balcon, the film thriller brought to the screen one of the most popular and celebrated forms of contemporary British fiction. For his famous sextet of thrillers made at Gaumont, Hitchcock adapted for the screen, among lesser known writers of the age, John Buchan, W. Somerset Maugham, and Joseph Conrad, an impressive trio of literary heavyweights.

On the other hand, the thriller form offered commercial advantages. Thrillers could be made effectively without the expensive production values of competing American "A releases." Neither high-priced stars nor elaborate sets were necessary for success at the box office. The form could make also good use of the stylistic elements that Hitchcock, in his first films, had adopted from the German cinema of the time, particularly the emphasis on expressive images that forcefully communicate without the need for extensive dialogue. Hitchcock's desire to have himself accepted as a director with "artistic" interests was served by such Continental connections—and more directly by his cultivation of the members of the British Film Society, whose meetings he began attending as his standing as Britain's finest director became quickly established by the end of the 1920s.

Working (though never exclusively) within the confines of the suspense thriller, moreover, Hitchcock could more easily concentrate or simplify his public image as a director with talent, associating his success with an infinitely repeatable form that was, in effect, "pre-sold." It was during the early stages of his career that he also fashioned another kind of image, the semi-abstract line drawing of his unmistakable portly figure that he then used for decades as a publicity device (much like the advertising icons used to simplify the marketing of today's so-called "high concept" productions). Hitchcock would later seek to define his version of the thriller through complex, perhaps even contradictory, definitions, of its affect, just as his contemporary Sergei Eisenstein sought to do with his theory of a montage of attractions. Though seeking commercial success and the various kinds of stability it would bring, Hitchcock was eager to be known as a director of quality, on the model of his European colleagues in Russia, Germany, and France. Through his association with the "artistic" directors of the British Film Society, he sought to distinguish himself from filmmakers uninterested in being more than craftsmen.

Through his several publications in the popular press, Hitchcock sought to impress those who, like himself, believed that film was an art form, not just mass entertainment. But that art form "included" the notion of a presiding creator inextricable from the very materiality of the text, as Hitchcock's eventual practice of weaving an image of himself into each new production established. This game of "find the director," as Thomas M. Leitch has termed it, made every new Hitchcock into a puzzle to be solved, one that led viewers to look eagerly for the director's now familiar face and figure (a persona and image—perhaps we should say logo—that he had carefully crafted).[2]

After he moved to Hollywood in 1939, Hitchcock, as Kapsis shows, continued these activities for the benefit of his new American audience, frequently discussing in radio interviews and journal articles his theories of suspense, while taking full advantage of the Hollywood publicity machine that was well-equipped to refine his image, increasing its box-office appeal. During the 1950s, Hitchcock's specialization in the suspense thriller worked against any acceptance of his films as more than riveting diversion by New York critics such as Bosley Crowther, who had become enamored of social realist forms of filmmaking in the wake of the life-and-death seriousness of the Second World War. Identified as a genre filmmaker, Hitchcock was denied the cultural and intellectual importance of directors like Fred Zinnemann and William Wyler, who in films such as *The Search* (1948) and *The Best Years of Our Lives* (1946) were applauded for engaging directly with the difficult social and political issues of the postwar era. Hitchcock showed little interest in this trend—even his *The Wrong Man* (1957), despite its authentic documentary stylizations and studied deglamorization in the tradition of Italian Neorealism, is more committed to exploring the mysteries of individual psychology than the social themes it only hesitatingly raises.

But at this point in his career, Hitchcock was fortunate to be taken up by the critics/filmmakers of the French New Wave such as François Truffaut,

Jean-Luc Godard, Eric Rohmer, and Claude Chabrol, who defended him as a master stylist and as a storyteller of intellectual, even spiritual depth, whose deceptively simple narrative surfaces were held to conceal the more complex thematic meditations of the committed moralist. As Chabrol and Rohmer put it in their famous 1957 study, which was the first book-length study devoted to him, "Hitchcock is one of the greatest *inventors of form* in the entire history of the cinema," and, not coincidentally, "an entire moral universe has been elaborated on the basis of this form and by its rigor." [3] The enthusiasm of the French for a filmmaker whom they saw as much more than a popular entertainer was soon shared by Robin Wood, the most articulate spokesman for a new generation of British critics, associated with the journal *Movie*, who also valued visual style. For Wood, Hitchcock was a master of the "cinematic," in the sense that he showed great talent in communicating meaning visually, not relying overmuch on the script. However, Hitchcock was also a storyteller of extraordinary talent who created characters of psychological depth (in the literary tradition of E. M. Forster's advocacy of "roundness"), putting them in stories that test moral values.

In Wood's view, an important element of Hitchcock's artistry was that he was able to deeply involve the viewer in these stories of moral failing and (at least often) ultimate redemption. Thus, Hitchcock's films met the criterion of thematic seriousness advocated by noted literary critic F. R. Leavis, a major influence at the time. As a popular entertainer, Wood argued, Hitchcock even bore comparison with a more famous and celebrated English genius and crowd-pleaser: William Shakespeare. In his last years, Hitchcock continued to enjoy the good opinion of academic and journalistic critics (including that of more than a few who, like Pauline Kael, had been converted to a taste for his work). He also received honors of all kinds from those within the industry. When he died in 1980, Hitchcock was, beyond dispute, the world's most famous director. He had overseen the production of a justly celebrated body of work within the radically different institutional contexts of two national cinemas—and had succeeded as well in establishing himself as an artist to be taken seriously. Thus, it is scarcely surprising that in the years since his death, Hitchcock's films have continued to exert a profound influence on other filmmakers and on film culture more generally.

. . . and After

Because of theoretical developments on the critical scene, now is a particularly propitious time for recognizing and analyzing the breadth of Hitchcock's influence, particularly the connection between his films and those of other directors. Different ways of usefully understanding and anatomizing the kinds of connections that may obtain between texts have been taken up within cinema studies in recent years, as the theoretical work of Mikhail Bakhtin, Julia Kristeva, Harold Bloom, Gérard Genette, and Fredric Jameson has emerged to prominence. And yet such key terms as influence, imitation, allusion, and pastiche (which all connect, if diversely, to the more global concept of intertextuality) have rarely, at least in a sustained and detailed fashion, been deployed to describe the "reach" that the work of any director has attained.

During the last decade, cinema studies have witnessed the move, as Robert Stam characterizes it, from "text to intertext." This change of focus takes as its point of departure Bakhtin's central observation about language: namely that every utterance, in ways too innumerable to anatomize, responds to those that have come before, even as it is answered, in turn, by those that follow. What Stam refers to is the shift away from analyzing individual works (formerly conceived as discrete and self-contained entities) to the relations of different kinds that obtain between texts:

> In the broadest sense, intertextual dialogism refers to the infinite and open-ended possibilities generated by all the discursive practices of a culture, the entire matrix of communicative utterances within which the artistic text is situated, and which reach the text not only through recognizable influences, but also through a subtle process of dissemination. . . . The intertext of the work of art, then, may be taken to include not just other artworks in the same or comparable form, but also all the "series" within which the singular text is situated. Any text that has slept with another text, to put it more crudely, has necessarily slept with all the texts the other text has slept with. Intertextuality theory is best seen as an answer to the limitations both of textual analysis and genre theory.[4]

In its exposure of the artificiality and permeability of textual "boundaries," the intertextual perspective provides a powerful description of the textual flow that characterizes the cinema. Intertextual theory certainly finds a suitable object in the multifarious relations of Hitchcock's films to those produced by filmmakers who are in some sense "after" him. In its more radical forms (particularly those developed by Julia Kristeva and Roland Barthes), intertextuality describes the ground of instability and infinite deferral of meaning that characterizes all uses of language in defiance of any individual's attempt to fix the sense of what s/he says. In a more restrictive sense of the term, taken up particularly by structuralist theorists like Gérard Genette, intertextuality provides the tools for analyzing the various relations that obtain among texts whose connections are established by the maker's (or remaker's) intentions. It is this less global meaning of intertextuality that the contributors to this book explore, as they demonstrate that it indeed does provide, in Stam's words, "an answer to the limitations both of textual analysis and genre theory."

The present volume takes a first, collective step toward an assessment of the textual "field" that those who followed Hitchcock have created. Hitchcock's films have been remade (even those of his British period such as *The 39 Steps* and *The Lady Vanishes*), provided with sequels (as in the *Psycho* "franchise"), made the object of respectfully humorous parody (Mel Brooks' *High Anxiety*, for example, is a take-off on *Vertigo* and *Spellbound*), and been redone in complex gestures of repetition and rejection (Francis Coppola's *The Conversation* is connected to the Hitchcockian thriller in general and *Rear Window* in particular). All subsequent productions of this kind are Hitchcockian in some sense; that is, they belong to the textual field that Hitchcock's films have inspired—and they exhibit his influence in some way.

The thirteen essays in this book, all published here for the first time, explore various aspects of that field, commenting on the forms that directorial influence can assume. The concept "after Hitchcock" organizes this book in two ways: as shorthand for "in the manner of" (as in the French concept of *après*) and as a historical signpost. Thus, the contributors to this volume have taken Hitchcock's career as an arbitrary point from which to measure the kind of textual reproduction that characterizes the cinema (and, of course, as intertextual theory has taught us, all forms of language). Most obviously, perhaps, such a heuristic reminds us that the cinematic present may always be understood by a glance backward (with the present text seen as containing, reusing, or challenging those of what Robert Stam terms the matrix in which it is situated). But it also positions textual production to be approached in the opposite direction, looking forward, as it were, and thus encouraging critics to ask interesting questions about both displacement (the rejection or transformation of models) and also succession (the installation of "new waves"). This makes a fundamental point about the role that Hitchcock (both the man and his texts) has played in film history. Thus, for the current generation of filmmakers, the famous director's accomplishments have been not only a source of inspiration or recyclable plenitude, but also at times a roadblock to individuation and growth into self-expression.

These opposed values of the Hitchcockian legacy are most famously (or notoriously, depending of your point of view) illustrated by Brian De Palma's engagement with some of Hitchcock's more celebrated films (and the themes such as voyeurism and misogyny that are often extracted from them). De Palma has often been thought a too-sincere admirer of the director he honored as his *maître* with a series of controversial films that are ostentatiously in the Hitchcockian vein. And yet De Palma's career garnered a huge amount of attention because he so straightforwardly confronted the difficulties and opportunities involved in rewriting Hitchcock through simultaneous gestures of imitation and displacement. Viewers of *Obsession, Dressed to Kill, Blow Out,* and *Body Double* are forced to retrace along with De Palma the paths back to Hitchcock's *Psycho, Vertigo,* and *Rear Window,* even as they discover that these paths finally lead to quite different destinations.

Such a critical perspective benefits from the pioneering work of Harold Bloom, who in his *A Map of Misreading* (which refines the perspective presented earlier in *The Anxiety of Influence*) makes a strong case for the oedipal nature of "belatedness," the sense that a new generation has of "coming after the event." If we substitute the term "director" for Bloom's "poet," then his description of the successor's artistic dilemma usefully describes those who are "after Hitchcock":

> A poet . . . is not so much a man speaking to men as a man rebelling
> against being spoken to by a dead man (the precursor) outrageously
> more alive than himself. A poet dares not regard himself as being *late,*
> yet cannot accept a substitute for the first vision he reflectively judges
> to have been his precursor's also.[5]

In *A Map of Misreading,* Bloom combines rhetorical and psychoanalytical concepts to anatomize the ways in which succeeding texts can be read as answers to those which have come before. The usefulness of such a theoretical model for analyzing the practice of Hitchcock's successors has just begun to be explored.

Across the films produced by the current generation falls Hitchcock's imposing shadow. Similarly, the essays collected here simply cannot avoid discussing Hitchcock even if their official concerns are elsewhere, thereby illustrating a central aspect of intertextuality: its multidirectionality, its de-privileging of what philologists once termed "the source." In his *Palimpsestes,* Genette anatomizes the different forms of "transtextuality," the relations that can obtain between texts, of which the most common—and important—is "hypertextuality."[6] Genette's most important contribution to the current theoretical examination of these issues is to be found in his discussion of this transformative connection, the way in which what he terms "hypotexts" are turned, in a variety of ways, into "hypertexts." Unlike older source theory, the hypo/hypertextual perspective is relational, never reducing what is transformed to inert "material." Similarly, the contributors to this book all return to the director's films from perspectives that relativize them by refusing them the status of art objects that exist somehow "in themselves," as analyzable outside the textual field whose creation they enabled.

In other words, the essays in this book contribute substantially to the continuing evaluation and analysis of the director's oeuvre. In tracing the Hitchcockian element in films that are so different in terms of both narrative and theme, the essays often highlight aspects of the famous director's own work that previously have either been neglected or required further discussion. And, of course, the look forward from the end of his career inevitably leads back to a consideration of its enduring value, providing both new perspectives for analysis and also different frameworks for judgment.

This book does not attempt to survey the entire range of Hitchcock's influence—an impossible task for any single volume. What it does attempt is to offer close analyses of the director's impact on particular films, filmmakers, genres, cycles, and even study of the medium itself. The different essays have been chosen to suggest something of the diversity and range of Hitchcock's impact, and their subjects include Italian, French, and Spanish works, as well as other Hollywood films. The topics considered here range, in historical terms, from the classical Hollywood of the 1940s to filmmaking to the contemporary post-studio, postmodern era. And they vary in kind from a focus on individual films, such as Gus Van Sant's "imitative" shot-by-shot remake of *Psycho,* to the more diffuse effect of Hitchcock on the subsequent history of the thriller, and even to the prominent place his films and the theories about them have come to occupy within the field of cinema studies, generating texts that are not films but theoretical tracts.

Thus, the focus in this volume is not always textual, narrowly conceived. The connection between Hitchcock's films and political violence in the 1960s is examined, as is his importance in the formation of cinematic poststructuralism, particularly as seen in the writings of Raymond Bellour and Slavoj Žižek. From current theoretical perspectives, this volume addresses fundamental questions of authorship and authority, genre and nationality, avant-garde as well as mainstream filmmaking. Our hope is that we have demonstrated here that Hitchcock's hard-won prominence in commercial filmmaking by no means dissipated with his death more than two decades ago, but has been kept alive within cinema culture by the many who have fallen under the spell of his genius and enduring accomplishments.

Notes

1. Robert Kapsis, *Alfred Hitchcock: The Making of a Reputation* (Chicago: University of Chicago Press, 1992).

2. Thomas M. Leitch, *Find the Director and Other Hitchcock Games* (Athens, GA: University of Georgia Press, 1991).

3. Eric Rohmer and Claude Chabrol, *Hitchcock: The First Forty-Four Films,* trans. by Stanley Hochman (New York: Frederick Ungar, 1979), 152.

4. Robert Stam, *Film Theory: An Introduction* (Oxford: Blackwell, 2000), 202.

5. Harold Bloom, *A Map of Misreading* (Oxford: Oxford University Press, 1975), 19.

6. Gérard Genette, *Palimpsestes: La littérature au second degré* (Paris: Seuil, 1982).

Norman (Anthony Perkins) shrinks from what turns out to be the specter of his own murderous assault in *Psycho*.

PART I: *PSYCHO* RECYCLED

Nothing more clearly suggests the extent of Alfred Hitchcock's ongoing influence than the legacy of *Psycho,* quite possibly the single most influential film of the past half century: like Norman Bates' mother, it just refuses to lie down and die. Constantine Verevis and Lesley Brill survey some of the diverse forms of its prolific afterlife. Verevis begins by reconsidering the generally hostile critical reception of Gus Van Sant's 1998 version, and then situates that most literal of remakes within a broader context ranging from the *Psycho* sequels (*Psycho II, III,* and *IV*), to homages and parodies like *Dressed to Kill* and *High Anxiety,* to Douglas Gordon's video installation, *24 Hour Psycho*. Brill then exhaustively examines the Hitchcockian resonances of a particular film, Jonathan Demme's *The Silence of the Lambs* (1991), and raises the central question of why our recognition of those resonances matters.

Van Sant's *Psycho* replicates much of its Hitchcockian model, whose most horrific scenes unfold in a Gothic mansion that is the image of an irrepressible past.

For Ever Hitchcock
Psycho and Its Remakes

Constantine Verevis

Much of the talk leading up to, and following, the release of Gus Van Sant's 1998 remake of the Alfred Hitchcock film *Psycho* (1960) was an expression of outrage and confusion at the defilement of a beloved classic. For fans and critics alike—for *re*-viewers—the *Psycho* remake was nothing more than a blatant rip-off: not only an attempt to exploit the original film's legendary status, but (worse) a cheap *replica* of "one of the best and best known of American films" ("*Psycho:* Saving a Classic"). These viewers consistently privileged the "original" *Psycho* over its remake, or measured the success of the Van Sant remake according to its ability to realize what were taken to be the "essential" elements of the Hitchcock text. This type of reaction seems consistent with a vast majority of critical accounts of film remakes which understand remaking as a one-way process: a movement from authenticity to imitation, from the superior self-identity of the original to the debased resemblance of the copy. Rather than follow these essentialist trajectories, some more recent approaches to cinematic remaking suggest that the remake, in its most general application, might (more productively) be regarded as a specific aspect of a broader and more open-ended intertextuality (see Frow, Mazdon, Stam, Stern, Verevis, Wills). As David Wills puts it: "The remake is [but] . . . a precise institutional form of the structure of repetition . . . that exists in and for every film" (148). Understood in this way, remaking might refer to any number of cultural and industrial activities, ranging from practices of allusion and quotation, to the repetition effects which characterize the Hollywood genre film, to the cinema's ability to repeat and replay the same film over and again. As a particular instance of this logic of cinematic repetition, the *Psycho* remake is a text initiated, negotiated, and stabilized—

but never totally limited—by a series of legal and critical institutions, such as copyright law and film reviewing, that are essential to the very existence of the film remake.

In recognition of these recent arguments around the nature of cinematic remaking, this essay seeks to sketch a *broad circuit* between *Psycho 60* and *Psycho 98*. That is, rather than accept the reductive negativity of majority accounts of the film remake, this essay seeks to understand Van Sant's replica of Hitchcock's *Psycho* as but "one aspect of a much wider process of cinematic reproduction" (Mazdon 151). The essay falls into four parts: the first looks at Alfred Hitchcock's artistic and authorial persona, and the way in which the author remakes himself (and *Psycho*) across a body of film and television work; the second part attends to Hitchcock's legacy to the contemporary slasher film, and how the *Psycho* sequels—*Psycho II, III,* and *IV*—remake not only their precursor but the conventions of the slasher movie genre; the third part looks at the nature of cinematic homage, specifically three films by Brian De Palma—*Dressed to Kill, Blow Out,* and *Body Double*—that remake aspects of *Psycho;* the fourth and final part considers the ongoing influence that Alfred Hitchcock and his masterpiece *Psycho* have had on contemporary art and film, in particular Pierre Huyghe's *Remake,* Douglas Gordon's *24 Hour Psycho,* and Gus Van Sant's *Psycho 98* replica.

* * *

Psycho is by no means the first or the only film of Alfred Hitchcock's to be remade (see Kerzoncuf, Condon, and Sangster). For instance, *direct, acknowledged remakes* of films from Hitchcock's early "British period" include such titles as *The 39 Steps* (Hitchcock 1935, Ralph Thomas 1956, Don Sharp 1978); *The Lady Vanishes* (Hitchcock 1938, Anthony Page 1979); and Hitchcock's own 1956 American remake of his earlier *The Man Who Knew Too Much* (1934). This type of remaking can be understood as a function of industry pragmatism whereby existing films are consistently thought to provide suitable models, and something of a financial guarantee, for the development of studio- (or television-) based projects. In a commercial context, Van Sant's *Psycho* remake is "pre-sold" to its audience because viewers are assumed to have some prior experience of the original story before engaging in its particular retelling (Altman 112). Even viewers with no direct experience of *Psycho* are likely to possess a "narrative image" of the film (Neale 48), or have some familiarity with the famous shower sequence and/or Bernard Herrmann's musical accompaniment of shrieking violins. This commercial orientation, whereby a new film seeks to duplicate past success and minimize risk by emphasizing the familiar, might account for the ubiquity of (Hollywood) remakes, but Hitchcock's revision of *The Man Who Knew Too Much* suggests that remaking might also be located in a filmmaker's desire to repeatedly express and modify a particular aesthetic sensibility and worldview in light of new developments and interests (Druxman 20). Michael Tarantino notes that during the early 1940s (the period in which Hitchcock was under contract to David Selznick) there was talk of remaking not only *The Man Who Knew Too Much*, but also *The Lodger* (1926), *The 39 Steps*, and *The Lady Vanishes* (25).

Stuart McDougal takes up this type of approach to remaking, describing Alfred Hitchcock as a director "who was continuously and obsessively remaking his own work" (52). This results not only in the repetition of specific shots, sequences, and themes, but in the case of Hitchcock's remake of *The Man Who Knew Too Much*, it provides the filmmaker with an opportunity to rethink "the relations between texts, between characters (real and fictional), and between the work of a younger, more exuberant director and a mature craftsman" (67). The centrality of remaking as a process across Hitchcock's work is evident not only at the level of the specific shot or individual film but also at a broader, generic level. For instance, Robert Kapsis notes that while Hitchcock's reputation as a director of thrillers can be traced back to *The Lodger* and *Blackmail* (1929), the 1934 version of *The Man Who Knew Too Much* inaugurated a cycle of six British thrillers now known as the "classic thriller sextet" (22). The high degree of continuity and consistency across these six films—*The Man Who Knew Too Much*, *The 39 Steps*, *The Secret Agent* (1936), *Sabotage* (1936), *Young and Innocent* (1937), and *The Lady Vanishes*—can be attributed to the house style of British Gaumont, but it also supports McDougal's claim that "Hitchcock remade his early work in a variety of ways, combining . . . the expressive potential of film with a desire for technical perfection" (52). Indeed, McDougal argues that it was Hitchcock's dissatisfaction with the climax of the earlier *The Man Who Knew Too Much* that led, first, to its *disguised and limited* remaking in the ending of *The 39 Steps*, and later to its *official and direct* remaking in *The Man Who Knew Too Much* (57–58). This approach, and the example of the classic thriller sextet, *would appear* to suggest that Hitchcock's authorship "lies in his ability to continually *remake* or recombine a basic repertory of narrative situations and cinematic techniques, thus creating a *characteristic world*" (Naremore 5, emphasis added).

Although *Psycho* might be seen as an amalgamation—a revision—of the bleaker tone of *The Wrong Man* (1957) and the ironic, antiromance of *Vertigo* (1958), several critics claimed that it "marked a darkening in the worldview of the director [Hitchcock]" (Rebello 47). *Psycho* certainly appears to be a departure from the interests and conventions of the "standard" Hitchcock thriller, especially the lavish, Hollywood productions of the 1950s—*The Man Who Knew Too Much, To Catch a Thief* (1955), and *North by Northwest* (1959)—that immediately preceded it. Hitchcock purchased the film rights to Robert Bloch's (then recently published) novel *Psycho* in 1959, but unable to secure an agreement under his existing contract with Paramount, he turned to Universal Studios, where his television series, *Alfred Hitchcock Presents* (CBS 1955–65), was filmed. Working within the constraints of a low budget, Hitchcock approached *Psycho* as an experiment in the making of a feature film along the lines of an expanded television episode, employing some of his regular television crew and working with multiple camera setups (Krohn 224, Rebello 25–30). Both Kapsis and James Naremore point to a number of continuities between Hitchcock's television work and *Psycho,* including such features as "the [film's] black-and-white photography, the moments of suspense, the sardonic wit and macabre humor, the ordinariness of its characters and the drabness of its setting" (Kapsis 60). Naremore argues that *Psycho* was "clearly influenced" by the format of *Alfred Hitchcock Presents,* and even finds in the film's first minutes "some echoes" of "Banquo's Chair," a 1959 episode of the TV series "which opens with the camera travelling across a row of buildings and moving in toward a doorway while words announce an exact place, date, and time" (26). In addition to this, Hitchcock's introduction and epilogue for each of the episodes for *Alfred Hitchcock Presents* had made him something of a household name. As Kapsis points out, the publicity campaign for *Psycho*—which included a six-minute trailer featuring Hitchcock leading a "tour" through the Bates house and motel (see Rebello 152–56)—would have given audiences familiar with the TV series every reason to believe "that *Psycho* would be in the tradition of Hitchcock's macabre little teleplays" (60).

    Psycho opened in the summer of 1960 to mixed critical reactions but immediately began to break box-office records, rapidly developing into a national phenomenon. Stephen Rebello states that *"Psycho* tapped into the American subconscious," provoking: "Faintings. Walk-outs. Repeat visits. Boycotts. Angry phone calls and letters" (162). *Psycho*'s massive domestic and international success ensured that it was one of the most talked-about films of 1960, cited in discussions on a range of topics, including "the rise in crime; the decline in sales of opaque shower curtains; the alarming upswing in violence, particularly toward women; [and] the downturn in motel stays" (172). *Psycho* immediately spawned a number of imitations: Rebello makes note of William Castle's *Homicidal* (1961), and Kolker describes J. Lee Thompson's *Cape Fear* (1962) as "a film that plays upon ... the atmosphere of *Psycho* and its reception" (40). In the wake of *Psycho*'s success, Hitchcock was interviewed and profiled as never before, but as Rebello notes "enshrinement for the movie and its director still lay several years ahead" (169). This is to say that it was not until *after* the re-evaluation of Hitchcock's work by the *Cahiers du cinéma* critics, and Andrew Sarris's popularization of the *politique des auteurs,* that Hitchcock would become one of Hollywood's most imitated directors (168–74). As Noël Carroll points out, the forging of a canon of films and filmmakers by auteur critics enabled allusion to film history, "especially as that history was crystallized and codified in the sixties and seventies," to become a major expressive device (52). This recognition of Hitchcockian themes and motifs enabled a filmmaker like Martin Scorsese to "recalculate" the Hitchcock formula (at least) twice: "*Taxi Driver* (1976) reformulates *Psycho* (while it simultaneously situates its narrative pattern in *The Searchers* [John Ford 1956])" and *Cape Fear* (1992) directly remakes the aforementioned 1962 Universal picture of the same name, but within this is "embedded a kind of remake of three minor Hitchcock films from the early fifties: *Stage Fright* (1950), *I Confess* (1953), and *Strangers on a Train* (1951)" (Kolker 40).

* * *

While the canonization of *Psycho* might account for the way in which the former version of a property can come to function as a kind of fixity against which its remake is evaluated, the suggestion that Hitchcock continually remakes or recombines a limited number of themes and techniques equally suggests that "there can never be a simple original uncomplicated by the structure of the remake" (Wills 157). More than this, John Frow argues that, at whatever level the intertext can be posited, "every remake simultaneously refers to and remakes the genre to which that intertext belongs, and this genre may itself be the only intertext." Taking this approach, Carol Clover situates *Psycho* within the broader context of film genre, describing it as the "immediate ancestor" to the cycle of slasher movies initiated by *The Texas Chainsaw Massacre* (Tobe Hooper 1974) and *Halloween* (John Carpenter 1978), and celebrated in the sequels and series that followed: notably, *Halloween II–VI* (plus *H2O* and *Halloween: Resurrection*), *A Nightmare on Elm Street I–V* (plus *Freddy's Dead: The Final Nightmare*), and *Friday the 13th I–VIII* (plus *Jason Goes to Hell: The Final Friday*). *Psycho* is taken as the benchmark for surveying each of the component categories of the slasher film genre: Norman Bates is the original *killer,* "the psychotic product of a sick family, but still recognizably human";

the Bates mansion is the *locale,* "the terrible place [that] enfolds the history of a mother and son locked in a sick attachment"; the carving knife is the killer's preferred *weapon;* Marion Crane is the first *victim,* "the beautiful, sexually active woman"; and her sister, Lila, is the *survivor,* "the final girl" or "the one who looks death in the face [but] survives the murderer's last stab" (Clover 192–205). As Clover points out, none of these generic particulars is exclusive to *Psycho,* "but the unprecedented success [*notoriety and canonization*] of Hitchcock's particular formulation, above all the sexualization of both motive and action, prompted a flood of imitations and variations" (192):

> The spiritual debt of all the post-1974 slasher films to *Psycho* is clear, and it is a rare example that does not pay a visual tribute, however brief, to the ancestor—if not in a shower stabbing, then in a purling drain or the shadow of a knife-wielding hand. (194)

Psycho's influence is nowhere clearer than in John Carpenter's low-budget stalker film *Halloween. Halloween*'s enormous commercial success—together with its transgression of the boundary between the psychological and supernatural monster (Neale 56)—made it the (more) immediate prototype for the slasher movies of the late 1970s and early 1980s. For instance, *Friday the 13th* (Sean S. Cunningham 1980) was described as a "bare-faced duplication of *Halloween*" (Pulleine 132) and the sequel *Friday the 13th, Part II* (Steve Miner 1981) was seen as "a virtual remake of the earlier movie" (138). The legacy of *Halloween* and its cycle in turn continued into the self-referential series of neo–slasher films of the 1990s, inaugurated by *Scream* (Wes Craven 1996) and culminating in the gross-out humor of *Scary Movie* and *Scary Movie 2* (Keenen Ivory Wayans 2000, 2001).

Halloween begins in a small Illinois town in 1963 where Judith Myers is brutally murdered by her six-year-old brother Michael. Fifteen years later Michael escapes from the asylum in which he has been held since the killing and makes his way back to his hometown where, on All Hallows E'en, he stalks a babysitter, Laurie Strode (Jamie Lee Curtis) and her teenage friends. Laurie is the only one to escape Michael's murderous knife attacks, and with the help of Dr. Sam Loomis (Donald Pleasence), the psychotic killer is stopped, at least for the moment. . . . *Halloween* repeats a number of the conventions or "rules" of the genre pioneered by *Psycho* (and parodied in *Scream*), but at the same time, Carpenter's film transforms and expands the formula, enlarging (in the character of Laurie) the role of the "final girl" (Clover 204). Although *Halloween* escaped what some critics saw as the "excesses" of Brian De Palma's early

homages to Hitchcock (see below), it nonetheless acknowledged its debt to
Psycho. It did this not only through theme and technique, but (more directly)
through the naming of the character of Dr. Sam Loomis after Marion Crane's
lover, and engaging in a kind of "genetic intertextuality" (Stam, "From Text,"
337) by casting Jamie Lee Curtis, daughter of *Psycho* star Janet Leigh, in the
role of Laurie Strode.

The late seventies' interest in the slasher movie subgenre, coupled with
the burgeoning home-video and cable-TV markets of the early 1980s, saw
the character of Norman Bates revived for a number of *Psycho* sequels. The
first of these, *Psycho II* (Richard Franklin 1983), was a low-budget joint ven-
ture between Universal Studios and a U.S. cable television company (Kapsis
172). *Psycho II* takes up the story of Norman Bates (played again by Anthony
Perkins) and tells of his return to the Bates Motel after spending twenty-two
years in a mental institution for the murder of Marion Crane (and others).
Norman secures a job at a local diner, but his attempt to begin a new life is
gradually undermined by Marion Crane's sister, Lila Loomis (Vera Miles),
and her daughter, Mary Samuels (Meg Tilly), who together conspire to drive
Norman back to the institution by masquerading as the deceased Mrs. Bates.
Back in the Bates mansion, Norman's behavior becomes increasingly erratic,
and following several grisly knife murders (subsequently blamed by police on
Lila and Mary), Norman is visited by the kindly Mrs. Spool, who explains that
she is his real mother, and the one actually responsible for the recent murders.
Norman kills her with a shovel, and carries the body up to Mrs. Bates' room
while the voice of mother gives Norman instructions on reopening the motel
(thus anticipating a further sequel). The film ends with a brooding shot of the
Psycho house and a scarecrow-like Norman silhouetted against the night sky.

Psycho II elects to provide part of its back story by opening with a black-
and-white shot of the Bates Motel neon sign (showing a vacancy) followed by
a replaying of the *Psycho* shower sequence, almost in its entirety. The prologue
begins with Marion Crane entering the bathroom and moving toward the
shower, and details her violent murder, omitting just two shots—the water
running past her legs to the bath drain and the famous dissolve to a close-
up shot of her eye—cutting instead directly to a shot of Marion's dead face
pressed against the tile floor. The first of the sequel's titles appears at the
end of the shower sequence as Hitchcock's camera begins its slow movement
from Marion's body in the bathroom to the folded newspaper with the stolen money on the night table and then out an open window to a silhouetted
view of the *Psycho* house and Norman's distant shouts of "Mother! Oh God,
Mother! Blood!" There follows a cut to the main title—*Psycho II,* in the same

bold, shattered letters of the original—and then the remainder of the credits are played out against a dark silhouette of the house (the first of the re-created shots), the night sky gradually turning through several colors to reveal a daylight view of the threatening mansion. The sequel's post-credit sequence takes up and develops the story of Norman's rehabilitation and release, but *Psycho II* also goes on to carefully remake further aspects of Hitchcock's *Psycho* through imitation and exact pastiche. Not only is there a replaying of elements of the shower sequence and its lead-up—Mary is treated by Norman to a supper of sandwiches and milk; Mary disrobes and showers as an eye watches through a hole drilled in the wall—but there is also the repetition of such details and shots as the silhouetted *Psycho* house, the overhead view of Norman carrying his invalid mother to the cellar, even a suitcase tumbling backward down the stairs in imitation of Arbogast's body.

While the publicity campaign for *Psycho II* attempted to identify it as a "quality film" (in the tradition of the Hitchcock thriller), upon its release it was dismissed by critics for its escalating violence—Mrs. Bates stabs Lila Loomis through the mouth, Norman draws his hands across the blade of a large knife (Kapsis 174–75). These aspects were seen to link the film to the (then) recent excesses of the slasher cycle, which included the heightening violence and multiple murders of such films as *Prom Night* (Paul Lynch 1980) and *Motel Hell* (Kevin Connor 1980). More than this, and despite its ending with a "paratextual" dedication—"The producers wish to acknowledge their debt to Sir Alfred Hitchcock"—the sequel (like *Psycho 98* fifteen years later) was condemned for its exploitative imitation of the master: "You don't have to be a Hitchcock idolater to see [that] this dumb, plodding pseudo-camp bore is a callous, commercial parasite" (Kroll qtd. in Kapsis 175). *Psycho II* (and the Norman Bates "franchise") nonetheless found enough of an audience to justify further sequels, both featuring Perkins: *Psycho III* (Anthony Perkins 1986) picked up from the narrative twist that Mrs. Bates was Norman's adoptive mother; and *Psycho IV: The Beginning* (Mick Garris 1990) functioned (through the use of numerous flashbacks) as a kind of "prequel" to the 1960 film. In addition to this, there was *Bates Motel* (Richard Rothstein 1987), an unsuccessful television feature and pilot for a proposed tele-series, in which Norman hands over management of the motel to a fellow mental hospital inmate (played by the wide-eyed Bud Cort).

Like the *Psycho* sequels of the eighties (each of which can be seen as a color update of *Psycho*) Van Sant's nineties' replica remakes Hitchcock's *Psycho*. But at the same time, at a higher level of generality, each one of these films re-peats—*replays and expands*—the generic corpus of the slasher film (Neale 56).

Released alongside such films as *Scream 2* (Wes Craven 1997) and *Halloween H2O* (Steve Miner 1998), *Psycho 98* might take the genre as its *only* intertext. Indeed, some of the transformations that *Psycho 98* effects upon its precursor are best understood in relation to the conventions of the contemporary slasher movie and its reformulation of the Hitchcock thriller. Although Hitchcock's frank treatment of Marion and Sam's sexual encounter and the shocking violence of the shower scene may have challenged (and contributed to the breakdown of) Hollywood's self-regulatory code of ethics, Hitchcock nonetheless had to work within the guidelines of the Production Code administered by the Motion Picture Association of America. For instance, Hitchcock had to remove, from Joseph Stefano's screenplay, a line of dialogue to be spoken to Marion by Cassidy, the Texas oilman: "Bed? Only playground that beats Las Vegas" (Rebello 77). This was restored to Van Sant's version, and a number of other *Psycho 98* modifications—nudity in the opening motel and central shower scenes, Norman masturbating as he watches Marion undress—would not have surprised a contemporary audience familiar with the amount of nudity and number of sexual themes that attend the slasher film. In a similar way, the role of the "final girl," prefigured only rudimentarily in *Psycho*'s Lila Crane, is reinterpreted in Julianne Moore's performance as the "spunky inquirer" (Clover 203), familiar to viewers of the genre from *Halloween*'s Laurie Strode to *Scream*'s Sidney Prescott (Neve Campbell).

* * *

In the early 1970s Brian De Palma began a cycle of films seen to be heavily indebted to those of Alfred Hitchcock: *Sisters* (1972) was a "very Hitchcock thriller" inspired by both *Rear Window* and *Psycho;* and *Obsession* (1975) was described by De Palma and co-writer Paul Schrader as "an homage to *Vertigo*" (Kapsis 193–96). The latter film—*Obsession*—can be seen as a kind of generic Hitchcock, reconstructing not only the "mood and manner" of *Vertigo,* but re-creating, too, some of Hitchcock's most visible stylistic characteristics: "tight plot construction, extended doppelgänger effects, precise control of point-of-view" (Rosenbaum 217). De Palma's next film, *Carrie* (1976), also had a number of borrowings from Hitchcock, in particular its opening—a variation on *Psycho*'s shower sequence—in which Carrie White (Sissy Spacek) becomes hysterical when she discovers in the high school showers that she has bleeding from her menstrual cycle. Across three subsequent films—*Dressed to Kill* (1980), *Blow Out* (1981), and *Body Double* (1984)—De Palma would go on to elaborately rework Hitchcock's famous shower sequence.

Released just a few months after Hitchcock's death in 1980, *Dressed to Kill* polarized viewers and critics alike, and demonstrated the extreme critical reaction to De Palma's ongoing revision of Hitchcock's oeuvre (Kapsis 201). *Dressed to Kill* was De Palma's most detailed invocation—a "virtual remake"—of *Psycho* (Combs 213). Andrew Sarris described *Dressed to Kill* as "a shamefully straight steal from *Psycho*" and noted several "Hitchcockian parallels in the plot," most notably the bloody slashing of the principal character, Kate Miller (Angie Dickinson), just a third of the way into the film, but also the nervously played meeting between Kate and Dr. Robert Elliott (Michael Caine) that has its equivalent in *Psycho*'s parlor room scene, and the psychiatrist's final revelation that Elliott is a transsexual driven to homicidal fury by any woman who arouses his masculine side. It is around these borrowings that the battle lines over *Dressed to Kill*—whether De Palma was "a consummate filmmaker or a rip-off artist"—were drawn (Kapsis 201). On one side, and in near identical terms to the kind of criticism leveled against *Psycho 98,* Sarris (and others) condemned "De Palma's shot-by-shot replicas for the cheap, skimpy imitations they [were]" (Sarris qtd. in Kapsis 207). On the other side, rival New York–based critics such as J. Hoberman and Pauline Kael celebrated De Palma's ability to "recalculate" the grammar of Hitchcock's work. Quoting the filmmaker, Hoberman noted: "De Palma reasonably asserts that his work is 'not a slavish imitation. . . . [Hitchcock] pioneered correct grammar. I use it because it's the best there is'" (Kolker 44).

The beginning of *Dressed to Kill*—Kate Miller in a languorous shower masturbation fantasy that ends in a violent awakening—is not just an outrageous reworking of *Psycho*'s famous murder sequence, but also a reprise of De Palma's own earlier tribute to Hitchcock: "[*Dressed to Kill*'s] showerbath sequence, with its swooning soft-porn atmosphere and adolescently overactive camera, actually starts out as a *homage* to *Carrie* before it becomes a cod *homage* to *Psycho* (with an attack that isn't)" (Combs 213). De Palma reprises the shower sequence at the end of *Dressed to Kill* in the nightmare Liz Blake (Nancy Allen) has of Elliott escaping from the mental institution and slitting her throat in the shower. It can be argued that, rather than slavishly imitating *Psycho*'s originary scene, this final sequence (like the larger gesture of *Psycho 98*) contributes to an elaborate circuit of *cinematic repetitions* in which "De Palma will become Hitchcock will become De Palma, *ad infinitum*" (Combs 213). More than this, De Palma cannily engages here not only with a sequence—the showerbath murder—that is part of a collective tradition, but also with its profilmic event: A "body double" was used for Angie Dickinson in some of the shower shots just as Hitchcock had hired, for the nude filming of *Psycho*'s shower scene, Marli Renfro, a professional dancer-model, to double for Janet Leigh (Rebello 104).

De Palma's next film, *Blow Out* (1981) is widely recognized as a variation on (an *unacknowledged remake* of) both *Blow-Up* (Michelangelo Antonioni 1966) and *The Conversation* (Francis Ford Coppola 1974), but in addition to this it replays—again—the *Psycho* shower sequence and its profilmic event. *Blow Out* begins—*Halloween*-style—with a knife-wielding murderer stalking young women through a dormitory to its steamy shower room. As the stalker draws back the shower curtain and raises his knife to strike, his victim lets out a pathetic scream. At this point, the scene cuts to a shot of Jack Terry (John Travolta), a sound recordist, watching a work-print of what is in fact a low-budget slasher movie titled *Coed Frenzy*. Jack's endeavor to replace some of the film's sound effects—the scream, but also eerie wind sounds—leads him to a secluded spot where he witnesses an "accident" in which a presidential candidate is drowned when his car plunges from a bridge (this sequence thus remakes, too, the Edward Kennedy Chappaquiddick incident of 1969). Jack rescues a female passenger, Sally Badina (Nancy Allen), from the water but she is later murdered while helping Jack attempt to unravel the conspiracy surrounding the candidate's death. At the end of the film, in an ironic reprise of the beginning, Jack finds his "voice double" in the dubbing of Sally's dying screams onto the soundtrack of his slasher movie.

De Palma's 1984 film, *Body Double*, is not only an extended reworking of the voice and body doubles of *Blow Out* and *Dressed to Kill* but arguably De Palma's "densest appropriation of Hitchcock's cinematic vocabulary and themes: voyeurism, pursuit, rescue, guilt, punishment, and the use of multiple identities or disguises" (Squiers 97). More particularly, in *Body Double* De Palma repeats elements of the narrative invention of both *Rear Window* (1954) and *Vertigo*. In the latter film—*Vertigo*—a wealthy industrialist, Gavin Elster (Tom Helmore), hires a former police detective, John "Scottie" Ferguson (James Stewart), to watch his beautiful wife, Madeleine (Kim Novak), because he believes she is suicidal. This triangular relationship of two men focused on a single woman is replayed in *Body Double*, where Sam Bouchard (Gregg Henry) points out to fellow actor, Jake Scully (Craig Wasson), that a woman in a distant house does a nightly dance and masturbatory routine that insists on being watched. As Carol Squiers points out, in both films the "watching" is a deliberate setup by the first man to make the second a witness to murder in order to cover up his role as the murderer. In both cases, the second man is stricken with a phobia that limits his actions at crucial moments. In both cases, the second man discovers that the woman he watched (in the lead-up to the murder) was a stand-in—*a body double*—for the murdered wife (97). More than this, in both cases, the first man is a "body double" for Hitchcock (and De Palma), the man who directs the audience—for which the second man is the body double—to watch the violence that the first has orchestrated and inflicted upon the woman.

Commenting on Hitchcock's films of the fifties, Dave Kehr explains that if cinema itself is the central metaphor that informs *Vertigo,* then "the dream of *Vertigo*—the dream of . . . a beautiful illusion that gives way to nothingness—is also the dream of the movies" (16). De Palma begins and ends not only *Body Double,* but also *Dressed to Kill* and *Blow Out,* with just such an illusion: a dream, a film-within-a-film. At the end of *Body Double,* De Palma returns to the horror movie set of the film's opening: A bat descends upon a bathroom where a young woman is showering, and transforms itself into a vampire, played by the actor Jake Scully. Just as the vampire is about to strike, the film's director (Dennis Franz, a De Palma regular) appears in the bathroom window, shouting for Jake to freeze. Jake holds a rigid pose as the actress in his clutches is replaced with a body double. The filming resumes and we see a montage: shots of Jake and the actress intercut with body shots of Jake and the body double, Jake sinking his fangs into the slender neck of the actress, blood streaming down the perfect breasts of the body double. At this point, *Body Double* does not lead in any direct way back to *Psycho,* but establishes instead the larger circuit of a kind of *dream-image,* a *transtextual* relay in which each image becomes legible in relation to the seriality of cinematic representation.

* * *

It seems curious that few (if any) of the commentaries at the time of the release of *Psycho 98* drew attention to the ways in which *Psycho 60* had *already* been "remade." These broader, intertextual relations range from the generic repetitions of *Halloween* and other slasher movies, to the careful acts of homage evident in *Body Double, Dressed to Kill* and *Blow Out,* to the various other limited remakings of *Psycho* such as the hilarious shower scene spoof in *High Anxiety* (Mel Brooks 1977) and the masochistic parody of the same in *Psycho Too* (Andrew Gluck Levy 1999). Van Sant's version of *Psycho* might well closely follow the form and narrative of Hitchcock's film and also repeat a number of its contexts: same soundstage, similar shooting schedule, no advance screenings, etc. But each of the aforementioned *other* revisions of *Psycho* suggests that the "original" text is never fixed and singular, and that Van Sant's *Psycho* remake differs textually (from this larger circuit of remakings) not *in kind,* but only *in degree*. As stated at the beginning of this essay, remaking might refer to any number of industrial and cultural practices: the remake is but a particular institutional form of the logic of repetition that is possible *for all films* (see Wills). Understood in this way, a broad conception of the remaking of *Psycho* would acknowledge, too, any of the several rereleases of *Psycho* (from 1965 onward) and its subsequent licensing by MCA for network and syndicated television screenings, and (later) sale to videotape and disc, as further revisions—remakings—of the film.

While all of the above establish a much broader set of relations between *Psycho 60* and *Psycho 98* (than that accorded it by most of its reviewers), there is another (perhaps) more interesting way to approach the Van Sant version. Rather than suggest, as its detractors have, that Van Sant's *Psycho* follows Hitchcock's film too closely—that it adds nothing to the "original"—it can be argued that Van Sant's *Psycho* is *not close enough* to the Hitchcock version. *Chicago Sun-Times* critic Roger Ebert explains:

> Curious, how similar the new version is, and how different. . . . The movie is an invaluable experiment in the theory of cinema, because it demonstrates that a shot-by-shot remake is pointless; *genius apparently resides between or beneath the shots* [emphasis added].

This suggestion—that an irreducible difference plays simultaneously between the most mechanical of repetitions—is best demonstrated by two earlier (and lesser-known) remakes of Hitchcock's work: *Remake* (Pierre Huyghe 1995) and *24 Hour Psycho* (Douglas Gordon 1993). The first of these, *Remake*, is a shot-by-shot remake, a video reproduction—"complete and literal but nonchalant, with a few jumps and discrepancies owing to its amateurism"—of Hitchcock's *Rear Window*. As in the case of Van Sant's *Psycho*, where the duration of the actors' performances were timed against those of a video monitor replay of their predecessors' movements, Huyghe instructed his nonprofessional actors "to repeat, to be doubles, to *reproduce*" (Royoux 22).

The second work, *24 Hour Psycho*, is a new version—an "exact" remake—of *Psycho 60*, but one that (as its title suggests) takes a full day to run its course. More specifically, Gordon's version is a video installation piece that reruns *Psycho 60* at approximately two frames per second, just fast enough for each image to be pulled forward into the next (see Taubin). As Stéphane Aquin points out, "stripped of its soundtrack, slowed down to the limit of tolerability, the film plays like a regression through the history of cinema, back to that threshold where black and white photography haltingly becomes a moving image" (174). Drawing upon the formal precedents of the North American "structural" film, notably Ken Jacobs's *Tom, Tom, the Piper's Son* (1969), Gordon's strategy is to demonstrate that each and every film is remade—that is, dispersed and transformed—in its every new context or configuration. Accordingly, Gordon does not set out to imitate *Psycho* but to *repeat* it—that is, to change nothing, but at the same time allow an absolute difference to emerge. Understood in this way, *Psycho 98* might be thought of not as a per-version of an original identity, but as the production of a new event, one that adds to (rather than corrupts) the seriality of the former version. If Hitchcock's work holds for its viewers some ongoing fascination, then it is perhaps because these viewers remake the work in its every reviewing, and this re-viewing may be no more or less than the genre labeled "remake."

Each of the above works—*Remake, 24 Hour Psycho,* and *Psycho 98*—is a kind of a homage to Hitchcock, "a recognition of the deep structure of his accumulated works, which speaks across generations and across artistic media" (Tarantino 25). As Paula Cohen notes, when critics declare that a better solution to Van Sant's remaking of *Psycho* would have been to rerelease a 35mm print of that film, they fail to realize that a *re*-viewing of *Psycho 60* is itself "a form of homage rather than a re-creation of the original experience": "Van Sant's film [is] a mechanism for catalyzing homage, as ingeniously designed to draw admiring attention to the original as anything Hitchcock might have come up with himself" (131). More than this, *Psycho 98*—indeed, *all* of the *Psycho* remakes—draw attention to the very nature of cinema, to the nature of cinematic quotation and cultural production, to the fact that every film, every film viewing, is a type of remaking.

Works Cited

Altman, Rick. *Film/Genre*. London: British Film Institute, 1999.

Aquin, Stéphane. "Hitchcock and Contemporary Art." *Hitchcock and Art: Fatal Coincidences*. Eds. Dominique Païni and Guy Cogeval. Montreal: The Montreal Museum of Fine Arts, 2000.

Carroll, Noël. "The Future of Allusion: Hollywood in the Seventies (and Beyond)." *October* 20 (1982): 51–81.

Clover, Carol. "Her Body, Himself: Gender in the Slasher Film." *Representations* 20 (Fall 1987): 187–228.

Cohen, Paula Marantz. "The Artist Pays Homage." *Hitchcock Annual* (2001–02): 127–32.

Combs, Richard. Rev. of *Dressed to Kill. Monthly Film Bulletin* 47.562 (November 1980): 213.

Condon, Paul, and Jim Sangster. *The Complete Hitchcock*. London: Virgin, 1999.

Druxman, Michael B. *Make it Again, Sam: A Survey of Movie Remakes*. Cranbury, New Jersey: A. S. Barnes, 1975.

Ebert, Roger. Rev. of *Psycho* (1998). http://www.suntimes.com. Accessed November 19, 2001.

Frow, John. Rev. of *Play It Again, Sam,* by Horton and McDougal. http://www.latrobe
.edu.au/www/screeningthepast/shorts/reviews/rev0799/jfbr7a.htm. Accessed November 19, 2001.

"Gus Van Sant vs. Alfred Hitchcock: A *Psycho* Dossier." *Hitchcock Annual* (2001–02): 125–58.

Hoberman, J. Rev. of *Dressed to Kill. Village Voice* (22–29 July 1980): 42, 44.

Horton, Andrew, and Stuart Y. McDougal, eds. *Play It Again, Sam: Retakes on Remakes.* Berkeley: University of California Press, 1998.

Kael, Pauline. "Master Spy, Master Seducer." *The New Yorker* (August 4, 1980): 68–71.

Kapsis, Robert E. *Hitchcock: The Making of a Reputation.* Chicago: University of Chicago Press, 1992.

Kehr, Dave. "Hitch's Riddle." *Film Comment* 20.3 (May–June 1984): 9–18.

Kerzoncuf, Alain. "Hitch and the Remakes." http://www.labyrinth.net.au/~muffin/remakes_c.html. Accessed November 19, 2001.

Kolker, Robert P. "Algebraic Figures: Recalculating the Hitchcock Formula." Horton and McDougal 34–51.

Krohn, Bill. *Hitchcock at Work.* London: Phaidon, 2000.

McDougal, Stuart Y. "The Director Who Knew Too Much: Hitchcock Remakes Himself." Horton and McDougal 52–69.

Mazdon, Lucy. *Encore Hollywood: Remaking French Cinema.* London: British Film Institute, 2000.

Milne, Tom. Rev. of *Psycho II. Monthly Film Bulletin* 50.596 (September 1983): 245–46.

Naremore, James. *Filmguide to* Psycho. Bloomington: Indiana University Press, 1973.

———. "Remaking *Psycho.*" *Hitchcock Annual* (1999–2000): 3–12.

Neale, Steve. "Questions of Genre." *Screen* 31.1 (1990): 45–66.

Psycho: Official Website. http://www.psychomovie.com. Accessed February 12, 1999.

Psycho: Saving a Classic. http://members.aol.com/montag17/psycho.html. Accessed February 12, 1999.

Pulleine, Tom. Rev. of *Friday the 13th. Monthly Film Bulletin* 47.558 (July 1980): 132.

———. Rev. of *Friday the 13th, Part 2. Monthly Film Bulletin* 48.570 (July 1981): 138.

Rebello, Stephen. *Alfred Hitchcock and the Making of* Psycho. New York: Dembner, 1990.

Rosenbaum, Jonathan. Rev. of *Obsession. Monthly Film Bulletin* 43.513 (October 1976): 217.

Royoux, Jean-Christophe. "Remaking Cinema." *Cinéma, Cinéma: Contemporary Art and the Cinematic Experience.* Eds. Marente Bloemheuvel and Jaap Guldemond. Stedelijk Van Abbemuseum, Eindhoven and Nai Publishers: Rotterdam, 1999.

Sarris, Andrew. Rev. of *Dressed to Kill. Village Voice* (22–29 July 1980): 42, 44.

Squiers, Carol. "Over Brian De Palma's Dead *Body Double.*" *Art and Text* 17 (1985): 96–101.

Stam, Robert. "Beyond Fidelity." *Film Adaptation.* Ed. James Naremore. London: Athlone, 2000.

———. "From Text to Intertext." *Film Theory: An Introduction.* Oxford: Blackwell, 1999.

Stern, Lesley. Rev. of *Play It Again, Sam,* by Horton and McDougal. http://muse.jhu.edu/journals/modernism-modernity/v007/7.1stern.html. Accessed November 19, 2001.

Tarantino, Michael. "How He Does It" (1976) Or "The Case of the Missing Gloves" (1999). *Notorious: Alfred Hitchcock and Contemporary Art.* Eds. Kerry Brougher, et al. Oxford: Museum of Modern Art, 1999.

Taubin, Amy. "Douglas Gordon." *Spellbound: Art and Film.* Ed. Philip Dodd with Ian Christie. London: Hayward Gallery and BFI, 1996.

Verevis, Constantine. "Re-Viewing Remakes." *Film Criticism* 21.3 (1997): 1–19.

Wills, David. "The French Remark: *Breathless* and Cinematic Citationality." Horton and McDougal 147–61.

Hitchcockian *Silence*
Psycho and Jonathan Demme's *The Silence of the Lambs*

Lesley Brill

Although by 1991 Alfred Hitchcock's last film was fifteen years past, his name was still synonymous with suspense, with movie (and TV) narratives of offbeat crime and terror. When an expensively produced crime-horror picture with marquee stars, a serial murderer, a generous dash of incongruous flippancy, and a strong psychoanalytic bent came out that year, one would have expected Hitchcock's name to be widely invoked. In reviews and numerous commentaries on *The Silence of the Lambs,* however, such was not the case. A number of critics noticed that Jame Gumb (Ted Levine), the serial killer of Demme's movie, "is the clear brother of Norman Bates."[1]; but beyond that observation and a provocative essay by Julie Tharp that compared sexual pathologies in *The Silence of the Lambs* with those in *Psycho,* little has been said of the connections between Demme's film and those of Hitchcock.[2] Nonetheless, Hitchcock's influence on *The Silence of the Lambs* is pervasive.

Why have Hitchcockian resonances in Demme's most successful film gone largely unnoticed? And why—if such resonances are indeed present—does it matter whether we notice them or not? As regards the first question, speculations about absences invariably suffer from a poverty of evidence, but I'll offer several guesses. First, the lack of references to Hitchcock may reflect a widely shared assumption that any movie thriller must have a Hitchcockian pedigree. Why belabor what's obvious? (Film critics and academics being who they are, however, one would not necessarily expect restraint about proclaiming the self-evident.) A more plausible hypothesis might be that critics encounter difficulty in distinguishing among the influences that come directly from Hitchcock's own films and those that come indirectly through the multitude of movies that Hitchcock influenced and that in their turn affected later films. In making the thriller his own, moreover, Hitchcock was a particularly effective conduit between his literary and cinematic legacies and the same material that appears in movies coming later. Hitchcock was not so much an inventor as a capacious crucible for recombining preexisting narrative elements. As Rohmer and Chabrol observed when Hitchcock's career as a filmmaker still had two decades to run, "The number of Hitchcockian stories in the world is certainly very great: a good third, if not a half, of all those that have been written until now." [3]

Another reason for the obliviousness of most commentators to Hitchcock's influence on *The Silence of the Lambs* may have to do with an uncomplicated popular understanding of him as the "master of suspense," "misogynist of murder," and so on. For the past ten or fifteen years, academic film studies has developed a thriving subspecialty around Alfred Hitchcock's career, turning out fifteen or twenty books and a multitude of articles. The varied, controversy-laden conception of Hitchcock's work that emerges from this industry seems hardly to have affected his nonspecialist audience. Many of the aspects of *The Silence of the Lambs* that may plausibly be called Hitchcockian have little to do with his reduction to the ironic icon who hosted television series and had Janet Leigh slaughtered in the shower.

Nonetheless, if the paucity of references to Hitchcock in most writing about *The Silence of the Lambs* reflects an undernourished conception of his work, it also partly reflects a sound instinct about something essential to most of Hitchcock's films and largely absent from Demme's: romantic love. That absence has been overstated by most commentators on Demme's film; but even so, romance in *The Silence of the Lambs* remains a low-wattage sidelight. In a Hitchcock movie, on the contrary, emerging affection (or romantic misfortunes) between leading woman and man, if not central from the beginning, tends eventually to displace murder, treason, or some other "MacGuffin" and to assume thematic top-billing. By my count, at least forty-three of the fifty-two surviving feature-length movies Hitchcock directed have love at or near their centers.

The second issue, why it matters if we detect Hitchcock's influence, can be more straightforwardly addressed. Perception of Hitchcockian resonances in the work of other directors improves our understanding not just of their films, but also of Hitchcock's. "Influence" includes, implicitly at least, interpretations of and responses to the precedent work. It includes, in short, an embodied criticism. For that reason, as T. S. Eliot famously proposed, thoughtful critics "will not find it preposterous that the past should be altered by the present as much as the present is directed by the past." [4]

To the case in point: where is Hitchcock in *The Silence of the Lambs*? I shall consider both clear borrowings and more diffuse affinities. Among the former, one may include the single widely noticed Hitchcockian aspect of Demme's film, the resemblance of its central serial killer to *Psycho*'s.

As Harold Schechter observes, "Gumb is a fictional incarnation of the real-life ghoul Edward Gein, whose ghastly crimes were the basis of Alfred Hitchcock's *Psycho* and Tobe Hooper's *The Texas Chainsaw Massacre*."[5] Norman and Jame both apply needle and thread to their fabric, the skins of the dead. Each is an overripe juvenile, a man-child who has not managed to grow up psychologically. Each tries to become the other person that he desperately needs. Through his taxidermy and sharing his identity with his Mother's remains, Norman attempts to provide himself with the parent whom he killed. After Jame has subdued his "next special lady," Catherine Martin (Brooke Smith), he cuts her blouse from her back to examine her hide. As he does, a close-up reveals a tattoo between his thumb and index finger: "Love." This word as flesh appears again as Gumb dances in front of his video camera, striving to be his own special lady. "Will you fuck me?" he asks himself. Then, a little later, "I fuck me. I fuck me so hard."

Despite the reflections bouncing between Bates and Gumb, their relation is not easy to fix. Jack the Ripper and other famous-in-their-day serial killers with sexual problems and a fondness for dissection preceded Ed Gein historically. Their fictional analogues in novels, short stories, and films also preceded his. One of those ancestors, indeed, motivates the action of Hitchcock's own *The Lodger* (1927). A descendent reappears forty-five years later in Hitchcock's next-to-last film, *Frenzy*. A kidnapper of young women who attempts to transplant their skin in Georges Franju's 1959 *Eyes Without a Face* anticipates Gumb's flaying and patching together the skins of his victims. Granting that "the notion of a killer propelled by psycho-sexual fury, more particularly a male in gender distress, has proved a durable one, and the progeny of Norman Bates stalk the genre [of horror films] up to the present day,"[6] we must also grant that their identifiable forebears have stalked both the horror film and its literary precedents since their beginnings. The story materials that later filmmakers take from *The Lodger*, *Psycho*, and *Frenzy*, they also take *through* Hitchcock from Hitchcock's own contemporaries and artistic ancestors.

Hannibal Lecter (Anthony Hopkins) has affinities both with Norman Bates and with another of *Psycho*'s figures, the psychiatrist who "explains" Mother-Norman. Rather as *Psycho*'s therapist pompously corrects the sheriff's deputy about Norman's being "a transvestite," Lecter oracularly declares that Gumb is not the transsexual he supposes himself to be, but instead the possessor

The intellectual as monster, a figure of repulsion and attraction, in Demme's *The Silence of the Lambs*.

of a far more dangerous pathology. Dr. Lecter also recalls and anticipates a host of murderous geniuses who precede and follow him, from the villains of *Dr. Caligari* and *Metropolis* through De Palma's *Dressed to Kill*, to the collectively brilliant evildoers of films like *The Terminator* and *The Matrix*. Bates lacks the conventional accoutrements of inspired insanity, but like Lecter he can be alternately perceptive and empathetic—as when he converses with Marion about "private traps"—and mercilessly savage, utterly without sympathy for victims. The same dichotomy is hinted at in Gumb, who almost weeps as Catherine Martin sobbingly pleads to "see my mommy" and then screams along with her.

After parallels to its characters, the most suggestive debts Demme's film owes to *Psycho* appear in significant props and settings. The apprehensive inspection that Clarice Starling (Jodie Foster) makes of Lecter's self-storage locker parallels Lila Crane's exploration of the upstairs of the Bates house. Each is similarly overstuffed with incongruously jumbled equipage. The climaxes of both films take place in dusty, roughly constructed cellars which contain the appalling corpses of women—although in *The Silence of the Lambs* the briefly viewed remains are putrefied in a mucky bathtub.

Again, however, we should be aware that such horrifying subterranean places are a common part of the folklore motifs that pervasively inform *The*

Silence of the Lambs—as Schechter shows—and that occur not only in *Psycho* but in much of Hitchcock's other work: the cellars of *Number Seventeen* (1932), *Notorious* (1946), and *Stage Fright* (1950), as well as numerous other off-kilter locations. If *The Silence of the Lambs* follows Hitchcock and *Psycho* in placing its violent resolution in Jame Gumb's cellar, we may say that Hitchcock's film is one of the springs through which flow currents that go back to the beginnings of film narrative, horror fiction, and narrative itself in the mortal descents of such heroes as Odysseus and Gilgamesh.

Both Jame Gumb and Norman Bates sink the corpses of their victims in muddy waters, Gumb in rivers (and the basement tub) and Norman in his slough. Water in Hitchcock's films repeatedly takes on associations of death or dissolution—dangerously in *Rebecca* (1940), *Strangers on a Train* (1951), and *To Catch a Thief* (1955), and comically in *Rich and Strange* (1932) and *Mr. and Mrs. Smith* (1941). Demme's camera pans across a river just after Clarice enters the house in which she will discover the Death's Head Moth that tells her she has found Buffalo Bill. As Thomas Harris's novel explains but the movie leaves us to notice ourselves, the moth's Latin name, *Acherontia styx*, invokes "two rivers in Hell. Your man, he drops the bodies in a river every time."[7]

The stuffed owl that confronts Clarice when she ventures into Lecter's self-storage locker repeats in pose and lighting the spread-winged owl in the parlor behind Norman's motel office. The same shape and position, transferred to human models, recur in *The Silence of the Lambs* when Lecter strings up the body of one of his murdered jailers and again during Gumb's autoerotic dance. More generally, avian imagery pervades both *Psycho* and *The Silence of the Lambs*. Such imagery in each tends to be associated with threatened or victimized women: Marion Crane "eat[s] like a bird" while surrounded by Norman's stuffed fowl and prints of captive women; the names of Clarice Starling and Catherine Martin emphasize their connection with birds, and Lecter directs Clarice, "You fly back to school now, little starling. Fly, fly, fly." At the home of Gumb's first victim, as Jhan Hochman notes, "several duck replicas 'walk' in the front yard, a thriving bird hotel stands on a pole out back, and a little wooden, wind-blown Indian paddles his canoe in full feathered headdress. Fredrica's father raises and kills pigeons."[8]

Neither in *Psycho* nor in *The Silence of the Lambs*, however, do birds serve exclusively as victims. They can be predators as well as prey, and some are both. The baleful owl duplicated from *Psycho* in Lecter's "Your Self-Storage" has its wings outstretched, as if swooping to attack. Hitchcock's birds include those that threaten to overrun the world in *The Birds* (1963). The sinister side of his avian imagery extends at least back to the "Cock Robin" cartoon of *Sab-*

otage (1936) and the screaming gulls around the corpse of a strangled actress at the beginning of *Young and Innocent* (1937). In *The Silence of the Lambs,* the imagery of birds *as* prey slides into that of birds *of* prey. Partly reversing Lecter's injunction to "fly, fly, fly," Clarice offers him an annual escape to an island where "terns nest." She and Catherine Martin play the roles of both predator and quarry in Jame Gumb's basement; Martin when she succeeds in capturing Gumb's small dog and Starling as at once hunter and hunted.

More often than not, Hitchcock's protagonists act simultaneously as the pursued (usually by the police) and the pursuing (usually after the true malefactor); so the three principal characters of *The Silence of the Lambs,* Starling, Gumb, and Lecter, all figure as both stalkers and quarries. Marion Crane begins by preying on her employer's obnoxious client, but her theft of his cash quickly transforms her into the target of those from whom she's stolen and, fatally, Norman Bates. He in turn is hunted by Marion's lover, her sister, and the detective Arbogast. In the opening sequence of *The Silence of the Lambs,* the camera that tracks a panting Clarice through misty woods invokes familiar thriller expectations. The audience is likely to suspect either that this as-yet-unidentified young woman will be attacked or that the shots following and running ahead of her will be revealed as originating from the point of view of some menacing stalker.[9] When the man who appears simply issues her an order to report to a superior, the absence of any obvious threat feels like a reprieve. The assignment she receives, nevertheless, will ultimately fulfill the menace of the opening sequence, casting her as both quarry and hunter.

The empathic capacity of "Hannibal the Cannibal" at once allows him to get into the heads of his prey and bespeaks his kinship with them. In Demme's movie of shifting, interpenetrating identities, Lecter acts and suffers variously as predator, protector, and quarry. So does Gumb, if one counts his protection of his pet "Precious." The same could be said of Norman Bates.

Norman's perpetual nibbling suggests something like the cannibalism that Lecter notoriously practices. It also suggests a connection with the hunger of birds that he alludes to during his conversation with Marion. Gumb's incorporation of his victims is as radical as Lecter's, but inverted; he wishes them to fully surround him. Again, the same could be said of Norman's relation to the Mother that he killed; he attempts to incorporate himself into her. The indignant threat Marion imagines being made by Cassidy, her robbery victim, comes close to cannibalism: "I'll replace it [the money] with her fine, soft flesh." Both the substitutability of flesh for other flesh (or money), and the desire to ingest or be ingested by another represent a radical form of unstable identity. Such desires and practices are the most extreme expression of the idea that predator and prey are finally one. As we shall see, this idea has close ties with another fundamental theme of both *Psycho* and *The Silence of the Lambs,* the attempts of their central figures to transform or re-create themselves.

Seizing and incorporation, wrote Elias Canetti, start with "the lying in wait for prey . . . [which] is contemplated, observed, and kept watch over."[10] Both *The Silence of the Lambs* and *Psycho* emphasize the predatory potential of looking. Norman's attack on Marion begins when he peeps into her room as she is undressing. In the last scene of the film, he sits as Mother, acutely conscious of the eyes of his captors. Lecter appeals to Clarice's experience both as object of visual desire—"Don't you feel eyes moving over your body, Clarice?"—and as one who desires—"And don't your eyes seek out the things you want?" Eyes and looking receive emphasis in *The Silence of the Lambs* quite as insistently as in such exemplars of scopophilia as *Peeping Tom* or *Rear Window*. Not only do people constantly look at Starling, but the camera tends to stay on their faces after she departs the frame, thereby emphasizing their watching. The abduction of Catherine begins with a subjective shot through Buffalo Bill's eyes, the strikingly green (perhaps envious) night eyes of his infrared viewers. Along with Gumb, the audience watches through the same green vision when he stalks Starling. In the storage space, the camera focuses repeatedly on eyes: Clarice Starling's, those of the stuffed owl, and the filmy, unnaturally wide-open eyes of the preserved head. The hometown of Gumb and his first victim harmonizes with the motif of eyes and seeing; it is Belvedere ("beautiful view"), Ohio.

The central characters of horror movies frequently strive for, and usually fail to achieve, some sort of self-transformation or re-creation. Such is the case in *Psycho* for Marion, whose attempt to transform herself from lover to wife costs her life; and for Norman, who does manage to metamorphose into Mother, but who loses himself in the process. A muted but insistent secondary evocation of transformation takes place with the character of Lila, who while attempting to find Marion drifts toward replacing her. "Patience," she declares, recalling the impulsiveness that led her sister astray, "doesn't run in my family." By drawing our attention to her general outlines and style, a series of reflections of Lila in mirrors and windows and as a back-lit silhouette serve to emphasize her physical similarity to her sister. When she and Sam register at the Bates motel "as husband and wife," they for a moment achieve the status for which Marion lost everything. An intensely ironic film, *Psycho* can be seen as a series of aborted transformations.

In *The Silence of the Lambs,* all three principal figures strive for some fashion of self-recreation. Hannibal Lecter explicitly introduces the idea of metamorphosis when he characterizes the evidence in the storage garage as "a fledgling killer's first effort at transformation." In his own practice of transformations, Lecter divides into two versions. As the first, he is an empathetic, preternaturally insightful psychoanalyst helping Clarice to understand and discover Buffalo Bill and to silence her torturing memory of screaming lambs. As the second, he changes his identity to escape his captors and to stalk them (and others) in turn. A Jekyll and Hyde figure who metamorphoses spontaneously without a potion, he is both Dr. Lecter and "Hannibal the Cannibal." [11]

Like the novice Buffalo Bill, Starling is also a "fledgling" at her profession. When Lecter raises the idea of transformation, she seizes upon it, "What did you mean by transformation, Doctor?" Her own "first principle," advancement, represents an important, difficult form of metamorphosis. Clarice descends into an underworld in search not only of a monster but also self-realization. After she has emerged into the fellowship of the FBI, Lecter, her instructor as well as antagonist, offers his congratulations. It was he, we remember, who mocked her "cheap shoes" and branded her—adopting an insulting drawl—as having sprung from "pore whaat trash." Now he renounces the power of the privileged, of the predator over former prey: "I have no plans to call on you, Clarice. The world's a more interesting place with you in it."

Buffalo Bill stuffs a pupa of the Death's Head Moth into the throats of his victims. Since he first began to kill, according to Dr. Lecter, "the significance of the moth has changed: caterpillar into chrysalis or pupa, from thence into beauty. Our Billy wants to change, too." [12] He cannot, because he is stuck in what Canetti in his discussion of transformation calls imitation. "Imitation relates to externals . . . [It] is nothing but a first step in the direction of transformation, a movement which immediately stops short." [13] The female body-mask that Gumb is constructing from the epidermis of his victims will turn him into a woman in externals only.

Insofar as he does achieve metamorphosis, his transformation goes backward. Like Gregor Samsa, he devolves from a person into a grotesque insect, bug-eyed in his infrared viewing apparatus, a creature of the dark. (Norman Bates' final transformation, famously, is also associated with an insect, the fly that Mother "wouldn't even hurt.") Contiguous sewing and moth rooms serve as workshops and emblems for Gumb's urgently desired transformation. Gumb is identified with his victims through the same vectors. He engorges them with pupae and he seems to have shared with some of them his passion for sewing. The head of his first victim (a male) is found in a car full of partly dismembered manikins, and a friend of the first young woman to have been flayed declares, "Sewing was her life." When Clarice is searching that girl's sewing room, the wallpaper there, significantly, is covered with pictures of butterflies. The dead girl also wanted to change. In her desire for self-transformation, she is like Jame Gumb, like Clarice Starling and Hannibal Lecter, like Marion Crane and Norman Bates, like humankind itself.

The film of *The Silence of the Lambs* adapts Thomas Harris's novel with remarkable fidelity and completeness; one might argue, therefore, that Hitchcock's influence on the movie derives largely from whatever effect he had on the book that the movie follows. While it remains possible that Harris knew and was influenced by Hitchcock's films, Demme's movie shows Hitchcockian influences that are specifically cinematic and that do not have analogues in its novelistic source.

Notable among those touches is Demme's management of camera and editing. In both *Psycho* and *The Silence of the Lambs,* the camera occasionally takes an active role, joining the human characters as another participant rather than functioning simply as a passive recorder. Its busy inquisitiveness in the opening shots of each film—its tracking of Clarice and its survey of Phoenix, followed by its plunge into the hotel window—anticipate other instances of such curious gazing. In *The Silence of the Lambs* it independently explores Gumb's basement lair well before Clarice undertakes the same exploration. Frantically active during Marion's murder in *Psycho*, Hitchcock's camera throughout that film asserts its presence both in its ability to convey fields of vision of the movie's characters and its own, independent of them.

At other moments, the camera in both films seems resigned to leaving its protagonists to their fates, as if it is unable to intervene and unwilling to watch. On its own agency, the camera retreats just after Clarice enters the house in which she will uncover Buffalo Bill. When it leaves her with Gumb, it shows the river, a swath of tripled railroad tracks, and a quiet, somewhat isolated house that offers nothing to raise suspicion. It appears for a moment to be abandoning her to a fate like that of Gumb's other victims. In doing so, it recalls a similar turning-away of the camera in Hitchcock's next-to-last movie, *Frenzy*. In that instance, the camera tracks a serial rapist and killer up a flight of stairs with his next victim, then backs down the stairway, through the entrance hall, and out into a busy street, unable even to watch after the killer closes the door on the doomed woman. Demme's camera, by contrast, soon returns to the inside of Gumb's dwelling. But even though it returns, it has made a similar point; no one passing the ordinary-looking house down by the tracks and the river will have any reason to go to Starling's rescue.

That she is truly alone with Gumb has only just been revealed after a sequence of deceptive, concealed parallel editing and camera placements that lead the viewer astray by implying that help is close in the form of her mentor Dr. Crawford. Similarly, Hitchcock's carefully planned high camera placements and editing during Mother's attack on Arbogast and when Norman carries her downstairs are intended to mislead the viewer of that movie as to the true source of danger. Insofar as they deceive the audience, their proper prey, Demme's and Hitchcock's cameras at such moments might be considered something like predators themselves.

However that may be, images of imagery—photos, video camera images in Demme's film, and paintings in *Psycho*—underscore the self-reflexivity of the cinematography in both movies and the involvement of their cameras with the desires and fears of the protagonists. Marion's room with its family photos and wallpaper at the beginning of *Psycho* and the ironically flowered wallpaper that is emphasized in her room at the Bates Motel resemble the bedroom of Gumb's first victim and the equally ironic butterflies that decorate the wallpaper of her sewing room. The photo of mother that Marion and Sam would turn "to the wall" must not witness their after-dinner lovemaking. The seminude photos of Gumb's first victim are hidden in her music box lid; they must not be witnessed. The photographs of houses in the real estate office where Marion works—"of homes, homes," as another forlorn Hitchcock protagonist murmurs in *Shadow of a Doubt*—represent the sad inability of the camera to solace those who look on its images. In *The Silence of the Lambs,* the bulletin board in Dr. Crawford's office is covered with newspaper clippings and photos of Buffalo Bill's crimes, photos that have no power to reveal the criminal. They are paralleled by similar photographs and some of the same clippings in Gumb's cellar. Like Gumb's videotaping of his dancing as a woman, they do not seem able to supply whatever it is he desperately wants.

At the same time, the images of images in both movies—including the numerous reflections in mirrors and on other glass surfaces of *Psycho*—have a quality of detachment that feels heartless in worlds abundant only in human need and grief. If the self-reflexive emphasis upon camera work and picture making in *The Silence of the Lambs* and *Psycho* embodies their directors' meditations upon their own art, we must conclude that Demme and Hitchcock represent themselves as ambivalent about the power of motion pictures to ameliorate or even to depict adequately the sorrows of the tangled web of human life.

Beginning with *Mr. and Mrs. Smith, Saboteur,* and *Shadow of a Doubt,* his third, fifth, and sixth U.S. films, Hitchcock took considerable interest in portraying American folkways and thinking cinematically about what it meant to be American. The great films that preceded *Psycho* in the fifties—*Strangers on a Train, Rear Window, The Trouble with Harry, Vertigo,* and *North by Northwest*—all make specifically American themes prominent. (After *Psycho,* Americana becomes less central thematically even in American settings—with the possible exception of *Marnie.*) The integration of meditations upon the United States into the action of Demme's thriller recalls the Hitchcock of 1940 to 1960. From the central role of the FBI, through a host of smaller details like Gumb's nickname and Catherine Martin's singing "She was an American girl," to insistent invocations of the USA in the mise-en-scène, *The Silence of the Lambs* puts the issue of American national identity, if not front and center, at least perfusively in its background. As Schechter asserts, "Just as *Psycho* and *The Texas Chainsaw Massacre* operate . . . as parables about the schizoid fifties and the paranoid sixties, *The Silence of the Lambs* offers insights into our own troubled time."[14]

In its color cinematography—largely through its handling of red, white, and blue—*The Silence of the Lambs* integrates its actions of threat and predation with American motifs in a manner that finds its most specific precedent in Hitchcock's similar treatment of those colors in *North by Northwest.* In that Hitchcock film, the threats frequently associated with red and the opposing plot movements toward safety or security that tend to be linked with blue or green are woven together with the use of red, white, and blue as an American national motif.[15]

For *The Silence of the Lambs,* the color of both light and objects has a similar significance. Contrasting, juxtaposing, and occasional apparent reversing of the symbolic associations of red and blue occur repeatedly throughout the film, from the blue-gray morning of its beginning to the blue-gray evening of its end. As in *North by Northwest, The Silence of the Lambs* connects red and orange with danger and predation while blue is given a variety of opposing associations: resistance, innocence, safety, counterattack. Interestingly, Lecter is connected at different times with both colors, depending upon whether he is acting as therapist or as cannibal. When he tells Clarice that her "bleeding has stopped," he emerges, illuminated by a blue light, in blue-green pants. When in his dangerous, predatory mode, on the other hand, Lecter appears in a literally different light. Under brilliant red and pink illumination at the Memphis airport, he arrives clothed in bright red pants, and he is transferred to a cage flooded with high-key, high color-temperature lighting. A little later, he will have murdered his two guards, killed two medical attendants, made his escape, and killed a passing tourist.

Integrating politics and character, Demme adds white to red and blue to invoke the United States. The huge red, white, and blue cloth that covers the old limousine in the storage garage joins opposing colors in the flag of the USA. Gumb's basement is filled with American flags and a poster of the American Nazi Party. The first symbolic object that Clarice sees when she enters his cellar is a map of the United States. The FBI also has such maps. The next-to-last sequence of the film, the graduation from the Bureau's training center, mixes the red, white, and blue in a cake frosted with the seal of the FBI. The members of the Bureau serve as both hunters of hunters and protectors of the hunted. An agency of the United States Government, the FBI is composed, like its country, of people who—potentially at least—are at once predator and prey.

As the great care in designing and photographing Gumb's basement reminds one of Hitchcock's scrupulousness, so do a number of less visual details. The twisting of language in *The Silence of the Lambs* and its ironic humor recall *Psycho* (which Hitchcock once famously called a comedy) and, generally, the wry wit that informs even Hitchcock's grimmest films. Deviations of language occur prominently in both *Psycho* and *The Silence of the Lambs*. The former is filled with Norman's semi-malapropisms—an office that is "too officious," a Mother who "isn't quite herself today," and significant stutterings like "fal-fal-false-falsity." As to *The Silence of the Lambs,* "the lowly pun," writes Karen Mann, "may be the best emblem for the way meaning functions in the film." [16] Besides his occasional puns, Lecter conceals meanings in another form of verbal metamorphosis, anagrams, which transform one word or phrase into another by rearranging letters.

Other bits of eccentric humor recall Hitchcock's characteristic playfulness. To the horribly disfigured policeman who seems to have survived Lecter's escape (actually, it's Lecter himself concealed beneath the flayed face of his victim), a hysterical young cop can only think to repeat, "You look real good there." Just before that escape, the camera briefly notes a copy of *Bon Appétit* magazine in Lecter's cell. The sheriff's gossipy wife and Marion's chatty fellow secretary in *Psycho* are but a pair of the quirky minor characters who pop up throughout Hitchcock's films. The incongruously patrician owner of the self-storage lockers and his chauffeur who "detests physical labor" recall Hitchcock's fondness for humorous incidental figures, as do the entomologists playing some curious game on a checkerboard with living beetles.

Let us end this discussion by turning to the aspect of Demme's film that seems most clearly to separate it from Hitchcock's practice, its absence of romantic love and—as is usual in Hitchcock's happy endings—the final conjunction of a central man and woman. This absence will be particularly noticeable to readers of Harris's novel, because the film omits the amorous connection that Clarice and the entomologist make at the end of the book. Nonetheless, a faint undercurrent of romance remains in the fact that Clarice does not reject the scientist's "hitting on" her; on the contrary, she invites him (and his colleague, who serves as her roommate's date) to her graduation from the FBI Academy. Clarice, who comes close to the horror-film role that Clover calls "the Final Girl," is not wholly uninterested in men, sexually attracted to her roommate (despite the assertions of some commentators), or, "in a word, boyish." [17] Rather, she is pointedly feminine: petite, attractive to men, conscious of her femininity, a user of perfume, and a purchaser of good handbags. That she is also energetic, enterprising, strong, and insightful does not make her less feminine.

From what filmmaker does one learn most clearly that last lesson? From Hitchcock, most of whose heroines are at once beautiful and responsive, and strong, tenacious, intelligent, prevailing: Young Charlie in *Shadow of a Doubt,* the characters played by Ingrid Bergman in *Spellbound, Notorious,* and *Under Capricorn,* Grace Kelly in her three Hitchcock films, and Blanche in *Family Plot,* to take some of the most obvious examples. Indeed, it was through Barbara Harris's shrewd, greedy, libidinous Blanche that Hitchcock offered his final adieu to his movie audience—an enchanting, ambiguous wink that sums up, as well as any single gesture could, the tone of his entire career.

By the end of most of Hitchcock's films—at least those that end happily— energetic heroines have firmly connected with a masculine counterpart. Before they achieve that connection, however, their circumstances usually cast them in the role of young women whose progress from the arms of fathers or father-figures to those of a lover has been somehow retarded. They find themselves dwelling too long in the parental home; drifting toward relationships with manifestly inappropriate, usually older, men; or being aggressed on by such figures—men who should be fathers or mentors rather than lovers. Constance in *Spellbound* is excessively attached to the father-figure of Dr. Murchison, for example, and Carol in *Foreign Correspondent* is acting as the companion and help-mate to her sinister father. Young Charlie in *Shadow of a Doubt,* Alicia in *Notorious,* and Eve in *North by Northwest* are each threatened or possessed by dangerous older men. At the end of *North by Northwest,* Cary Grant must rescue Eve from the "formidable" embrace of Vandamm. In *Notorious,* he must carry Alicia away from her marital incarceration by the aging but still maternally dominated Sebastian—whose own need to declare independence from his parent is emphatically not achieved by his counterfeit marriage.

The relation of Clarice to Dr. Lecter recalls the threats from older males faced by Hitchcock's heroines. (Such threats, of course, are the standard fate of the heroines of a great many romantic fictions, from Persephone and the princess in *Rumpelstiltskin* to Satine, the heroine of Baz Luhrmann's recent *Moulin Rouge.*) The "first meeting [of Hannibal and Clarice] always seems to me to have elements of a perverse flirtation reminiscent of the scene in Norman's parlor," suggests David Boyd.[18] Indeed, Lecter begins their relationship on a sexual note by insisting that Clarice repeat Miggs' claim, "I can smell your cunt." To that Lecter adds, with an insolent gallantry, "I myself cannot." He will continue to return aggressively to matters sexual, asking if the rancher who took her in as a foster child molested her, remarking that she must be aware of eyes gliding over her body, and suggesting that Dr. Crawford might "want to fuck you." The latter suggestion receives no support from any of Dr. Crawford's actions, but for the audience it does raise the possibility of such a mismatch. Coming from Lecter, it suggests more his own sexual suspicion than the likelihood of an April-September connection between Clarice with her boss and former professor. Lecter's jealousy is directly and chillingly expressed when Miggs flings his semen onto Clarice. Like an implacable lover or husband revenging the violation of a mate, he manages—by the unlikely expedient of persuading Miggs to swallow his tongue—to kill Clarice's sexual assailant. With his congratulatory telephone call to Clarice's graduation party, Lecter seems to have retreated into a more paternal role, but his declaration that "the world's a more interesting place with you in it, Clarice" does not wholly shelve the possibility of ongoing amorous interest.

Nonetheless, despite the presence of a potential mate at the end of the film and the threats of an unsuitable one at the beginning, the fact remains that there's little billing and cooing or other love interest in *The Silence of the Lambs.* We should recall, however, Northrop Frye's argument that comedies are narratives of social integration and that the marriages or other couplings with which so many of them end are emblems for the broader coming together of young and old, rich and poor, male and female, and all the parties whose contentions fuel their plots. Hitchcock's romantic comedy–thrillers, in addition to their frequent creation of a heterosexual couple, almost always also include the wider social integration that Frye found to be essential to comic actions. False accusations are finally refuted, parents abandon their skepticism and beam approvingly at formerly dubious offspring, crowds and nations—implied or explicit—enthusiastically welcome back the central figures they formerly pursued. The richness and complexity that Hitchcock was capable of bringing to the confluence of the social and the romantic is well exemplified by the doubled ending of *Shadow of a Doubt,* in which a congregation celebrates the benevolence of Uncle Charlie inside the church while on its steps the lovers at once puzzle over his evil side and implicitly acknowledge their love.

The comic plot of *The Silence of the Lambs* ends with its penultimate scene, Clarice's graduation. It typifies the social integration and acceptance that signifies successful conclusions to romantic comedies. Having been plunged into absolute darkness and stalked to the point of death, Starling emerges from her ordeal to be certified, in the next shot, as a full-fledged agent of the FBI. She is welcomed into its fellowship by her mentors, the doctors. Crawford and Lecter, and by the memory of her dead parent; for to his own applause Crawford adds, "Your father would be proud of you." Whatever subdued amorous overtones may remain, Hannibal Lecter raises only therapeutic issues when he asks Clarice if she has achieved her other longed-for transformation, into one who hears not the screaming but the silence of the lambs. Like most of Hitchcock's heroines, in defeating her antagonists she has been cured of what ailed her. Moreover, she and her roommate have dates. Not an un-Hitchcockian resolution, after all.

Notes

1. Carol J. Clover. *Men, Women, and Chain Saws* (Princeton: Princeton University Press, 1992), 233.

2. Julie Tharp, "The Transvestite as Monster: Gender Horror in Jonathan Demme's *The Silence of the Lambs* and *Psycho*," *Journal of Popular Film and Television* 19, no. 3 (Fall 1991): 105–113. Tharp argues that "Many of the elements that made *Psycho* a horrific experience for its original audience have been magnified and in some cases collapsed into one another in *The Silence of the Lambs*." (106).

3. Eric Rohmer and Claude Chabrol. Stanley Hochman, trans. *Hitchcock: The First Forty-Four Films* (New York: Frederick Ungar, 1979), 134. Originally published in France in 1957.

4. T. S. Eliot. "Tradition and the Individual Talent" in *The Sacred Wood: Essays on Poetry and Criticism* (1920; rpt. London: Methuen & Co., 1946), 50.

5. Harold Schechter, "Skin Deep: Folk Tales, Face Lifts, and *The Silence of the Lambs*," *Literature, Interpretation, Theory* 5, no. 1 (1994): 23.

6. Clover, 5.

7. Thomas Harris. *The Silence of the Lambs* (New York: St. Martin's Press, 1988), 239.

8. Jhan Hochman, "*The Silence of the Lambs*: A Quiet Bestiary," *Interdisciplinary Studies in Literature and Environment* 1, no. 2 (Fall 1993): 57.

9. As Carol Watts writes, "the assault course sequence . . . encodes a feeling of threat in classical fashion; the camera stalking the lone runner/victim through the woods." "From Looking to Coveting: The 'American Girl' in *The Silence of the Lambs*." *Women: A Cultural Review* 4, no. 1 (1993): 68.

10. Elias Canetti. *Crowds and Power* (New York: Farrar, Straus and Giraux, 1984), 203. Originally published by Victor Gollancz Ltd., 1962.

11. "Lecter's role in the film," observes David Sundelson, "is perfectly ambiguous." "The Demon Therapist and Other Dangers," *The Journal of Popular Film and Television* 21, no. 1 (Spring 1993): 13.

12. Judith Halberstam notes that Gumb "is waiting . . . for his beautiful metamorphosis" and that "Hannibal too attempts a transformation." "Skinflick: Posthuman Gender in Jonathan Demme's *The Silence of the Lambs,*" *Camera Obscura* 27 (September 1991): 48.

13. Canetti, 369–70.

14. Schechter, 25.

15. For an extended discussion of Hitchcock's use of color in *North by Northwest,* please see my article, "Canetti and Hitchcock: *Crowds and Power* and *North by Northwest.*" *Arizona Quarterly* 56, No. 4 (Winter 2000): 119–46.

16. Karen B. Mann, "The Matter With Mind: Violence and *The Silence of the Lambs,*" *Criticism: A Quarterly for Literature and the Arts* 38, No. 4 (Fall 1996): 601.

17. Clover, 40. On page 233, Clover declares Starling to be "masculine in both manner and career, uninterested in sex or men."

18. David Boyd, editorial suggestion, April 2002.

PART II: THE RETURN OF THE REPRESSED

Although Hitchcock consistently shunned the horror tradition of vampires and werewolves, an element of the Gothic lies buried just beneath the surface of many of his films. Adam Knee and Ina Rae Hark examine the return (or disinterment) of this repressed element in two very different films. Possibly the oddest of all Hitchcockian remakes, Paul Landres' low-budget 1958 horror film *The Return of Dracula* replays the pervasive vampiric suggestions of *Shadow of a Doubt* in perfectly literal and explicit terms, while Kenneth Branagh's *Dead Again* similarly literalizes the metaphorical reincarnations of figures like Rebecca de Winter and Madeleine Elster. When the repressed returns, however, it does so in oddly disguised and distorted forms, and much of the interest of these films lies in the unusual nature of the intertextual relationships they involve. *The Return of Dracula,* Knee suggests, is less like a remake than like a parody, whereas *Dead Again,* according to Hark, "imagines a Hitchcockian scenario that escapes Hitchcock's usual solutions, and then applies a post-Hitchcockian fix."

The Return of Dracula is pervaded by the themes and images of the horror film, yet betrays a strong Hitchcockian sensibility in its dark humor and social satire.

Shadows of *Shadow of a Doubt*

Adam Knee

The *Return of Dracula* (1958) is hardly a distinguished film as American horror films go—a low-budget production at a time of a low ebb in the genre, horror having been largely supplanted by science fiction throughout the 1950s. Both in fact remained largely disreputable genres during the decade, rarely commanding "A treatment" and instead serving as fodder for drive-in double bills. The seventy-seven-minute film mentioned here, produced by the small independent company Gramercy Pictures, was itself variously released (by United Artists) on double bills with the genre films *The Flame Barrier* (1958) and *House of the Living* (1958).[1] As such low-budget fare goes, however, *The Return of Dracula* is a reasonably entertaining film, with passable acting, an intermittently strong sense of atmosphere, and several extremely striking scenes—none more so than a staking scene where the film stock suddenly switches from monochrome to color in a gloriously bloody close-up. Moreover, in its attempt to resurrect a moribund genre and give it a New World context, *The Return of Dracula* utilizes the novel plot device of having the vampire find lodging with a California family who think he's a long-lost relative and only gradually become aware of his true nature. This means of getting the vampire to the west coast of the United States is all the more unusual in that it strongly echoes a central premise of a major Hollywood success of fifteen years earlier—the Alfred Hitchcock film *Shadow of a Doubt* (1943)—and it is for this reason that this largely marginal horror film will receive closer scrutiny in this essay.

In fact, not just the central premise—murderous relative comes to live with unsuspecting California family—is borrowed; numerous elements of the earlier film seem to be resurrected here in vampiric—or, perhaps more to the point, vampirized—form. There is again an opening flight from the authorities, an arrival at a California train station involving disguise and subterfuge. There is again a relationship with a teenage woman in the household who feels a deep connection to the visitor and for whom the visitor represents excitement. There is again a visitation to the household by a less-than-forthcoming government agent in pursuit of the visitor. There is again eventually an attempt by the visitor against the young woman's life, which ends when the visitor has a fatal fall. Certainly many audience members familiar with the Hitchcock text could have drawn the connection. Indeed, there is even a marked allusion to a celebrated Hitchcock transition in one of the opening sequences of the film: when the vampire claims his first victim on a train, there is a cut from the screaming victim to the scream of the train's whistle, much like the cut from the scream of the landlady finding a corpse in *The 39 Steps* (1935).

On the surface this may sound like a relatively self-conscious remake—citing both a prior film and the renowned style of the director of that film—and a later interview with the scriptwriter in fact confirms that the Hitchcock film "had an influence."[2] Nevertheless, *The Return of Dracula* differs from most remakes in quite a few ways and therefore makes an interesting "test case" for our understanding of what constitutes a remake and how it functions with respect to its sources. A first difference is that the film's credits make no acknowledgment of any prior source (neither the original story for *Shadow of a Doubt* by Gordon McDonnell, nor its screenplay); it simply lists an original story and screenplay by Pat Fiedler. Thomas M. Leitch argues that it is a central tendency of remakes to disavow the prior film text, citing instead the shared literary source material, as a strategy to simultaneously suggest both similarity and superiority.[3] One could in one sense describe *The Return of Dracula*'s not even citing a shared source as an extreme instance of such disavowal. However, I think the functioning of this disavowal is a bit different than in the texts Leitch cites: *Return* doesn't really have pretenses to be a superior version of *Shadow*. If it is to be described as a remake, it would have to be as a debased one, a degeneration of an "A picture" by a top director to a "B picture" from a marginal production outfit.

One reason for the lack of acknowledgment of prior texts may be that *The Return of Dracula* is not conceived of as a remake in the usual sense, that it sees itself more as an adaptation, of sorts—from one cultural realm (widely accepted) to another (marginalized exploitation fare) and indeed from one genre (crime thriller) to another (vampire film).[4] This is evident from the fact that the film was not marketed as a Hitchcockian product, but rather as an horrific exploitation film, United Artists copying from other exploitation advertising campaigns in its suggestion that insurance companies were refusing to cover liability stemming from fright during the film.[5] Clearly, the film's not positioning itself as a remake also engenders financial savings—and it was presumably able to get away with this in part because its particular form of circulation was in an entirely different realm than that of the Hitchcock film, because it would have been "off the radar," so to speak, dwelling in the shadowy recesses of the exploitation world. But again, even if some of the motivations are pecuniary, the nature of its differences from the earlier film are such that *The Return of Dracula* doesn't quite fit the usual rhetoric of the remake, as Leitch describes it. What the film does to the prior text(s) might in fact be more fruitfully compared to what a parody does; it reengages elements of a specific prior text, but in a different generic mode, and therefore gives these elements rather different functions than they had before.

Or perhaps not all that different. The vampire thriller is not that far apart in the generic universe from the crime thriller—both offering thrills and suspense, shadowy visuals, and a fascinatingly transgressive (even attractive) antagonist—and *Shadow of a Doubt* in particular has many elements that readily lend themselves to a reworking as horror (as indeed, the director himself became more and more associated with that genre in later decades).[6] *Shadow of a Doubt* even has a direct, if seemingly incidental, reference to the vampire genre, when one of the detectives investigating the murderer gets some privacy with the protagonist by sending her precocious little sister away to tell someone "the story of Dracula." While this may at first seem a throwaway line, the reference to vampirism does in fact resonate at several levels of the text—and Bill Krohn (noting that the reference in the shooting script had been, rather, to Jekyll and Hyde) has suggested the line is "a clue inserted in the dialogue by Hitchcock."[7] Indeed, David Sterritt and James McLaughlin have both offered convincing analyses of the film which posit the vampire references as central to its structure and signification.[8] As one who murders wealthy widows for their money, Uncle Charlie feeds upon others for his sustenance, and manages to do so by making himself attractive to them, just as the vampire is able to elicit the cooperation of those he feeds upon by making himself irresistible to them through hypnotism, itself often sexually charged. Like Dracula, Uncle Charlie is a master of dissemblance, appearing to be something other than what he really is—and he takes his most genuine form in the filmic discourse in a scene that occurs at night, a scene where he accompanies his suspicious niece (also Charlie) to a disreputable cocktail lounge. (That, significantly, is a scene in which Robin Wood sees the film's own internal generic tensions—between small-town Hollywood drama and film noir—as especially pronounced.⁹) And Uncle Charlie's aversion to the camera as an apparatus which may unmask him has a corollary in the vampire's similar aversion to mirrors (and, in some films, cameras) for the same reasons. (Indeed, in *The Return of Dracula* it is a photograph which finally proves to authorities the interloper's vampirism.) Charlie herself fits into the role of the attractive young female threatened by the vampire but often rescued from him just in time—sometimes even being instrumental in the destruction of the vampire (as, for example, when Nosferatu cannot resist drinking the blood of an innocent past the cock's crow in the films that bear his name [1922 and 1979]). In such cases, the female often falls under the sway of the vampire in part because a small amount of his blood has been introduced into her system. In *Shadow of a Doubt*, similarly, Uncle Charlie pleads for sympathy from his niece, even as she becomes repulsed by him, with the reminder that "the same blood flows through our veins." But at the same time (as McLaughlin emphasizes), both Charlie's and Dracula's victims collude in their own victimization: both on some level desire interaction with the victimizer, Charlie believing she has somehow telepathically summoned her uncle to rescue her from the doldrums.¹⁰

In this light (or, more appropriately, under this shadow), *Shadow of a Doubt* appears a film that already has a vampiric subtext: rather than radically shifting the prior material, *The Return of Dracula* in effect unearths what is already there in repressed or hidden form, making it explicit. In a sense then, it seems to be trying to offer a more complete drawing-out of the prior text's implications, making a new "attempt to get it right," to use Ira Konigsberg's description of the impulse to revisit an earlier story.¹¹ Konigsberg is in fact dealing with the singular case of the extreme popularity of *Dracula* as a source for remakes, arguing that the compulsion to return to it must be related to a deeper attraction that the character and the narrative elements have—an attraction that goes beyond a need to remake any single literary text. The story of *Shadow* obviously hasn't had the same obsessive attraction for filmmakers as that of *Dracula* (though, as shall be touched on further, *The Return of Dracula* is *also* a remake of *Dracula*)—but *Shadow* can be argued to likewise suggest a need for extension or completion, to more fully work out some of the themes it suggests.

Though Konigsberg's emphasis is on the transcendent, near-mythic resonance of the *Dracula* narrative, he does allow that a remake may also be seen as "a reinterpretation to fit a changing time and culture," and I think this emphasis is especially pertinent for understanding the remaking of *Shadow of a Doubt*—not only because it was *not* remade with obsessive frequency, but because (as shall be discussed further) it was in fact remade *twice* in 1958, which surely points to a particular historical resonance for some of its elements.[12] It therefore seems to me that the most critically productive questions to ask about a remake (or adaptation or extension) such as *The Return of Dracula* concern the cultural relevance of the processes of retelling and transforming: Why was the Hitchcock film remade in the way it was and at the time it was? What are the culturally resonant/relevant emphases of this resurrected form of *Shadow of a Doubt*? In asking such questions I concur with Robert Eberwein's position that we need to return to the cultural contexts of the texts in question, to see the films' temporal connections to the semiotic fields in which they have operated over time.[13] Before I attempt to explore such contexts, however, I would like to specify my approach a bit further: I do accept that *The Return of Dracula* is, in part, a remake of *Shadow of a Doubt*—but it is simultaneously involved with remaking/reworking/adapting other texts, engaging other contemporary discourses as well, in a complex, multilayered process. Most obviously, the film also remakes other vampire and Dracula films and engages in a late-1950s exploitation film discourse. Rather than simply a transformation of a prior text, then, I think it would be more fruitful—and more precise—to discuss *Return* as being involved in the kind of "intertextual dialogism" Robert Stam ascribes to some film adaptations. This "activist" form of adaptation, as Stam describes it,

is less an attempted resuscitation of an originary word than a turn in an on-going dialogical process. The concept of intertextual dialogism suggests that every text forms an intersection of textual surfaces. All texts are tissues of anonymous formulae, conscious and unconscious quotations, and conflations and inversions of other texts. In the broadest sense, intertextual dialogism refers to the infinite and open-ended possibilities generated by all the discursive practices of a culture, the entire matrix of communicative practices within which the artistic text is situated, which reach the text not only through recognizable influences, but also through a subtle process of dissemination.[14]

Borrowing from Stam (himself borrowing from various theorists of intertextuality) then, I would like to emphasize the multiplicity of *The Return of Dracula*'s referentiality and textual borrowing, even if it is also reasonable to posit references to *Shadow of a Doubt* as a "dominant" within its textual system; and I would further like to emphasize that these textual references mesh with, indeed are a component part of, the broader web of contemporary discourses which produce this particular text.

The title of the remake in question here draws attention to a textual "return," one going back at the very least to Bram Stoker's story, which, like the film (and unlike *Shadow of a Doubt*) involves the antagonist's journeying from his old dominion to achieve new conquests in a foreign land. The screenwriter herself mentions the influence of the Stoker text, pointing to "the angle about the friendship of the two girls"—two victims of the vampire in the film, as in the prior story.[15] This emphasis in the 1958 film is arguably taken up in such a way that it speaks to that film's expected teen audience[16]—while there isn't near the same level of emphasis on Charlie's relationship with any of her girlfriends in the 1943 film. Indeed, the whole notion of a distinct teenage identity was largely the creation of the 1950s, given one of its most significant articulations in that era's teen-oriented exploitation film.[17] Thus, in *The Return of Dracula,* there is the representation of protagonist Rachel Mayberry's distinctly teenage behaviors, most significantly her courtship and dating rituals with teen neighbor Tim, always at the ready with his big-finned convertible to give a lift whenever she might need one, and her volunteer work at the local parish house. Not surprisingly, the vampire's chief threat in this film is against teenagers—and his conversion of Rachel's virginal (and blind) friend Jenny into a vampiric (and seeing!) evildoer, along with his potential to do the same to "clean teen" Rachel, clearly aligns him with the threat of teenage loss of morals and teenage delinquency so often played up in that time period. In sharp contrast, *Shadow of a Doubt*'s protagonist Charlie is clearly presented as a "young adult," as opposed to a part of a (not yet existent) distinctly teen demographic; indeed, that earlier film seems to want to emphasize the protagonist's dressing as an adult and showing judgment and behavior that in many ways mark her off as the most emotionally mature member of her family, in spite of her age.

The other textual influence Pat Fiedler refers to, *Shadow of a Doubt,* she interestingly describes as "Thornton Wilder's film for Hitchcock." Perhaps this emphasis on celebrated author over celebrated auteur reflects the fact that she herself is a scriptwriter, but it also suggests that she found some of the salient features of the film text to be "Wilderian" rather than Hitchcockian; one could conjecture, for example, that she took interest in the portrait of the rituals of small-town American life, associated with Wilder in the wake of the 1938 stage production and 1940 film of *Our Town,* as much as in its Hitchcockian suspense and drama. And *The Return of Dracula* does indeed seem, within the modest confines of its genre and budget, interested in some appreciation of small-town life in the 1950s plausibly inspired (directly or indirectly) by Wilder—the aforementioned courtship rituals of Rachel and Tim, for example, and the preparations for and execution of a costumed Halloween dance at the parish house. Such details, moreover, are hardly incidental in a film about an evil external force which threatens life in the town: the cherished rituals are precisely what are threatened. The influence of Thornton Wilder's work (in conjunction with Cold War angst) makes its way into *The Return of Dracula*'s textual nexus in another, more circuitous, way as well. The production designer for the 1940 film of *Our Town* was William Cameron Menzies. A fence at the opening of that film, which serves as a visual correlative of the social order of the region being marked off by the narrative, is very strongly echoed (visually and thematically) by a fence prominent in the Menzies-directed 1953 science fiction film *Invaders from Mars*—a fence which seemingly separates the domestic and alien realms. In that exceptional, and exceptionally paranoid, work—Menzies' follow-up to his anticommunist thriller *The Whip Hand* (1951)—the old small-town way of life is put in imminent danger from both the secretive atmosphere fostered by military-based industries and an actual alien invasion. As producers of a number of teen-oriented 1950s science fiction and horror films, the makers of *The Return of Dracula* would certainly have been aware of that film and its thematic emphases; indeed, the producer and director of *Return* had themselves at one time been involved in preproduction on *Invaders from Mars* before losing the option on the property.[18]

This brings us back to the generic frame of reference so central to the film's intertextual negotiations. Themes of threatening external invasion were paramount in the science fiction genre with which horror was so closely allied in the 1950s—some horror-themed films (including Gramercy Pictures' previous film *The Vampire* [1957]) even bringing in science-fictive explanations for the existence of their (formerly supernatural) monsters. As has often been noted, 1950s science fiction films use alien invasions as a cipher for a range of fearful and potentially invasive forces of the age—foreign governments and ideologies (particularly communism) among them. Like these science fiction films (and significantly unlike *Shadow of a Doubt*), *The Return of Dracula* draws from contemporary generic and other popular discourses to figure its antagonist likewise as a foreign, invading agent; and as Cyndy Hendershot rightly notes, the vampire's representation in the film more specifically likens him to a communist threat.[19] There are references, for example, not only to his desire to wield control over a small community, but his more ambitious aims of "spreading his evil dominion ever wider" (according to voice-over narration) and of "starting a chain of domination" in the United States (according to a European official). The vampire's Eastern European origins would also appear to allude to a communist threat, while the opposition to Christianity he represents (discussed further below) is itself consonant with perceptions of communism as godless. As this discussion might suggest, the contemporary anticommunist (or "Red Scare") films, often lurid thrillers dealing with various forms of communist infiltration and subversion, are another generic intertext engaged here; *My Son John* (1952) indeed seems a particularly strong point of reference, as it too deals with a formerly absent relative's returning home, only to arouse (fully founded) suspicions of a dark secret (his indoctrination into Communism).[20]

This characterization of the vampire as interested in conquest is markedly different from that of the antagonist of *Shadow of a Doubt;* Uncle Charlie hardly has any grand designs to spread his influence. His is strictly a one-man operation—of which, as he intimates to his niece, he himself has grown weary—and he has come to small-town America purely to elude pursuing authorities. The cause of Uncle Charlie's predations, that film suggests, is mental illness (as opposed to vampirism)—indicated in a reference to a childhood skull fracture after which Uncle Charlie was never the same. This tendency to do evil is not, like vampirism, a spreading malignancy—but the film goes out of its way to darkly suggest that the potential exists in all of us, lurks behind the scrubbed-clean façade of small-town America. As Uncle Charlie explains to his niece in the smoky environs of the cocktail lounge (itself emblematizing the underside of Santa Rosa), "You live in a dream. You're a sleepwalker, blind. How do you know what the world is like? Do you know the world is a foul sty? Do you know if you ripped the fronts off houses you'd find swine?" The detective who pursues Uncle Charlie as a criminal and Charlie as a wife makes some comments at the close of the film which are intended to assuage the young woman's concerns about her uncle's claims, but in effect really confirm some of them. He says that the world is "not quite as bad" as the uncle makes out, "but sometimes it needs a lot of watching. It seems to go crazy every now and then. Like your Uncle Charlie." The detective himself appears to hold such a potential, as suggested in his admittedly irrational outburst when he professes his love for Charlie. And Charlie for her part, in both her seemingly telepathic intimacy with the killer and in her extreme emotional confusion as the film progresses, appears to even more strongly hold such a potential; in fact, by the time she is fully disillusioned with her uncle, she is able to calmly inform him, "I'll kill you myself," and she eventually does—albeit not as a result of any plan. This potential for "madness" and mortal violence also resonates in the historical context of the Hitchcock film. Where vampirism appears allied to the malignant spread of communism in *The Return of Dracula,* the potential for violent mental imbalance in all of us seems allied with a context of global military violence in *Shadow of a Doubt;* while the World War II context is never directly addressed by the characters, it is everywhere evident in Hitchcock's Santa Rosa—in the servicemen we continually see, in the war bond posters which adorn the bank and public library—and it is also present in the contemporary Hitchcockian intertext of *Foreign Correspondent* (1940) and *Saboteur* (1942).

Thus, while in the Hitchcock film, the small-town American way of life is under threat from the potential madness of human nature—an *inherent* human proclivity for violence—which resonates with the contemporary hot war, in the 1950s vampire film, the small-town American way of life is under threat from vampirism—an *alien* malignancy—which resonates with the contemporary Cold War. In keeping with Hitchcock's essentially darker view—that the potential for evil is something that must be regulated within all of us—*Shadow of a Doubt* repeatedly (albeit often humorously) offers the suggestion that all might not be completely right with its all-American family, to which Uncle Charlie does indeed belong. Charlie's father, for example, has a ghoulish and childish preoccupation with mystery stories and, in particular, effective methods of murder; he also appears rather weak-willed and disconnected from his family life in general. Nor is Charlie's mother (Uncle Charlie's sister) much more of an authority figure in the household; though evidently well-meaning (like her husband), she is also often emotionally overwrought and seemingly overwhelmed by the various family pressures upon her. We can therefore readily understand when Uncle Charlie tells his niece, "You're the head of your family, Charlie; anyone can see that." But, as already noted, the darker side of her character is also suggested. In their turn, her uncomfortably precocious younger sister has an obsession with books which, we later learn, echoes one Uncle Charlie had in his youth, while her younger brother suffers from being doted upon as the youngest just as Uncle Charlie too had been: unfortunate family patterns persist. Then there is the borderline incestuous attachment both Charlie and her mother have to Uncle Charlie, their comportment toward him in a number of scenes appearing to suggest more a romantic than a familial relationship.

In substantial contrast, such darker undertones are largely absent from the representation of the family in *The Return of Dracula*. This bastion of American values is under threat here not because of any inherent moral flaw but because its lack of a father (he has died), in a decade when the nuclear family is a culturally and institutionally enforced norm, leaves it open to an invasion by an alien element—a substitute father in the form of a long-lost cousin.[21] Quite significantly, this is not a true blood relative, but an impostor—a fact which both takes away any suggestion that the malignancy is inherent within the family and engages contemporary discourses about communist agents disguising who or what they really are (a discourse taken up likewise in contemporary science fiction films where aliens disguise themselves as specific humans). Nor does Dracula genuinely take up residence in the home as Uncle Charlie does; the Mayberrys give him a room, but he in fact stays in his coffin in a cavern at a distance from the house.[22] Rachel is attracted to the foreigner's evident classiness and exoticism (a fictitious background in the Parisian art world) and does eventually begin to fall under the vampire's sway, even giving him some aid in his evildoing after she has been hypnotized, but the suggestion is that this is because of her innocence more than any inherent moral flaw; she is vulnerable as a fatherless teen and therefore must be protected from alien influence. Significantly, this protection comes in the form of a would-be husband; it is the boyfriend Tim (rather than the female protagonist, as in *Shadow of a Doubt*) who causes the villain to fall to his death. In the 1950s, all is made right with the world not when a young woman comes to greater wisdom and independence, but when she is safely positioned within a potential nuclear family unit.

Another significant axis of connection between the two films is their emphasis on themes of religion and morality, a number of commentators arguing the influence of Hitchcock's Catholicism on *Shadow of a Doubt*.[23] Uncle Charlie and Dracula alike are figured as embodiments of evil, and the church (in contrast) is repeatedly shown as a moral and architectural cornerstone of Santa Rosa. Uncle Charlie himself, not surprisingly, does not attend services, commenting sarcastically to his namesake, "Show's been running such a long time, I thought maybe attendance was falling off." Interestingly, Hitchcock's camera never takes us inside the church; in scenes at the church (always bathed in bright sunlight), those people who are involved in the combat of evil (in the form of Uncle Charlie) hold their conversations outside of and back away from the building. It is almost as though those involved in the "good fight"—Charlie and the policemen—need to have a broader, more catholic view of things, need to literally see beyond the town's complacent moral center to perceive and counter the underlying darkness. The religious motifs are more explicitly foregrounded and less nuanced in *The Return of Dracula*, the product of an era of religious revivalism.[24] Part of what makes Rachel's own morality beyond question is her continuous involvement in parish house activities, volunteering, for example, to read to the blind Jenny and to make costumes for the Halloween party. The parish's reverend seems a central figure of authority in this small community, one whom a European police agent goes to for local assistance in tracking down Dracula. As in many a vampire film, the fight for the vampire's victims is discussed as a fight for their "souls," in which a key weapon is the cross itself. When Rachel is finally influenced to toss her cross to the ground, Dracula's response makes his identity as an Antichrist unequivocal: "You shall rise reborn in me." The vampire's death moments later thus not only allows the return of nuclear family stability (as noted), but of Christian moral authority as well—in a close which hardly suggests the complex moral shadings of the Hitchcock film.

One further contemporary discourse from *Shadow of a Doubt* which *The Return of Dracula* finds of use for its own context is that regarding the proper limits of individual freedoms when national security is at stake—especially against a backdrop of (hot or cold) international conflict. In *Shadow,* the issue comes up in part when Uncle Charlie asserts his right not to be photographed, not to have his individual privacy invaded. He explicitly makes the connection between this demand and American conceptualizations of individual rights later on, when he bids farewell to the detective: "Have a nice trip, Mr. Graham. And don't take any more photographs without permission. Rights of man, you know, freedoms?" Detective Graham's response is that "we'll have to talk about freedoms some day." The detective's later comments about the world needing a lot of watching suggests what his (and the film's) position on these freedoms might be—that individual liberties must often be balanced with security concerns in order to ensure their continuation in an unstable and potentially violent world, as evidenced by the conflict overseas. On another level, this is a lesson that Charlie herself has learned. She opens the film feeling trapped, listless, and bored, needing excitement and freedom from the dull confines of Santa Rosa. Her wishes are answered in the form of her uncle—but she comes to learn that what is exciting and refreshing is also (as often the case in a Hitchcock film) dangerous; as a result, at the close of the film she appears ready to set aside some of this impulse for personal freedom in favor of the safety and security represented by a potential marriage to the detective.

Charlie's later counterpart, Rachel, also feels constrained by her small-town existence and is thrilled by the exotic and glamorous possibilities represented by her supposed relative; and she too learns that with the freedom to break away comes danger. In *The Return of Dracula*'s Cold War context, the discourse about freedom is now linked to an opposition between a free America and an oppressive Communist bloc. A would-be immigrant artist from Eastern Europe (soon to be killed and have his identity stolen by the vampire) comments on this opposition at the film's opening, declaring, "At least in America, I will be free to paint what I like." Upon his arrival in California under the guise of an artist, Dracula himself claims (with much double entendre), "My life has been confined. That's why I've come here. For freedom. I must have it." Later on, when a Department of Immigration official comes to the Mayberry residence to inquire after him, he pardons the intrusion, indicating that he is used to them. The official takes the opportunity to respond, "Yes, that's the big difference between our countries. You see, over here we don't like to investigate a man unless it's absolutely necessary." The sentiment is echoed later in the reverend's unintentionally humorous line, "We don't want to make unjust accusations until we are sure." Certainly the Hitchcock text does subtly suggest a similar American perspective—the detectives, for example, do try to respect Uncle Charlie's wishes within reason—but this Cold War text feels a need to work overtime to make the point. The need for this new level of emphasis, one could readily surmise, is that such values had so visibly and publicly come under pressure in the McCarthy years of the early 1950s, with many people accused of political subversion with little or no evidence. The discourse from the earlier film thus remains quite relevant indeed, while taking on new kinds of resonances (and needing to be dealt with in a new fashion) because of intervening historical events. Another way the discourse about individual freedoms is reconfigured to meet the needs of the 1950s is through the connection made to contemporary concerns about conformity. It is commonplace that concerns over the pressure to conform—both at home and in the corporate world—had substantial currency in the decade of the "Organization Man." *The Return of Dracula* makes a nod to this discourse both in having its two "free spirits" (Rachel and Dracula) be artists (longstanding figures of nonconformity), and in having Dracula respond to the mother's concern about his evident emotional distance with the following little speech: "And is this the price for your acceptance? For me to conform? To be as you would want me to be?"

The basic premise here that aspects of the prior text are resurrected because they are in some way pertinent to (or have a potential cultural use-value for) a new historical context is, as noted earlier, bolstered by the fact that another remake of *Shadow of a Doubt*, this one more authorized in the usual sense, appeared in the same year. *Step Down to Terror* remains in the same genre as the Hitchcock film and explicitly acknowledges a prior text (the story upon which *Shadow* is based) as its source material—thus engaging the kind of triangular textual relationship Leitch describes as often obtaining with remakes.

Step Down to Terror is, like *The Return of Dracula,* a low-budget production clearly intended for the "program market," as the *Variety* review describes it, but it is also not as industrially or culturally marginal as the vampiric remake[25]: It is an in-house production of Universal Studios and is, as noted, an authorized remake and not in as disreputable a genre as the teen horror exploitation film.

Compared with *The Return of Dracula,* however, *Step Down to Terror* is by far the more "lifeless" film. Where *The Return of Dracula* has the freedom (that its characters themselves refer to) as an unauthorized text to do what it wants to with the original and thereby to explore its horrific undertones to an imaginative extent, *Step Down* appears to feel constrained from substantially reworking the (disavowed) Hitchcock film—or, as an obvious factory product, to simply be uninspired to do so. After an opening which, given its visual similarities to *Shadow of a Doubt,* might have been intended to allude to the earlier film, many key scenes are re-created, but with little sense of narrative aim or focus; likewise, lines of dialogue similar to those of the earlier film are rattled off but with little sense of emotional connection to them by the actors.[26] The overall effect is that this text feels *less* plausible than the vampiric version of the narrative, its characters far more lacking in color.

Setting such sticky questions of "quality" aside, however, one can notice that once more the remake performs some adjustments upon the original that speak to a late 1950s historical context. Once more, for example, the visited household in California is seen as vulnerable to negative influences because it is lacking a father figure; indeed, in this film the lack is doubly felt, as the family matriarch has lost a husband several years previously and a son one year back, and she now lives with her widowed daughter-in-law (Helen, the film's female protagonist) and fatherless grandson. Helen's son indeed openly complains about being the only man in the house, and all are eager to welcome Johnny, the brother of Helen's late husband, into the household. If there is a warping of the earlier narrative by an ascendant contemporary genre here, it is by what is now called the family melodrama[27]; *Step Down to Terror* is plainly set up for a focus on a potentially lurid struggle concerning the continuation of the family line, with all of the adult men dead or (in the case of Johnny) criminally insane, and the female protagonist not (as in the other films) a blood relative of the visiting outsider (and hence a potential wife).

Also as in the vampire film, there is a lessening here of the Hitchcock film's broader sense of moral duality or uncertainty. Helen, unlike Charlie, has not felt an earlier, profound attachment to the criminal figure; she has hardly ever seen Johnny before his visit, and when she observes clues about Johnny's true nature, she is quick to dismiss him as a potential suitor. (The problem with this shift from the earlier film, in dramatic terms, is that it removes all of the interesting ambivalence felt by both Charlie and Rachel at having to turn against the visitors to their respective homes; Johnny is a threatening killer Helen hardly knows, so of course she is ready to see him apprehended.) Johnny does (now very quickly, on a suburban sidewalk) give a version of Uncle Charlie's speech about ripping the fronts off houses (he finds "selfish, miserable animals" instead of "swine"), but the film no longer offers any dark context in which the claim resonates (as it does indeed in *Shadow of a Doubt*); instead we are forced to see it merely as part of the increasingly unreasoning nature of Johnny's various outbursts, as part of his mental illness. Most strikingly, the detective's final comments to Charlie suggesting a universal potential to "go crazy" are now replaced by comments from a detective to Helen suggesting that Johnny was a singular aberration of the kind that needs to be erased from suburban America: "He was just a very sick man. Let's be thankful he's at rest now."[28]

However, one morally darker undertone which *Step Down to Terror* retains from the Hitchcock film, and perhaps even amplifies, is that of incestuous attraction. Aside from the fact that Johnny has a romantic interest in his late brother's wife (and she in him), there is the film's repeated emphasis on the fact that both Helen and Johnny's mother answer to the same name (Mrs. Walters) (a case of doubling, one could note, in a film that doubles a film itself known for its doubling). Johnny and his mother indeed appear to have an unusually strong, and unusually sensual, bond to one another, his mother caring for him, doting over him, making suggestions about his behavior—and fussing over him, stroking him, massaging him when he is upset. This shift from the earlier film too is very strongly related to contemporary perspectives—in particular certain negative discourses about overbearing motherhood. Michael Rogin has shown, for example, how such discourses (popularized in the 1940s under the term "Momism" by Philip Wylie) circulate within the aforementioned anticommunist films of the 1950s, the mother sometimes receiving some narrative blame for the son that has gone politically awry.[29] Images of Mrs. Walters feminizing her grandson at the film's opening— commending him for fetching flowers for his visiting uncle and requesting that he kiss his uncle when he meets him—are clear signals of such Momism, and the boy himself is evidently cognizant of the dangers of "being the only man in the house," when he complains, with Freudian self-consciousness, that the situation "was starting to give me a complex." Although Johnny's mental illness is most directly and explicitly attributed to his accident, it is clear that his own unhealthily intense relationship with his mother may be to blame for his maladjustment as well.

What remains most consistent in both 1958 retellings of the *Shadow of a Doubt* narrative is the emphasis on a small-town family's response to a dangerous visitor. The Hitchcock film's themes of suspicion over an outsider, desire to achieve family stability, and concern over the integrity of individual freedoms in a small-town context all quite clearly have strong potential use-value for the popular mediamakers of the 1950s. *The Return of Dracula*'s unauthorized remake in a generically shifted form gives the filmmakers free reign to utilize the narrative's resonance for the 1950s context and to draw out some of its horrific implications to a far-reaching extent; it transforms the earlier film's anxiety-ridden World War II subtext into a corresponding Cold War subtext, while also rendering the material in a more popularized (if arguably debased) form. *Step Down to Terror*, on the other hand, is more a genuine step down from the earlier text in not fully or convincingly revisiting its implications—but it too is plainly aware of the continued resonance of the Hitchcock film for the uneasy suburban framework of the 1950s.

Notes

1. *The Flame Barrier* is cited as a co-feature in Bill Warren, *Keep Watching the Skies!: American Science Fiction Movies of the Fifties*, vol. 2 (Jefferson, NC: McFarland, 1986), 71. *House of the Living* is cited in Thomas Doherty, *Teenagers & Teenpics: The Juvenilization of American Movies in the 1950s* (Boston: Unwin Hyman, 1988), 171.

2. Tom Weaver, *Science Fiction Stars and Horror Heroes: Interviews with Actors, Directors, Producers and Writers of the 1940s through 1960s* (Jefferson, NC: McFarland, 1991), 89.

3. Thomas Leitch, "Twice-Told Tales: Disavowal and the Rhetoric of the Remake," in *Dead Ringers: The Remake in Theory and Practice,* ed. Jennifer Forrest and Leonard R. Koos (Albany, NY: State University of New York Press, 2002), esp. 49. (A revised version of Leitch's "Twice-Told Tales: The Rhetoric of the Remake," *Literature/Film Quarterly* 18 (1990–91): 138–49.)

4. The precise relationship between a "remake" and an "adaptation" has not yet been definitively characterized, some seeing these as discrete categories, others seeing them as overlapping in various ways. Let it suffice for now to say that I concur with James Naremore's assertion that the same critical issues obtain with both forms, that "the study of adaptation needs to be joined with the study of recycling, remaking, and every other form of retelling in the age of mechanical reproduction and electronic communication," to ultimately work toward a "general theory of repetition." Naremore, "Introduction: Film and the Reign of Adaptation," in *Film Adaptation,* ed. James Naremore (New Brunswick, NJ: Rutgers University Press, 2000), 15.

5. "Mad, Mad Doctors 'n' Stunts," *Variety*, 23 July 1958, 7. (Reference brought to my attention in Doherty, 171.) The original review in *Variety* also makes no mention of the Hitchcock film: Powe, review of *The Return of Dracula, Variety*, 23 April 1958.

6. Carl Royer and Diana Royer's recent discussion of Hitchcock's relationship to the horror genre in fact puts particular emphasis on *Shadow of a Doubt* as engaging horror-related motifs. "'And I Brought You Nightmares': The Play of Horror in Hitchcock's Films," conference presentation, Popular Culture Association Conference, Toronto, Canada, 15 March 2002.

7. Bill Krohn, *Hitchcock at Work* (London: Phaidon Press, 2000), 62.

8. David Sterritt, *The Films of Alfred Hitchcock* (Cambridge University Press, 1993), ch. 3; James McLaughlin, "All in the Family: Alfred Hitchcock's *Shadow of a Doubt*," in *A Hitchcock Reader*, ed. Marshall Deutelbaum and Leland Poague (Ames: Iowa State University Press, 1986), ch. 11. (Expanded from version in *Wide Angle* 4, no. 1 [1980].)

9. Robin Wood, "Ideology, Genre, Auteur," in *Film Genre Reader*, ed. Barry Keith Grant (Austin: University of Texas Press, 1986), 69. (Originally in *Film Comment* 13, no. 1 (1977): 46–51.)

10. McLaughlin, 143.

11. Ira Konigsberg, "How Many Draculas Does It Take to Change a Lightbulb?" in *Play It Again, Sam: Retakes on Remakes*, ed. Andrew Horton and Stuart Y. McDougal (Berkeley: University of California Press, 1998), 250.

12. Konigsberg, 250.

13. Robert Eberwein, "Remakes and Cultural Studies," in Horton and McDougal, esp. 15–20.

14. Robert Stam, "Beyond Fidelity: The Dialogics of Adaptation," in Naremore, 64.

15. Weaver, 89.

16. The Powe review in *Variety* makes explicit reference to an assumed teen audience.

17. See Doherty, esp. ch. 3.

18. Weaver, 87.

19. Cyndy Hendershot, *I Was a Cold War Monster: Horror Films, Eroticism, and the Cold War Imagination* (Bowling Green, OK: Bowling Green State University Press, 2001), 50–51.

20. For an overview of this cinematic trend (and a specific discussion of *My Son John*), see Nora Sayre, *Running Time: Films of the Cold War* (New York: The Dial Press, 1982), ch. 3.

21. On the family ideology of the 1950s, see, for example, Douglas T. Miller and Marion Nowak, *The Fifties: The Way We Really Were* (Garden City, NY: Doubleday, 1977), ch. 6.

22. This cavern dwelling is, interestingly, a noticeable pattern among creatures in 1950s science fiction and horror films—evident in *It Conquered the World* (1956), for example.

23. See Wood, 66–70.

24. On this revivalism, see Stephen J. Whitfield, *The Culture of the Cold War* (Baltimore: Johns Hopkins University Press, 1991), ch. 4.

25. Powe, review of *Step Down to Terror*, *Variety*, 17 September 1958. This review also does not mention the Hitchcock film.

26. In at least one published interview, Hitchcock indicates his awareness of the existence of *Step Down to Terror*—and responds to an interviewer's comment that "it was exactly the same story line, but it was very dull" by observing, "You see, in a remake, they strip it of all its detail." Andy Warhol, "Hitchcock," in *Alfred Hitchcock Interviews*, ed. Sidney Gottlieb (Jackson: University Press of Mississippi, 2003), 210–11. (Originally in *Interview*, September 1974.)

27. For an overview of the genre, see Thomas Schatz, *Hollywood Genres: Formulas, Filmmaking, and the Studio System* (New York: Random House, 1981), ch. 8.

28. Another interesting, though more modest, change to the 1950s context here: while Uncle Charlie arrives by train and is killed in a fall from one, Johnny arrives in a big 1950s convertible and is killed when it crashes.

29. Michael Rogin, *Ronald Reagan: The Movie and Other Episodes in Political Demonology* (Berkeley: University of California Press, 1987), ch. 8.

Psycho or Psychic?
Hitchcock, *Dead Again,* and the Paranormal

Ina Rae Hark

W ere a court proceeding to be conducted on the issue, the *Dead Again* attorneys would have to stipulate that there are Hitchcockian echoes in that film. On the DVD commentary track, director Kenneth Branagh speaks of the film's evocation of "a bit of Hitchcock black Gothic" and admits that the film throughout was infused with "a lot of Hitchcock and Welles." Composer Patrick Doyle modeled his score on those of Bernard Herrmann, who worked with both these directors. On her track, producer Lindsay Doran remarks that the importance of objects in the film reflects Hitchcock's theories about "plastic material." A Google search of reviews of the film and its DVD release turned up over five hundred which noted Hitchcockian elements in *Dead Again.*

Specific nods in Hitchcock's direction include extended riffs on *Rebecca* (1940), *Spellbound* (1945), *Dial M for Murder* (1954), *Vertigo* (1958), and *Psycho* (1960). The Strauss mansion was envisioned "à la Manderley" Branagh says, and it houses a hostile housekeeper in conflict with her employer's second wife. He also thought of *Spellbound*'s "big dramatic score, the Salvador Dali designs, the dramatic lighting" (Hartl). Moreover, "Grace's" amnesia and memory flashes to a murder have a corollary in "John Brown's" emotional collapse in that film. The identity of an apparently sympathetic therapist as the actual killer links Dr. Murchison to hypnotist Franklyn Madson. The Strauss murder weapon is a pair of scissors, as it was in *Dial M;* screenwriter Scott Frank had wanted that Hitchcock film to play on Inga's television as she told Mike the truth about Margaret Strauss's death, but the rights would have been too steep for the budget to accommodate. "Grace's" apparent possession by a dead woman and her fright at the sight of a nun allude to Madeleine

Elster's supposed fixation on Carlotta Valdes. Mother-obsessed Madson seems a nod to Norman Bates, and the more generalized "traditionally pernicious" assignment "of murder, violence, and blame to the figure who conjures up the spectre of same-sex sexuality" (Fischer and Landy 18) recalls such sexually ambiguous Hitchcock villains as Handel Fane, Alex Sebastian, Bruno Anthony, Philip Vandamm, and Bob Rusk, whom audiences and critics are all too eager to read as "murderous gays," in Robin Wood's punning formulation (336).

Nevertheless, while "*Dead Again* owe[s] much to the films of Alfred Hitchcock ... even Mr. Hitchcock never attempted a thriller where people's past lives come back to haunt them" (Vivona). Whatever its Hitchcockian accessorizing, *Dead Again* is premised on the reality of reincarnation and the accessing of past lives through hypnotic regression. There is no comparable Hitchcock text that unequivocally posits the existence of supernatural or paranormal phenomena, although there are a number that leave the possibility of such occurrences ambiguously open. Looking at how *Dead Again* works the certainty of reincarnation into the paradigm of the Hitchcockian thriller can, by juxtaposition, help us trace the parameters of Hitchcockian supernaturalism, a subject that has received relatively little attention in Hitchcock studies.

If a person encounters evidence of paranormal phenomena, and wishes to discount it, three general sorts of explanation occur. The apparent occult manifestations may be the result of faulty perception, of psychological projection, or of fraud. When Gavin Elster tells Scottie Ferguson about Madeleine's odd behavior in regard to Carlotta Valdes, Scottie runs through the first two immediately:

> *Gavin:* Scottie, do you believe that someone out of the past, someone dead, can enter and take possession of a living being?
> *Scottie:* No.
> *Gavin:* If I told you that I believe this has happened to my wife, what would you say?
> *Scottie:* Well, I'd say take her to the nearest psychiatrist or psychologist or neurologist or psychoan—or maybe just the plain family doctor. I'd have him check up on you, too.

Madeleine's death raises the possibility that there was a ghostly power at work after all, but in the end the third explanation holds true. Elster and Judy have conned Scottie in order for Elster to get away with the murder of his wife.

Dead Again, on the other hand, incorporates the alternate explanations in support of, rather than contradistinction to, the existence of paranormal

The descent into the dark past in *Dead Again* features the apparent "possession" of the living by the dead, as in Hitchcock's *Vertigo*. Courtesy of Paramount Pictures.

events, in this case the reincarnation of Roman Strauss as Amanda Sharp/ "Grace" and of Margaret Strauss as Mike Church. The revelation of this supernatural occurrence is provided by a con-artist hypnotist, Franklyn Madson, who usually brings forth the past lives of his customers to help him find valuable antiques. Because hypnotism has long been associated both with psychotherapy and with charlatanism, it is the perfect vehicle by which to reveal the story of Roman and Margaret and to link the position that belief in the paranormal results from neurosis with the position that it is perpetrated as a deception. Lucy Fischer and Marcia Landy point out that "in the case of *Dead Again,* the occult also becomes a further strategy to undermine the stability of medical and psychiatric knowledge. The hypnotist turns out to be a contradictory figure who assists the woman in uncovering her identity but who is himself tainted and complicit" (7).

However the film goes one step further when it reveals that Madson has indeed tapped into Mike and Amanda's former lives. Reincarnation's questionable validity is confirmed by Cozy Carlisle, a former psychiatrist who has lost his license for sleeping with his female patients and who gives his expert opinion to Mike while they sit in a supermarket meat locker surrounded by the carcasses of butchered animals. As played by Robin Williams, Cozy seems as much in need of therapy as qualified to dispense it, as is also true of Madson, who is revealed to be a psychotic killer as well as a gifted hypnotist. Yet the film does not posit the equivocal nature of these two proponents of the truth of reincarnation as reasons for the audience to equivocate about whether reincarnation is possible. As Fischer and Landy acknowledge, "the film's emphasis on the occult, its insistence on the possibility of reincarnation is never dispelled" (10). Indeed, the mainstream distrust of the existence of paranormal phenomena is seen in *Dead Again* to result in only marginalized individuals being willing to believe in past lives and profit from tapping into them. (The closest Hitchcock comes to duplicating this thesis is with the con-artist medium Blanche Tyler in *Family Plot,* whose ability to channel the dead may or may not be genuine.) Although Cozy and Madson never meet in the film, Cozy corroborates the antique dealer's statement that "hypnosis can take us back to our past lives as well as our past." "You stick with the junk man; he's on the right track," the disgraced shrink advises.

This right track naturalizes reincarnation by turning forgotten past lives into a mere variant of traumatic events in a current life that have been buried in the subject's subconscious. When Madson's mother Inga tells Mike about the therapist in England who treated her son's stuttering, she also equates repressed memories with repressed former lives: "The guy used hypnosis to cure him. He told him about reincarnation and the subconscious." Cozy converted to a belief in reincarnation when he tried to find the hidden psychic trauma responsible for a female patient's claustrophobia. An initial regression revealed that she had been molested in a closet at age five by an uncle. Yet bringing this repressed trauma to the surface does not cure her neurosis. Further sessions take her back to a previous life in 1832, when her brother tormented her by locking her up in the empty coffins in their undertaker father's funeral parlor. Made aware of both repressed memories, the woman is no longer claustrophobic. Thus the personal past and the person's previous incarnations are elided. Unearthing a memory from 1832 in an adult alive in 1991 is no more remarkable than unearthing a memory from, say, 1982. The "flashes" from Roman and Margaret's lives, the triggering effect of scissors on Amanda, don't function much differently than the parallel lines in *Spellbound* or the red stains in *Marnie*. Despite the paranormal origins of the former and the subconscious origins of the latter, both have an equal ability to produce the frisson of uncanniness and fear in the audience. Freud's essay on the "unheimlich" observed the resemblance of the uncanny to the manifestations of repression: "An uncanny experience occurs either when infantile complexes which have been repressed are once more revived by some impressions, or when primitive beliefs which have been surmounted seem once more to be confirmed" (249). Most of the hallmarks of uncanniness which the essay details crop up in *Dead Again:* repetition, doubling, the "haunted" house, as well as a seeming affirmation of the belief in reincarnation that late twentieth-century Americans like Mike and Amanda have "surmounted." Freud also shrewdly observes that he would "not be surprised to hear that psychoanalysis, which is concerned with laying bare these hidden forces [of neurosis and madness], has itself become uncanny to many people for that very reason" (243).

Thus *Dead Again*'s "occult" belief in reincarnation does little to nullify its Freudian and psychoanalytic premise. In fact, another borrowing from *Spellbound* occurs with Madson's formulation about opening a door to access the memories of the past. The title card for the Hitchcock film defines the methodology of psychoanalysis as inducing "the patient to talk about his hidden problems, to open the locked doors of his mind." Later in the film, repression is described as "put[ting] the horrible thing behind a closed door." (Slippages in vocabulary that frequently conflate the subconscious and the supernatural go both ways, however. In *Spellbound*, "John Brown" speaks of being "haunted" by the traumatic event he can't quite remember.) *Dead Again*'s quasi-therapist searching out the root of hysteria simply has a number of childhoods from which to excavate, rather than the one we usually assume an individual to have lived through. That traditional psychoanalysis does not accept this fact just shows its insularity and closed-mindedness. Cozy assures the skeptical Mike, "There's a lot more people on this planet who believe in past lives than don't."

Nor are we to see reincarnation as something that occasionally happens when a previous life is cut short by violence or otherwise diverted from fulfillment. By double-casting several background roles in both the 1940s and 1990s sequences, Branagh indicates that every soul that dies is reborn. Because of its determination to naturalize the supernatural, the film moreover limits its manifestation to psychic locations without the necessity to violate any physical laws. There are no ghostly presences walking through walls or levitating furnishings. Nor do we experience the uncanny aura that a psychologically susceptible mind can project onto the mundane world. The second Mrs. de Winter's exploration of *Rebecca*'s bedroom or Scottie's forced "reincarnation" of the dead Madeleine by his reinscription of her "look" on Judy's body are far spookier in their affect than anything in the present-time narrative of Mike and Amanda. Only the repetition involved when we juxtapose the flashbacks-as-repressed-memories of the story of Roman, Margaret, Gray Baker, Frankie, and Inga to the present-day interactions among Amanda, Mike, Madson, and the aged Baker and Inga causes that prickle at the back of the neck. It's an understandable slip of the tongue that Mike, after hearing much of the murdered Margaret Strauss, might address as Margaret the nameless amnesiac who resembles her and seems to share her memories. However, with the '40s scenes suggesting that a Roman who looks very much like Mike was the killer, the slip, and "Grace's" terrified response of backing up against the wall, gun pointed at Mike, became one of the sure-fire scream-inducing moments of the film (Doran and Frank).

Even though *Dead Again* stipulates that we all have lived before, it does not suggest that memories of these past lives ordinarily break into conscious memory or that they even surface through nightmares and neuroses. Only past-life traumas have this effect, just as only painful memories during a single lifetime get locked behind the door. The film advances a psychic theory stemming from its premised universal reincarnation which does, however, depart from a Freudian paradigm. This occurs in its evocation of a determinist theory of karmic repetition and payback. As Cozy explains it, "Thanks to fate, the only cosmic force with a tragic sense of humor, you burn somebody in one life, they get a chance to burn you back in this one. It's the karmic credit plan. Buy now, pay forever." In other words, even if the memories of the past lives never surface into the conscious mind, people are doomed to replay with variations one ur-text of their lives forever. Thus the reincarnated Roman and Margaret are inexorably drawn to the former Strauss mansion, now the St. Aubrey School for Boys, and to each other, with it similarly fated that the still-living Frankie Madson who killed Margaret and framed Roman will come into their orbit and try to destroy them a second time before they can destroy him. The doubling that we see so frequently in Hitchcock's transference of guilt scenarios is displaced from the temporal simultaneity of those films to the endlessly reincarnated scenarios that bind antagonists in *Dead Again*'s universe. Whereas the Hitchcockian worldview mandates that so-called karmic debts be worked out through struggles between alternate versions of the self in one lifetime, *Dead Again* replaces multiplicities of the various aspects of the self with later repetitions of the same selves in new guises. Despite its use of Buddhist and New Age concepts on the one hand, and nuns and priests on the other, *Dead Again* expresses an essentially Calvinist theology, in contrast to the Catholicism Rohmer and Chabrol saw in Hitchcock.

Although the "karmic credit plan," which promises an endless replay of past lives with no hope of redemption, paints a generally more grim picture of human existence, it at least preserves the autonomy of each originary human soul. One may fight the same battles through eternity, but at least they are one's own battles. In those instances when Hitchcock allows for the possibility that the dead may somehow influence events in the world of the living, they inevitably do so by manipulating or even possessing the minds of others. "Do you think the dead come back and watch the living?" Mrs. Danvers asks Rebecca's quaking successor. While Danvers' actions, including the destruction of Manderley, can be ascribed to her obsessive devotion to her former mistress, the narrative could accommodate the alternative explanation that Rebecca's vengeful spirit has directed the housekeeper's seemingly deranged action. Were she not a hoax, Carlotta Valdes' return from the grave would have the consequence of consigning Madeleine to it. Nor can we rule out the possibility that "Mother" Bates has taken over Norman's mind not just as psychotic delusion but as actual demonic possession. The brief superimposition of her corpse's skeletal visage over Norman's face at *Psycho*'s conclusion is as chilling as any shock effect from a cinematic ghost story.

Reincarnation doesn't colonize anyone else's psychic space, but its determinism is also not the stuff of date movies, which *Dead Again*, hoping to capitalize on the surprise blockbuster success of *Ghost* (1990), aims at being, along with doing its riff on the Hitchcockian psychological melodrama. In one of Scott Frank's very early drafts of the screenplay, one of the reincarnated lovers does kill the other, as had happened in their previous life. (Frank fell in love with the title of that early draft and stuck with it, he noted on the DVD, even though the point of the final version is that neither of the two doomed Strausses dies young in the next life; to be accurate but awkward, the title would have to be revised as *Not Dead This Time*.) Such a gloomy denouement is suggested by Cozy, who advises Mike to kill Amanda before she can kill him, as she is otherwise fated to do. The detour around such a sobering finale to arrive at the concluding embrace of romantic comedy is accomplished in several ways. So as not to discredit the operations of the karmic credit plan *Dead Again* has been at such great pains to validate, the film reveals that Roman did not in fact kill Margaret. Thus the karmic retribution plays out in their struggle to kill Frankie/Franklyn Madson before he can cause them to fall "dead again." Secondly, persistence of souls after death is linked to an alternative form of occultism, one which is mystically romantic rather than part of a perpetual cosmic balance sheet. On their wedding night Roman gives Margaret an antique anklet. The old man who sold it to him claimed that "when a husband gives this to his wife they become two halves of the same person, nothing can separate them, not even death." The anklet and its magic spell thus render Roman and Margaret special cases, so that their reincarnations have a unique resonance. It also enables the play with gender and with gendered point of view that separate *Dead Again* decisively from its Hitchcockian and Wellesian influences and make it very much a film of the early 1990s, an era these directors may have continued to influence but whose zeitgeist they did not live to make films about.

* * *

Looking back at *Dead Again* more than a decade after its release, we can recognize that it comes near the end of a very important cycle of paranormal films that began in the 1980s and that the striking plot twist that made it stand out among those films marked it as among the first in a series of films prevalent in the 1990s and 2000s (for instance *The Usual Suspects* [1995], *The Sixth Sense* [1999], and *Memento* [2000]), which at a certain point in their narratives completely redefined audience assumptions about the nature of the characters through whom they access the narrative's events. Because Mike and Amanda are played by the same actors who play Roman and Margaret (a concept not in the original script, but insisted upon by Branagh), we assume that the traumatized Amanda is suffering from flashbacks to the brutal murder of herself in her former life as Margaret. When Mike allows himself to be regressed in an attempt to prove that he is not the murderous Roman reborn, he looks into a mirror and discovers that he is in fact *Margaret* reborn, so Amanda must be the reincarnated Roman, leaving Mike to realize that he better find out quickly whether the husband killed his wife in order to protect his own life.

One of the pleasures of filmic texts that foreground "brilliance of [a] highly crafted point-of-view system" is to go back and review them, checking up on how spectators were both deceived and alerted to the deception without ever being explicitly lied to (Fischer and Landy 16). As Fischer and Landy point out, *Dead Again* does not wholly deliver those pleasures because "quandaries proliferate" so that "the point of view game cannot be played successfully" (16). I would argue that some of the issues they regard as quandaries are in fact explicable within a fair-play reading of the film, but it nevertheless does resort to considerable contrivance in its presentation of the events of Roman and Margaret's relationship, to an extent that a viewer can legitimately cry foul.

The biggest cheat comes early. When Madson first regresses "Grace," she screams out "somebody help me" and wakes from the hypnotic trance. The viewer does not glimpse what she has seen in her recovered memory. Madson then suggests that she narrate what she is remembering in the third person. As she begins the tale of Margaret and Roman's first meeting in voice-over, the film fades into black-and-white footage that presents the story of their

Hypnotic regression dominates a séance overseen by a morally ambiguous investigator (played by the film's director, Kenneth Branagh). Courtesy of Paramount Pictures.

romance from an omniscient point of view, including, as will all the representations of what "Grace" accesses while hypnotized, not only scenes that Margaret could not have been witness to but also scenes that Roman could not have been witness to, as well as scenes, like the conversations between Gray Baker and his photographer, that neither could have observed firsthand. Throughout the film, the black-and-white footage may either represent one of "Grace's" nightmares, what she or Mike see when hypnotized, or a generalized flashback to events that occurred between the moment Margaret and Roman met and the day of Roman's execution. Branagh's dodge is to intermix objective flashbacks into subjective dreams and repressed memories without clearly demarcating them. This obfuscation combines with the two other misapprehensions initially imposed on the viewer, that "Grace" must be Margaret reborn, and that Roman murdered Margaret. The result is that until the truth is revealed to Mike by Inga and the interpolated 1940s scenes clearly are marked as flashbacks, reading any of the monochrome sequences as either a first-time deceived viewer or a subsequently enlightened one will produce inconsistencies.

Let us consider the opening sequence of the film. It is monochrome and opens in Roman Strauss's prison cell. A long shot of a wall papered with news clippings about the murder and Roman's trial and conviction reveals the location of the Gray Baker articles shown in close-up during the credit sequence. As a guard cuts Roman's hair in preparation for his execution, Roman is giving a last interview to Baker. The points he makes are that "I loved my wife and . . . I'll love her forever"; that, quoting Whitman, "To die is different from what anyone supposes and luckier"; and "what I believe, Mr. Baker, is that this is all far from over." When Baker asks him for a definitive answer as to whether or not he killed his wife, Roman leans over and apparently whispers something in the reporter's ear. As Roman is led out to the electric chair, Baker notices that the scissors are missing. He is too late to prevent Roman from stabbing a woman seen in soft focus, as he says, "These are for you." Cut abruptly to color as "Grace" awakens screaming.

As the viewer traverses various points in the unfolding narrative the meaning of this sequence changes. At first we believe it either to be the primary narrative itself (oh, a period piece in black and white) or a flashback. Then we believe all of it to be the hysterical woman's nightmare. Because we have not yet seen Margaret Strauss's face, we do not notice that "Grace" is her double and presumably connected to her in some way. When the first hypnosis session suggests that "Grace" is Margaret reincarnated, then the symbolism of the dream work seems logical. A woman murdered by her husband fears that he may reach out from beyond his own grave to threaten her again in her new life, thus his statement that death is not what we think it to be and that "this" is far from over. The proclamation of eternal love runs in the face of this, but after all, a husband who murders out of jealousy may be said to have an obsessive and exaggerated love for his wife. Later, however, the book written by the prison guard demonstrates that the conversation with Baker is not a nightmarish projection. It really happened, with the details exactly as shown to the audience. How, we wonder, could Margaret be aware of them so precisely? When the surprise twist is revealed, that difficulty vanishes. Roman would remember, of course. Unfortunately another difficulty takes its place. Why would Roman be terrified of being stabbed by himself? Is he perhaps living out his crime again and again in his subconscious? No, that won't work, because Roman didn't commit the crime after all. With the narrative ended and all secrets disclosed, the film still hasn't explained why the reincarnated Roman Strauss should appear as a menacing, scissors-wielding figure in his own repressed memories.

An answer can be found, I believe, in the competing reincarnation paradigms of the karmic credit plan and of souls bound eternally by love, and in the gendered implications of each, allied as they are to the blatantly Freudian scissors on the one hand and anklet on the other. In each of the nightmares, the figure of Roman may appear to be an assailant, but he represents himself as someone transferring ownership: "These are for you." In Amanda's subconscious mind resides the knowledge that the soul that once lived in Roman has been reborn in a female body. His phallic sexuality, his "scissors," now exists internally as female sexuality. The terror that accompanies this transaction can reasonably be interpreted as a castration anxiety now literalized. Secondly, the scissors were taken from Roman in order to deprive him of his beloved other half and then falsely reassigned to him to deprive him of his own life. By psychically passing them on to his next incarnation, he is arming her for the inevitable combat with the unknown (to Roman) murderer that must ensue in the scheme of karmic payback. Indeed, once Roman's memories start bleeding into Amanda's subconscious, she abandons her paintings of seascapes and begins obsessively to paint and sculpt scissors; one of the sculptures turns out to be the weapon that kills Franklyn Madson. The one absolute early fair-play clue that "Grace" reincarnates Roman is that the only words she utters in her hysterical state are "die Schere," the German that is inscribed on Roman's scissors in Roman's native language.

As advocated by Cozy Carlisle, the karmic credit plan is very phallic and aggressive. Cozy himself, we recall, was discredited for exploiting his female patients sexually. He was caught by an undercover policewoman, and misogynistic rhetoric surfaces in his dialogue. "Fuckin' do her, man, blow her away," is how he phrases his warning to Mike to kill Amanda before she kills him. He speaks of one female patient who was sexually abused by an uncle in childhood, and inherits money from a male patient with impotence problems. Although he is not fazed to learn of the gender switch, he still insists that a compulsory heterosexualism and binary opposition inform the workings of karmic reincarnation: "It all makes perfect sense. Yeah, I mean this gender switching shit happens all the time. You can be Bob in one life and then Betty in the next, you can be husband in one life and the wife in the next." Apparently if one switches from Bob to Betty, one's partner from the one life must switch from Jane to Jim, and not Jane to Janet.

The legend of the anklet, on the other hand, decrees that male and female do not oppose but complement, that a husband and wife linked by the gift of this piece of jewelry by the former to the latter makes them two halves of the same person, thus asserting an essential androgyny of the human spirit which true love metaphorically brings into being. As the one associated with the anklet, which is torn from her along with her life, the soul of Margaret, reborn in Mike, makes itself felt in a radically different fashion than the

vengeance-seeking soul of Roman. Mike has no nightmares and certainly no
bouts of hysterical amnesia. The boundaries between his past and present lives
seem far less permeable. Even when a Madson regression reveals to him that
he is Margaret reincarnated, he abruptly brings himself out of the memory.
Despite his urgent need to know who killed Margaret, he doesn't undergo
hypnosis again, but solves the crime in the present by finding first Gray Baker
and then Inga, who is finally the source of true memory about the night of
the murder. As one might expect from a reborn soul that had died violently,
he was a troubled youth, whom Father Timothy had to straighten out, and
we see flashes of a hot temper, but the drive that characterizes his life is the
search for completion. Orphaned, he becomes first a policeman on the missing persons squad, and then a private detective specializing in the discovery
of lost heirs. These impulses position him to be the one who is assigned to
discover "Grace's" identity and thus the severed half of his own soul. She has
misread the repressed Roman's offer of the scissors of retribution/self-defense
as a threat; when Mike, bearing Roman's face but Margaret's soul, enters her
waking world and says, "This is for you," he is not bearing a "sharp" instrument of revenge and rending—scissors are singular yet divided, a pair, thus
"this" should be "these." Mike instead offers the closed circle of the anklet to
make the two of them whole as one.

And then Amanda shoots him, with a gun given to her by Madson, who
has been planning the whole time to stage a second performance of his double
murder of Roman and Margaret in order to ensure a repetition of "fate"
rather than a karmic redress of grievances. Madson is also a figure who desta-
bilizes heterosexuality and fixed gender identity. When he shows up at Mike's
apartment in response to the story about "Grace's" amnesia, the detective
sarcastically inquires whether Madson is claiming to be her grandfather; "No,
I'm not her grandfather—nor her grandmother for that matter," he replies
breezily. While there are certainly fifty-something unmarried male antique
dealers living with their mothers who are not homosexual, these details repeat
enough of what Wood labels "popular (and generally discredited) heterosexist
mythology" for a viewer reasonably to conclude that the film is coding him as
homosexual (336). To read Madson as gay also provides an additional motive
for his savage murder of Margaret. He told his mother, and she tells Mike, that
he blamed Margaret for diverting Roman's love from its rightful object, Inga.
In this way, Katherine Fowkes contends, she also deprives Frankie of a father
figure and proper oedipalization: "The murder weapon, scissors, becomes the
highly charged, yet paradoxical symbol by which to castrate but also to attempt to gain the unattainable phallus" (114). Given the centrality of the emo-

tion of jealousy to the whole Strauss scenario—it is the subject of the opera Roman composes and is playing while the murder takes place in an upstairs bedroom—I would suggest that Frankie may in fact desire Roman as a lover rather than a father. After the murder he disavows the phallic scissors, wiping off his fingerprints and leaving them for Roman to pick up, but he steals the anklet, the symbol of Roman's undying love for Margaret.

Despite his continuing murderousness, this melodramatically intense Frankie of the '40s metamorphoses into the playful, ironic Madson, brilliantly portrayed by Derek Jacobi, who functions as Mike and Amanda's Cupid as well as their nemesis. More faithful to the androgynous, unifying spell of the anklet than he realizes, he is the catalyst to bring together what he has himself torn asunder. Even his death occurs only with his own assistance. Neither Mike nor Amanda brings him down with their successive stabbings of him with the scissors that killed Margaret. He is only stopped when he slips and impales himself on a giant, bladed sculpture made by Amanda and positioned beneath him by Mike.

Amanda only wounds Mike when she shoots him, and her gun misfires when she tries to defend herself against Madson. This should not surprise us, Fischer and Landy's analysis indicates, because poor Amanda is an overdetermined emblem of the castrated woman represented by patriarchy—hysterical, mute, amnesiac, unable to access the truth her previously male soul is trying to tell her. Fischer and Landy's ultimate take on *Dead Again* is a harsh one:

> When one looks for enlightened difference in the film's addresses to
> such issues as psychoanalysis, gender, and sexuality, one finds the
> reinscription of common motifs (in a terrain redolent with familiar
> ideological landmarks). The film's treatment of its female protagonist,
> its view of the mother, its presentation of embattled but ultimately tri-
> umphant heterosexuality; its imbrication in the codes of masculinity, its
> reanimation of cinema history are all mired in residual discourses, despite
> the film's postmodern pyrotechnics. (21)

I would agree that the film's project involves an initially transgressive set of gender relations that become naturalized under patriarchy at the end. I would also argue that, when read historically, we can recognize *Dead Again* not as a reactionary text trying to pass itself off as radically postmodern but as part of a larger project of U.S. cinema in the 1980s to carry off what Susan Jeffords describes as "the remasculinization of America." If one strain of this movement spawned the hard-body films of Stallone and Schwarzenegger, another delineated tales of adult men who either become disembodied ghosts or are re-embodied as women or children. In all these films, the male is rendered ineffectual and powerless relative to his properly embodied state. Fowkes discusses a number of them, including *Dead Again,* in her *Giving Up the Ghost.* She argues that they play out a masochistic fantasy in which "the male ghost repudiates its likeness to the guilty father and instead attempts to access that which recalls the pre-oedipal bliss with the mother" (77). The "guilty" father is certainly the failed masculine American enterprises of the 70s, and, by occupying with some pleasure the position reserved for the female under patriarchy, the dis- or reembodied male cedes any pretense to phallic authority, thus clearing the way for the emergence of a new, uncastrated incarnation of patriarchy. Ghost films, Fowkes notes, tend to proliferate in times of "a crisis in male power" when Hollywood films wish to correct "gender imbalance through a reassertion of patriarchy" (152). This is not an operation that is in any way progressive, but one might note that it is an operation that *Dead Again* accomplishes with considerable virtuosity.

In *Flatlining on the Field of Dreams,* his study of Reagan-era cinema, Alan Nadel describes the dis/reembodied male protagonist's character trajectory in the following terms: "Having failed to secure the home during the tenure of his recent history, he returns in diminished form to echo a past . . . that will affirm domestic security through a series of strategies all of which rely on a central act of faith: that we must trust the patriarch to accomplish in death that which he failed at in his vitality" (50–51). Roman certainly fails to secure his home and does return in diminished form—a mute amnesiac female. Nevertheless he does not accomplish the restoration of domestic security without help from his other, female half. Indeed Roman is, throughout the film, a site of masochistic disempowerment; it is Margaret who reclaims patriarchy for them both via her masculine rebirth as Mike.

More than most of the diminished patriarchs whom Nadel discusses, Roman has his masculine insufficiencies while alive enumerated in detail in the diegesis. We first see him, a man imprisoned and condemned, being shorn by the guard. The earliest chronological flashback in which he appears shows him as the powerful orchestra conductor, shot from a low angle while he stands on the podium, baton in hand. Everyone was afraid of him, "Grace" narrates— except for Margaret, who looks up from her piano and winks at the ostensibly terrifying "maestro." As Roman's career in America proceeds, he fails to succeed in composing acceptable film scores or in finishing his opera. There are money worries, rumors that his fortune was inherited from his first wife, and fears that Margaret is having an affair with Gray Baker. In a scene that echoes the one in the prison cell, we see Margaret giving him a haircut at the same time Roman catches her in a lie about a call from Baker. Ultimately Roman's scissors are taken from him by a stuttering, androgynous teenager in order to destroy the person Roman loves most at a time when Roman is rapturously absorbed in his own composition, a state characteristic of patriarchy's conception of female overidentification with the work of art. He is helpless to save Margaret ("somebody help me" were *his* words when he discovered her body) and to save himself; he chooses not to testify in his own defense. He did not whisper the truth about the murder into Gray Baker's ear, but instead planted a kiss on his cheek. One begins to wonder if "Roman" is supposed to suggest "no man."

Reborn as a woman, Roman becomes also "A-man"da (see Fischer and Landy 15). Frank and Doran point out on the DVD commentary that Amanda is frequently seen wearing Mike's male clothing and with her hair wet and slicked down mannishly. Like her fixation on representing scissors, these masculinizing traits portray Amanda as a female screen through which the trapped and castrated Roman is trying mightily to reassert his male identity and power. There is an asymmetry here, as there is very little in the way of feminization to identify Mike as a male screen through which Margaret is trying to reassert her femininity. He uses scissors with ease, wears casual "guy" clothes, and is a tough cop/detective. The only hints of anything slightly feminine come in his friend Pete's teasing about how he doesn't like anyone to "mess with [his] stuff," his interest in antique furniture, and his efforts to give up phallic cigarettes. The film seems to endorse a sexist ideology by which a man reincarnated as a woman would be horrified and eager to assert his masculinity, whereas a woman reincarnated as a man would figure that she had it made. More precisely, however, if no less sexist, the message of *Dead Again* asserts that souls are without gender, but they manifest varying attitudes and capabilities that patriarchy erroneously attributes to biological sexuality. It's no wonder that Roman, having enjoyed male privilege although not spiritually suited for it, would try to get it back. The film's judgment, however, is that he will be much happier as a woman. Margaret, conversely, gets the chance as Mike to exercise those "masculine" strengths that we see her exhibit in the '40s sequences. Frank and Doran made the decision to have Margaret be English, so that Emma Thompson could use her natural accent. She is thus the only one of the four main characters whose way of speaking is not a masquerade, and in a film where, as Fowkes points out, impaired speech is a motif this must be significant (86). The spirit that animates Margaret/Mike is the strongest of all the players in the initial Strauss melodrama, and it is the one that in its male reincarnation solves the mystery and defeats Frankie.

Compared to many films in this paranormal cycle, *Dead Again*'s sexism is somewhat muted. While in most of them the diminished male either moves on to the next world after restoring patriarchal heterosexuality or returns to his own adult male body, the feminized Roman of the '40s remains the female Amanda, still subject to "the passivity, poor communication and ineffectuality [that] all already belong to woman under classic patriarchal structures" (Fowkes 118). And even though Margaret gets her "scissors" in her next life, the film fairly consistently interrogates phallic masculinity. Scissors carry their own castrating powers with them, and cigarettes rob Gray Baker of his speaking voice just as Roman's kiss deprived him of his ability to speak in print. ("And I haven't written a word since.") It is only when Madson impales himself that "the door just closed" and Mike and Amanda can reunite the two halves of a single person under the benevolent spell of the female circlet of the anklet, their karmic debts decisively settled for their present incarnations at least.

Fowkes speculates that the reemergence of ghost films in the 80s also signaled a desire to return from "a detour in the portrayal of purely romantic love, as sex became divorced from love in the popular imagination" and "the sexual revolution helped shift the emphasis toward an ideal of uncommitted sexual freedom" (151). Certainly films like *Always* (1986), *Truly, Madly, Deeply* (1991), and *Ghost* are preeminently romantic, but the romance is by necessity bittersweet. The ghost cannot linger indefinitely with his living loved one, and such films often end with her finding another man and getting on with her life. If audiences needed a reminder that love could be spiritual as well as physical, the pendulum swing to love that could only occur on a spiritual level was not wholly satisfying either. By gambling that it could overcome viewer skepticism with its insistence on reincarnation in a tale of lovers who both meet unjust and untimely deaths, *Dead Again* is unique among this large number of paranormal films in finding a way for a couple eternally united on a spiritual plane to take up where they left off in their new, if reconfigured, physical bodies. Thus the last shots of the film are of Margaret and Roman kissing in profile, with their black-and-white image coming to life as color, and this image in turn fading into a kiss between Mike and Amanda.

* * *

Does *Dead Again*'s Reagan–Bush era gender project then render its Hitchcockian echoes as mere intertextual bric-a-brac? I would say rather that it imagines a Hitchcock scenario that escapes Hitchcock's usual solutions, and then applies a post-Hitchcockian fix. For the story of Roman and Margaret

Strauss, Gray Baker, and Frankie and Inga runs very close to those big melo-dramatic '40s Selznick films that Branagh cites, *Rebecca* and *Spellbound*. How easy it might have been for Mrs. Danvers to lure the second Mrs. de Winter to her death, and for Max to be convicted of Rebecca's murder because the shady doctor was never found. John Ballantine *is* convicted of Dr. Edwardes' murder. Had Dr. Murchison not turned the gun on himself but somehow disposed of Constance without being apprehended, we would once again be looking at a replica of what happens to the Strausses, with the Frankie charac-ter also getting away with his crime. If whatever fate, providence, or luck and cunning that preserves (some) Hitchcock heroines from deranged killers and that clears "wrong man" heroes from looming miscarriages of justice nods for an instant, the Hitchcock romance would be shattered. The reuniting of Roman/Amanda and Margaret/Mike has much the same resonance as one of those romances, as Lesley Brill defines them: "Humans, injured and deficient by nature, can be healed and made whole only by the mundane miracle of love. It follows, since the love must be reciprocal and not adulterous, that both partners before their meeting are to some degree ill and in need and that their redemption must be mutual"(9). *Dead Again* merely reimagines Hitchcock's providence as karma, saving lovers only after having doomed them. Like so many of the other '80s and early '90s films about reembodied consciousnesses or spirits returned from the grave, it asserts the benevolent and redemptive effects of such paranormal manifestations.

Although he never made a film that unequivocally postulated the existence of ghosts, Hitchcock did not categorically deny the power of the return of the repressed, whether it be a psychological phenomenon or a psychic one. He tried after all for many years to make a film of James M. Barrie's *Mary Rose,* a tale of a young woman mysteriously frozen in time for twenty-five years who returns to her family still in the first bloom of youth while they have all aged. What Hitchcock did have doubts about was whether the power could ever be harnessed for beneficial results. Like Barrie's heroine, "the person who exerts influence from beyond the grave ... is often a woman" in Hitchcock's films, and her influence is inevitably a baleful one. Tania Modleski, author of the words quoted above, goes on to say that "his films are always in danger of being subverted by females whose power is both fascinating and seemingly limitless" (1). Mary Rose's return would have been "very sad," Hitchcock told Francois Truffaut, unlike the joyful and redemptive joint return of the formerly male and female souls in *Dead Again*. Moreover, Hitchcock admit-ted that "it's not really Hitchcock material. What bothers me is the ghost." And then he says, "Because the real theme is: If the dead were to come back, what would you do with them?" (Truffaut 232). It is a question to which *Dead Again* responds with a sly wink, "Oh, you'd be surprised."

Works Cited

Branagh, Kenneth. "Commentary." *Dead Again* DVD. Los Angeles: Paramount DVD, 2000.
Brill, Lesley. *The Hitchcock Romance: Love and Irony in Hitchcock's Films*. Princeton: Princeton UP, 1988.
Doran, Lindsay, and Scott Frank. "Commentary." *Dead Again* DVD. Los Angeles: Paramount DVD, 2000.
Fischer, Lucy, and Marcia Landy. "*Dead Again* or A-Live Again: Postmodern or Postmortem?" *Cinema Journal* 33, 4 (Summer 1994): 3–22.
Fowkes, Katherine. *Giving Up the Ghost: Spirits, Ghosts and Angels in Mainstream Comedy Films*. Detroit: Wayne State UP, 1998.
Freud, Sigmund. "The Uncanny." *The Standard Edition of the Complete Works of Sigmund Freud,* vol. 17, ed. James Strachey. London: Hogarth P, 1955: 219–52.
Hartl, John. "Branagh Moves from the Past to a Past Life." *Seattle Times,* (August 18, 1991).
Jeffords, Susan. *The Remasculinization of America: Gender and the Vietnam War*. Bloomington: Indiana UP, 1989.
Modleski, Tania. *The Women Who Knew too Much: Hitchcock and Feminist Theory*. New York: Methuen, 1988.
Nadel, Alan. *Flatlining on the Field of Dreams: Cultural Narratives in the Films of President Reagan's America*. New Brunswick, N.J.: Rutgers UP, 1997.
Rohmer, Eric and Claude Chabrol. *Hitchcock: The First Forty-Four Films,* trans. Stanley Hochman. New York: Ungar, 1979.
Truffaut, Francois, with Helen G. Scott. *Hitchcock*. New York: Simon and Schuster, 1967.
Vivona, Steve. "The Latest DVD: Dead Again." September 11, 2002.
Wood, Robin. *Hitchcock's Films Revisited*. New York: Columbia UP, 1989.

PART III: THE POLITICS OF INTERTEXTUALITY

Although most critics have seen Hitchcock's films as engaging more seriously with sexual politics than with those of the national and international spheres, these works nevertheless exercised a profound influence on the more overtly political thrillers of later generations. But the model of the Hitchcock thriller, as R. Barton Palmer and Walter Metz demonstrate, was radically transformed in response to a changing, and increasingly dark, social and political climate. Palmer argues that films like Francis Ford Coppola's *The Conversation* (1974), Alan J. Pakula's *The Parallax View* (1974), and Brian De Palma's *Blow Out* (1981), as well as the wave of "paranoid thrillers" which followed in their wake, pose "Hitchcockian problems, but cannot win through to Hitchcockian solutions." Metz deals with what may well seem a very different kind of thriller, but finds a similar process of transformation at work in James Cameron's *True Lies* (1994), a generic hybrid of action-adventure film and domestic family melodrama, which rewrites Hitchcock's geopolitical thrillers of the 1950s, particularly *North by Northwest,* for the post–Cold War era.

In *The Parallax View*, the "wrong man" must hide from a powerful institution bent on his destruction.

The Hitchcock Romance
and the '70s Paranoid Thriller

R. Barton Palmer

Emerging in the Hollywood of the 1970s to enjoy a popularity that has now lasted for three decades, the "paranoid thriller" is commonly considered thoroughly Hitchcockian, especially since at least three of the films in this series, all directed by Brian De Palma, are more of less imitative homages to the "master of suspense."[1] A variety of the "suspense thriller," these are films, according to Charles Derry, that have all been "made in the shadow of Alfred Hitchcock."[2] Though never contested, the view that the shadow of Hitchcock looms over the appearance and flourishing of the paranoid thriller does seem problematic when the texts in question are closely scrutinized and compared. For if, as Robin Wood has shown, a key theme of Hitchcock's films is that they tell stories "built upon the struggle to dominate and the dread of impotence," upon, more specifically, "the form of man's desire ... to dominate the woman," then it is difficult to imagine how such an oeuvre could have exerted a formative influence on the paranoid thriller, which thematizes powerlessness in the face of ubiquitous and omnipotent institutional control.[3]

Once the thematic differences between his films and their successors have been properly accounted for, however, the influence of Hitchcock on the genre is revealed as both unquestionable and deep. The intertextual tie that connects the two bodies of texts is, in fact, fundamental, but it is defined more by the reorientation of characteristic narrative structures than by shared subject matter.

Except for the De Palma replications (which also make intertextual space for other extended "references"), paranoid thrillers certainly depart substantially from the Hitchcockian concept of the thriller, such as it can be inferred from his decades of practice. Most important, paranoid thrillers are more concerned with politics, broadly conceived, than with the romantic relationships that constitute Hitchcock's most common, if not exclusive, subject. The paranoid thriller does not foreground the man's compulsion to possess and control (as he, perhaps, also contests the woman's urge to do the same to him). It explores instead his struggle to maintain or regain an untrammeled individuality and independence of action in an America that, while ostensibly "free," subjects its citizens to what Ray Pratt terms "total surveillance and unlimited government access."[4]

The harried males of the paranoid thriller do not pursue "the power and the freedom" that Gavin Elster (Tom Helmore), the successful adulterer and murderer of Hitchcock's *Vertigo,* affirms that men once possessed by right in a bygone, perhaps Edenic past. Elster, ironically, is Hitchcock's most eloquent (or at least most direct) spokesman for what the men in his films customarily desire, and it is certainly not insignificant that he endures as the unpunished villain of the piece. Elster's bold statement about what men want speaks for many of the director's other male characters, especially, perhaps, Mark Rutland in *Marnie* and T. R. Devlin in *Notorious,* both of whom are obsessed with remaking and possessing absolutely the "fallen women" with whom they fall helplessly, and somewhat shamefully, in love.

In *Vertigo,* however, Hitchcock offers what is arguably his most penetrating and disturbing statement about the discontents of the contradictory male impulse toward power (with its possession of the woman) and freedom (with its rejection of the emotional ties that bind, weaken, and feminize). This self-canceling movement away and toward the object of desire becomes the film's central figure, as expressed in the famous zoom in/track out that characterizes the main character's perceptual malady, his disorienting and paralyzing vertigo. Like the protagonists of the paranoid thriller, the main male characters of *Vertigo* are no doubt harried. Yet the loss of power and freedom in the world Elster inhabits is only apparent, lamented by this dissimulating schemer for effect. Though he pretends to his erstwhile friend and helper Scottie Ferguson (James Stewart) that he has lost control over his wife, Elster has actually set an elaborate plot into motion to murder this woman who has now become inconvenient, in fact already "replaced" by his female accomplice so that the scheme can move forward. Not long afterward Elster will easily shed his helpful mistress, buying her off with money and jewels. In this way, Elster uses his power (a force that is exerted on the bodies of two women) in order to establish his freedom. Power and freedom also define the sexual politics that Elster's double, the narrative's ostensible hero, Scottie Ferguson, unquestioningly embraces: first by appointing himself psychiatrist to a self-destructive woman and, later, having failed to cure the living, by persisting in his role as a desolate lover. Like a maniacal Pygmalion, Scottie resurrects his dead beloved in order to satisfy an otherwise inconsolable desire. In this "achievement," he rivals Elster's complete control of the female body; although "free from the past" in the end, he is, ironically enough, delivered to a bleak, loveless solitude.

Elster and Scottie are invested with a power and freedom that are deployed exclusively in dominating the narrative's two women, who play a most primeval role in the relationship between the men; that is, they are essentially objects of exchange. The men never confront one another, though Elster is the master plotter who exploits Scottie's weakness in order to fulfill his aims. In their several scenes together, the two men are, instead, always united by either their joint concern to control Elster's wife or their grief at their failure to do so (which is, of course, a mirage since the woman/women in question do not elude male domination in the end). Elster first entrusts his wife Madeleine (the woman is actually Judy, Elster's accomplice) to Scottie's care, while Scottie later takes control of Judy, whom, like Elster, he remakes into Madeleine.

These two unfortunate women are thus victims (Judy, of course, also becomes a victimizer, but only at the instigation of the exploitative Elster). They are both delivered to destruction, and one is remade in the image of the other to facilitate her killing. Both women are discarded by Elster when they prove no longer desirable, and Judy is forcibly recruited to serve Scottie's therapeutic needs, even as she had been enlisted to further Elster's scheme to escape marital bondage. The "remade" Madeleine even furnishes Scottie with the means to punish his tormenting double, for she provides the object for revenge, albeit only symbolic, against Elster. Remaking Judy into Madeleine rewrites past exploitation and cures Scottie of the instability and impotence, the vertigo that had seized him. It is because of that disabling vertigo that Elster makes him part of the murder plot, but Scottie's wielding of the power and freedom that had allowed Elster to remake himself likewise permits a "cure" to emerge for his vertigo. The narrative ends with both having become "new men," in an ironic contrast to the remaking that destroys the identity first of the real Madeleine and then of Judy. Their power and freedom are confirmed by the erasure from the narrative of both women, who each tumble from the church tower (an identical fate that indicates their interchangeability). Yet neither man suffers a corresponding "fall" into dissolution. Even though a similar descent for the male figure into a terrifying abyss is predicted by Scottie's nightmare, this is a fate that Elster and Scottie separately escape. Theirs is the opportunity, theirs the power and the freedom, to descend the tower after they have mounted its peak, where they separately bear witness to the deaths of the women they love and hate.

Vertigo's key moral point takes shape from Hitchcock's characteristic focus on the hero's dark doppelgänger, as in *Strangers on a Train*, *The Wrong Man*, and, perhaps most chillingly, *Shadow of a Doubt*. As opponent but fellow traveler, this double represents the underside of official respectability and order; he acts out of a forceful, compulsive desire that the Hitchcockian protagonist always resists initially, but to which, in the darker films, he in the end also falls victim. *Vertigo* climaxes in a deeply ironic fashion, as the hero reenacts both Elster's rejection of Judy and his escape to freedom and riches. Like Elster, Scottie becomes "free of the past," which, in terms of the film's pervasive anti-oedipalism, can happen only when the woman, who draws him to love (that is, in the terms of the text, also to obsession and madness), is herself drawn to destruction.

In stark contrast, when confronted by collective and organizational forces they can scarcely fathom, much less control, the protagonists of the paranoid thriller find themselves compelled to abandon "any illusions of the possibility of a free, private, personal space."[5] In such films, the dark underside of life, that chaos moral and physical to which ordinariness can suddenly and irrevocably be delivered, is represented not by erotic self-abandonment and its discontents, but by unfathomable institutions bent on relentless surveillance and control. If they are driven by an urge to dominate, the men in the paranoid thriller do not seek control over (but then escape from) beautiful, enigmatic women. Instead, their aim is both more global and unattainable: the power to define who they are and how (or indeed whether) they live. Their struggle is to retain (or regain) the liberty to remain self-directed moral beings in a totalizing society, where the individual is beginning to possess only an instrumental value for the conscienceless elites in control.

Though they are not the first films in this series, two 1974 productions, *The Conversation* (Francis Ford Coppola) and *The Parallax View* (Alan J. Pakula), certainly established its main themes.[6] Even the most striking and topical paranoid thrillers of recent years, such as *The End of Violence* (Wim Wenders, 1997), *Enemy of the State* (Tony Scott, 1998), and *Lost Highway* (David Lynch, 1997), simply put a contemporary spin on these innovative narratives from an earlier decade. *The Conversation* and *The Parallax View* demonstrate how an intrusive electronic surveillance (or a sophisticated mind control dependent on insidious personality evaluation) makes it possible for "corporations," whether private or public, to control vulnerable private citizens for their own, usually mysterious aims, whose pursuit requires a ruthless violence. In this world of relentless persecution, even if the institutions of government do not oppress or persecute, they offer no protection from violence, being either too weak or themselves too invested in the conspiracy to preserve the rights and freedoms guaranteed to citizens in a modern society by the rule of law.

The Conversation traces the descent from control into paralyzed inaction of a renowned private snoop, Harry Caul (Gene Hackman), whom the film first presents orchestrating in masterly fashion the video and audio surveillance of a young couple. Caul has been asked to record and decipher their conversation for his employers, the director of an unnamed corporation (Robert Duval) and his assistant (Harrison Ford). Caul must piece together several separate recordings and eliminate the noise that makes some of what the couple says indecipherable. As he uses all his expertise to complete this difficult assignment, Caul reveals himself as an unhappy loner who, though desiring intimacy, is unwilling to surrender the power he wields over others. His assistant quits because he refuses to share his professional knowledge, and his girlfriend abandons him when he refuses to answer any questions about himself. Determined to be the only one who "knows," and thus exert a power over others, Caul is desperate as well to avoid responsibility for terrible sin. In the past, information he supplied led to the horrible murder of innocent people.

Caul's unending suspicion of those around him, his seeming paranoia, is soon justified when he infers correctly from the "conversation" and from his reading of the director's intentions that a murder is to be committed, involving him in mortal sin once again. It does not seem that Caul will ever be "free of the past." And yet his discovery affords him a moment of control. In the end, however, his knowledge turns out to be mere illusion because the attractive young couple whom Caul thinks will be murdered are actually plotting to murder her husband, a startling reversal (and further proof of his impotence) that Caul discovers only after the fact. Even when finally possessed of the truth, he proves unable to bring his erstwhile employers to justice. For Caul discovers that they are now surveilling him in his own home—by means that he cannot discover despite his considerable expertise. After wrecking his apartment in a fruitless attempt to locate the "bugs," Caul resigns himself to suffering the endless gaze of his persecutors in exchange for being left alive.

The Parallax View begins in spectacular public fashion, with the murder on Independence Day of a youthful, self-described "independent" presidential candidate that is carried out in full public view during a campaign fund-raiser in the restaurant atop Seattle's Space Needle. The actual assassin, whose actions are revealed only to the viewer, frames another man who seems to be his colleague (both men are waiters dressed in identical uniforms and, with knowing looks, cross paths in one shot). The unfortunate dupe ascends the monument attempting to escape and falls to his death, in an opening sequence that recalls the eye-popping finales of Hitchcock's *Saboteur* (1942) and *North by Northwest* (1959), whose pursuits climax with the fall of villains from the Statue of Liberty and Mount Rushmore, respectively. Lacking an alternative explanation (or perhaps prevented from exploring one), a national blue ribbon commission decides the crime is the work of a single assassin.

Joe Frady (Warren Beatty), a maverick journalist with good reason to distrust the police, whose illegal tactics he is eager to expose, does not doubt at first that the committee's finding is correct, especially since he was present at the rally that day. But the unlikely deaths (all ruled accidents or the result of natural causes) of many others who were there convince him some months later that his own life is in danger. He then discovers evidence that confirms a wider conspiracy is involved, finding that these plotters are eager to cover their tracks by eliminating anyone who could challenge the official verdict. An attempt is made to murder Frady while he is investigating one of the so-called accidents, and, confirming his distrust of authority, the would-be killers turn out to be the local police, from whom he escapes, in an appropriately symbolic gesture, by stealing a prowl car.

Further leads encourage Frady to seek the advice of a friend in the FBI, and from him he learns that the Parallax Corporation, a mysterious organization, is suspected of providing assassins, perhaps to serve the aims of some other group(s). Posing as an eager psychopath, Frady allows himself to be recruited as an operative so that he can infiltrate the organization and bring its workings to light. Interestingly, he does well on the "entrance exam." Frady is asked to watch a film of value-laden images and title cards, intercut into different patterns (some socially conventional, others not). Making use of the Kuleshov effect, this film is designed to elicit from the viewer characteristic emotional reactions, which are measured by sensors in the seat. Parallax is, of course, looking for discontented sociopaths, those who resent authority and believe the country is threatened by its leaders. Ironically, Frady fits this bill and is immediately enrolled. Now one of Parallax's operatives, he has the chance to disrupt their plans.

Much like Harry Caul, however, Frady soon falls victim to more powerful plotters. He follows one of Parallax's assassins and manages to prevent him from exploding a bomb on an airliner full of innocent people, one of whom is yet another prominent senator and potential presidential candidate. Frady's luck runs out when he trails the man to a political rally in an exhibition hall.

Here the candidate is shot down before his eyes, even as the would-be hero is framed for the killing. A second assassin, posing as a security guard, then kills Frady before the police can capture him. Thus, the scenario of the first political murder repeats itself, but this time with Frady as the fall guy. *The Parallax View* ends with yet another blue ribbon commission reaching the same predictably incorrect finding: that Frady, a known troublemaker whose recent erratic behavior is the proof of deep disturbance, acted alone in committing the murder of the candidate.

The Conversation and *The Parallax View* identify manipulative, murderous, and conspiratorial organizations as the agents of political and social instability whose goals can never be fathomed, only glimpsed. With their apparent wealth and wide influence, such entities lie beyond the official and visible regulating powers of government and law enforcement, of which, perhaps, they are covert elements. Significantly, Harry Caul never considers going to the authorities even before he is frightened into silence, and the only lawmen Joe Frady encounters are in the pay of Parallax. Desperate to avoid moral responsibility for some terrible crime and eager to preserve those he thinks innocent, Harry Caul attempts to assert his independence of his employers by withholding the evidence his surveillance and powers of highly technical interpretation have produced. The elaborate precautions he takes to ensure his personal security, however, are easily breached—and not only by them, but also by his snoopy, if well-wishing, landlady, a demonstration that his wish to remain private and unobserved cannot be fulfilled. And if even "the most famous bugger on the West Coast" (as one character calls him) cannot protect himself from surveillance, then who is safe, who can enjoy privacy? Further proof of his vulnerability is that the tapes are easily stolen from him, appropriately enough by a woman who preys on Caul's residual desire for intimate human contact.

Even so, Caul knows when the murder is to take place (some few days hence) and where (a local motel). Like Frady, he attempts to stop the crime from happening; however, he does this because of his horrified desire to avoid responsibility for sin, not because he fears for his life and feels empowered to bring down wicked authority wherever he finds it. Though Caul manages to install himself in an adjacent room and uses his surveillance equipment to overhear what transpires, he finds neither the will nor the strength to save the intended victim. After all is quiet, he can only search the murder scene for the crime's hidden gore, which gushes out from the room's toilet to index his moral responsibility. A more conventional thriller hero, Frady proves able to defeat, for a while, the forces of Parallax, but such victories prove illusory in a world where the individual counts for nothing. His heroic efforts provide in the end only the ground for defeat and misidentification as the perpetrator of a terrible crime. Much like Harry Caul, Frady winds up furthering the conspiracy that destroys him despite his best intentions. The "power" Frady acquires ironically deprives him of his "freedom," which he was allowed to possess only while it was irrelevant to the aims of the malevolent institution he arrogantly thought to defeat.

If *The Conversation* treats the treacherous plotting of corporate politics, tracing what turns out to be a hostile takeover of sorts, *The Parallax View* engages a larger issue, the supposed existence of groups powerful enough to subvert the democratic process by assassination, even as they convert the discontented and dissenting in contemporary America to their own purposes. In the process, the film offers an "explanation" for the rash of political murders that blighted American life in the sixties, thematizing a more public and "historical" form of the violence that lies at the center of *The Conversation,* whose motives seem to be personal, not political. The pattern for the Parallax fall guys is furnished by Lee Harvey Oswald and Sirhan Sirhan, both of whom were determined to have "acted alone" in murdering John and Robert Kennedy respectively, at least according to official judgments that were widely disbelieved (especially in the case of Oswald). Like the theorizers of extended conspiracy in both cases, whose findings filled many hugely popular books published after these assassinations, *The Parallax View* offers another kind of explanation, one that seemed more plausible to many Americans.[7]

Films like *The Parallax View* and *The Conversation* are not paranoid in the sense that they treat the pathological experiences of delusional characters who only imagine they are the victims of malevolent plotting, in the manner of the lonely young woman in Roman Polanski's 1965 film *Repulsion* whose hallucinations cause her to murder an innocent suitor and a snoopy landlord. Such films are, instead, culturally paranoid, in that they justify a fear of oppressive organizations which they "prove" responsible for horrendous public crimes. In this fashion, the two films provide textual resolutions for "inadequately explained socio-historical traumas." The paranoid thriller thus responds, in Pratt's apt formulation, to a "structure of feeling that seeks to illuminate hidden dimensions of history."[8] This desire for a deeper knowledge is predicated upon the belief that the whole truth about the chaos and violence in American society is withheld from the public. Such a structure of feeling characterizes the consciousness of those powerless to control themselves and their culture at a time of incomprehensible threat and widespread uncertainty.

Hitchcockian thrillers are never political in this deeper sense. The director's expressed aim was never to probe and thus shed light on otherwise "hidden dimensions of history," but to produce an engaging cinema of finely calculated affect. Granted, Hitchcock's oeuvre does offer at least one exception to the general rule that he was uninterested in political films as such: *Lifeboat* (1944).[9] But this film was made and released under very particular historical conditions that exerted a profound effect on Hitchcock's approach. A brilliant piece of wartime propagandizing designed to limn the dangers of a seductive and complex fascism, *Lifeboat* is a morality play that deploys a democratic microcosm forced into collective action. Its rousing narrative offers the argument that those in the free world must resort to a grim, distasteful violence if they are to retain their liberty. Espionage, to be sure, is, or at least can be, political, and it is a common enough theme in Hitchcock's thrillers—perhaps even their most common theme. But the concern with espionage in these films does not make them political. It would be misleading, in any case, to suggest that the director engages more than superficially with the various issues connected with the covert acquisition of vital information. In all his spy films, Hitchcock's intellectual and artistic interests lie elsewhere.

This is a large claim, impossible to defend at length here, but let us consider the evidence in part. Contrast, for example, how Hitchcock and Martin Ritt (adapting a popular novel by John Le Carré) explore the moral implications of the spy's double life, his inhabiting of a professional identity that must compromise his commitments as a human being to others. In *The Spy Who Came in from the Cold* (1965), Ritt takes pains to transfer intact to the screen the novel's detailed evocation of the labyrinthine betrayals necessitated by the Cold War, particularly the "Free" World's decision to sacrifice official ideological commitments (including its supposed reprehension of anti-Semitic fascism) in order to defeat communism. The narrative turns, in fact, on just this moral point, when the already disillusioned agent Alec Leamas (Richard Burton) determines to side with the victims (those who are brutally used to gain geopolitical advantage) rather than the victors. Spurning safety, Leamas chooses to share the destruction visited upon them not by the enemy but by his own comrades.

Hitchcock's *Torn Curtain* (1966), also written and produced during this intense period of Cold War rivalry, deals with much the same materials, following a trend in "secret agent" films begun by the James Bond series some years before. Spy Michael Armstrong (Paul Newman) must be faithless like Alec Leamas. When duty calls, he must suddenly abandon his unsuspecting fiancée, Sarah Sherman (Julie Andrews), in order to carry out his covert mission to steal a secret formula. Yet this desertion is only superficially developed by the narrative, as Sarah's investigation of Michael's strange behavior soon leads her to conclude correctly that he has undertaken to spy on his East German colleague and is only pretending to be a defector. Joining him in East Germany, she decides to help him fulfill his mission. At this point the film becomes a simple narrative of pursuit and escape as the couple, like Nick and Nora Charles of *The Thin Man* series, embark on an odyssey of strange adventures from which they emerge unscathed, if against all odds.

Like Alec Leamas, Michael Armstrong is "remade" or "misidentified" to suit the momentary needs of the West for scientific knowledge that will prevent their falling behind in the arms race. Hitchcock refuses, however, to probe the moral effects of Armstrong's willing assumption of a covert identity, including the violation of professional ethics that the theft of a colleague's discovery involves. Unlike Hitchcock's more complex romances, Armstrong's experience is neither substantially therapeutic nor penitential; at story's end, he and Sarah are safely back in the Western Europe from which they had originally departed.

Espionage as a theme, of course, furnishes the character types and narrative structures that most characterize the Hitchcockian thriller. In masterpieces such as *The 39 Steps* and *North by Northwest,* villainous conspiracies of spies emerge to, first, threaten the protagonist's independence and, then, oppose his struggle to exculpate himself. And yet the misidentification to which they subject him is constructed more as a barrier to his romantic fulfillment rather than as microcosmic proof of the individual's random persecution by malevolent organizations. In other words, the conspiracies function not to identify a political threat to the hero's independence, making a comment about "modern life." Instead, the conspiracies are "blocking" elements that the hero must overcome in order to take possession of the woman. Like the fantastic and improbable *avantures* of medieval romance, the cabals of foreign agents are more important for what they do, not for what they are. They normally generate the narrative's "MacGuffin," the disposable motor that is quickly forgotten by the audience once the plotting, in both senses, comes to an end.

It is emblematic of this "blocking" function that the master spy in *North by Northwest* who seeks the death of Roger Thornhill (Cary Grant), wrongly thinking him an American agent sent to undo him, also rivals him for the woman's affection and loyalty. However, Vandamm (James Mason) is more properly the evil monster that has carried off the beautiful princess (whom he intends to murder) than the spy conveying important information out of the country on microfilm. What is on the microfilm, in what ways its theft contributes to the ultimate aim of Vandamm and company, and how the interests of the United States are thereby threatened—all these are questions

Hitchcock shows little interest in raising, much less in answering. His hero is preoccupied with getting the girl, not foiling the spy's plans and absconding with their secrets (which he winds up obtaining, as it were, by accident).

Significantly, the protagonists of Hitchcock's most effective thrillers, from Roger Thornhill to Richard Hannay (Robert Donat) in *The 39 Steps* and Johnny Jones (Joel McCrea) in *Foreign Correspondent,* are not spies, though they are forced at times to adopt or, perhaps better, "play at" that role. *Torn Curtain* is not one of Hitchcock's more successful productions, and the film's (at least partial) failure perhaps results from its departure from a successful pattern, thereby raising questions of motivation and behavior that neither Hitchcock nor writer Brian Moore was able, or interested enough, to resolve effectively. In most cases, the protagonists of Hitchcock's thrillers are, above all else, romantic heroes.

Hitchcock's politics are sexual politics. As Lesley Brill, following Northrop Frye, characterizes the underlying structure of Hitchcock's films, "the plot of romance leads to adventure, with the killing of a hyperbolically evil figure the usual penultimate action and the winning of a mate the conclusion."[10] While the Hitchcockian oeuvre can be approached through its enactment of archetypal patterns, Brill does not deny that the director's inflection of the male urge to dominate the woman (which is the underlying theme of most forms of romance) is also intriguingly personal. In fact, his perceptive study shows how varied and complex is Hitchcock's engagement with the conventions of romance. Hitchcock's presentation of the male urge to dominate is thus a subject fit for an auteurist analysis, even though this theme, certainly a central element within patriarchy, is therefore "in the culture," as even the erstwhile auteurist critic Robin Wood concedes.[11]

In contrast, the paranoid thriller's treatment of the individual's helplessness in the face of oppression by institutions private and public transcends individual authorship. In some sense a reemergence of a central component of the dark vision of film noir,[12] this theme finds its shape and meaning within a series of works by various directors that unfolds in time and in response to changing social conditions, which it "constructs" (or perhaps better "reconstructs") in response to the desires and fears of its viewers, of which it is a culturally prominent expression. Such a cinematic development calls for a sociocultural explanation, as Pratt correctly recognizes, but he proves unable to supply it.[13] For him the "political basis of noir paranoia," the cultural ground of the paranoid thriller's appearance three decades later, is connected to a number of factors, the most influential of which is what he terms the "Hollywood Left perspective." However, explaining a film genre's rejection of official American optimism by resorting to a kind of group auteurism depends too heavily on conscious political theorizing as the crucial, determining element in their production. Pratt gives short shrift to questions of reception and popularity, though, as is true with any genre or series, it is the acceptability to a broad public of such narratives and the sociopolitical vision that the films promote that account for the longevity of the series and the vector of development it follows.

David Cochran has persuasively outlined what shape such a more balanced explanation of the paranoid thriller's genesis might take. Cochran concentrates on the emergence and nature of the "structure of feeling" in question, to use the Raymond Williams term that Pratt judiciously employs.[14] As it has entered critical discourse in the last three decades, a structure of feeling is what characterizes "the lived experience of the quality of life at a particular time and place." Moreover, at any historical moment there will be a number of structures of feeling current in a social formation, corresponding both to differentiated class experience and the overlapping of epochs, which means that residual structures of feeling and those just coming into play coexist with what is presently dominant.[15]

In Cochran's view, which I here simplify for the sake of brevity, Americans in the immediate postwar era experienced beyond all else the cumulative effects of an uninterrupted series of crises beginning with the Great Depression. The dominant structure of feeling at this time was thus a profound sense of uncertainty, of life being ruled by chance rather than by either design or desire. The country, like the individuals of which it was compromised, was forced to react to events that it could not master because they imposed themselves from without—unfathomable economic forces resulting in widespread economic breakdown, the sudden rise of expansionist fascism and militarism in both Europe and Asia, the eruption of global war that required American intervention, and then the abrupt transformation of a wartime ally into a bitter geopolitical rival, with a cold war replacing its just-concluded hot counterpart and reversing the moral poles of "good" and "evil" as former enemies were quickly recruited as important friends.

Film noir, in Cochran's account of the genre's rise to popularity, gave cinematic shape to this uncertainty by evoking a dark underworld of anomie and malaise populated by the criminally minded, who are always ready to entrap and destroy the unwary among the more respectable. This is why this emerging genre, although a striking if minority element of wartime Hollywood production, became so prominent in the immediate postwar era, with a remarkable run of profitable "A" and "B" features from 1946–1949. Although he does not mention this parallel development in popular literature, it is precisely during this same period that the *série noire* fiction of writers such as Cornell Woolrich, David Goodis, and Raymond Chandler, offering a grim vision of contemporary American life that had previously primarily appealed to the readers of pulp magazines, became acceptable to a broadly midcult public in hardback form. The sudden fashionability of *série noire* writers indicates that the structure of feeling Pratt identifies was widely shared across class lines, even among those who had by no means been left out of the American dream.

Cochran suggests that film noir came to an (only temporary) end when the emergence of a political consensus, shaped by the exigencies of the Cold War, made unpopular the critical and pessimistic view of American society it delineated. That consensus, however, had its dark underside, the structure of feeling emphasizing a "vision marked by chaos, anxiety, and alienation," which was accorded different forms of expression. The social criticism hitherto such an important element of high art was aestheticized (as modernism attained social acceptability and abstract expressionism replaced more "engaged" forms of realism in the plastic arts). Pessimistic accounts of conflicts or rifts in American society were banished from middlebrow culture because artists on both the right and left united in supporting the free world against the perceived threat from world communism. But the dark view of the American scene that had found such widespread expression during the forties still exerted some appeal (for threat and uncertainty had not come to an end), and it thus found a place in the work of maverick filmmakers like Sam Fuller and pulp writers such as Richard Condon and Chester Himes, all of whom worked—and with profit, it might be added—on the margins of "respectable" cultural production.[16] Condon's breakthrough novel, *The Manchurian Candidate* (1959), with its terrifying evocation of pervasive communist infiltration of American institutions, including the far right of the Republican Party and an ostensible Medal of Honor recipient, set the tone (if it did not establish the structure) for the paranoid thriller films of later decades, one of which, *Winter Kills* (William Richert, 1979), is based on a Condon novel that offers an idiosyncratic take on the waves of assassinations that shook the foundations of American democracy in the sixties. As an explanatory narrative, addressing itself to history's "hidden dimensions," *Winter Kills* bears close comparison to *The Parallax View,* as indeed do most of Condon's novels, which are thoroughly political in this sense.

For Cochran, the social dislocations and discontents of the late sixties and early seventies, especially the costly inconclusiveness of the Vietnam War and the loss of faith in government institutions that was the legacy of shocking revelations about the immorality of the Johnson and Nixon administrations, led to the breakdown on the Cold War consensus and the reemergence in the seventies to prominence of that "vision marked by chaos, anxiety, and alienation." Once again this structure of feeling was widespread enough to be addressed in substantial fashion by the institutions of popular literature and film, which, as Fredric Jameson theorizes, are not "escapist" in the sense that they offer "empty distraction." Instead, such popular objects perform "a transformational work on social and political anxieties and fantasies which must then have some effective presence in the mass cultural text in order subsequently to be 'managed' or repressed."[17] Clearly, the fashion in which the dark vision of this structure of feeling is most often managed in the paranoid thriller (or in the comparable literary series) is to display the irresistible power of institutions bent on the instrumentalization of the individual. The nightmare of surveillance and manipulation never ends, or if some unlikely hero gains a victory over totalizing control, there is no hope that it is more than local or temporary. Paranoid thrillers offer, to use Jameson's term, fantasies of disaster.

From a vantage point some thirty years later, it is easy to survey the literary and cinematic consequences of the cultural transformations that took place in the seventies. The last two decades have witnessed the sudden appearance and then widespread popularity of midcult or masscult fiction that explores, even as it continues, the tradition of the forties hardboiled writers and their successors in the fifties and sixties such as Condon, Richard Stark, and Jim Thompson. This development Woody Haut has aptly termed "neon noir," and some of its prominent practitioners are among our most widely read authors of popular fiction: Elmore Leonard, Michael Connelly, and James Ellroy. Similarly, the nation's screens have seen the rediscovery of film noir traditions, first in the form of the paranoid and, subsequently, the erotic thriller.[18] In fact, even the briefest informal survey of profitable films from the last decade suggests that the thriller in both its incarnations persists as the genre with the most widespread and assured popularity in contemporary Hollywood.

The determining energy behind the appearance and development of the paranoid thriller has thus been "cultural" rather than "artistic." If these are indeed films "made in the shadow of Hitchcock," the paranoid thriller series did not principally arise (the replications of Brian De Palma certainly excepted) through the decisions of filmmakers to continue the work of the renowned director, attaching their films to his oeuvre by deliberate and self-conscious intertextual gestures of one kind or another. Instead, it is because Hitchcock had established the basic narrative patterns of the cinematic thriller that the paranoid thriller displays a deep indebtedness to the director's work.

Let us consider these patterns. Hitchcock's films, we have seen, are not political and can almost always be understood as romances whose major theme is the desire of men to dominate women. But even a quick look at his work in the genre reveals two general modes, as Brill has suggested. In its "comic" mode, the Hitchcockian romance ends with the (re)constitution of the couple. *Torn Curtain* is exemplary in this respect, as the hero and heroine are delivered not only to safety but are reunited, passing through grave dangers together, including "certain death" at the very end, in order to take on the more enduring commitment of marriage. In its "darker" mode, the Hitchcockian romance ironizes the conventional conclusion in which deliverance and possession are such important elements. But even the gloomier and less socially conservative of Hitchcock's narratives differ substantially from the paranoid thriller in emphasizing the protagonist's power and freedom rather than his weakness and submission. I agree with Brill that *Psycho* and *Vertigo,* certainly the director's darkest films, "subvert most thoroughly the romantic plots, images, and structures that recur throughout his work," and yet it seems clear to me that in both films the man attains his desire to dominate the woman, even as he establishes his right to "the power and the freedom" to dispose of her as he would.[19] The reversal in both *Vertigo* and *Psycho* of the director's customary polarities, in other words, did not provide a model for the different kind of dark film represented by the paranoid thriller.

In *Vertigo,* Hitchcock certainly interrogates the value and moral worth of the male prerogative, but he does not dispossess his hero of his dominating position. In *Psycho,* Hitchcock probes the psychopathology of the male urge, the way in which through the discontents of the mother/child relationship the drive to dominate can become reoriented toward a violence that destroys the object of desire even before it is possessed (Scottie at least consummates his relationship with Judy before leading her up to her destruction). Despite initial appearances (and the startling gender "reversal" of the film's conclusion), the violence in *Psycho* is male in the traditional sense, even though (or, perhaps, especially because) it results from the paradoxical "possession" of the man by his mother. With cosmic irony, this possession leads to the destruction of threatening females, including the mother herself.

For the mother's power is generated by a transvestite performance. "She" is nothing more than a projection of homicidal energy fueled by the conflict between guilt and desire that consumes Norman Bates (Anthony Perkins). The male identity that Norman conceives to be the object that "Mother"

seeks to dominate is delivered to Norman's absolute control at the very moment when "she" takes him over. Like Scottie, Norman becomes "free of the
past" by surrendering absolutely to his own version of it. His attendant loss
of self is thus the paradoxical index of complete self-possession. In this way,
even *Psycho,* I would argue, is about "the power and the freedom" men desire
and, albeit in a horrifyingly ironic sense, secure. In the end, the power (and
even the existence) of the women in Norman's life has been destroyed (just
as in *Vertigo*), while he remains alive, free within the space of his own unim-
prisoned consciousness. Hitchcock chillingly evokes this freedom in one of
cinema's most horrifying voice-overs, and he does so just before showing the
automobile containing the dead body of Marion Crane being pulled from its
underwater tomb. Like *Vertigo,* this film ends with the startling juxtaposition
of living man with murdered woman.[20]

Unlike Scottie and Norman, the protagonists of the paranoid thriller discover that they dispose of no real power to act—and that such freedom as
they once had has been taken from them. The thematic trajectory of the
Hitchcockian romance develops in quite the opposite direction, reaffirming a
socially conventional, patriarchal "truth," however problematized, ironized,
or dissected, that the paranoid thriller undermines. And yet in terms of narrative pattern, the paranoid thriller is thoroughly Hitchcockian, as some further
brief discussion of both *The Conversation* and *The Parallax View* will readily
demonstrate.

First, however, I must make one last point about Hitchcock's thematics
since they are in some sense continued by the paranoid thriller. Many would
agree with Robin Wood that his films are "disturbing" in the sense that the
director's concern is to show how "good and evil are seen to be so interwoven
as to be virtually inseparable," which has its affective reflex in the desire to
make us, his viewers, "aware . . . of the impurity of our own desires."[21] The
moral complexity evident in the world of the story, which is made an experience of those who gaze upon that world, is sometimes given a teleology
through an emphasis on some form of therapy (or sometimes, more properly speaking, penance). The protagonist sheds his "weakness or obsession by
indulging it and living through the consequences."[22] Moreover, Hitchcock
makes his viewers share that experience at times through identification, but
at others he asks them to sit in judgment when he either deploys a more objective presentation of the character's trials or deploys dramatic irony. Such a
"moral" structure is typical of Hitchcock's later films, not of his earlier assays
of the thriller form; for in works such as *The 39 Steps,* the heroes are "quite

unpredictably and abruptly plunged into hair-raising adventures, but the adventures bear no really organic relationship to the men."[23]

From John Buchan's *The 39 Steps* Hitchcock borrowed the device of the double pursuit, which he uses in many of his later thrillers, especially *North by Northwest*. Such a narrative begins with the main character's misidentification as criminal or agent; in *North by Northwest*, Roger Thornhill is first mistaken by Vandamm's operatives as the spy George Kaplan, but soon after wrongly identified again, in his actual identity as Roger Thornhill, as the murderer of UN diplomat Lester Townsend (Philip Ober), who is actually killed by one of Vandamm's henchmen. This double "miscasting" means that Thornhill must pursue the villains in order to exculpate himself even as he is himself pursued by the police, who are eager to have him prosecuted for his "crime." The adventures in which Thornhill becomes embroiled, however, are hardly conceived ultimately as "accidental," but, instead, as therapeutic since they deliver a man, in the beginning too self-concerned and immature for a proper relationship with a woman, to an enduring love that he risks his life to preserve. The trials and humiliations Thornhill undergoes do not exemplify the global truth about modern life that the paranoid thriller trades in: that an underworld of chaos and threat can suddenly sweep up and over any unsuspecting individual who happens to beckon at the wrong moment for a cocktail lounge waiter (or be present at a political rally when a candidate is gunned down).

In a number of notable Hitchcock thrillers, however, there is no double pursuit motored by the protagonist's misidentification, because the protagonist, like a questing knight, seeks out adventures that correspond to his obsessions or weakness. In *Rear Window* (1954), for example, photojournalist L. B. Jefferies (James Stewart) has been sidelined by a broken leg. Gazing at the windows in the apartment house across the courtyard, he transforms them into narratives, one of which turns out to be a murder mystery that he solves with the help of girlfriend Lisa Fremont (Grace Kelly). The investigation in which they become embroiled teaches Jefferies to appreciate the rougher and readier virtues of the woman he thought was merely a glamorous fashion plate, even as he, living out his obsession, is punished for his presumptions with a second broken leg.

We might say, then, that Hitchcock actually developed two forms of the thriller, one in which the main character is, at first, relatively passive and the other in which he provides the energy that sets the narrative moving. In the first, adventures threaten his identity with chaos and dissolution, and in the second, his obsessions lead him to seek out (perhaps, in the case of

L. B. Jefferies, to create) what will give them form. In this way, he can free himself from their controlling power. In both patterns, the cure follows (can this be an accident?) what seems a Catholic (because semi-Pelagian) conception of spiritual recovery, with the living out of misorientation, weakness, or sociopathology requiring a penitential suffering that leads, according to the hero's rejection or acceptance of change, to therapeutic regeneration (Jefferies), self-destruction (Uncle Charlie [Joseph Cotton] in *Shadow of a Doubt* [1943]), or a paralyzed suspension between the acceptance of a restored moral order and the nearly irresistible urge for dissolution (Scottie Ferguson in *Vertigo*). In those films, such as *Shadow of a Doubt*, where a main character refuses the possibility of redemption, his double, in this case his niece and namesake young Charlie (Teresa Wright), seizes the chance to reform, rejecting the obsession or evil within that finds its more solid representative in a doppelgänger figure. The reform may be partial or inconclusive, as in the case of Guy Haines (Farley Granger) in *Strangers on a Train* (1951) or Richard Blaney (Jon Finch) in *Frenzy* (1972), but the main character, however flawed, still comes to occupy the moral high ground. His reward, then, is possession of the woman (and, naturally, the power and the freedom to dispose of her when, or as, he sees fit).

Of these two Hitchcockian patterns, *The Conversation* focuses on the obsessive hero who sets out on a penitential journey, while *The Parallax View* offers a reconceived version of the Hitchcockian "wrong man," selected by "accident," who passes through adventures that threaten him with death but also hold out the promise of achieving dominance. And it is through the imitation or borrowing of narrative patterns from these two early paranoid thrillers that the Hitchcockian oeuvre has come to exert considerable influence on the subsequent history of the genre.

Harry Caul, like L. B. Jefferies, lives out his obsessive desire to surveil, know, and control. In fact, he has chosen to persist in the profession that so well suits his fear of intimacy and urge for power despite his fears of eternal damnation. For his experience has shown him that, while his urge to discover the truth cannot be resisted because of his technical ingenuity, he can exert no control over the knowledge he acquires once he turns it over to those who engage his services. Just like him, they seek a power over others. Only what he is now made to experience forces Caul to understand the irony of this "double bind." It is his very assertion of control that leads, once the transaction is complete, to his moral dependence on others, who can involve him in terrible sin.

Again like Jefferies, Caul finds in the "truth" that his skills enable him to uncover exactly what answers to his preoccupation. For Hitchcock's hero, the rooms across the courtyard display at first only the varied discontents of romance. His observations are hardly objective, but instead generate a series of "readings" that respond to his unresolved relationship with Lisa, the beautiful woman from whom he diverts his gaze in order to project his concerns on others. One of these narratives, as he constructs it, is perhaps his darkest, most desperately unacknowledged imagining at this turning point of his life when he feels the pressure of Lisa urging him toward marital commitment: the woman construed as wife, as a burden so heavy, disagreeable, and insupportable that a disgruntled husband must rid himself of it by cold-blooded murder and gruesome dismemberment. By projecting his fears onto the killer, Thorwald (Raymond Burr), Jefferies manages to exorcise them. It is hardly an accident that the satisfying denouement to his own adventure (in which Lisa's willing and daring participation convinces him of her worthiness to share the unconventional life of an action photojournalist) is matched by his "observation" of happy (or humorously conventional) endings for the other narratives. Among the "characters" involved is the woman he names "Lonelyheart," who finally "meets a man" in what is perhaps meant as a correlative to Jefferies' own escape from immobilized solitude.

Caul's experience, however, leads not to this kind of redemption and release, though this is what he desires. Like Scottie Ferguson at the close of *Vertigo*, he gets a "second" chance after a devastating failure. He looks for and discovers the opportunity to free himself of the past by reliving it, thereby overcoming the weakness that before had prevented him from falling into sin. Scottie's experience with that second chance, of course, is developed ironically by Hitchcock, in that his failure manifested itself in two ways: he could not save Madeleine from falling because, disabled by vertigo, he could not climb the stairs. Scottie does climb the tower a second time, but his concern is not to save the "Madeleine" he forces to accompany him. Thus Scottie's recovery of power leads to the same failure he experienced when he could not "get to the top" that first time. Caul's failure in the past also resulted from two related actions: his delivery of damning information to his employers, who then murdered in ghastly fashion a number of people, including some who were innocent. After discovering the murder plot, Caul has the chance to save himself from further moral danger either by withholding what he discovers or by otherwise thwarting the villains' plans.

Attempting both courses of action, Caul manages to succeed at neither, thus prefiguring the final immobilization that, while imposed by others, is the correlative of his own incapacity. Arriving at the corporate office to complete the deal, Caul is at first reluctant to give up his tapes of the conversation because the director is not there to take personal delivery. His suspicions aroused, Caul does further work on the tapes, now deciphering a previously unclear part of the conversation. He listens in horror as the young man turns to the woman and says, "He'd *kill* us if he had the chance." That night, however, the tapes are taken from him. A second trip to the corporation's office confirms Caul's fears; as he collects his money, the director is listening to the tape, hearing the evidence of his wife's infidelity. Caul asks, "What will happen to her?" And the director says nothing, but the young man's voice on the tape repeats, "He'd *kill* us if he had the chance." Horrified, Caul goes to the fateful hotel at the appointed time, but, listening to angry words and then screams in the next room, he can manage only to eavesdrop on the murder and then pull the covers over his head and turn on the television set to drown out the noise. Only later, appearing once again at the corporate office, does Caul realize his error. It is the "innocent couple" who have arranged the murder of an inconvenient husband. Caul had misheard the young man, who actually said, "He'd kill *us* if he had the chance."

The surveillance expert, it seems, has not only failed to prevent others from involving him in a terrible crime; he has also proved unable to comprehend its true nature. Unlike either L. B. Jefferies or Scottie Ferguson, Harry Caul thus achieves no mastery, not even over the facts of the case. Living out his obsession, Caul cannot shed it, but instead finds himself trapped in a Dantean *contrapasso*. With "no exit" from his existential impasse, Caul becomes the object of the same instrumentalizing surveillance he had made others endure; the effect of his sin is justly turned upon him. As in the Hitchcockian thriller, the theme of *The Conversation* is the urge to dominate, but Coppola's protagonist, in league with those who seek power over others, discovers that the price he must pay is the loss of his own freedom, even as he forfeits any chance at redemption.

In *The Parallax View*, by way of contrast, Joe Frady lives out the role of the Hitchcockian "wrong man," but the adventures in which he becomes embroiled never deliver him to power and freedom, or to the full identity that his Hitchcockian counterparts attain. He is at first "misidentified" as a target for assassination simply because he was in the wrong place at the wrong time, but he later allows himself to be "miscast" as a homicidal sociopath. Frady embarks upon a double pursuit, evading the "accidental" death that surely awaits him, even as he seeks out those who are plotting against him. He assumes control over his own fate when he successfully penetrates (or so he thinks) the Parallax Corporation; the generic expectation is that Frady will use his false identity to solve the mystery of this series of assassinations and attendant murders, emerging in the end as "himself." But that expectation will not be fulfilled.

This turning point in the narrative recalls a similar movement in the plot of *North by Northwest*. Finally informed by government agents that the beautiful Eve (Eva Marie Saint) is actually playing a double role, pretending to be Vandamm's mistress even as she spies upon him for American counterintelligence, Thornhill is persuaded to save the woman he now loves from the suspicion he has helped cast upon her. And so he agrees to play out the role of the American spy Kaplan, in reality only a pseudoidentity that can readily accommodate him. Now Kaplan, Thornhill engages in further theatrics, pretending to fall into a violent lovers' quarrel with Eve when Thornhill meets with Vandamm. Eve "shoots" Thornhill with a gun loaded with blanks, thus eliminating him as a threat (or so Vandamm is meant to think).

The irony, of course, is that not only Vandamm but also the U.S. agent (Leo G. Carroll) believe that henceforth Thornhill has been written out of the plot. Eve is to accompany Vandamm out of the country, and her erstwhile lover must accept that she will continue to perform her role as the villain's kept woman. Thornhill, however, will not accept this projected version of the narrative and goes beyond the parts that have been written for him by both sides. Escaping from government custody, he proceeds to abduct Eve "as himself," rescuing her from Vandamm, who has discovered her pistol was loaded with blanks. Thornhill works free from other possible selves to do things his own way, in the process asserting his power over the villains and gaining possession of Eve. He literally rips her from his rival's deadly embrace.

Frady, however, never comes to dominate the narrative in such a fashion. Like Harry Caul, he offers in microcosm the social evil that confronts him. When Thornhill occupies the role of a fictitious American agent, it is a role that would not suit him—except that the emotions he is required to express in the confrontation leading up to his shooting by Eve (namely anger, jealousy, passion) are those he actually feels for Eve. The romantic hero is indeed a part that Thornhill can play convincingly because it is the one toward which he actually aspires. But Frady is not really "misidentified" as a sociopathic loner—this is the part we actually see him playing earlier in the film, when he sets himself against the police and, by his iconoclastic demeanor, against the establishment. There is no other identity he aims to assume. Unlike Thornhill, he can be finally accommodated to the role assigned him by the villains because its suits him. His opposition to the "power structure" mirrors their own.

To put this in Hitchcockian terms, Frady is never really the "wrong man." As far as Parallax is concerned, he fits perfectly the personality profile they require for their fall guys, even as he remains incapable of shedding his obsessions by living them out, never becoming the "right man" who can win through to wholeness. The plot in which he becomes involved thus can offer no cure for his discontent, only a larger stage on which it may be played out—and to the advantage of those he seeks to destroy. This finale corresponds to Frady's firmly held view that American society is thoroughly corrupt, especially its official institutions, whose power he can therefore not summon up to help him oppose the machinations of the Parallax Corporation.

One way of understanding the narrative and thematics of the paranoid thriller is that these films pose Hitchcockian problems, but cannot win through to Hitchcockian solutions. A successful entrepreneur in the surveillance industry that has deprived Americans of the privacy that is their right, Harry Caul cannot rid himself of the obsession for power, and the resultant powerlessness its exercise imposes on him. Written into a narrative that demands his destruction, Joe Frady is unable to offer his enemies a version of himself that they cannot use to destroy him. But this is perhaps appropriate. For *The Conversation* and *The Parallax View* do not correspond to an essentially moral view of the human condition, as Hitchcock's films characteristically do. Instead, the two films, as well as their many successors in the genre, answer to a widespread lack of faith in the public and private spheres. Paranoid thrillers deploy narratives that customarily lead only to immobility and death, in the process adapting the Hitchcockian inheritance to a darker, collective vision of human (im)possibility than the master of suspense ever thought to bring to the screen.

Notes

1. I refer to *Obsession* (1976), *Body Double* (1984), and *Blow Out* (1981). Among other commentators, Ray Pratt terms the films in question "paranoia thrillers" in his *Projecting Paranoia: Conspiratorial Visions in American Film* (Lawrence, KS: University Press of Kansas, 2001): 124. I prefer the slightly different term "paranoid thriller" because such films, in my view, focus more on paranoid characters than on the psychological/cultural state of paranoia. The connection between Hitchcock and the New Hollywood thriller cycle has been addressed by Robert Kapsis in *Hitchcock: The Making of a Reputation* (Chicago: University of Chicago Press, 1992), esp. pp. 176–215. Kapsis, however, examines neither Hitchcock's influence on *The Conversation* and *The Parallax View,* nor on the paranoid thriller cycle that these two films inspire.

2. The influence of Hitchcock on the suspense thriller (a larger category that subsumes the

paranoid thriller) is so pervasive, in fact, that Charles Derry laments the failure of criticism to deal with them as a genre or series apart from the famous director's body of work: "Perhaps the most important contribution to this critical lack is that Alfred Hitchcock's reputation as a suspense thriller director has been so great, that any genre concerns have unfortunately been regarded as irrelevant," *The Suspense Thriller: Films in the Shadow of Alfred Hitchcock* (Jefferson, NC: McFarland, 1988): 4.

3. Robin Wood, *Hitchcock's Films Revisited* Revised Edition (New York: Columbia University Press, 2001): 21.

4. Pratt, 8.

5. Pratt, 8.

6. Three films directed by John Frankenheimer in the sixties undoubtedly inaugurated the paranoid thriller: *The Manchurian Candidate* (1962), *Seven Days in May* (1964), and *Seconds* (1966). Though Hitchcockian touches can be detected in all three, the key influence on Frankenheimer was undoubtedly literary: the political fiction of Richard Condon and his imitators.

7. These nonfiction and cinematic trends find their apotheosis in Oliver Stone's *JFK* (1991).

8. Pratt, 9.

9. It would be easy to make the case that *Lifeboat* belongs more to the oeuvre of producer Darryl F. Zanuck, who made the film in part to show his bona fides in supporting the war effort; it is certainly questionable how Hitchcockian the production in fact is. In the category of Hitchcock's political work, we might also include two (mostly regrettable) efforts also made during World War II for propaganda purposes: *Bon Voyage* and *Aventure Malgache*, both 1944. Another wartime production, *Saboteur* (1942), it might be argued, also departs from the standard Hitchcockian thriller with its discernible overlay of democratic themes and "messages" melded to a plot modeled on the earlier *The 39 Steps*.

10. Lesley Brill, *The Hitchcock Romance: Love and Irony in Hitchcock's Films* (Princeton: Princeton University Press, 1988): 6. Brill draws on Frye's views of romance as expressed in several of his studies, but especially Northrop Frye, *The Secular Scripture: A Study of the Structure of Romance* (Cambridge, MA: Harvard University Press, 1976).

11. Interestingly, weight is given to the director's supposed "misogyny" even in a semiotically oriented study like Tania Modleski's *The Women Who Knew Too Much: Hitchcock and Feminist Theory* (London: Methuen, 1988).

12. For further discussion of paranoia as a theme of classic film noir, see Richard Maltby, "The Politics of the Maladjusted Text," in Ian Cameron, ed., *The Book of Film Noir* (New York: Continuum, 1993), and Paul Jensen, "The Return of Dr. Caligari: Paranoia in Hollywood," *Film Comment* 7, no. 4 (Winter 1971–72): 36–45.

13. See especially pp. 65–80.

14. David Cochran, *American Noir: Underground Writers and Filmmakers of the Postwar Era* (Washington: Smithsonian Institution Press, 2000): 1–15.

15. Michael Payne, ed., *A Dictionary of Cultural and Critical Theory* (Oxford: Blackwell, 1996): 518. Williams offers a full account of this concept in his *Marxism and Literature* (Oxford: Oxford University Press, 1977).

16. Cochran, 8.

17. "Reification and Utopia in Mass Culture," in *Signatures of the Visible* (New York: Routledge, 1992): 25.

18. Woody Haut, *Neon Noir: Contemporary American Crime Fiction* (London: Serpent's Tail, 1999) offers a comprehensive account of the literary scene, while Foster Hirsch's *Detours and Lost Highways: A Map of Neo-Noir* (New York: Limelight, 1999) offers a useful anatomy of cinematic developments.

19. Brill, 200.

20. For some interesting discussion/debate along similar lines see Linda Williams, "When

Women Look: A Sequel" in Steven Jay Schneider, ed., *Freud's Worst Nightmares: Psychoanalysis and the Horror Film* (Cambridge: Cambridge UP, forthcoming). See also Schneider's "Manufacturing Horror in Hitchcock's *Psycho*," *CinéAction!* 50 (1999), especially the comments on p. 75.

21. Wood, 67.

22. Wood, 71.

23. Wood, 133.

Exposing the Lies of Hitchcock's Truth

Walter Metz

Introduction

As a helicopter descends into an isolated trailer park, commandos storm into one of its residences. Inside, a man and a woman scream as armed troops surround them. The woman is whisked into a van and driven away. Later, this woman is taken deep within an intelligence agency's headquarters. She is placed inside a dark, cavernous room where she is interrogated by two men who remain hidden behind a one-way mirror. The men's voices are grotesque, distorted by computer technology. The woman cries hysterically, desperately trying to convince her abductors that she is not a spy.

Is this torture scene from a recent Tom Clancy adaptation, in which evil Soviets have kidnapped a brave American spy as part of a Cold War battle? While its imagery certainly draws from such Cold War films, this scene in fact comes from James Cameron's *True Lies* (1994), a generic hybrid of post–Cold War action-adventure film and domestic family melodrama. The torturers are the film's two Arnolds—Tom (as in Roseanne's ex-husband) and Schwarzenegger (as in big muscles). They play two Omega Sector (a CIA-like antiterrorism organization) agents: Schwarzenegger is Harry Tasker and Tom Arnold is his sidekick, Gib. The woman being tortured is Harry's wife, Helen, played by Jamie Lee Curtis. The scene is part of a lengthy subplot early in the film that depicts Harry using the technologies of his agency to cure Helen of her adulterous tendencies.

The cruelty of this subplot—as vicious as the film's main plot about Arab terrorists attempting to detonate nuclear devices on American soil—belies an instability in the narrative structure of the Cold-War spy thriller in the post–

Cold War era. With the end of the Cold War, an espionage plot such as the one *True Lies* attempts to activate needs to be rewritten in a number of ways. One such method is to refocus attention on the spy's home front. In doing so, *True Lies* returns to the roots of the Cold War thriller, namely to the geopolitical thrillers of Alfred Hitchcock (such as, for example, 1959's *North by Northwest*). Like *True Lies*, these 1950s films also express their Cold War intrigues within the framework of the domestic melodrama.

Toward an Intertextual Hitchcock Criticism

At the end of "Ideology, Genre, Auteur," Robin Wood engages in a defensive critical exercise, attempting to shield his bravura reading of Hitchcock's *Shadow of a Doubt* (1943) against appeals to intentionality. Wood argues,

> My final stress is less on the evaluation of a particular film or director than on the implications for a criticism of the Hollywood cinema of the notions of interaction and multiple determinacy I have been employing. Its roots in the Hollywood genres, and in the very ideological structure it so disturbingly subverts, make *Shadow of a Doubt* so much more suggestive and significant a work than Hitchcock the bourgeois entertainer could ever have guessed. (72–73)

My reading of *True Lies* as a Hitchcockian thriller rejects the functioning of genre that Wood takes for granted, and replaces this largely formalist concept with the more post-structuralist concept of intertextuality. Whereas Wood uses his formalist reading of *Shadow of a Doubt* to transcend the intentional claims of the author, this essay uses intertextual criticism to trace how a contemporary Hollywood film engages in a wide variety of discursive reactivations. This historical and political reading of Hitchcock goes far beyond what even Wood in his later Lacanian incarnation could ever have guessed about Hitchcock's political significance. I use this observation to reconceptualize the "genericity" of *True Lies*. For even though *True Lies* is most superficially an Arnold Schwarzenegger action-adventure film, it also reactivates the geopolitical-thriller trajectory of such films as *North by Northwest* and *Notorious;* for this reason, *True Lies* is a film of great interest to film studies; far greater than it would appear at first glance.

This replacement of genre by intertextuality is what Jim Collins has in mind in his essay, "Genericity in the Nineties." Collins argues that Hollywood films in the 1990s follow two discrete paths in activating a generic intertext:

there are those that engage in eclectic irony, and those that activate a "new sincerity." The films that are most prominent are those of the former type, of which he sees *Back to the Future III* (1990) as a prototype. With respect to this film, Collins argues,

> We enter a narrative universe defined by impertinent connections, no longer containable by one set of generic conventions. We encounter, instead, different sets of generic conventions that intermingle, constituting a profoundly intertextual diegesis, nowhere more apparent than in the shot of the DeLorean time machine being pulled through the desert by a team of horses, the very copresence of John Ford and H. G. Wells demonstrating the film's ability to access both as simultaneous narrative options. (249)

Collins argues that the semiotic loss of stability of genre as a unified meaning-making system has produced a narrative structure built around intertextual webs of references. *True Lies* engages in such postmodern referencing of Hollywood's past, most prominently following the traditions of the James Bond Cold War thriller, the Hitchcockian geopolitical thriller, and the Arnold Schwarzenegger comedy-action-adventure film.

My source of inspiration for building this historical intertextual approach linking 1950s Hitchcock to the 1990s post–Cold War action film has been Robert Corber's *In the Name of National Security: Hitchcock, Homophobia, and the Political Construction of Gender in Postwar America*, a bravura examination of the politics of the 1950s Hitchcock films. Of acute annoyance to traditional Hitchcock scholars, which delights me to no end, Corber's book argues that the Hitchcock films constitute and are constituted by various Cold War practices of surveillance and gender containment. The book succeeds admirably in demonstrating that Cold War discourses regulating the sexual behavior of Americans were just as crucial to national security as regulating outright political dissent, and that this repressive ideology dominates the beloved Hitchcockian quadrangle: *Rear Window, Vertigo, North by Northwest,* and *Psycho*.

In the present essay, I argue that Corber's frame for reading Hitchcock's geopolitical thrillers offers a way of studying *True Lies* and its attempt to rewrite the thriller into a post–Cold War landscape. *True Lies* inverts the principles of the Hitchcockian thriller (which Corber argues at least ambiguously critiques discourses of the national security state), thus collapsing gender politics, national security, and family values into one ideological problematic.

For example, *True Lies* concerns a spy who is masquerading as a family man in order to be a more convincing spy. This directly inverts *North by Northwest,* wherein Roger Thornhill, a self-centered businessman too busy for a family, is mistakenly identified as a spy by the communists. The American spies, taking advantage of the situation, force Thornhill to work in the interest of national security. At the end of the film, Thornhill is reformed of his selfish ways and settles down to raise a family with fellow American spy, Eve Kendall. Conversely, *True Lies* begins with a dysfunctional nuclear family in which Helen is about to have an affair, and ends with her reformed into both the good wife and the good spy. *True Lies* thus demonstrates that defending the interests of the national security state is one and the same as instilling good family values, which in turn is bound inevitably to ensuring the continuation of patriarchy.

Thus, my reading of *True Lies* intertextually analyzes the Hitchcockian system in order to examine the implications of the film's gender representations. An application of Robert Corber's reading of Hitchcock's 1950s films demonstrates that *True Lies* and Hitchcock films are part of a matrix of Hollywood representational practices which link discourses of gender and national security. In the case of *True Lies,* the forces of national security enforce rigid gender role behavior via a complete mastery of high technology.

Robert Corber's *In the Name of National Security* applies a historical methodology to Alfred Hitchcock's films of the 1950s. Unlike the psychoanalytic frameworks that have dominated Hitchcock criticism in recent years, Corber argues that the films respond in diverse ways to the rise of the national security state in the postwar era. He argues that Hitchcock's films both ambiguously critique and yet also participate in propagating Cold War discourses. Specifically, the films engage those Cold War gender discourses which attempt to regulate the sexual behavior of average Americans by arguing that everyday behavior directly influences the well-being of the national security state.

Corber traces the causes of this fundamentally conservative containment of gender and sexuality to the writings of the so-called Cold War liberals. The radical change in political alignments created after World War II produced a centrist coalition of liberals whose primary focus was bent on fighting Communism and maintaining political order.

Corber's main contribution to the historical understanding of this period involves linking the Cold War liberals' fight against Communism to issues of sexuality at home. The Cold War liberals' attempted to distance themselves from the pre-war 1930s Leftist "fellow travelers" by siphoning off unwanted traits onto a scapegoat, namely gay men and lesbians. Such homophobia becomes a virtual trope in Cold War liberal writing. For example, in *The Vital Center* (1949), Arthur Schlesinger compares the American Communist Party to the gay male subculture, wherein a communist would "cruise" for dates as would a gay man. In this way, the Cold War liberals effectively linked national and gender identity, defining communism as "unnatural," and complimentarily arguing that engaging in "perverted sexual practices was un-American" (qtd. in Corber, 20).

Corber applies this insight linking national security to gender identity to a much wider realm of discourses, and then reads the Hitchcock films from this framework. For example, he sees *Rear Window* (1954) as a film about the national security state. Corber argues that the film ambiguously critiques McCarthyism, "by constructing Jeff as a McCarthyite subject and then pathologizing [his] behavior" (90). Jeff forwards the goals of the national security state by spying on his neighbor, making sure he does not commit any affronts to family values (such as, perhaps, murdering his wife!), thereby threatening the security of the nation. Because communists, the logic goes, could attack inside America at any morally weak point (including gay men, working women, and indeed wife-murderers), it was important for people to spy on their neighbors.

The Hitchcock criticism that has attempted intertextual arguments with reference to even traditional views of Hitchcock has offered a good start, but such work needs to be pushed in new directions. Intertextuality scholar Robert Stam reveals the limitations of more traditional intertextual criticism: "The concept of intertextuality is not reducible to matters of 'influence' by one writer on another, or by one film-maker on another, or with 'sources' of a text in the old philological sense" (204). The most prominent of this traditional intertextual criticism with respect to Hitchcock has involved Brian De Palma homages. For example, in "Twice-Told Tales: The Rhetoric of the Remake," Thomas M. Leitch argues, "Brian De Palma's remakes of Hitchcock's *Vertigo* and *Psycho* . . . show the celebratory impulse increasingly complicated by an impulse to develop, to elaborate, and (in *Body Double*) to combine motifs from the original films in a way that marks the frontiers of the homage" (144–45). Certainly, there is nothing inherently wrong with explorations of the connections between Hitchcock and De Palma. However, the consideration of Hitchcock's relationship with New Hollywood seemingly begins and ends with De Palma. Such a literal assessment of what constitutes intertextuality has produced a limited criticism, which needs to be pushed in new directions.[1]

This paper moves intertextual Hitchcock criticism in a dialogic direction, using Corber's insight into the national politics of the 1950s films to interrogate *True Lies* as a post–Cold War geopolitical thriller in the tradition of such Cold War narratives as *Notorious* (1946) and *North by Northwest*. Stam states,

"The intertext of the work of art, then, may be taken to include not just other artworks in the same or comparable form, but also all the 'series' within which the singular text is situated" (204). Identifying a "series" of Cold War thrillers from Hitchcock through *True Lies* allows a focus on those films that link interests of gender and national security.

National Security, Gender Politics, and Technological Terrorism

The conservative nature of the gender politics of *True Lies* can be most clearly seen as the adultery subplot unfolds. This sequence develops through a number of action beats, all of which engage Hitchcockian imagery. First, upon discovering that his wife is about to have an affair, Harry uses the surveillance technologies of the Omega Sector to follow her. Next, Harry leads a commando mission to kidnap Helen and her would-be lover Simon. Then, Harry questions Helen inside the Omega Sector's interrogation room. As punishment for her transgression, Harry sends Helen on a fake spy mission, which leads her to a motel room where she is forced to perform a striptease for a mysterious spy, who unbeknownst to her is Harry.

As represented in this subplot, *True Lies* works to contain and mold women's sexuality, masking patriarchal imperatives behind the interests of national security. From an intertextual perspective, the structure and imagery of the adultery subplot in *True Lies* is forced to reveal Hitchcockian slippages between the maintenance of patriarchal control and that of national security. Unlike Hitchcock, however, this containment is enforced by the technological apparatus of the national security state. Harry punishes his wife for her moral transgressions with the help of the technological superiority of the Omega Sector. Harry's torture of Helen continues until she acquiesces to his will. This effectively demonstrates the power of technology-based coercion to convert a formerly transgressive family unit into both a literal and a moral apparatus for defending the national security.

Upon discovering Helen's intentions to have an affair, Harry uses an Omega Sector helicopter to pursue the would-be lovers to Simon's trailer-park home. The helicopter is a state-of-the-art surveillance tool, complete with infrared vision technology. The film's narration itself participates in Harry's pursuit of Helen. The film image at times consists of the helicopter's infrared imaging screen, so that we see from the point of view of Helen's pursuers.

In another of the images during the pursuit, we see in extreme long shot the helicopter chasing Simon's red convertible. The U.S. Capitol Building is featured prominently in the background of this image: the mise-en-scène

The darkly comic romance in *True Lies* recycles many elements of the Hitchcockian thriller.

here reveals that issues of national security are at stake in Harry's pursuit of his wife.

Immediately before this sequence, Gib had tried to convince Harry not to deploy the agency's resources on this personal mission. Gib argues that pulling the units off of the anti-terrorist project is "a breach of national security." What Gib does not understand, and what both Harry and the mise-en-scène of the film do, is that the wife's breach of her marriage vows is to be seen as a breach of national security. Harry must divert units from watching the Arab terrorist leader, Aziz, in order to police his own wife. This results directly in the agency's ignorance of Aziz's location, and thus indirectly results in Harry and Helen getting kidnapped by him later in the film. Helen's affair, the initial breach of national security, will eventually lead to more serious consequences, namely a nuclear device being detonated in the Florida Keys. The film thus enforces domestic morality by revealing the high stakes in transgressing family values.

In several sections of *In the Name of National Security,* Robert Corber argues that using national monuments as signifiers of the importance of national security is a recurrent trope of the Hitchcockian system. Both *North by Northwest* and *Strangers on a Train* (1951) engage in this representational practice. In examining *Strangers on a Train,* Corber assesses that it was very important for Hitchcock's adaptation of Patricia Highsmith's novel to move the setting from New York City to Washington, DC. In the film's imagery, the national monuments function to link its homophobic subtext to national security discourses: "Bruno is dwarfed by the size of the Monument, but his black shadow on the white Monument creates a blemish on the nation" (72).

True Lies slightly alters this Hitchcockian representational strategy. The gender threat to national security is now the adulterous wife instead of the gay man. However, such an attitude toward the central female character is very much in keeping with the Hitchcockian system. Corber argues that in *Strangers on a Train,*

> Miriam represents the sexually "deviant" woman demonized by Cold War political discourse because she resists confinement to the private sphere. Not only does she continue working when she no longer needs to, but she refuses to restrict her sexuality to the privatized space of the nuclear family. (76)

Corber argues that despite the homophobic construction of Bruno as a weak gay man susceptible to communist influence, the film sees Miriam's independence as the real threat to national security: "Hitchcock's film ... attributes the homosexual menace not to the gay men and women who were employed by the federal government and passed [as straight] so much as to those American women who positioned themselves as subjects rather than as objects of desire" (78). Corber concludes his analysis of *Strangers on a Train* by arguing that its solution to this crisis in gendered identity, "lay not in the expulsion of gay men and women from the government so much as in a stricter regulation of female behavior" (80).

Strangers on a Train constructs the gay Bruno as a threat to national security, which serves to mask the deeper extent of the crisis in gendered identity expressed via the film's minor female character's rebellious behavior. No such masking of the threat of the female character exists in *True Lies*. The direct threat to national security during the subplot is Helen's refusal to remain in the stifling private realm of her own home.

As the subplot progresses, it becomes clear that Helen has only agreed to have an affair with Simon out of boredom with her domestic life. Inside the trailer, Simon works to seduce her, claiming to be a dangerous spy. Her resistance to him seems about to evaporate as he tells her to "do it for your country." However, Helen comes to her senses and refuses to continue any further. As she is about to kick Simon off of her, Harry and the commando team break into the trailer to catch her in the act. The film thus seems about to argue that Helen is a virtuous and moral woman, that Harry's regulation of her sexuality is not necessary after all. But Harry's activities turn out to be desperately necessary, to which Corber's analysis of *Notorious* attests.

Corber reads the plot of *Notorious* through the frame of Sigmund Freud's "A Special Type of Choice of Object Made by Men," a case study in which a man engages in a rescue fantasy where his lover is attached to another man. The subject of the case study must rescue her away from the other man, and reform her of her promiscuous ways. Freud argues that in this fantasy, the subject is replaying his pre-oedipal attachment to his mother. Corber argues that this is the subtext of *Notorious,* as Devlin must rescue Alicia away from her evil Nazi husband, Alex. Corber claims that the state enforces Devlin's participation in national security by making him relive his pre-oedipal stage via his love for Alicia: "The similarities between Devlin in *Notorious* and the type of man described by Freud suggest that Devlin remains libidinally invested in his activities for the American government because they create a fantasy scenario that re-stages his pre-oedipal attachment to his mother" (207).

This plot trajectory is reenacted in Harry's rescue of Helen from Simon. Harry must extract his seemingly promiscuous wife from Simon and reform her. *True Lies* thus again inflects the Hitchcockian system in a new direction. Unlike Devlin, Harry's cooperation with the national security state has already been assured. Harry's loyalty to national security is not at stake, but Helen's is. She must be made to see that being faithful to her husband is in the interest of national security. The film accomplishes this in the end by turning Helen into a spy as well, making her join the national security family.[2]

In the subplot's next phase, Harry takes Helen prisoner, and questions her in the Omega Sector's interrogation room. This is a horrific torture sequence: Harry, sitting behind a one-way mirror, interrogates his wife about the affair.[3] The fact that Harry uses the technology of his agency to regulate the sexual behavior of his wife is analogous to the Cold War liberal's use of anticommunism rhetoric to contain Americans' sexuality in the 1950s. By arguing that being gay or being a working mother contributed to the communist threat, 1950s intellectuals essentially regulated morality from behind a distant screen of national security. In a very similar way, Harry, interrogating his wife inside a torture chamber, uses the apparatus of national security to police her sexuality.

Not surprisingly, this misogynist scene is driven by the dynamics of voyeurism. Helen cannot see Harry through the mirror. Yet Harry, due to his technological gadgetry, can see many facets of Helen. He has an oscilloscope that graphs Helen's voice and a thermal sensor hooked up to a color monitor that graphs the temperature of the regions of Helen's head. In addition, Harry can see Helen in the room through the one-way mirror, as well as via a video surveillance camera.

In *Discipline and Punishment: Birth of the Prison,* the historian Michel Foucault discusses Bentham's panopticon prison, in which the centrally-located warden can see all of the prisoners under his control. In *New Vocabularies in Film Semiotics,* Stam connects the panopticon to Hitchcock's *Rear Window* by arguing that both the panopticon and the cinema are voyeuristic machines: "Since the panopticon installs an asymmetrical, unidirectional gaze—the scientist or warden can see the inmates but not vice versa—it has been compared to the voyeuristic situation of the film spectator" (212). Stam argues that Jeff in *Rear Window* serves as the warden of the prison: "L. B. Jefferies, at the beginning of *Rear Window,* overseeing the world from a sheltered position, subjecting his neighbors to a controlling gaze, becomes the warden-spectator, as it were, in a private panopticon, where he observes the wards ... of an imaginary prison" (212–13).

Harry's interrogation of Helen in the torture scene reinvents the voyeurism of *Rear Window,* inscribing it within the domestic dispute between a husband and his adulterous wife. *True Lies* presents us with a *technological panopticon,* in which technology has compressed the prison to only one cell. The husband-warden interrogates the wife-prisoner, seeing the many sides of her via his technological devices. The cinema itself is represented in this panoply by the video surveillance camera. In all three panoptica—Foucault's, *Rear Window*'s, and *True Lies*'—the warden looks, but is never looked at. *True Lies* demonstrates the logical conclusion of rendering a personal dispute as an issue of national security. The oppressive relationship between husband and wife in the patriarchal family is technologized to the extent that the husband can summon his own personal panopticon to correct his wife's criminal behavior.

The patriarchal desires to which this scene gives voice are astoundingly defined by the popular debate over the film's sexism, as reported in *Entertainment Weekly.* James Cameron, defending the interrogation scene, claims, "I don't think every scene in a movie has to present itself as an example of political correctness ... I've had a lot of guys say, '*I need one of those rooms at my house*' [my emphasis]" (qtd. in Broeske and Hajari, 7). In addition to being a poor defender of the scene's gender politics, Cameron expresses an even deeper sexism by claiming that a torture chamber would be a good mechanism for making women behave.[4]

When terrorizing Helen for her transgression proves a failure, the film resorts to a more coercive strategy of containment. Purportedly as a joke, Harry assigns Helen to a spy mission to repent for being found with Simon. The lasting effect of this sequence is to convert Helen into a spy; she is coerced into acting in the direct interest of the national security state, rather than working indirectly against it via her loose morality. This is a gendered inversion of the Hitchcockian system, in which it is usually a man who gets mistaken for a spy and gets lured into acting for the national security apparatus.[5] In *North by Northwest,* for instance, Roger Thornhill is mistaken for a spy, and must complete his mission before he is allowed to return to his domestic life.

Left without a choice—she is understandably terrified—Helen agrees to the plan. She is to pose as a prostitute and attempt to obtain information from an unknown male spy. Of course, that unknown man turns out to be Harry, who, hidden in darkness, asks Helen to perform a striptease for him. She obliges. The visuals of this scene engage a voyeuristic dynamic. Harry sits in the shadows to look at Helen's striptease. The lighting scheme is completely different when we look at Helen. High-key lighting illuminates Helen for maximum visibility, while Harry is lit with low-key lighting in order to shroud him from Helen's returning gaze.

This scene is also reminiscent of Foucault's poetic description of the panopticon: "[It consists of] small captive shadows in the cells of the periphery" (qtd. in Stam, 213). *True Lies* inverts the power relations within the panopticon. Harry the warden is now the one in the shadows, while Helen is where the prisoner should be. The film again works to construct Harry as the victim of his wife's adultery.

Corber's examination of the psychoanalytic readings of *Rear Window* helps to further situate this scene's negotiation of the relationship between sexuality and national security. Corber argues that *Rear Window,* contrary to the now-traditional Lacanian reading of the film, "does not so much critique the voyeuristic economy of the cinematic apparatus as try to retrieve the cinematic apparatus from its contamination by the emergence of the national security state" (98). In the Hitchcock film, Jeff's looking can no longer be purely sexual, but must automatically engage the mechanisms of surveillance. Corber argues that Jeff is not sexually interested in Lisa until she goes into Thorwald's apartment, where he can look at her through his lenses. His looking is not sexual, but is instead grounded in his investigation of Thorwald's murder of his wife. Because Jeff is the perfect McCarthyite neighbor, he is driven to look by Thorwald's affront to family values, which is of course an assault on national security.

The striptease segment in *True Lies* makes similar connections between the national security state and private sexuality, except this film makes no attempt to critique the contamination of voyeurism by surveillance. *True Lies* instead collapses this distinction. Whereas Jeff is a private citizen, Harry's voyeuristic activity is accomplished under the guise of his role as protector of the national security. Furthermore, it is his abuse of that position, his use of the agency to attempt to seduce (or rape, since Helen's participation is involuntary) his wife, that directly leads to a breach of national security. At the moment Harry reveals himself to Helen, the Arab terrorists storm into the room and kidnap them both. This scene directly mirrors Harry's previous commando raid on Helen's adulterous affair, constructing a visual logic that implicates her as responsible for the kidnapping. It is Helen's breach of family values that functions to set off the chain of events that will threaten the security of the United States.

The terrorists' kidnapping of Harry and Helen moves the film out of its domestic subplot and into its national security main plot. The trajectory of the rest of the film is geared toward finishing Helen's transformation from immoral housewife into a spy working for the national security. The film's penultimate scene, after Harry has rescued his daughter and killed the remaining terrorists, demonstrates the benefits of Helen's transformation. The scene involves Harry, Helen, and daughter Dana sitting at their dining room table engaging in a playful game of thumb wrestling (which of course Harry wins). The scene demonstrates that the experience fighting the terrorists as a family has proved therapeutic, bringing the transgressive mother and daughter into line with the interests of both patriarchy and national security.[6]

This scene expresses the extent to which Helen and Dana have been reformed by having each woman wear a string of pearls. Whereas Dana formerly wore grubby clothes, the experience of fighting the terrorists for both her dad and her country has caused her to completely adopt the bourgeois American lifestyle that she so obviously rejected at the film's beginning.

Beyond the costuming, this scene's narration also expresses the film's gender politics. After Harry has killed all the terrorists, he lands his Harrier jet and rushes to Dana's side. He hugs her and says, "It's over."[7] We dissolve to an exterior shot of the Taskers' white, picket-fenced house. The camera cranes forward, and moves into the house through the dining room window.

This expository camera movement, of course, mimics the famous opening of Hitchcock's *Psycho* (1960). By contrasting *North by Northwest* (1959) and *Psycho* (1960), Corber argues that the control over behaviors of gender and sexuality that had dominated the 1950s was about to break down during the 1960s. Corber argues that *North by Northwest* demonstrates that, "the discourses of national security virtually guaranteed that gender and nationality functioned as mutually reinforcing categories of identity." Conversely, *Psycho* places "emphasis on the breakdown of the practices and discourses that anchored and guaranteed the construction of gendered identity in the 1950s" (191). The opening camera movement in *Psycho* begins outside an apartment window and ends inside a bedroom, revealing a half-dressed Marion with her lover Sam at the conclusion of a lunch-time tryst. Sam is married, and Marion has been attempting to convince him to get a divorce so that they can themselves get married. The beginning camera movement of the film serves to introduce an upheaval of proper family values. Marion eventually pays with her life for this transgression.

In *True Lies'* reactivation of this sequence, the potential breakdown of morality is repressed. The tracking camera through an open window is used to end this film, not begin it. The political effect is therefore inverted—whereas *Psycho's* camera movement brought us into a world of moral disequilibrium, *True Lies'* usage of this device demonstrates the ideological closure whereby the interests of the national security and of Harry's domestic security have been brought into alignment.

This one intertextual equivalence effectively summarizes the differing gender politics of *True Lies* and the Hitchcock films. Whereas Hitchcock's films, especially *Psycho,* at least ambiguously critiqued the linkage between national security and the patriarchal containment of sexuality, *True Lies* fully collapses the distinction. *True Lies,* seen from this intertextual perspective, fully endorses the Cold War liberals' contention that to act against the interests of national security is immoral, and conversely, that to act against the interests of the patriarchal family is a threat to national security.

Conclusion

This essay has demonstrated that a historical approach to intertextuality can illuminate the textual connections between *True Lies,* a post–Cold War action film, and various 1950s Hitchcockian thrillers. However, if my interest in *True Lies* lay in the purely formalist system of filmic references, an intertextual criticism of the film would be a meaningless exercise. Instead, reading *True Lies* via the Hitchcockian thriller brings to light a political implication of *In the Name of National Security* which Robert Corber does not pursue. Corber's book concludes with speculations as to why his insights are relevant today, citing Pat Buchanan's speech at the 1992 GOP national convention, which argued that gays and working mothers are responsible for the decline of national morality, and therefore, national strength. Since Corber argues that the domestic politics of the Cold War were constituted by this very same conflation of gender and national security discourses, he concludes that the Buchanan speech represents an attempt by conservatives to *prolong* Cold War discourses into the post–Cold War world.

This is a stunning reflection that opens up a fertile ground for intertextually relating Cold War representational strategies to post–Cold War films. *True Lies* attempts to prolong Cold War discourses of social containment. Like the 1950s Hitchcock films, *True Lies* conflates discourses of national security with those of national morality. In the kidnapping sequence with which this essay begins, one of the most misogynist sequences in a major Hollywood release since Hitchcock's shower scene, an American agent uses the surveillance technologies of the United States government to terrorize his wife for contemplating adultery. *True Lies*' use of this Hitchcockian conflation of morality and national security discourses reaffirms Corber's suspicion that the so-called post–Cold War era is actually a prolongation of the Cold War's major discursive articulations.

Furthermore, by activating yet subtly transforming the Hitchcockian plot as described by Corber, *True Lies* seems to pine for the "peaceful" days of the Cold War, when all that was at stake was a few lives and some microfilm (as is the case in *North by Northwest*). In direct contrast, in *True Lies*' chaotic post–Cold War world, the loss of the superpowers' stalemate has destabilized hegemonic control over nuclear weapons, resulting in the stakes being radically raised: toward the end of the film, the terrorists detonate a nuclear bomb off the coast of the United States. In a symptomatic case of papering over ideological contradictions, the film rapidly denies the environmental consequences of this event. The film quickly attempts to return to its Cold War, Hitchcockian womb, wherein the conflict concerns ideological battles over gender and national identity, not global annihilation.

However, within the post–Cold War landscape, with the evacuation of the Soviet threat, the ideological concerns almost exclusively collapse onto the domestic morality of the family members. As the bomb goes off, Harry kisses his wife. The film teaches us, if nothing else, that the love between a man and a woman will protect them from any of the world's new dangers. And it can't hurt if they happen to be spies.[8]

Notes

1. For other examples of studies wherein De Palma serves as the major intertextual example with respect to Hitchcock and New Hollywood, see Laurent Bouzereau, *The De Palma Cut;* Ann Cvetkovich, "Postmodern Vertigo"; Robert E. Kapsis, *Hitchcock: The Making of a Reputation;* and Kenneth MacKinnon, *Misogyny in the Movies: The De Palma Question.*

2. Of course, *Notorious* also turns Alicia into a spy. But in that film, as in most of Hitchcock's geopolitical thrillers, the spying is only a temporary situation. In *True Lies,* Helen's conversion into a spy is permanent. Her job with the national security agency is the linchpin around which her moral containment is assured.

3. The film attempts to repress through comedy the fact that this is the most horrific moment of the film. The contradiction is that these actions are carried out by the purported heroes of the film. As this scene demonstrates, the Omega Sector agents are the real terrorists of this film, regardless of how much the film attempts to vilify the behavior of the Arab nationalists.

4. A further irony is that the previous issue of *Entertainment Weekly* featured an article that gushed over Cameron's strong heroines. The article quotes Cameron, explaining the method he uses to create these "strong" women: "I never find it hard to write female characters. I project myself into the situation, and then another part of my mind says, 'Women see things differently, they create life,' and it has to be modified." (qtd. in Thompson, 33). Cameron's sexism is apparently only outdone by his essentialism.

5. With the notable exception of *Notorious*'s Alicia, which I discuss above.

6. Dana is also coded early in the film as a transgressive presence in the family. She dresses like a grunge rocker, has a biker boyfriend, and engages in petty thievery. In her first scene, she steals money from Gib's wallet. Interestingly, it is a high-tech surveillance device that uncovers this early indicator that the values of the family are breaking down. Gib's microscopic camera, hidden in a pack of cigarettes, exposes Dana's immorality.

7. While the motivation for this line at the level of the surface plot is obviously that the trauma of her kidnapping by the terrorists is over, at the ideological level, Harry is really telling Dana that her transgressive behavior is now over.

8. This essay was written in 1994, and promptly sent to a number of film studies journals for publication, where it was rejected repeatedly for relying too much on Corber's political reading of Hitchcock. I have refrained from rewriting the paper to point out the obvious connections to September 11, 2001, and the United States' barbaric response to that event. In 1994, the depiction of Arab terrorists as infantile horrified me. Today, I am more horrified by Americans' inability to theorize the political meanings of their own culture, a skill that is brilliantly displayed by Corber's book, and hopefully, although too late, by this meager essay.

Works Cited

Bouzereau, Laurent. *The De Palma Cut: The Films of America's Most Controversial Director.* New York: Dembner Books, 1988.

Broeske, Pat H., and Nisid Hajari. "Burden of 'True'." *Entertainment Weekly* 234 (August 5, 1994): 6–7.

Collins, Jim. "Genericity in the Nineties: Eclectic Irony and the New Sincerity." In *Film Theory Goes to the Movies.* Eds. Jim Collins, Hilary Radner, and Ava Preacher Collins. New York: Routledge, 1993. 242–263.

Corber, Robert. *In the Name of National Security: Hitchcock, Homophobia, and the Political Construction of Gender in Postwar America.* Durham, NC: Duke UP, 1993.

Cvetkovich, Ann. "Postmodern *Vertigo*: The Sexual Politics of Allusion in De Palma's *Body Double*." In *Hitchcock's Rereleased Films: From Rope to Vertigo.* Eds. Walter Raubicheck and Walter Srebnick. Detroit: Wayne State UP, 1991. 147–162.

Foucault, Michel. *Discipline and Punishment: Birth of the Prison.* New York: Vintage, 1979.

Freud, Sigmund. "A Special Type of Choice of Object Made By Men." In *The Standard Edition of the Complete Psychological Works of Sigmund Freud.* Volume XI (1910). Trans. James Strachey. London: Hogarth, 1957. 163–175.

Kapsis, Robert E. *Hitchcock: The Making of a Reputation*. Chicago: U of Chicago P, 1992.

Leitch, Thomas M. "Twice-Told Tales: The Rhetoric of the Remake." *Literature-Film Quarterly* 18.3 (July 1990): 138–149.

MacKinnon, Kenneth. *Misogyny in the Movies: The De Palma Question*. Newark: U of Delaware P, 1990.

Schlesinger, Arthur Jr. *The Vital Center: The Politics of Freedom*. Boston: Houghton Mifflin, 1949.

Stam, Robert, Robert Burgoyne, and Sandy Flitterman-Lewis. *New Vocabularies in Film Semiotics*. London: Routledge, 1992.

Thompson, Anne. "5 True Lies about James Cameron." *Entertainment Weekly* 233 (July 29, 1994): 27–33.

Wood, Robin. "Ideology, Genre, Auteur." In *Film Genre Reader*. Ed. Barry Keith Grant. Austin, TX: U of Texas P, 1986. 59–73.

PART IV: FOUND IN TRANSLATION

Although Hitchcock's influence may be most easily recognized in Hollywood movies, he has had an equally significant impact on European cinema. The essays in this section suggest something of the diversity of that impact, investigating the varied ways in which Hitchcockian elements have been inflected in a range of different social and cultural contexts. Hitchcock first emerged as a major figure in European film culture in France during the 1950s, and Richard Neupert explores the centrality of Hitchcock's place in French critical debate before turning his particular attention to critic-turned-director Claude Chabrol's adaptation of Hitchcockian themes and techniques in *The Unfaithful Wife* (1968) and *The Butcher* (1969). Frank Tomasulo traces the remarkably detailed narrative and stylistic similarities between *Rear Window* and Michelangelo Antonioni's *Blow-Up* (1966), emphasizing in particular their shared reflexivity as meditations on cinema. Ernesto R. Acevedo-Muñoz examines the way in which allusions to Hitchcock films emerge at key moments of crisis and revelation in Pedro Almodóvar's *Women on the Verge of a Nervous Breakdown* (1988), structuring it and functioning as part of an emerging multicultural aesthetic. And finally, Philippe Met explores the intertextual links connecting Hitchcock, modern American horror, and the Italian *giallo,* that florid fusion, as Met characterizes it, of "estheticism and sleaze, realistic violence and abstract stylization" best known in the films of Mario Bava and Dario Argento.

Red Blood on White Bread
Hitchcock, Chabrol, and French Cinema

Richard Neupert

Hitchcock and the French

No British or American director has been more important to French critics and theorists than Alfred Hitchcock. Since the 1940s, Hitchcock has been at the center of every major debate and every critical movement in French theory, from auteurism to structuralism, psychoanalysis, feminism, and beyond. Moreover, Hitchcock's highly structured narratives and manipulative cinematic techniques inspired several generations of French filmmakers to offer pastiches of shots, scenes, and even whole movies "à la Hitchcock." Thus, there is no more fertile ground for evaluating the impact of Alfred Hitchcock on world cinema than testing his ties to French film criticism and practice. This chapter reminds us how crucial Hitchcock's movies were for the formation of the French *politique des auteurs* in the 1950s, but also how fundamental his narrative strategies proved for a variety of directors ever since, and especially for, Claude Chabrol.

Just what "Alfred Hitchcock" means to French critics, however, is not necessarily the same as for many American and British scholars. It was not so much his label as "master of suspense" that initially intrigued French critics, so much as his formal rigor and narrative strategies. During the 1950s, much of the critical interest in Hitchcock involved having to excuse his work in genre filmmaking, while trying to provide evidence of thematic concerns that went deeper than the surface of his technically polished suspense films. However, not all French critics were willing to look beyond the façade. French leftists in particular have long attacked his brand of apolitical, manipulative filmmaking. Two firm camps were quickly entrenched in France. At the same time in the 1950s that *Cahiers du cinéma* was devoting great praise and attention to Hitchcock, their rival, *Positif,* attacked his "neo-Nazi" themes and failure to connect with social reality. A Hitchcock movie was too much like a roller-coaster ride, a well-constructed studio product.[1] Regardless of which side of the Hitchcock debate one was on, there was no denying that he played a vital role in the formation of cinema criticism. The heated disagreements over Hitchcock's movies often forced his biggest supporters to make bold claims about hidden themes and personal symbolism as they tried to counter complaints of his shallow conservatism. Many of these passionate defenses came from a new generation of reviewers who staked their careers on proving that Hitchcock was a central figure in the modern cinema. Alfred Hitchcock and the young French critics of *Cahiers du cinéma* both benefited from this unparalleled association in the 1950s and 60s.

Alfred Hitchcock was interested in France long before French critics became so interested in him. As James M. Vest points out, Hitchcock was a Francophile all his life. For him, France was the place of temptation, deception, and the appealing, passionate sides of life. French culture, including its language, wines, literature, and foods, was intriguing to him, and by Vest's calculations, one fourth of all Hitchcock films "included substantial allusions to France or sequences in French."[2] Not surprisingly, it was during the 1950s that Hitchcock's love of France became more and more pronounced, including frequent visits to Paris for the premieres of his films, at the very moment when French critics, and *Cahiers du cinéma* in particular, were valiantly championing his artistry. Not only did he revel in the very rewarding experience of being the center of attention at French press conferences, but he began to carry issues of *Cahiers* around the globe with him as a marker of his new status in world cinema. But that auteur ranking was the result of a slow and often controversial process initiated by a handful of particularly adept and fanatical young critics in Paris.

During the 1940s there were only a few sporadic attempts to elevate Alfred Hitchcock as a major auteur, and certainly one factor that delayed his ascendance in France was that his American movies were not readily available until after the war. But soon Hitchcock's more recent movies, along with the newly discovered American *films noirs,* swept across French screens and prompted widespread discussion. According to Vest, twenty-four Hitchcock films played in Paris between 1945 and 1954. The new prevalence and power of *ciné-clubs,* film journals, and review columns in the popular press guaranteed that a great deal of attention and a wide range of critical perspectives would be devoted to this steady stream of movies. For the French, the cluster of *Rope* (1948), *Under Capricorn* (1949), and *Stage Fright* (1950) proved particularly significant for fueling debate either for or against Hitchcock.[3]

During 1948 and 1949 a subset of French critics, including André Bazin, Jacques Doniol-Valcroze, and Pierre Kast, began giving increased coverage to American directors, including Hitchcock, although he was still regarded as a skilled commercial technician in contrast to William Wyler or Orson Welles. Strangely, it was an article in the leftist journal *L'Ecran français* by Jean-Charles Tacchella and Roger Thérond that helped solidify Hitchcock's reputation. They acknowledged he was maturing with *Rope,* becoming "audaciously sure of his audacity," but they also claimed that it was pretty much a "pre-fab" project forced on him by the studio system. For them, it helped that Hitchcock shot *Rope* quickly, and below budget. This proved he had an artisanal directorial economy through which his own personal style could nonetheless shine.[4] Rohmer had already praised Hitchcock in several journals, including Auriol's *Revue de cinéma,* but for many at *L'Ecran* it was going too far to offer so much attention to American movies which were also beginning to dominate the French box office. By 1950 the divisions at *L'Ecran* over treatment of American cinema had gotten so deep that the editors complained that some of their critics cared more about empty form than social themes: for them, pro-Hollywood critics seemed ready to throw away national independence. In such a world, they argued, France's future would surely see the triumph of Coca-Cola, American cinema, and U.S. atomic military bases on French soil![5] An exodus of pro-Hollywood critics, including Bazin, from *L'Ecran* changed the critical climate in France as they moved on to form other journals.

Eric Rohmer was the most persistent in praising Hitchcock, so when Doniol-Valcroze and Bazin asked him to write for *Cahiers* in 1951, he built a critical perspective that included Hitchcock as a central figure. He and Jean-Luc Godard were quick to argue that Hitchcock's *mise-en-scène* reflected a certain realism of character and theme, creating a modern depth that revealed truth and a moral universe.[6] According to Vest, "Rohmer saw Hitchcock as a consummate practitioner of the plastic arts, as a formalist for whom design was at least as important as content, and whose rhythms and skilled use of metaphor testified to his artistry."[7] Bazin, struggling to assess Hitchcock in light of all the praise lavished on him by Rohmer, Godard, Claude Chabrol, and François Truffaut, even met with Hitchcock in 1954. He still dismissed some of Hitchcock's more commercial movies, but did reevaluate other films based on themes mentioned by his young critics: "The identification of a weaker character with a stronger one had moral and intellectual implications that moved those films beyond the realm of simple thrillers to encompass something more intellectually compelling."[8] This was a major victory for Rohmer and his cohorts at *Cahiers*. Rohmer would go on to coauthor with Claude Chabrol an exemplary study of Hitchcock as auteur, published in 1957. Thus, by the mid-1950s, nearly every critic working at *Cahiers*, from Doniol-Valcroze and Bazin on down, had closely evaluated the films of Alfred Hitchcock, granting him privileged auteur status.

In 1954, Jacques Rivette admitted that Hitchcock, like Howard Hawks, was tough for critics to evaluate. So just what was it about Hitchcock's cinema that proved so essential for these young French critics? They practiced a brand of auteurism which argued that film analysis requires locating key, central themes behind a work. Ideally, a director will have consistent concepts as well as consistent narrative or stylistic formal strategies. But working in the wake of World War II, they also felt compelled to prove that their favorite directors were in one way or another engaged in moral issues, reflecting real-world concerns. Realism, however, was hardly a trait most people associated with Hitchcock's flashy style and implausible stories. Establishing Hitchcock as an important figure became a double challenge. First, they had to prove that their new brand of close analysis worked on American cinema; second, they had to reveal that Hitchcock was as much an auteur as Jean Renoir and Ingmar Bergman. Eric Rohmer was among the most successful at this, claiming Hitchcock's films were modern because they employed a realism that reveals the deep inseparability of the material and spiritual orders. For him, movies such as *Shadow of a Doubt, Under Capricorn,* and *I Confess* presented "a landscape of souls" undergoing moral torment. Rohmer struggled to show Hitchcock was as complex and intellectually compelling as Roberto Rossellini, though he admitted that fate, sin, and redemption were harder to find in these Hollywood movies.[9]

Given that these Young Turk critics were fed up with much of contemporary French film production, they staked their own reputations on proving Hitchcock had aesthetic and moral value for contemporary audiences. "Our idea was that the author of a film was its director," explains Chabrol. "Thus his personality had to be strong enough to appropriate the film completely, even if he was not its scriptwriter."[10] Evaluating this Hollywood director was the perfect test case since he worked in a much more industrial context than European directors. Finding marks of narrative and moral unity in a collection

of genre films made for various studios would prove not only the good analytical abilities of the critics, but also that their hunches about Hitchcock were
correct all along. In 1955, Truffaut and Chabrol, armed with their new auteurist tool, a portable tape recorder, interviewed Hitchcock and tested several of
their hypotheses about his recurring themes involving guilt and redemption,
hypotheses they were already exploring in their reviews. They consciously
moved French criticism forward with their attention to *mise-en-scène*, realism,
form, and authorship in Hitchcock. As Bazin pointed out to their skeptics,
these Young Turks managed to locate "the film's very material, an organization of beings and things that are its meaning, which is to say moral as well as
aesthetic" within Hitchcock's visual style.[11] Proving his auteur status valorized
the young critics' aesthetic judgment and *Cahiers*' good sense for supporting
these seemingly blasphemous reviewers.

 Godard's 1952 review of *Strangers on a Train* is typical of the praise for
Hitchcock: "I know of no other recent film, in fact, which better conveys the
condition of modern man, who must escape his fate without the help of the
gods."[12] His review tries to placate leftist social critics such as Georges Sadoul
who complained that Hitchcock only delivered apolitical entertainment. Bazin had gradually been won over, up to a point, by such arguments, and in
particular by Truffaut and Chabrol's idea that Hitchcock's American movies
were built around central themes of the transfer of identity through paired
characters and situations. Domination, manipulation, and identification cir-
culated among and between characters, and these themes were reflected in the
setting, casting, editing, and camerawork, especially with subjective point of
view shots. Godard, in particular, praised Hitchcock's centrality of voyeurism:
"Cutting on a look is almost the definition of montage ... It is in effect, to
bring out the soul under the spirit, the passion behind the intrigue, to make
the heart prevail over intelligence by destroying the notion of space in favor
of that of time. The famous sequence of the cymbals in the remake of *The
Man Who Knew Too Much* is the best proof."[13] Later, in a review of *The Wrong
Man*, Godard connected "looking" with real life experience: "To look around
oneself is to live free. So the cinema, which reproduces life, must film characters who look around."[14] *Rear Window* also provided an ideal example for
Godard, who wanted to concentrate on Hitchcock's revelatory power rather
than his amusement park–like effects.

 For Truffaut, who spent fifty hours interviewing Hitchcock in 1962, his
movies display a clarity of purpose and persuasive power that pervade everything he does, but here too it was always tied to a sort of realism: "Hitchcock

chooses to express everything by purely visual means . . . Because of his unique ability to film the thoughts of his characters and make them perceptible without resorting to dialogue, he is, to my way of thinking, a realistic director." Truffaut explains that most dialogue in real life is empty or superficial, so movies built around earnest dialogue scenes are by definition unrealistic, in contrast to Hitchcock. This opened up one avenue for critics to compare Hitchcock to Renoir: Rather than using deep space and long takes to reveal complexity, Hitchcock exploited his own arsenal of visual tactics (including the heavy reliance on eyeline matches). "Hitchcock is almost unique in being able to film directly, that is, without resorting to explanatory dialogue, such intimate emotions as suspicion, jealousy, desire, and envy. And herein lies a paradox: the director who, through the simplicity and clarity of his work, is the most accessible to a universal audience is also the director who excels at filming the most complex and subtle relationships between human beings." Truffaut finds "an exchange of looks" in Hitchcock has the power to convey "that one of the two characters dominates, is in love with, or jealous of, the other." The resulting scenes follow a natural, sensitive rhythm.[15] No wonder Bazin continued to have reservations toward Hitchcock, given that much of the praise from Truffaut and others was based on how his use of montage or conventional continuity editing generated a "rich realism."

Chabrol and Hitchcock

Claude Chabrol was as deeply engaged in plumbing the depths of Hitchcock as any of his friends at *Cahiers* and was less afraid to praise genre films. He saw "the crime" in a Hitchcock thriller as a test for all the characters, and pointed out the spiritual or moral itinerary of temptation, suspicion, and deliverance at work in each movie. For him, Hitchcock's characters were lost in a modern world full of symbolic objects.[16] Chabrol's own films would eventually echo these spiritual journeys. We should remember that these *Cahiers* critics were also influenced by Catholicism. Even Truffaut's most famous article, "A Certain Tendency of the French Cinema," attacks contemporary French directors for their immoral themes. Chabrol worked to prove a moral Christian framework present within Hitchcock. His 1955 review of *Rear Window* connects themes of love with morality. Chabrol establishes that the courtyard is a projection of the idle Jeff's "amorous fixation," with each apartment representing one possibility of a full range of emotional relationships, from solitude to honeymoon bliss to hatred to longing. But Hitchcock's perspective is proven by "three biblical quotations" spoken by characters, proving for Chabrol that this auteur has a metaphysical core, presenting a Christian world. Chabrol even discusses the plot as a "trinity:" the romance, the thriller, but also the "realist painting of the courtyard." He explains that the structure linking *Rear Window*'s events, from the murder of a wife to the death of a dog, is Hitchcock's personal call for a more committed, neighborly, responsible world.[17] This is a perfect example of the way the *Cahiers* critics connected narrative structure, style, and moral vision to Hitchcock's authorship. Later in his career, Chabrol wrote, "Hitchcock delivers his worldview, that of a bourgeois puritan . . . What is beautiful is that Hitchcock does not blurt out the basic [metaphysical] concept but gives it form."[18] As a director, Chabrol gradually turned more cynical and distanced himself from redemptive Christian themes, though he still liked to point out the moral failure inherent in modern life. What he retained from Hitchcock was his use of structural oppositions between characters and their moral stances, as well as the formal unity of theme and visual style.

Evidence of the concrete effects of all this auteurist interest in Hitchcock can be witnessed in Louis Malle's neo-noir crime drama, *Ascenseur pour l'échafaud* (*Elevator to the Gallows*, 1957). Malle explains that for his first feature film he wanted to make a good thriller but also pay homage to his favorite directors: "The irony is, I was really split between my tremendous admiration for Bresson and the temptation to make a Hitchcock-like film. So there's something about *Ascenseur* that goes from one to the other . . . I was emulating Hitchcock in trying to do, even if slightly ironically, a thriller that works."[19] That Malle should consider Alfred Hitchcock alongside the prestigious modernist Robert Bresson proves that the critical campaign begun by Rohmer, Chabrol, Godard, and Truffaut had succeeded. Hitchcock's reputation had been elevated to the point where he was just as worthy an influence on new French cinema's stories and styles as any European art cinema auteur.

But even Alfred Hitchcock helped prove the very real contacts between France and his own cinema. By fall of 1959, when the New Wave was dominating the French film scene, Hitchcock, touring to promote *North by Northwest,* continually compared himself to "other young filmmakers" and even stated that his next movie, *Psycho,* would be shot like the New Wave, quickly and cheaply, in black and white. He went so far as to compare his juxtaposition of scenes occurring miles apart late in *North by Northwest* as comparable to Alain Resnais' montage in *Hiroshima mon amour.* "Hitchcock would return to that conception of himself as innovator and even as model to New Wave filmmakers in the years to come."[20] The young *Cahiers* critics had used Alfred

Hitchcock to jump-start their critical careers, but by the end of the decade, he was exploiting their ideas and even their new filmmaking tactics to his own advantage. According to Vest, "Hitchcock was well aware of *Cahiers'* particular contributions to his well-being and that of his work. He was also aware of changes in filmmaking represented by the young French writer-directors who were now commanding worldwide attention for their films, and he took steps to link himself to them in new ways."[21] However, while those young directors regularly pastiched his work, they rarely simply tried to "be" Hitchcock. They each wanted to become auteurs in their own rights, so adapted lessons from Hitchcock, Bazin, Renoir, and others into their new, experimental film styles.

Hitchcock's Effect on Claude Chabrol

Claude Chabrol has consistently been the director most clearly influenced by Hitchcock, in part because he tells so many domestic crime stories, but also because of his exploration of guilt, eroticism, and point-of-view structures. "Alfred Hitchcock takes seriously the subjects I take seriously."[22] Rohmer and Chabrol's unifying idea for their 1957 book on Hitchcock was that his diegetic worlds, narrative structures, and even visual style are built around an exchange. "The idea of 'exchange,' which we find everywhere in his work, may be given either a moral expression (the transfer of guilt), a psychological expression (suspicion), a dramatic expression (blackmail—or even pure 'suspense'), or a concrete expression (a to-and-fro movement)."[23] Exchange is a process, evident when one character gets caught up in some problem begun by someone else, but also when a spectator observes the preparation of a crime. Thanks to the structures of voyeurism, the viewer becomes implicated in the act of dreading and yet desiring a violent crime. Suspense makes such participatory exchanges even stronger.

Hitchcock's manipulation of a character's subjective vision, which then becomes the audience's point of view, was one of his key strategies, according to Chabrol. He points out that most shots in a Hitchcock thriller reveal what characters see. A favorite example of this "subjective base" in Hitchcock's form comes from *Notorious*. Chabrol describes the scene when Devlin (Cary Grant) locates Alicia (Ingrid Bergman), drugged in her room. In the first shot she sees him in the dim light, in the second shot he sees her and the camera approaches her bedside as he does. For the third shot, which encircles them, the shot has been passed from their subjectivity over to ours, so that even an objective shot functions in a subjective manner, implicating us in their visual narrative space.[24] This "subjective/objective" strategy fits well alongside the other traits identified by Chabrol's summaries of Hitchcock, and would play a key role in Chabrol's own filmmaking.

Hitchcock's influence is clear in each of Chabrol's fifty-plus films. Some of his characters even remind us of figures from Hitchcock's worlds (the shrewish older woman in *Innocents with Dirty Hands* [1975] recalls the vicious matrons of *Rebecca* and *Notorious,* for instance) and everyday objects take on great significance (shiny cigarette lighters, a bloody handkerchief, tell-tale whiskey bottles . . .). There are also many pairs of male characters who share or exchange some guilt, beginning with *Le Beau Serge* (1958), *The Cousins* (1959), and *The Third Lover* (1962). But rather than listing scores of intertextual references and plot devices, it is more productive to condense Chabrol's central observations about Hitchcock and apply them to two features that were central to reviving his career in the late 1960s: *La Femme infidèle* (*The Unfaithful Wife,* 1968) and *Le Boucher* (*The Butcher,* 1969). Both of these stories are founded on Chabrol's sense of Hitchcock principles, including that everyone can turn evil, while violence lurks just beneath the surface of the most banal, everyday events.

Other traits, already outlined by Chabrol's reviews of Hitchcock, are also evident in *The Unfaithful Wife* and *The Butcher:* his characters are tested by some crime, often leading them on a path from temptation to suspicion to some sort of deliverance; themes of exchange between characters, but also the viewer and the fictional world, are reinforced by voyeurism; and characters are lost in a world filled with symbolic objects. However, one crucial difference between Chabrol and Hitchcock is that Chabrol is much more intrigued by the criminals and their predicaments than with beautiful couples who end up in each other's arms. If Chabrol had made *Rear Window* he would have been tempted to place the camera in criminal Lars Thorwald's apartment, instead, to show how and why he killed his wife. At the close of a Chabrol movie, characters are usually punished, isolated, or dead, yet we feel perverse sympathy for them. In some ways, *Psycho* might be said to be the most "Chabrolian" of Hitchcock's films.

Chabrol isolated the full range of emotional relations that unify *Rear Window,* and such a range is equally important to *The Unfaithful Wife.* In this movie, an upper-middle-class family man, Charles (Michel Bouquet), suspects, then discovers that his wife Hélène (Stéphane Audran) is having an affair with Victor (Maurice Ronet). Charles secretly kills Victor and dumps his body in a swamp, in a scene reminiscent of *Psycho*. Hélène, sad now, believes she has been abandoned by the absent Victor. As the police close in, both wife and husband independently have something to hide: she the affair, he the murder. But Hélène learns that her meek husband has killed her handsome lover to preserve their family life. For the first time in the movie she shows some affection for her husband as he walks away with the police detectives at the close of the film. Chabrol's films often involve killing off unwanted spouses and lovers (*The Third Lover, Innocents with Dirty Hands, Wedding in Blood, Poulet au vinaigre, L'Enfer*, etc.) in acts that leave no one above some sort of direct or indirect guilt.

Importantly, Chabrol's stories owe much to the formal patterns of Hitchcock movies, and are typically built around carefully structured sexual and personal relations. The range of options individuals and couples in *The Unfaithful Wife* face are as rigorous as those in *Rear Window*. We have a devoted but sexually lazy husband, Charles, madly in love with his wife. She, however, seeks physical satisfaction from Victor, but he turns out to be a poor family man: he is divorced and a disinterested father, which shocks Hélène. The men have other key differences: Victor lives in the city, Charles lives in the country. Each believes he has the home Hélène prefers. Victor also lets Charles know he is quite pleased physically with Hélène: "She's a great little girl." Further, Charles' partner at work, Paul, has slept with their sexy secretary, Brigitte, but he explains to Charles that she has more willingness to please than real skill in bed. Every sort of option is explored between men and women, but no combination works perfectly and everyone becomes ridiculous in some setting. Chabrol's story is organized around clear, binary oppositions. The entire plot structure is carefully doubled, with its range mostly restricted to Charles in the first half and Hélène in the second part. Such a binary structure, plotting out a story by comparing and contrasting characters, also fits with the sense of narrative unity and efficiency that Chabrol respected so much in Hitchcock.

The result of the story's parallels between couples and its strict manipulation of the range of information is a series of exchanges in which one character's action (Hélène's adultery) leads to another's crime (Charles' murder of Victor) and a final sense of empathy between the estranged couple, as Charles walks away with the police. Chabrol's films end with more ambivalence than those by Hitchcock, but his characters in *The Unfaithful Wife* nonetheless go through a sort of spiritual journey. Hélène begins with a period of lying and illicit pleasure, then sinks into depression, followed by fear and regret, before ending with a newfound love for her husband. Similarly, Charles goes from blind happiness to suspicion to panic to murder to a new pride and even happiness as he declares that he loves his wife madly. The audience develops alignment with both Charles and Hélène at various points throughout the plot, only to end with Charles walking off with the police, disrupting the happy family album pose of mother, father, and son Michel in the rose garden. This ending breaks from Hitchcock's generic resolutions, but does exploit a visual device used by Hitchcock in *Vertigo* and *Marnie*. As Wood and Walker observe, "The complex and moving last shot of the film is a fine example of the creative use to which Chabrol puts the lessons of Hitchcock . . . We are placed subjectively (in effect) in Charles' position as he is led away, watching Hélène standing with son Michel among the shrubs Charles had been pruning. As the camera moves back, the zoom-in towards Hélène slowly begins and gradually gains ascendancy over the pull backwards: the effect is that while the husband is *physically* led away he is *emotionally* reaching back towards wife and family . . . The film's tragic sense of simultaneous gain and loss is beautifully summed up."[25]

Chabrol had praised the mixing of subjectivity and objectivity in all the voyeuristic camera setups in Hitchcock, and he explores the options here as well. His camera tends to anticipate the action rather than follow it, which lends some of the sense of stylization to the narrative space. Several times in the film characters walk into what we had assumed were their own point-of-view shots, as when Hélène goes into the garden to burn a photo of Victor. But perhaps the most stunning example of Chabrol's playful style is the murder scene, when Charles is overcome with nausea and becomes disoriented in Victor's apartment, especially upon seeing his bed. He also discovers that Hélène gave Victor the huge cigarette lighter Charles had once given her. It is at this point that Charles impulsively grabs a small bust and cracks Victor's skull, bringing the irony together: a man who does not smoke is killed because his mistress gave him a cigarette lighter, and a fake head breaks his real head. After two relatively long takes, there is a burst of activity as Charles lunges toward the bust, the camera quickly pans to follow him clubbing Victor, who then falls in two jump cuts. But the rest of the scene plays out slowly as Charles cleans up after the crime.

This scene foregrounds symbolically charged objects, including the whiskey bottle and bust, but especially the huge lighter which has passed, like Hélène's body, from Charles to Victor: "She said you had forgotten it even existed." The movie's most amazing shot may be the blood pouring down the white floor, like paint on a canvas. There is also the blood running down the drain during the cleanup, recalling *Psycho,* though the only sounds here are the practical, diegetic sounds. Chabrol does not employ melodramatic music to heighten suspense or guide the audience's emotions. But where Chabrol truly parallels Hitchcock, without following his model, is in Charles' exit from the apartment. Charles looks up to see a man across the street washing windows, in what seems like the perfect spot to observe Charles struggling to drag the wrapped-up body out to his car. But Chabrol never again shows Charles look up at the potential witness, nor does he reveal whether that man sees anything, so no Hitchcock-like "suspense" is created. Chabrol has the *shots* Hitchcock would use, but does not combine them for suspense, and the "getaway" scene becomes more pathetic than exciting. Many reviews noted the Hitchcock touches in *The Unfaithful Wife,* including *France Soir,* which pointed out the Hitchcockian precision with which Chabrol revealed how to kill and then dispose of the body.[26] Shock, humor, sympathy for the murderer, and suspense all result from the murder scene. In one way or another, all the traits Chabrol the critic praised in Hitchcock reappear in *The Unfaithful Wife.*

The Butcher provides further opportunities to prove Chabrol's clever methods for reworking and lending homage to Hitchcock's influence. *The Butcher* reverses the order of many genre films by beginning with a wedding and ending with a death. The single school teacher, Hélène (Audran), lives above the school (like Annie in *The Birds*) in a town in southwest France. At a local wedding she meets Popaul, the village butcher, recently returned from the army. This thirty-something pair is attracted to one another, but both are inept at beginning a relationship. In the meantime, several young women, including the recent bride, are murdered in the area. Hélène gradually realizes Popaul is the killer, but promises not to turn him in. In a disorienting scene in the school, however, Popaul ends up stabbed with his own knife. Hélène then drives him to the hospital where he dies. The final shot reveals her standing at night, alone, near the river. Chabrol has often stated that the best way to express complex issues is with the simplest form, and *Le Boucher*'s plot becomes a perfect example of this principle. There are only two main characters, Popaul the butcher and Hélène the teacher, making a clear distinction between nature and culture. He provides the town's more basic needs while she feeds their minds. Both characters are damaged emotionally, with barriers to any sexual fulfillment.[27] Further, *The Butcher* offers only the one possible criminal throughout, which makes the movie more about the formal process of revealing information and character relations than about any suspense over a "wrongly accused man." Any possible happy, last-minute salvation of the couple is impossible.

Le Boucher is also a very unified film built around several concepts tied to sexual desire and violence. In this story, both Popaul and Hélène are tested by the situation. Popaul apparently displaces perversely his frustrated desire for Hélène onto the bodies of other young women he kills, almost as sacrificial offerings to her. Hélène gradually comes to suspect Popaul is the serial killer, a suspicion that seems confirmed when she discovers a cigarette lighter she had given him near one of the bodies. The lighter, like those in *Strangers on a Train* and *The Unfaithful Wife*, proves a trigger for action. There is a shared guilt, a sort of exchange in Chabrol's terms, and there are highly significant objects, but the ending again remains more ambivalent toward the characters than Hitchcock typically allows. There is also a young boy, here a surrogate son, the student Charles, who stays late at the school and gets along well with both the butcher and the teacher. His presence suggests a potential ideal family that can never exist. *Le Boucher*, like *The Unfaithful Wife*, has a pathetic yet somewhat endearing man who murders, impulsively, for love. Two key scenes help illustrate the combination of Chabrol's Hitchcock traits: Hélène's discovery of a body and the cigarette lighter, and the stabbing of Popaul near the end.

On a school outing to visit the cave paintings just outside of town, Hélène explains to the children, deep in the cave full of wall paintings, that Cro-Magnon man was indeed human, with feelings and intelligence, but the big difference was his instinctual need for survival. The students and teacher ponder whether a Cro-Magnon man could survive in today's world. Once outside in the bright sunshine, the class gathers high on a cliff overlooking the Dordogne River. As one blonde girl, dressed in blue and white just like Mme. Hélène, begins eating her sandwich, drops of blood splatter her outfit, bread, and face. The shot of red blood on the buttered bread is one of the tightest close-ups in the movie, providing a condensation of the color pattern for this scene which evokes the French tricolor (blue, white, red) as well as a reference to the blood dripping in beer from *Rio Bravo* (Hawks, 1959). The scene is also built around a rapid series of eyelines between Hélène, the girl, the other students, and finally their looks up at the bleeding hand on the cliff above. The murder victim, dressed in white, is the woman whose marriage brought Popaul and Hélène together earlier. At the murder site, Hélène sees Popaul's lighter on the ground, picks it up, and there is a fade to black. Staging the setting high on this precarious cliff recalls both the Mount Rushmore scene from *North by Northwest,* and also the children put at risk at the birthday party in *The Birds.* Tolling church bells follow, which is an audio motif that often introduces new scenes in *The Butcher.* Hélène is shown withdrawn, practicing yoga, when the police arrive at the school to question her. She pretends to know nothing, hiding evidence just as the Hélène of *The Unfaithful Wife* had, which now implicates her in the crime.

Once Hélène realizes that Popaul knows she has his lighter, she fears for her life. In a very expressionistic night scene, with harsh shadows and Popaul steaming up the windows from outside, pleading to talk with her, a frightened Hélène locks all her doors. He manages to get in, however, explaining that he is now lost. The desperate-looking Popaul shows her the large switchblade knife he used to kill the women, and tells her the impulse to kill falls over him like a nightmare. He cannot breathe again until he shoves his knife in them. He blurts out in a sort of confession that things can never be the same now between them. He cannot tolerate this situation. Hélène looks down at the knife during the silence that follows and Chabrol cuts the scene into six shots, including one of her closing her eyes, in almost sexual resignation, and three short shots that each fade to black: one on the knife, one of his face, and another on hers, with only silence on the soundtrack. Slowly the image fades back up on Popaul with the knife in his stomach, claiming he has killed himself. The discontinuity has distorted the action and time, blurring the responsibility, in a scene very reminiscent of *Sabotage,* where the husband is stabbed in the offscreen space. Ironically, one of the most romantic and intimate moments of the movie occurs as she drives him to the hospital. He rambles on about his love for her, but also about his lifelong fascination with blood, even as the blood is leaving his body. During the ride there are out of focus point-of-view shots of the road, either Hélène's view, blurred by tears, or Popaul's failing vision. These shots recall the point-of-view shots from drunk-driving scenes involving Alicia in *Notorious* and Roger Thornhill in *North by Northwest,* though Chabrol's instance is more extreme, melding and confusing the look of two characters at once.

By the end of *The Butcher,* Hélène kisses Popaul's sweaty, deathly blue face, but the flashing red elevator, like his beating heart, stops and signifies his death as he is taken up to the emergency room. Chabrol's "beauty" is left alone without her "beast" and we are unsure just what she finally thinks of him. The color palette is reduced to red (she wears a red dress) and white (the hospital); blood and death. Rohmer in particular had argued that French filmmakers should learn to use color cinematically, and look to *Rear Window* for inspiration (he particularly liked Miss Lonelyheart's green dress). Chabrol was equally impressed with controlled color schemes that exceeded mere referential realism, and became active narrative devices. His story structure and visual style are influenced by Hitchcock in such a variety of ways that most scenes and most devices can be read back as a reaction or tribute to Hitchcock. Yet Chabrol avoided generic endings. His Hélène seems to be waiting until morning when she will have to face the police. Will she make up some story, or confess to having hidden evidence of the murderer? Or will she follow Popaul's example and sacrifice herself, leaping into the river? Hitchcock would never leave the audience with such ambiguity. Chabrol's strength is that he exploits some essential strategies from Hitchcock, but synthesizes them into his own brand of specifically French thrillers.

Conclusions

While French criticism helped launch the detailed attention to formal aspects of Alfred Hitchcock's thrillers, those same cinematic strategies and structures influenced the subsequent film styles of French directors. Louis Malle, Eric Rohmer, and François Truffaut, among many others, reveal deep debts to Hitchcock. Nonetheless, it is through Chabrol's practice, as *The Unfaithful Wife* and *The Butcher* prove, that we can best see the concrete results of film criticism practice. Today, French psychological thrillers continue to rework and play with the lessons from Hitchcock. One of the best recent examples would certainly have to be Dominik Moll's *With a Friend Like Harry* (2000). The script is indebted to the doubling from Patricia Highsmith plots, Hitchcock's form and humor, and Chabrol's pacing and sense of the bankruptcy of the bourgeois marriage, which nonetheless seems to be the only viable option, regardless of its faults. Even American movies have gained significantly from the Hitchcock/Chabrol pairing, as is obvious in Adrian Lyne's remake, *Unfaithful* (2003), which revises *The Unfaithful Wife* considerably in some respects, but also replicates some of Chabrol's sequences shot-for-shot.

Hitchcock managed to retain a biting sense of ridicule toward humanity in his best films, and Chabrol expands on that derision and social satire. French directors, including Chabrol, continue to respect the precision, unity, and manipulation revealed by *Cahiers du cinéma* back in the 1950s. But they also situate their own stories in a context that is specifically French, with more bold attacks on middle-class values, and more art-cinema touches, synthesizing the lessons they learned from a wide range of auteurs they helped champion. Many aspects of the genre film are lifted from the Hitchcock arsenal, but the endings in particular refuse to tack on the happy termination points required of Hollywood. Had Chabrol made *Suspicion,* the milk would have been poisoned; had he made *Strangers on a Train,* Guy would not be rewarded with the wealthy, devoted Ann, and if he had made *Notorious, Spellbound,* or *North by Northwest,* the couples could not have successfully weathered all the problems and ended with the promise of successful sexual unions. Chabrol and other French directors work to retain the perverse sense of fate and even humor that Hitchcock often had to renounce or repress by the close of his narratives. It is worth noting, however, that French directors became stronger thanks to their detailed knowledge of world-cinema history, from which they have borrowed so productively. Alfred Hitchcock has simply been one of their most enduring referents.

Notes

1. Antoine de Baecque, *La Cinéphilie* (Paris: Fayard, 2003): 120.
2. James M. Vest, *Hitchcock and France: The Forging of an Auteur* (Westport, CN: Praeger, 2003): 2.
3. Vest 12.
4. de Baecque 98. *Rope,* however, was chosen and produced by Hitchcock.
5. de Baecque 105.
6. de Baecque 110.
7. Vest 85.
8. Vest 77.
9. de Baecque 110, 113.
10. Wilfrid Alexandre, *Claude Chabrol: La Traversée des apparences* (Paris: Félin, 2003): 89.
11. André Bazin, "Comment peut-on être Hitchcoco-Hawksien?" *Cahiers du cinéma* 44 (February, 1955): 18.
12. Jean-Luc Godard, *Godard on Godard,* trans. Tom Milne (New York: Viking Press, 1972): 23.
13. Godard 39–40.
14. Godard 51.
15. François Truffaut, *Hitchcock* (New York: Touchstone, 1967): 11–12, 13.
16. de Baecque 113–14.
17. Claude Chabrol, "Serious Things," *Cahiers du cinéma: The 1950s,* ed. Jim Hillier (Cambridge: Harvard University Press, 1985): 137–38.
18. Claude Chabrol, *Et pourtant je tourne* (Paris: Robert Laffont, 1976): 131.
19. Philip French, Ed., *Malle on Malle* (London: Faber and Faber, 1993): 14, 16.
20. Vest 190.
21. Vest 200.
22. Chabrol, *Et pourtant je tourne* 133.

23. Eric Rohmer and Claude Chabrol, *Hitchcock: The First 44 Films* Trans., Stanley Hoch-man (New York: Ungar, 1979): ix.

24. Chabrol, *Et pourtant je tourne* 134.

25. Robin Wood and Michael Walker, *Claude Chabrol* (New York: Praeger, 1970): 120.

26. Robert Chazal, "*La Femme infidèle,*" *Avant-scène Cinéma* 92 (May 1969): 40.

27. Joel Magny, *Claude Chabrol* (Paris: Cahiers du cinéma, 1987): 133.

Like his counterpart in *Rear Window,* the photographer in Antonioni's *Blow-Up* "sees" more than he first intends.

"You're Tellin' Me You Didn't See"
Hitchcock's *Rear Window* and Antonioni's *Blow-Up*

Frank P. Tomasulo

Alfred Hitchcock's influence on international culture and especially on other film directors has been enormous. Whether the filmmaker perceived trends ahead of his time or the contemporary zeitgeist just happened to catch up with his feverish fantasies (perhaps because of the popularity of his paranoid movies) is somewhat irrelevant. What *is* important is that the "Age of Anxiety" proclaimed by poet W. H. Auden and composer Leonard Bernstein found its cinematic "Artist of Anxiety" in Alfred Hitchcock. Critic Richard Schickel summed it up in the title of an article in the *New York Times:* "We're Living in a Hitchcock World, All Right." If Schickel meant that over the past century mankind has become as anxious, paranoid, and obsessed as the characters in (and the director of) Hitchcock's films, there is probably no denying that world wars, massacres, nuclear weapons, and the Holocaust have become part and parcel of the cruelty of life on our planet in the twentieth century and beyond (the director was born in 1899).

Whether Hitchcock's morbid vision actually changed the course of human events and made the world a scarier place is open to debate. What is less debatable is that Hitchcock's oeuvre has had a profound impact on the world of international cinema. Some of the diverse films and film directors influenced by Hitchcock include: Francis Ford Coppola (*The Conversation*), Alain Resnais (*Muriel, Last Year at Marienbad*[1]), Roman Polanski (*Repulsion*), Stanley Donen (*Arabesque, Charade*), François Truffaut (*The Bride Wore Black, Fahrenheit 451, Mississippi Mermaid, Finally Sunday!*), Orson Welles (*The Stranger*), Henri Clouzot (*Diabolique*), Akira Kurosawa (*High and Low*), Mel Brooks (*High Anxiety*), Colin Higgins (*Foul Play*), Paul Verhoeven (*Basic Instinct*), Martin Scorsese (*Cape Fear*), Goran Marković (*Déjà Vu*),

Adrian Lyne (*Unfaithful*), Slobodan Šijan (*Strangler vs. Strangler*), Richard Marquand (*Jagged Edge*), Jerzy Skolimowski (*The Lightship*), Anthony Perkins (*Psycho III*), Claude Miller (*Alias Betty*), and, of course, the James Bond series, Claude Chabrol (*Leda, Les Cousins, The Third Lover, Le Boucher, La Femme infidèle, La Cérémonie, L'Enfer*), and Brian De Palma (*Sisters, Obsession, Dressed to Kill, Body Double, Blow Out*). The list could go on and on. The plots, characters, and cinematic style of Hitchcock's films have been borrowed, plagiarized, spoofed, incorporated into, and used as intertext in many of the world's best (and some of its worst) movies.

* * *

Consider the following scenario, for instance: An isolated and alienated male protagonist, a professional photographer, comes to believe that he has witnessed or uncovered a murder in a major metropolis. Despite conflicting evidence, he investigates the alleged crime using the tools of his trade, only to discover that the corpus delicti has been removed from the scene. The hero's relationship with fashion models is an important part of the plot, as is his identity crisis. Indeed, his personal problems exhibit themselves primarily in his contemptuous and sexist treatment of women. In the end, the murder is revealed to have taken place, but many other issues remain unresolved.

In style, the color film is strikingly visual and frequently uses the gaze-object-gaze editing regime and a fairly rigid (albeit complex) point-of-view camera perspective to establish identification with the protagonist, whose chief preoccupation is looking intently at the world for clues to its significance. We are stuck, for the most part, in the consciousness of the main character for most of the film's 112-minute running time. A meticulous, yet minimalist, soundtrack emphasizes natural and urban sounds to comment on the action and create suspense. The music track, which consists of both instrumental and vocal renditions, comments subtly on the action, theme, and characters.

In theme, the movie provides a subtle and self-reflexive metacommentary on the art and process of cinema itself by foregrounding the voyeuristic viewing of the photographer-protagonist (a surrogate filmmaker), his attempts to impose a narrative on the events he witnesses through his camera lens (the usual province of a film director), and the activity of the spectator in the theater watching the film. The anomie, alienation, and ambiguity of modern life are important subjects. Despite these abstruse and serious themes, there are light, humorous moments in the film, which provide enjoyment and entertainment value to a mass audience. The movie goes on to become the most commercially successful release of the auteur filmmaker, who was raised in a restrictive Roman Catholic environment.

In a book devoted to the films of Alfred Hitchcock, the plot, characters, themes, and director described above would be assumed to be those of *Rear Window* (1954). Yet these same elements are also present in *Blow-Up* (1966), directed by Michelangelo Antonioni.

Both Alfred Hitchcock's *Rear Window* and Michelangelo Antonioni's *Blow-Up* are about isolated male photographers who come to believe that they witnessed a murder. While the former movie can be classified as a relatively conventional and easy-to-follow Hollywood thriller and the latter as a "difficult" modernist European art film, the two films have more in common than their protagonists' occupation and that there may have been homicides. Although both films were based on separate short stories by internationally known authors—Cornell Woolrich's "Rear Window" and Julio Cortázar's "Las babas del diablo" (The Devil's Drool), respectively—they share remarkable characterological, narratological, cinematic, and thematic similarities.[2]

Character

In both *Rear Window* and *Blow-Up,* the protagonists—L. B. Jefferies (James Stewart) and Thomas (David Hemmings)[3]—are professional photographers who come to question their own vision (mediated and unmediated) during epistemological quests for certainty in an ambiguous world of sense perceptions. They both seem to cross the line between fantasy and reality, imagining murders where evidence beyond a "shadow of a doubt" is lacking. Furthermore, both men suffer "identity crises," especially with regard to their masculinity and their relationships with women. In *Rear Window,* Jeff's broken leg (or "swollen foot," the English translation of the name "Oedipus") confines him to a wheelchair, but it also causes him to question his long-time "engagement" to fashion model Lisa Carol Fremont (Grace Kelly).[4] Thomas, the high-fashion photographer in *Blow-Up,* is also involved with female models, and treats them with the same sexist disdain and negativity displayed in Jefferies' framed photographic "negative" of a female model for the cover of a *Life*-like magazine. At a haute-couture modeling session at his studio, Thomas shouts rudely at the anorexic women, roughly positioning their limbs into static poses, and struts smugly around the set like a martinet.[5] Thomas whistles loudly to get the attention of his models and refers to them contemptuously as his "birds." He keeps Veruschka, one of the world's leading fashion models, waiting for almost an hour. Two teenyboppers, who come to have

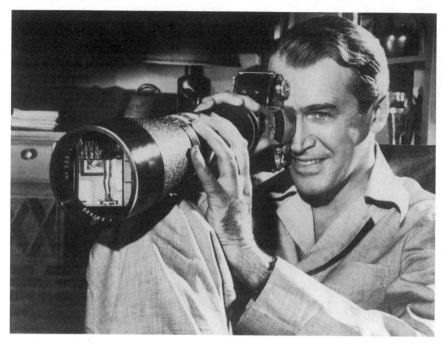

The sidelined cameraman in Hitchcock's *Rear Window* becomes a law-enforcing Peeping Tom.

their pictures taken, end up having sex with him, and are dismissed without any photos. In short, he bullies and disrespects women and cannot seem to relate to Jane (Vanessa Redgrave) unless he is posing her. Antonioni himself has said that "in *Blow-Up,* eroticism occupies a very important place, although the focus is often placed on a cold, calculated sensuality. Exhibitionism and voyeuristic trends are particularly underlined" ("It Was Born" 90). Thus, in both movies, modern masculinity is in crisis.

That male crisis is figured through the use of phallic icons and objects in both films. In *Rear Window,* for instance, Jefferies is unable to pop the cork on a bottle of wine, and his repeated attempts to scratch under his leg cast with a back scratcher can be likened to masturbation. Jeff's long 400mm telephoto lens is another instance of a phallic substitute, especially when it is seen resting in his lap. In *Blow-Up,* Thomas is attracted to mechanical phallic symbols, such as a propeller ("I *must* have it!") and a guitar neck (an icon of castration). In London's Maryon Park, Thomas passes a mannish-looking woman in male work clothes who picks up refuse with a pointed spear; here, the female has the phallus again—and a job other than modeling.

Jefferies also has "issues" with women. Stella the nurse (Thelma Ritter) explicitly states that Jeff must have "a hormone deficiency" because "those bathing beauties you've been watching haven't raised your temperature in a month." Even when his girlfriend, Lisa, plans to stay overnight, the photographer is forced to say "I won't be able to give you any . . . pajamas." When Lisa becomes the sexual aggressor and kisses Jeff repeatedly, he virtually ignores her and talks incessantly about the Thorwald case. There are so many verbal and nonverbal clues in *Rear Window* about Jeff's "abnormal" aversion to marriage (Stella's phrase) or his "problem" (Lisa's phrase) that Robert Samuels contends that "Jefferies looks at women but he doesn't get turned on by them" (118). Whether or not *Rear Window* is a repressed homosexual text, L. B. Jefferies is no 1950s John Wayne icon of masculinity.

Unlike Jefferies, on the surface, Thomas appears to possess the macho swagger of the "real man." Beneath his gruff exterior, however, there is evidence that Antonioni's photographer only plays at sex but cannot sustain a meaningful relationship with a woman. Like Jefferies in *Rear Window,* Antonioni's photographer often seems preoccupied with other things and virtually ignores the women who throw themselves at him throughout *Blow-Up*— Veruschka, Jane, the teenyboppers, the antique-store owner, and his neighbor, Patricia (Sarah Miles). This is seen most clearly in the ersatz sex scene between Thomas and the model Veruschka. After mounting the model and stimulating her verbally and physically to perform for his camera lens, he finally screams out *his* pleasure ("Yes! Yes!"), then nonchalantly dismounts the woman and walks away. The cut is to a view of Veruschka sprawled out on the floor, as the photographer lies collapsed on the sofa in the background. A phallic wooden beam appears to emerge from the woman's crotch, suggesting the impersonal, "wooden," and unconsummated nature of their make-believe "intercourse," as well as that bugaboo of the male psyche, the phallic woman. Here, Antonioni's subtle mise-en-scène reveals Thomas's career-driven, locked-up ego, as well as his male anxiety in the face of modern female sexuality.

In addition to treating women badly, the photographer makes disparaging remarks about two gay men he spots walking their dogs ("Already there are queers and poodles in the area"). If, as Wilhelm Reich suggests, repressed homosexuality is the etiology of the phallic narcissist—proving to himself that he is not gay by acting the part of a macho man—then Thomas may fit that description. In a way, both he and Jefferies seem to prefer their women at a distance and through a camera lens. Ultimately, both characters are ciphers, men whose personas contain ambivalent and contradictory traits and motivations.

Thomas, of course, is even more of a "man without qualities" than Jeff.

Silent through much of *Blow-Up,* the photographer expresses his narcissistic worldview mainly through sneers, dismissive gestures, and occasional curt remarks to the human beings who pass through his visual field. Jefferies, at least, quips and talks to a variety of friends, acquaintances, and associates. Several contrasting examples will illustrate this difference, all involving telephone conversations.

Thomas speaks several times on his car phone (a relatively new technology in 1967). He always identifies himself as "Blue 4-3-9," his code name and number, rather than by his given name, a device that both conceals his identity from the audience and makes him appear to be part of a dehumanized technological society that devalues real communication. Although these car-phone calls are usually professional messages, Thomas's personal telephone "conversation" with the woman he calls his wife betrays the same "failure to communicate" evident in all his telephone (and face-to-face) interactions. Furthermore, Jane, whom he is about to seduce, is physically present in his loft, so he addresses her as well.

The scene begins with Thomas and Jane seated in his loft. The telephone rings. At first, Thomas coolly ignores the persistent sound; then, suddenly, after a half-dozen double rings, he suddenly becomes animated and scrambles all over the floor looking for its source. After he locates the telephone and picks up the receiver, he hands it to Jane without a word. The following incoherent exchange ensues:

> *Jane:*   Is it for me?
> *Thomas:* It's my wife.
> *Jane:*   Why should I speak to her?
> *Thomas* (into phone): Sorry, love, the bird I'm with won't talk to you.
> (He hangs up.)
> (to Jane) She isn't my wife really. We just have some kids . . . No, no kids . . . Sometimes, though, it feels as if we had kids. She isn't beautiful; she's . . . easy to live with. [pause] No she isn't. That's why I don't live with her.

Jefferies' phone conversations are more direct and focused, but, like Thomas's, they do not bring any clarity to the issues at hand. Jeff's dialogues with his friend, police detective Tom Doyle (Wendell Corey), for example, mainly consist of him strenuously trying to persuade the expert criminologist that a murder has taken place, while Doyle calmly presents the facts he has uncovered (train tickets, postcards, etc.) and the accumulated wisdom of years of criminal investigations. Jeff even calls Thorwald at one point to create a ruse that will get the murderer out of his flat, but the plan backfires when Thorwald returns unexpectedly and catches Lisa snooping in his apartment.

Beyond the depiction of the male protagonists, both films share a similar vision of women, although not necessarily the misogynistic tendencies both directors have been accused of exhibiting. The evidence on-screen suggests a more complex attitude toward women. To the extent that Hitchcock's views about women can be equated with Jefferies' troubling and vicious dialogue and male fantasies (like so many other male leads in Hitchcock's oeuvre) and Antonioni's intentions are derived from the obnoxious and macho behavior of his "hero," then maybe there is reason to criticize both directors' representations. But, as Tania Modleski so persuasively argues in *The Women Who Knew Too Much*, Hitchcock's depictions of women also reveal their oppression under patriarchy, as well as their wisdom and tolerance; furthermore, his portrayals of men are hardly paeans to the male psyche but, rather, sharp and incisive critiques of male scopophilia, fetishism, and sexual insecurity. Modleski argues that in *Rear Window*, Lisa is the stronger and more dominant figure: "It is the man who is motionless and the woman active and animate ... She towers over Jeff in nearly every shot" (76–77). Stella is also a very strong character; she lectures Jeff and even participates in the potentially dangerous investigation of Thorwald.

Similarly, Antonioni's pre–*Blow-Up* films were often hailed as proto–women's liberation movies; indeed, one female film critic referred to the director as "the poet of matriarchy" (Fernandez 158–60). Whereas those earlier films often followed feminine protagonists, in *Blow-Up*, Antonioni chose to explore the male psyche. In short, both Jefferies and Thomas may not be the positive role models they were perceived to be when *Rear Window* and *Blow-Up* were initially released; in fact, in retrospect, they may both have been offered as negative images of men at a time when assertive and domineering males tended to be valorized.

In *Rear Window*, Jefferies frequently ogles a neighbor across the courtyard whom he has named "Miss Torso" based primarily on her shapely physical attributes and her scanty attire. Hitchcock treats the photographer's peeping ambiguously. On the one hand, there are sexy views of Miss Torso and, for that matter, of Lisa. On the other hand, this indulgent voyeurism on the part of the diegetic protagonist, as well as the heterosexual male viewer, is punished repeatedly.[6] Jeff wins the verbal scorn of Stella (who tells him that "we've become a race of Peeping Toms" and that "in the old days, they used to put your eyes out with a red hot poker"[7]) and Lisa for his prurient peccadilloes, and ends up with *two* broken legs for his sins.

This objectification of the female body sees its match in *Blow-Up* when

Thomas leads the teenyboppers up the stairs to his studio and Antonioni's camera (from Thomas's point of view) leers up their skirts at their leotarded legs. Later, as the photographer tussles playfully with the would-be models, pubic hair can be seen for a fleeting second—a prohibited sight in mid-sixties cinema. But although Antonioni clearly shows the female body here as the object of the male gaze, he is also critiquing that gaze in the process. As in *Rear Window*, the director's camera both participates in the male gaze (of the diegetic character and of the straight male spectator) and simultaneously provides a "cold shower" by showing that the unsatisfied protagonist is a sexist reprobate and vicarious voyeur.

Apart from the visual portrayal of the male gaze of these characters, their words and actions evince the retrograde stance of the male chauvinist. As Fawell observes, Jefferies "spouts a great deal of sexist diatribe that we might . . . identify with Hitchcock" (10). For example, when Stella the nurse opines that "one day maybe [Miss Lonelyheart] will find her happiness," Jeff cynically responds, "Yeah, and some man will lose his." Like many of the director's other heroes, Jeff is "cruel to women, stereotype[s] and pigeonhole[s] the woman who loves him, underestimate[s] and judge[s] them unfairly" (Fawell 11). His negative and sexist comments are mainly directed at Lisa ("She's *too* perfect . . . *too* talented, *too* sophisticated") but many apply to the female gender in general. Likewise, in *Blow-Up*, Thomas's gaze is often affixed on Veruschka, the other beautiful models in his studio, the teenyboppers, his neighbor, the antique-store owner, and Jane. These "admiring" looks are in sharp conflict with his physical and psychological treatment of and cutting comments about women ("I'm fed up with those bloody bitches").

Another interesting parallel between the two protagonists is that initially both men believe they are witnessing romance and love instead of murder. Thomas even assumes that his voyeuristic "snaps" (taken from behind fences, hedges, and trees) of Jane and her older male companion hugging and frolicking in the park represent something "very—peaceful, very still," when what he is actually documenting is a murder scene. Similarly, Jefferies initially views the honeymoon couple across the way as engaging in a loving and tender scene of marital bliss; later, he thinks that same couple is argumentative and quarrelsome and the Thorwald marriage is murderous.

In addition to all the personality traits noted above, both films proffer unrelenting depictions of their respective protagonists' points of view. There are few scenes (or even moments) in either film that do not take place in the presence or visual field of the male hero. This physically claustrophobic restriction is justified in the case of *Rear Window* by Jeff's literal confinement to a wheelchair; in *Blow-Up*, Thomas is highly mobile—he drives and romps around London without physical restraint—yet he is *psychologically* confined by his congenital narcissism. In both cases, the viewer spends almost two hours "in the moccasins" of the main character, thus providing a strong basis for emotional identification and empathy—even with basically flawed and weak individuals.

Needless to say, most films depict more than the trials and tribulations of one or two main characters; as social documents, movies tend to address cultural issues by personifying those larger themes in the stories of a few individuals. Thus, L. B. Jefferies and Thomas stand in for and represent a much larger subset of men—those of the postwar generation who have yet to adjust adequately to the changing gender dynamics of their eras. As such, the protagonists of both *Rear Window* and *Blow-Up*, although from different epochs, personify an age-old conundrum—the eternal crisis of masculinity—yet they also signify variations on that universal dilemma in the specificity of the 1950s and the 1960s.

Narrative

In both *Rear Window* and *Blow-Up*, the crisis of masculinity is intimately bound up with a mysterious murder plot and its resolution. Both men believe that they have witnessed or uncovered a murder. Both rely on their cameras to try to solve the hermeneutic but find that they cannot trust the mechanical apparatus of vision—the camera—to resolve their doubts, or their personal identity crises. (In fact, in *Rear Window*, the hero's crisis of masculinity, his impotence and symbolic castration, is signified by both his broken leg *and* his smashed camera.) Ultimately, Hitchcock seems to resolve the murder narrative—Jefferies exposes the murderer figuratively and photographically (with the help of his girlfriend and his flashbulbs), and the police arrest the culprit. Toward the end of *Blow-Up*, Antonioni shows us a dead body, but the real closure takes place on a more metaphysical plane—Thomas capitulates to the postmodern world of the simulacrum, represented by his increasingly abstract blow-ups and imaginary tennis ball in the finale. Both films have "open" endings: *Rear Window* concludes with *both* of Jeff's legs in plaster casts and Lisa, now in male attire, reading fashion magazines; *Blow-Up* ends with Thomas putting down his camera and putting more trust in his imagination. That said, with the exception of its ambiguous conclusion, *Blow-Up* is clearly Antonioni's most carefully and traditionally structured film (with the possible exception of *Il Mistero di Oberwald*, 1980).[8] Indeed, *Blow-Up* is somewhat anomalous in Antonioni's work because it follows an almost classical narrative trajectory of exposition (in which the protagonist's occupation and character are introduced), point of attack (what happened in that park?), discovery (the grainy blow-ups seem to reveal a gun and a dead body), reversal (the blow-ups are stolen), and falling action (the corpse is gone and the photographer plays with the mimes). The one difference from the Aristotelian, Scribean, and Syd Fieldsian dramatic norms is that there is no catharsis or resolution step at the end. This uncustomary faithfulness to narrative norms may be the result of the genre—the mystery film or thriller—in which Antonioni chose to work. But despite what appears to be a relatively conventional plotline (until the end), the director himself seemed to think that he was breaking all the rules: "I don't believe that the old laws of drama have validity any more. Today, stories are what they are, with neither a beginning nor an end necessarily, without key scenes, without a dramatic arc, without catharsis. They can be made up of tatters, of fragments, as unbalanced as life itself" (Billard 5).

Rear Window follows the traditional pattern even more closely, although somewhat less than the average Hitchcock thriller. Indeed, John Fawell concludes that "*Rear Window* [is not] too immaculate, so highly unified and tightly constructed as to be lifeless . . . The viewer's mind has more free play [because] *Rear Window* operates so fluidly on so many different levels—as psychological study, treatise on modern alienation, rumination on the nature of film going, and autobiographical statement" (7). (In this latter regard, it is worth noting that Antonioni has explicitly stated that *Blow-Up* "is [his] most autobiographical film" [qtd. in Brunette 111]).

One other subtle narrative connection between Hitchcock and *Blow-Up* involves the street address of Thomas's studio in London. At one point, the photographer pulls up to the building in his Rolls-Royce and the camera holds on the entrance door for some time, much longer than necessary to establish that the photographer has reached his destination. As the static shot remains on the screen, the viewer tries to make sense of the numeral that fills the frame: 39. William Arrowsmith once suggested that this number had both spiritual connotations and historical significance. The number three has important meaning in the Roman Catholic religion (the Holy Trinity—the Father, Son, and Holy Spirit; the Holy Family—Jesus, Mary, and Joseph; the three domains of the afterlife depicted in Dante's *Commedia*—Heaven, Hell, and Purgatory; etc.). Three squared (nine) would thus have even more import in that cosmology. Thirty-nine would combine two already symbolic numbers, three and nine, and add up to another mystical integer, twelve (as in the twelve apostles of Christ). Arrowsmith's primary interpretation of the number

39, though, was a bit idiosyncratic. He claimed that Antonioni was trying to communicate that he was "a 39er," that is, an individual whose worldview was dramatically shaped by the experiences of living in Europe in the fateful year 1939 and, subsequently, during World War II (Arrowsmith 1982). In the context of this essay, though, another equally idiosyncratic reading is possible: the 39 may refer to Hitchcock's early British film *The 39 Steps* (1935). After all, Hitchcock's film, like Antonioni's, is a thriller about a murder in London witnessed by an innocent protagonist who has nothing to do with the intrigue but who is drawn into the affair by a mysterious woman and feels compelled to solve the riddle.

Theme

In a sense, both films share the metatheme of self-reflexivity; indeed, they can both be called meditations on the movies, commentaries on the camera. In *Rear Window*, Jefferies stares at the many (thirty-one) rear-window views of his neighbors and sees a variety of screens across the courtyard. He projects film plots (love stories, comedies, murder mysteries) and characters (the Newlyweds, Miss Torso, Miss Lonelyheart) onto the mindscreen of his imagination. As Hitchcock himself once observed, "What he sees is a mental process *blown up* in his mind" ("*Rear* Window" 18, emphasis added). All are projections of Jeff's own possible future: an unsatisfying marriage,[9] loneliness, despair, and maybe even a homicide. Similarly, in *Blow-Up*, Thomas's still camera is a metaphor for the motion picture apparatus. He "edits" his *blown-up* photographs in his mind to tell a story—one in which he is the hero who has prevented a murder. Indeed, the cuts from one enlarged image to another follow the montage regime of classical Hollywood (and classical Hitchcockian) cinema in that we follow Jane's gaze to the bushes and then to the victim and in both cases see what she sees: a hidden revolver in the foliage and a dead victim under the tree.

Just as Jefferies sees a projection of a possibly unsatisfying marriage to Lisa as he observes the Thorwald household through his camera, Thomas sees a reflection of his own views on love and marriage in his blow-ups; he believes they are the invention of duplicitous females, such as his (maybe) ex-wife, who lead men on only to destroy them. (He sees Jane literally leading her victim to his death by pulling him up a hill and toward the tree.)

Both films, then, are self-reflexive in two important ways: as metacommentary on the voyeuristic/scopophilic act of watching films as a spectator and as metadiscourse on the process of filmmaking from the point of view of the cinematographer-director-editor. Like film viewers, who must always perform hermeneutic work to interpret the events before them, both protagonists are forced to actively engage with the text of the events they are witnessing. Jeff is clearly a surrogate for a film viewer, as has been pointed out in much of the scholarly literature on *Rear Window,* with the windows across the way being the movie screens he watches (Belton, Douchet, Fawell, Modleski, Palmer, Sharff, Wood, et al.). The much-discussed opening shot shows the bamboo curtains being raised, like the curtains in a theater, as the credits appear; those same shades are lowered at the conclusion of the film as the end credits roll. No human agency is in evidence as these shades go up and down.

In *Rear Window,* Jefferies "sits behind his camera, weaving fantasies with the people on the other end of the lens" (Fawell 135). He even gives them stage directions ("Go ahead, Thorwald, answer it" [the phone]). As such, Jeff functions like a film director, who tells a story primarily through visual images. More than that, because of his injury-imposed isolation, Jefferies *lives* through his camera (like Alfred Hitchcock) and does not have much contact with the real world.

In *Blow-Up,* Thomas is also a filmmaker figure, if not an explicit avatar for Antonioni. This is, of course, most evident in the scenes in which the photographer takes pictures in his studio or on location (functioning like a cinematographer); when he poses and coaches his models, Jane, and the teenyboppers (acting as film director, acting coach, and casting agent); and when he arranges his blown-up images to tell a story (performing the work of an editor/auteur). The scene in which Thomas has an encounter with Jane (Vanessa Redgrave), the mystery woman from Maryon Park, in his loft epitomizes this idea that he is acting as a film director. At the beginning of the scene, the photographer treats Jane in the only way he knows how to relate to a female—as a model. He wants to see "how she sits," poses her against a mauve backdrop, and directs her to "keep still" and to move "slowly, slowly, against the beat" of the mood-enhancing music playing on his stereo. In this sense, Thomas orchestrates the scene like a cinema director; indeed, he orchestrates the scene like Michelangelo Antonioni, who in many respects treats his performers like models (if not mannequins). In addition, Thomas's schizoid photographic work in two ostensibly antithetical genres—documentary (the doss-house and park pictures) and illusionism (the high-fashion work)—replicates the early history of the cinema, when Lumière and Méliès vied for the attention of audiences around the world.[10]

Both *Rear Window* and *Blow-Up* derive from source stories that are dark meditations on contemporary city life, as seen through the eyes and lenses of

bored still photographers. Woolrich and Cortázar both created claustrophobic settings and situations and obsessive protagonists who insist on solving
the riddles they photographed. Thus, both stories evince, albeit in very different ways, a sort of "urban spectatorship" (Brand 124), especially when their
city views are given plastic form on film. Although Hitchcock's immobilized
hero does his obsessive urban spectating from a wheelchair and Antonioni's
flaneur does his Benjaminian exploring on foot or from behind the wheel of a
Rolls-Royce, they share an ennui about "civilized," "cosmopolitan" life in the
modern metropolis and find excitement only in the ambiguous possibilities of
a murder mystery.

Cinematic Style

One of the most consistent connections between *Rear Window* and *Blow-Up*
is their cinematic style, especially the film's all-but-ceaseless use of a single
character's perspective on the action. Not only do Hitchcock and Antonioni
show Jefferies and Thomas throughout most of their respective movies, but
the action that is depicted is literally seen through their eyes for most of the
screen time. In particular, the point-of-view shot and the gaze-object-gaze
editing regime—pioneered and developed by Alfred Hitchcock—is on display as the visual armature of characterological identification throughout both
films. As a prototypical modernist film, *Blow-Up* ambiguates that point of view
in several instances. However, Hitchcock also deviates from the classical paradigm in some key moments, thus creating a tense and uncertain situation for
the spectator that is as problematical as that found in *Blow-Up*.

One of the first instances of an ambiguated POV occurs at the beginning of
Blow-Up. Thomas moves toward the door of his studio, ostensibly to photograph supermodel Veruschka. Framed in a tight close-up, Thomas looks into
the studio through the narrow doorway. By all the codes and conventions of
traditional (e.g., Hitchcockian) editing structures, this "gaze" shot would be
followed by an "object" shot showing the attention of the photographer's
look—presumably the inside of the studio. And at first glance, that is what
we appear to get: a view of a bored Veruschka seated on the floor near a large
sheet of Plexiglas. However, after a few seconds, Thomas enters the shot from
the background, retrospectively changing the ostensible subjectivity of the
view to a more objective one. What we thought was the protagonist's perspective now turns out to be a more impersonal view. The conventional char-
acter-based gaze-object-gaze axis is thus elided in favor of a frame-breaking
autonomous camera regime. Beyond that, Antonioni plays even further with

the viewer's sense perceptions. What appears to be Veruschka's body is actually her *reflection* in the Plexiglas, a point that is made obvious when Thomas snaps his fingers on the sheet, causing it (and her image on it) to vibrate.

Although the commercial "master of suspense" generally follows most of the accepted POV protocols in order to guide the attention of his viewers, Hitchcock himself is not above confusing his audience at times. The opening images of *Rear Window,* for instance, beg the question of who is watching this scene. The camera pans right to left around the Greenwich Village courtyard in the daylight, seemingly from the perspective of the rear-window view of our hero.[11] When the pan finally concludes, the camera settles on the sleeping figure of L. B. Jefferies, whose back is to the courtyard and whose name is inscribed on his leg cast. So, not only could he not be the point of origination of the panning shot because he is asleep, but by showing him facing away from the window, he cannot be the source of the gaze. As in *Blow-Up,* the assumed POV is retrospectively changed from an ostensibly subjective view to a more detached regard. This happens again later in *Rear Window* when, once again, the camera pans around the courtyard (this time at night) only to reveal that Jeff is asleep, facing away from his window. A detached and omniscient authorial camera seems to be the source of these images, a different perspective from what we expect in a Hitchcock opus.

Antonioni's set design also manifests the Hitchcock influence. Generally speaking, Hitchcock's films use minimalist, utilitarian décor, probably to focus attention on the interactions of characters. A white shower stall (*Psycho*), a bare-bones telephone booth (*The Birds*), a nondescript flat that becomes the site of murder (*The 39 Steps*), an unadorned train compartment (*The Lady Vanishes*), a lifeboat (*Lifeboat*), a middle-class dinner table (*Shadow of a Doubt*), an austere British courtroom (*The Paradine Case*), a tidy three-room New York apartment (*Rope*), Scottie Ferguson's functional home and hearth (*Vertigo*), and many more examples illustrate Hitchcock's penchant for stark environments that serve as mere backdrops for desperate human dramas. For Hitchcock, sets round out the picture of his characters and situations but do not generally contribute directly to the thematic histrionics of his films. His characters are often trapped and isolated by their environments but their surroundings are rarely metaphors for or commentaries on the characters' predicaments. Indeed, the director often selected especially prosaic settings so that when evil broke out in them the contrast would be especially telling.

In *Rear Window,* the courtyard is considerably more expressionistic than the sets in other Hitchcock works.[12] The sky is an unnatural and unrealistic orange, the alleyway and tavern across the street look like a studio set, and the unlikely coincidences that occur behind the many apartment windows in the courtyard all suggest that the setting is unrealistic. Taken in toto, the many boxlike windows function as visual correlatives by which to convey the theme of urban isolation and alienation. Add to this the diegetic soundtrack, which consists of "incidental" sounds that all bear obvious reference to the plot and characters, and we can see the artistry of Hitchcock at work.

In *Blow-Up*, Antonioni takes similar care with his set design and soundtrack, although for this filmmaker, environment is no mere backdrop to the main action and characters; in many ways, environment (rather than character) is *destiny*. The director even went to the extreme length of painting the grass in Maryon Park green to create just the right artistic atmosphere and mood. Throughout the film, though, the desaturated color scheme comments on the restricted personality of its protagonist. As a case in point, the mannequins in the shop window wear relatively colorless clothes and their stiff appearance reflects Thomas's dead-in-life lifestyle. In addition, even though Thomas is "out and about" London through most of the film, he is often alone in his car, alone in his studio, alone in a crowd. Antonioni's mise-en-scène and set design portray his anomie by isolating him in the frame.

The odd neon sign seen in the park when Thomas investigates the corpse is another example of how Antonioni uses the environment to create ambiguity. The sign looms over Thomas, but its precise meaning and signification remain vague. (Is it FOA or TOA? Is it an advertisement? A corporate logo? A work of modern art?) The sign is reminiscent of the "Eyes of Dr. T. J. Eckleburg" billboard in F. Scott Fitzgerald's *The Great Gatsby* that presides over a symbolic ash heap like the gaze of a *deus absconditus*, a dumb commercial god without pity or remorse surveying its "ash-gray" subjects. Such metaphysical speculations are apt in that both Hitchcock and Antonioni can be seen as post-deist auteurs who were raised in the Roman Catholic liturgy but created fictive universes in which God is dead.

Barrier images are used throughout both films to portray the alienation of characters from each other. The bank of separated windows in *Rear Window* is the most obvious visual device used to convey the loneliness of the residents. But even within those individual apartments, Hitchcock separates cohabitants. Thorwald and his wife, for instance, are frequently shown in the same film frame but through separate windowpanes.[13] Similarly, after Miss Lonelyheart evicts her "gentleman caller" for "getting fresh," he is seen in the hallway sadly rubbing his slapped cheek while Miss Lonelyheart weeps poignantly on the other side of the door frame.

Antonioni is, of course, a master of using barrier images and constricted frames to illustrate his grand theme of modern alienation. Ted Perry has traced such "barrier-isolation" motifs in *Eclipse* (1962), but they are also found in *Blow-Up* ("A Contextual Study" 256–62). Whether or not such compositions are directly attributable to the influence of Hitchcock remains an open question. However, the similarities in visual architecture and theme point to a convergence between him and Antonioni that has not been mentioned in the scholarly literature. Examples of Antonioni's use of barrier images in *Blow-Up* include door frames that frequently delimit the space of his characters (e.g., the doorway through which Thomas observes Patricia and Bill having sex), the clear and smoked Plexiglas sheets in the photographer's studios, the windshield of the Rolls-Royce, the fence and trees used to conceal Thomas's surreptitious photography in the park, the fence around the tennis court at the film's coda, and the wardrobe rack that comes between the protagonist and the teenyboppers.

The soundtrack of *Rear Window* is almost entirely diegetic—composed of "incidental sounds," as Fawell notes (25). There is some music, but it emanates mainly from the composer's piano across the courtyard or from radio broadcasts and phonograph recordings ("That's Amore," "To See You Is to Love You," "Lover," "Waiting for My True Love to Appear"). Although a nondiegetic jazz theme opens the film as the credits roll (as in *Blow-Up*) and while the camera pans around the complex, for the most part *Rear Window* depends on "natural" tones. This is not to say that these sounds are not highly selective and carefully chosen for their thematic relevance; quite the contrary. Hitchcock's artistic control over his sealed-off universe is never more evident than in the soundtrack of *Rear Window*. For example, the plaintive wail of a distant foghorn expresses the loneliness and sadness of most of the denizens of this Greenwich Village courtyard. (Fawell reads this soundtrack articulation as "the sad exhale of a distant god watching the pathetic struggles of humans" [29]). The patter of gently falling raindrops coursing down a gutter also conveys the pathos of Lars Thorwald's situation as he comes and goes, removing his wife's body parts from the scene of the crime. Thus, even "realistic" sounds that are justified by onscreen events convey meaning and mood. Elizabeth Weis notes Hitchcock's fondness for "asynchronous" and "contrapuntal" sounds that add "variety, denseness, tension, and . . . irony" to his visual images (109, 19).

Natural sounds also convey theme and meaning in *Blow-Up*. When Thomas first sees the corpse in the park, the rustle of wind through the trees adds to the ominous mood of the scene. The offscreen cracking of a twig causes Thomas to turn his head in the direction of the snap, but it is unclear whether another human being (a Peeping Tom spying on Thomas, for instance) or a local squirrel made the noise.

Like Hitchcock, Antonioni also uses nondiegetic sound sparingly. The most obvious instance of its use is in the final moments, when Thomas "hears" the "ping" of an imaginary tennis ball (or is it the click of a camera's shutter?). Although in many ways the moral of the entire film is summed up in that sound, its meaning is imprecise and ambivalent.

Antonioni also uses contrapuntal sound to comment on a situation and to expound on his theme. For example, as Thomas approaches the Riki-Tiki Club in search of Jane, whom he spotted on the street, we hear the anticipatory sound of a driving rock beat. However, when he enters the discotheque, the young patrons are inappropriately silent. In fact, they are rigidly immobile, except for one interracial couple who dance listlessly to the pounding beat. Although the youngsters' clothes are visually "loud," we cannot hear their voices. The music and lyrics of the Yardbirds seem to speak for the youngsters and seem to convey an apposite thematic message from the director—"You're tellin' me you didn't see"—which exactly fits Thomas's predicament vis-à-vis what he saw (or "didn't see" in the park). But even the song is not communicated properly. A technological failure causes the rock group's performance to go sour as an electric guitar malfunctions, producing annoying static. This failure of technology to create or improve the rapport between people mirrors the protagonist's own overreliance on his ineffective camera apparatus.

It is only when the rock performer smashes his obstreperous instrument to bits and hurls the guitar neck into the statuelike crowd that the youngsters react. This direct frontal assault on their zombielike state provokes them to shout and scream loudly and to chase after the prop, which ends up in Thomas's besieged hands. However, the noisy pandemonium and all the impassioned movements of the crowd do not communicate anything more than the mimes' histrionic excess. They are still dead-in-life characters, like Thomas, who are stirred by ersatz phallic symbols (the propeller, the guitar neck) to move or shout inarticulately, but they do not share authentic intimacies or joy with their fellow human beings. Thus, the overwrought soundtrack in this scene suggests that despite all the ostensible Sturm und Drang, human beings still experience "failure t' communicate."

Both directors also utilize silence in artistic ways, in contrast to the talkathon dialogue in most mainstream movies. Indeed, both filmmakers have commented in interviews on this aspect of their work. Hitchcock once said that "silence is often very effective and its effect is heightened by the proper handling of music before and after" (Gottlieb 242). Similarly, Antonioni once said, "My aim is to achieve the suppression of outward physical action . . . and, where possible, eliminate dialogue" (qtd. in Gessner 396). Hitchcock's influence on Antonioni's soundtracks can be noticed throughout his oeuvre, but it is especially evident in *Blow-Up*.

It has been estimated that 35 percent of *Rear Window* contains no dialogue (Sharff 2). The opening is a classic example of Hitchcock's ability to convey information to the viewer without resorting to verbal communication. Visual clues and images predominate as the director sets the stage, establishes the "backstory," and reveals details about the lifestyle and situation of the protagonist. After the camera pans the entire outer courtyard, Hitchcock continues the camera movement into Jefferies' apartment. The shot holds in tight close-up on a bead of perspiration on Jeff's forehead before revealing his leg cast ("Here lie the broken bones of L. B. Jefferies"), his smashed camera, photographs of the race car crash that immobilized him, and other shots—including one of a nuclear mushroom cloud—that establish his dangerous occupation. A wall thermometer indicating a ninety-four-degree day and a framed negative of a model alongside the positive print on the cover of a magazine tell us more about the protagonist than just the temperature and his profession; they suggest the superheated nature of his confinement and foreshadow his "negative" attitude about Lisa, who happens to be a model.[14] There is no dialogue throughout this expository shot, although the voice of a radio announcer is heard: "Men, are you over forty? When you wake up . . . do you have that listless feeling?" This advertisement bears directly on Jeff's status in the world and, as in *Blow-Up*, establishes a commercialized consumer culture that impinges on people from the outside.

The very first sequence in *Blow-Up* also establishes a conflict between sound and silence, as Antonioni crosscuts between a group of youthful, noisy Rag Week students who look like mimes and a group of older, quiet derelicts exiting a doss-house. The Rag Week students are not, technically speaking, mimes since they are rather boisterous—kinetically and aurally—especially in the opening scene. They run through the streets and shout exuberantly. Their shouts, however, do not communicate much more than their excitement and passion within staid, stiff-upper-lip British society (epitomized by the Royal Guard, African nuns, and other solemn people they pass on the streets). In the opening, the mummers "converse" with Thomas exclusively through gestural synecdoche and other unspoken means. Nonetheless, their shared gazes—their imploring requests for a donation and Thomas's lackadaisical facial response—establish a silent, ambiguous link between them that convinces the photographer to give them some cash at the beginning of the film and to retrieve their invisible tennis ball at the end. Like Antonioni, who uses atypical "wires" to communicate meaning and character, the mimes use atypical channels to convey information about themselves.

Finally, screen performance, or acting style, must be considered as part of a film's overall style. This is one of the clearest connections between Hitchcock and Antonioni, since both directors eschew histrionics and "Method" acting. Hitchcock, of course, is equally famous for saying that "actors are like cattle" and then for amending that statement by stating that he meant to say that "actors *should be treated* like cattle." In seeking a neutral, minimalist performance style that was conducive to his cinematic vision, the director often instructed performers to "drain their faces of all expression" ("The Dark Side," Spoto 291) so that he could *create* emotion using camera, editing, music, or mise-en-scène. As the director put it, "The screen actor . . . has to submit himself to be used by the director and the camera . . . The best screen actor is the man who can do nothing extremely well" ("Direction" 35). In interviews, Hitchcock often invoked his notion of "pure cinema," which relied on Kuleshovian montage and restrained acting, especially in facial close-ups, so that when the cut was made to what the character was looking at, *the viewer* would experience the emotion directly, through identification, rather than by observing the actor's artifice of sentiment. Both classical actors, like John Gielgud, Laurence Olivier, and Gregory Peck, and so-called Methodists, like Montgomery Clift and Paul Newman, complained that Hitchcock wanted to destroy their craft by insisting that they unlearn their carefully honed techniques and deliver a "less-is-more" performance. Hitchcock admitted this tendency to François Truffaut: "[Paul Newman] is a 'method' actor, and he found it hard to just give me one of those neutral looks I needed to cut from his point of view" ("Direction" 313).

Antonioni also relies on a combination of mise-en-scène, découpage, camera angles, color, lighting, set design, soundtrack articulations, music, *and* pared-down performances to construct his singular cinematic language of characterization. As he once put it, "Only one person fuses in his mind the various elements involved in a film . . . the director. The actor is one of those elements, *and sometimes not even the most important*" ("A Talk with Antonioni," Antonioni 144). Most naturalistic film directors exploit the theatrical codes of their actors' facial expressions, gestures, and vocal intonation in dialogue to effectuate audience understanding and empathy. In contrast, Antonioni uses a cinematic syntax that problematizes such clarity. For him, "It is much more cinematographic to try to catch a character's thoughts by showing his reactions, whatever they may be, than to wrap the whole thing up in a speech, than to resort to what practically amounts to an explanation" (Leprohon 96). The viewer is thus presented with a paradoxical modernist morphology, a minimalism that ultimately underplays his characters' individuality and "personality." Indeed, an Antonioni character is often just a small part of a larger visual and social field, a "figure in a landscape" as Ted Perry called it ("Men and Landscapes" 3).

A basic tenet of Stanislavskian/Method acting is that the actor is the auteur (Carnicke 80), or, as Tony Barr has said in discussing screen acting, "The actor's primary function is to communicate ideas and emotion to an audience" (3). However, in the work of Antonioni, the communication of ideas and emotion has become the job of the filmmaker, not the performer. Antonioni has stated this directly: "Actors feel somewhat uncomfortable with me; they have the feeling that they've been excluded from my work. And, as a matter of fact, they have been" (*Blow-Up* 8). This may be because the director believes that his actors are only one part of a larger composition: "I regard [the performer] as I regard a tree, a wall, or a cloud, that is, as just one element in the overall scene" ("A Talk with Antonioni," Antonioni 36). Antonioni has explained his work methods on the set as follows: "The film actor ought not to understand, he ought to *be* . . . The director owes the actor no explanations except general ones about the character and the film. It is dangerous to go into details" (Leprohon 101–03).

Examples of Antonioni's use of subdued, nonverbal gestures abound in *Blow-Up* ("Sounds of Silence," Tomasulo 94–125). At the start of the Veruschka photo session, for instance, Thomas gestures with a shrug of his head for Reg, his assistant, to open the blinds and let in some light, not even deigning to speak to the hired help. Throughout much of the film, Hemmings' face remains expressionless and deadpan, neutral in the Hitchcock-Kuleshov manner. As just one example, when he goes back to the park at night to search for the corpse, he slowly and deliberately approaches the tree where he saw the corpse. The camera tilts down to reveal the dead body. When Thomas kneels down and gently touches the cadaver, the photographer is mute and his face is impassive—as impassive as the dead man's. Thomas is equally emotionless when he stares at the enlargements hung about his loft like the stations of the cross. Hemmings' face at this point expresses at most slight curiosity, conveyed by his slightly knit brow; the shot composition communicates the character's situation more directly. Thomas's face is trapped between two of the blow-ups, which impinge on his "personal space" and occupy most of the frame. As such, his entrapment by the mystery in Maryon Park is presented in a graphic visual manner, rather than through any overt techniques in David

Hemmings' performance. Although it would be difficult to prove a direct influence from Hitchcock, both directors certainly appear to be "working in the same idiom" of cinematic performance codes. They clearly share, in both their public pronouncements and their films, a resolute exteriorization of emotion and a deemphasis on verbal communication.[15] Even when there is dialogue, Antonioni's methods of working with actors are such that "they appear to recite their lines with the monotonous detachment of non-performers who have no involvement with what they are saying" (Scott 88), as evinced in the exchange between Thomas and Patricia cited above.

Differences between Hitchcock and Antonioni

In an interview with me, Antonioni said, "Hitchcock's films are completely false, especially the endings ... Life is inconclusive" ("Life Is Inconclusive," Tomasulo 64). Although many scholars have argued that the ending of *Rear Window* is less definitive than that of many other Hitchcock films, it is still rather different from the conclusion of *Blow-Up*. As *Rear Window* concludes, the murderer has been captured and the protagonist is chastened by his experience; after falling from the window ledge, Jeff is surrounded by Lisa, Stella, and Doyle in a composition reminiscent of a pietà tableau. Furthermore, the fates of all the other apartment dwellers are revealed. The future of the romance between Jeff and Lisa is the only plot line that remains somewhat unresolved: although Lisa seems to be Jeff's dutiful wife or companion as she reads a travel book on the Himalayas, she conceals a copy of *Harper's Bazaar,* the fashion magazine, indicating that her transformation is not entirely complete and that her relationship with Jeff may be on a rocky foundation. Nonetheless, the epistemological quest embodied in the murder mystery is resolved and Jeff can return to life as usual—once his *two* broken legs heal.

In contrast, the last scene of *Blow-Up* is a classic modernist stopping. None of the ravelings and unravelings of the plot have been resolved, and narrative closure is avoided so much that it has come to represent (along with Truffaut's final freeze-frame in *The Four Hundred Blows*) the inconclusiveness of the European art cinema. Of course, this pattern of anticlosure has been a hallmark of Antonioni's oeuvre throughout his career; the director has even commented on it by quoting Anton Chekhov: "Give me new endings and I will reinvent literature!" ("Life Is Inconclusive," Tomasulo 64). In particular, Thomas's ambiguous facial expression has been interpreted as indicating either negative capitulation to the delusionary forces (represented by the mimes and marijuana) eating away at his grasp of reality or his positive revelation that he must give up observing life through his camera and make contact with other human beings. Between these antipodes, the Antonioni literature is filled with differing interpretations about what the imaginary tennis ball signifies and what Thomas is thinking about after he "returns" it to the mimes.

In *Blow-Up*, neither the murder subplot nor Thomas's epistemological questions are resolved. We know there was a murder (and a corpse), but the evidence (the dead body and the blow-ups) disappear without a hint of who the victim was or what the motive for the crime might have been. Hitchcock, of course, could not end a commercial American genre film made in the 1950s without fulfilling his audience's expectation of who committed the murder and why. By the late 1960s, though, Antonioni *could* provide an open-ended modernist finale so that in *Blow-Up* the classical *anagnorisis* of Greek drama is elided in favor of a polysemic metadiscourse on the nature of reality. One does not have to "make sense" of this *in medias res* ending, especially since the protagonist vanishes from the screen in an enigmatic fade-out. The modernist ending is, after all, usually more immanent than imminent, evoking a mood of epistemological despair rather than narrative closure and characterological certainty. Indeed, for Thomas and for the viewer, the final frame does not end the search for meaning.

In both films, the two protagonists' cameras figure prominently in the denouements, albeit in markedly different ways. Jeff *picks up* and uses his photographic apparatus, especially his flashbulbs, to stave off the menacing Lars Thorwald. As Thorwald approaches the wheelchair-bound Jefferies, the photographer triggers his flash attachments one by one, thus temporarily blinding and delaying his murderous attacker. Throughout the film, Jeff had used his camera as a means to distance himself from others and to observe life without participating in it. In contrast, at the end of *Blow-Up* Thomas *puts down* his camera to commune with the mimes by tossing back their imaginary tennis ball. Of course, Thomas, like Jeff, had used his camera as an alienating device—to keep him at a remove from the people he encountered. Ironically, when he finally puts down his lens, he is able to make creative contact with the outside world and with other human beings, even if only on the level of a game. In both cases, the protagonists move on and are allowed to grow and overcome their alienation—one by using his camera in an imaginative way, the other by using his imagination and *not* his camera.

One of the chief differences between *Rear Window* and *Blow-Up* is in the depiction of the protagonist. Although L. B. Jefferies has a dark and disturbing side, as do many of the subsidiary characters in *Rear Window*, there is nonetheless "a warmth of characterization . . . a credibility and an emotional wholeness, a heart and a humor" in the movie—"characteristics that other Hitchcock films ... conspicuously lack" ("Dark Side," Spoto 374). Donald Spoto attributes this light touch and generosity of spirit to Hitchcock's screenwriter, John Michael Hayes, who also wrote *North by Northwest*. Jeff may be a suspicious and sexist Peeping Tom, and he may declaim against his fate and his loving girlfriend through most of the narrative but, as personified by Hollywood Everyman James Stewart, he is likeable and agreeable. When he first asks Lisa to "shut up for a minute," it comes out of his frustration over not being able to get a word in edgewise and is spoken with a gentle mien; a few moments later, he raises his voice and tells her more directly: "Shut up!"[16] Nonetheless, even his most cutting comments are tinged with sly wit, humor, and a delivery that indicates he is just teasing and not intentionally trying to be cruel.

The same cannot be said about Thomas. Although some spectators have apparently been taken in by his mod-ish "charm," rugged good looks, and glamorous occupation, he is clearly a boorish and egotistical workaholic who despises the people (especially the women) he works with, drives past, and encounters in the course of his daily routine. He calls his female Asian assistant (and most of the other women he meets) "love," in the patronizing idiom of the 1960s, but he mainly orders her around. Although Thomas never tells anyone to "shut up," he does tell his models to keep their eyes shut while he leaves the studio and verbally abuses them ("You, arm down!" "Terrible!" "Smile!"). Viewers may forgive Thomas (and David Hemmings) for his uncouth qualities and misogyny, but his dark side is clearly more visible (and more risible) than that of L. B. Jefferies.

Conclusion

The impact of Alfred Hitchcock's oeuvre has been enormous, both on international culture in general and on other filmmakers in particular. Scholars and critics have pointed out the most obvious examples of motion picture directors who have appropriated or satirized the Hitchcock legacy—De Palma, Charbol, Truffaut, Brooks, Higgins, et al.)—especially when those auteurs have specifically acknowledged their debt to the master of suspense. Establishing a Hitchcock influence on other directors is a more difficult task, one that is made more complicated by differences in nationality, era, themes, and cinematic styles. Nonetheless, just as it is important to attempt to trace such patterns and document the "anxiety of influence" in poetry and prose, there are rewards to be gained by studying the intertextual and self-reflexive "borrowings" that are passed down from one generation of film auteurs to another (Bloom).

Without denying the clearly visible distinctions between a Classical Hollywood filmmaker like Hitchcock and a European modernist cineaste such as Antonioni, it is instructive to note the tangible textual (and subtextual) similarities in narrative, character, theme, and cinematic style that pervade their most commercial movies, *Rear Window* and *Blow-Up*. It would be wrongheaded to say that the latter is merely an artistic "remake" of the former; it would be just as wrongheaded to conclude that there is no connection between the two films. How that influence happened—whether it was intentional or unconscious, direct or indirect, productive or destructive—is open to debate and discussion. This study, along with the other chapters in this collection, has attempted to open the door to future research on "the Hitchcock factor" in world cinema. Furthermore, investigating the lineage of *all* the artistic inheritances in the historical evolution of the film medium is a worthy, albeit daunting, goal for scholars and critics alike.

Notes

1. There is even a humorous, though subtle, homage to the "master of suspense" in the otherwise dour *Last Year at Marienbad*: a shadowy cardboard figure of Hitchcock. No doubt Resnais was offering a tribute to a filmmaker who shared his aesthetic predilections for puzzling narratives and both long takes and montage editing.

2. Although I originally noticed the resemblances between the two films when *Blow-Up* first came out in 1967 and even presented the comparison in various conference papers during the early 1980s, this is the first time I have published these ideas. While conducting final research for this chapter, I noticed that at least three authors had briefly called attention to the similarities: Thomas Harris (60–63), William J. Palmer (102), and Charles Derry (237–38). In addition, Francesco Casetti makes a comparison/contrast between Hitchcock's "fruitful" use of narrational agency in *Stage Fright* (1950) and Antonioni's "erratic" self-reflexivity in *Cronaca di un amore* (1950). See Casetti, especially 6.

3. One of the most common ways to convey character semes—the proper name—is absent in *Blow-Up*. The two main characters are never identified by name within the diegesis, although their first names—Thomas and Jane—are noted in the film's published screenplay and in most of the scholarly literature. The very absence of a cognomen provides symbolic inferences, just as it does in the modernist novels of Kafka (K. in *The Trial*) or the plays of Samuel Beckett. Since one's name is often associated with one's identity (Who are you? John Doe), the failure to provide an appellation suggests a characterological anonymity or veritable nonexistence. This namelessness (also found in *The Passenger* [the Girl], *Il Mistero di Oberwald* [the Queen], and *all* the family names in *L'Avventura*, *L'Eclisse*, *Il Deserto Rosso*, and *Zabriskie Point*) bespeaks a lack of or loss of personal identity that Antonioni thematizes throughout his work.

By providing extratextual information about the characters' names through the *Blow-Up* script and interviews, however, the director encourages individual associations that attach to those designations: "doubting" Thomas, "peeping" Tom, or "plain" Jane, all of which have some resonance with the people in *Blow-Up*. In combination, however, Thomas and Jane are sexually charged names to readers of D. H. Lawrence's *Lady Chatterley's Lover,* in which Mellors, the groundskeeper, uses "John *Thomas*" and "Lady *Jane*" to designate, respectively, the male and female sex organs: "John Thomas! Dost want *her*? Does want Lady Jane?" (252). Neither the script nor the film, however, offers a surname for either character (or for any other character in the entire film), thus setting them apart from any roots, traditions, or family ties, and makes them modern tabulae rasae.

4. Hitchcock has been quoted as saying that he modeled (pun intended) Lisa's character on supermodel and businesswoman Anita Colbey (Samuels 118). Another report has the director basing the Jeff-Lisa romance on the real-life relationship between still photographer Robert Capa and actress Ingrid Bergman (Cohen 2–7).

5. This was, of course, the era of the rail-thin British fashion model, with Twiggy and Jean Shrimpton being the most renowned exemplars of the Mod look. The Hemmings character was apparently based on a real-life British fashion photographer, David Bailey, who was notorious for his demanding persona.

6. Jefferies is not the only male in *Rear Window* prone to scopophilia. At the beginning of the film, some men in a helicopter hover over Jeff's apartment complex, hoping to get a view of some sunbathing women—a scene that seems to have been "borrowed" by Federico Fellini for the opening of *La Dolce Vita* (1959). Later, even upright Lieutenant Doyle stares across the courtyard at Miss Torso until Jefferies asks "How's your wife?"

7. It was, of course, the fate of Oedipus to have his eyes plucked out as punishment for his taboo activities.

8. This may partially explain the film's international success at the box office, along with its daring (for the time) depiction of "sex, drugs, and rock 'n' roll."

9. Although the Thorwald marriage—with its constant bickering, physical separation, and eventual murder of the wife—is the most obvious example of a bad marriage, even the rapturous newlyweds end up quarreling over money by the end of the film. There are even hints that the older couple, who love their dog like a child, are sexually alienated from each other; they are introduced sleeping on their fire escape but facing in opposite directions—the bed positions assumed by another sexless couple: Leopold and Molly Bloom in James Joyce's *Ulysses* (1922).

10. Indeed, Angelo Restivo has pointed out the similarity between the Lumière brothers' *Workers Leaving a Factory* (1895) and the shot of Thomas and the derelicts exiting the doss-house at the beginning of *Blow-Up* (109).

11. This right-to-left direction is "against the grain" of the natural movement of the eye in western societies, where reading is inculcated as a left-to-right activity. Robert Stam and Roberta Pearson point out that Hitchcock uses this "counterclockwise" pan around the courtyard no less than *six times* in *Rear Window* (199).

12. Although far from the extreme found in German Expressionist cinema of the 1920s, it is important to note that Hitchcock worked at UFA in the silent period and observed the dramatic set designs of that era.

13. They are, in fact, usually in separate rooms—Mr. Thorwald in the living room and his wife (an invalid like Jefferies) in the bedroom. The background walls in both rooms are painted in contrasting colors to further illustrate their differences.

14. Hitchcock introduces Lisa as a negative force, by showing her casting a deep shadow over Jeff's sleeping countenance when she first enters his apartment.

15. "No Words" was painted on the stolen airplane in Antonioni's *Zabriskie Point* (1969), an apt expression for the director's cinematic goals.

16. Jefferies' rudeness to Lisa in this scene rhymes with Thorwald's earlier injunction to the sculptress: "Why don't you shut up?!" Several commentators have pointed out the doppelganger relationship between Jeff and Thorwald.

Works Consulted

Antonioni, Michelangelo. *Blow-Up*. New York: Lorrimer, 1971.
———. "It Was Born in London, but It Is Not an English Film." In *The Architecture of Vision: Writings and Interviews on Cinema*. Ed. Carlo di Carlo and Giorgio Tinazzi. New York: Marsilio, 1996. 89–91.
———. "A Talk with Michelangelo Antonioni on His Work." In *The Architecture of Vision: Writings and Interviews on Cinema*. Ed. Carlo di Carlo and Giorgio Tinazzi. New York: Marsilio, 1996. 21–47.
Arrowsmith, William. "Antonioni." Unpublished paper. Symposium on Michelangelo Antonioni, Cornell University, 1982.
———. *Antonioni: The Poet of Images*. New York: Oxford University Press, 1995.
Barr, Tony. *Acting for the Camera*. New York: Harper & Row, 1986.
Belázs, Béla. *Theory of the Film: Character and Growth of a New Art*. Trans. Edith Bone. New York: Dover, 1970.
Belton, John, ed. *Alfred Hitchcock's "Rear Window."* Cambridge: Cambridge University Press, 2000.
———. "The Space of *Rear Window*." In *Hitchcock's Rereleased Films*. Ed. Walter Raubicheck and Walter Srebnick. Detroit: Wayne State University Press, 1991.
Billard, Pierre. "An Interview with Michelangelo Antonioni." In Michelangelo Antonioni, *Blow-Up: A Film*. New York: Simon and Schuster, 1971. 5–10.
Bloom, Harold. *The Anxiety of Influence*. New York: Oxford University Press, 1973.
Brand, Dana. "Rear-View Mirror: Hitchcock, Poe, and the Flaneur in America." In *Hitchcock's America*. Ed. Jonathan Freedman and Richard Millington. New York: Oxford University Press, 1999. 123–34.
Bresson, Robert. *Notes sur le cinématographe*. Paris: Editions Gallimard, 1975.
Brunette, Peter. *The Films of Michelangelo Antonioni*. Cambridge: Cambridge University Press, 1998.
Cameron, Ian, and Robin Wood. *Antonioni*. New York: Praeger, 1969.
Carnicke, Sharon Marie. "Lee Strasberg's Paradox of the Actor." In *Screen Acting*. Ed. Alan Lovell and Peter Krämer, London: Routledge, 1999. 75–87.
Casetti, Francesco. "Antonioni and Hitchcock: Two Strategies of Narrative Investment." http://substance.arts.uwo.ca/51/51cas. April 29, 2003.
Chatman, Seymour. *Antonioni or, the Surface of the World*. Berkeley: University of California Press, 1985.
Cohen, Steve. "*Rear Window:* The Untold Story." *Columbia Film View* 8.1 (winter/spring 1990): 2–7.
Della Vacche, Angela. *Cinema and Painting: How Art Is Used in Film*. Austin: University of Texas Press, 1996.
Derry, Charles. *The Suspense Thriller: Films in the Shadow of Alfred Hitchcock*. London: McFarland, 1988.
Doane, Mary Ann. "The Voice in the Cinema: The Articulation of Body and Space." *Yale French Review* 60 (1980): 33–50.
Douchet, Jean. "Hitch et son Public." *Cahiers du cinéma* 113 (November 1960): 7–15.
Dyer, Richard. *Stars*. 2nd ed. London: British Film Institute, 1997.
Fawell, John. *Hitchcock's* Rear Window: *The Well-Made Film*. Carbondale: Southern Illinois University Press, 2001.
Fernandez, Dominique. "The Poet of Matriarchy." In Leprohon, *Michelangelo Antonioni*. New York: Simon and Schuster, 1963. 158–60.
Gessner, Robert. *The Moving Image: A Guide to Cinematic Literacy*. New York: Dutton, 1971.
Gottlieb, Sidney, ed. *Hitchcock on Hitchcock: Selected Writings and Interviews*. Berkeley: University of California Press, 1995.

Harris, Thomas. "*Rear Window* and *Blow-Up:* Hitchcock's Straightforwardness vs. Antonioni's Ambiguity." *Literature/Film Quarterly* 15 (1987): 60–63.

Hitchcock, Alfred. "Direction." In *Focus on Hitchcock*. Ed. Albert J. LaValley. Englewood Cliffs, NJ: Prentice-Hall, 1972. 32–39.

———. "*Rear Window*." *Take One* 5.2 (1976): 18–20.

Jameson, Fredric. *Signatures of the Visible*. London: Routledge, 1992.

Knight, Arthur. "Three Encounters with *Blow-Up*." *Film Heritage* 2 (spring 1967): 3–6.

LaValley, Albert J., ed. *Focus on Hitchcock*. Englewood Cliffs, NJ: Prentice-Hall, 1972.

Lawrence, D. H. *John Thomas and Lady Jane: The Second Version of* Lady Chatterley's Lover. New York: Viking Press, 1972.

———. *Lady Chatterley's Lover*. New York: Grove Press, 1959.

———. *The Letters of D. H. Lawrence*. Ed. Aldous Huxley. London: William Heinemann, 1956.

Leprohon, Pierre. *The Italian Cinema*. Trans. Roger Greaves and Oliver Stallybrass. New York: Praeger, 1972.

———. *Michelangelo Antonioni: The Man and His Work*. New York: Simon and Schuster, 1963.

Marcuse, Herbert. *One-Dimensional Man: Studies in the Ideology of Advanced Industrial Society*. Boston: Beacon Press, 1964.

Marx, Karl. *Capital,* vol. 1 (New York: Modern Library, 1936).

———. *The Communist Manifesto*. In *Essential Works of Marxism*. Ed. Arthur P. Mendel. New York: Bantam, 1965. 13–44.

———. Preface to *A Contribution to a Critique of Political Economy*. In *Early Writings*. Trans. Rodney Livingstone and Gregor Benton. New York: Vintage, 1975. 424–28.

Meeker, Hubert. "*Blow-Up*." In *Renaissance of the Film*. Ed. Julius Bellone. New York: Collier, 1970. 121–40.

Metz, Christian. *The Imaginary Signifier: Psychoanalysis and the Cinema*. Trans. Ben Brewster. Bloomington, IN: University of Indiana Press, 1982.

Modleski, Tania. *The Women Who Knew Too Much: Hitchcock and Feminist Theory*. New York: Methuen, 1988.

Naremore, James. *Acting in the Cinema*. Berkeley: University of California Press, 1988.

Nowell-Smith, Geoffrey. *L'Avventura*. London: British Film Institute, 1997.

Palmer, R. Barton. "The Metafictional Hitchcock: The Experience of Viewing and the Viewing of Experience in *Rear Window* and *Psycho*." *Cinema Journal* 26.2 (winter 1986): 4–29.

Palmer, William J. *The Films of the Seventies: A Social History*. Metuchen, NJ: Scarecrow Press, 1987.

Perry, Ted. "A Contextual Study of Michelangelo Antonioni's *Eclipse*." Ph.D. dissertation, University of Iowa, 1968.

———. "Men and Landscapes: Antonioni's *The Passenger*." *Film Comment* 11 (July–August 1975): 2–6.

Pudovkin, V. I. *Film Technique and Film Acting*. New York: Grove Press, 1970.

Restivo, Angelo. *The Cinema of Economic Miracles*. Durham, NC: Duke University Press, 2003.

Rifkin, Ned. *Antonioni's Visual Language*. Ann Arbor, MI: UMI Research Press, 1982.

Rohdie, Sam. *Antonioni*. London: BFI Publishing, 1990.

Rohmer, Eric, and Claude Chabrol. *Hitchcock: The First Forty-Four Films*. Trans. Stanley Hochman. New York: Frederick Ungar, 1979.

Samuels, Robert. *Hitchcock's Bi-textuality: Lacan, Feminisms, and Queer Theory*. Albany: State University of New York Press, 1998.

Schickel, Richard. "We're Living in a Hitchcock World, All Right." *New York Times Sunday Magazine,* Oct. 29, 1972, 22–32.

Schrader, Paul. *Transcendental Style in Film: Ozu, Bresson, Dreyer*. Berkeley: University of California Press, 1972.

Scott, Michael Alan. "Michelangelo Antonioni's *The Passenger:* A Film Analysis." Ed.D. dissertation, Columbia University Teachers College, 1979.

Sharff, Stefan. *The Art of Looking in Hitchcock's* Rear Window. New York: Limelight, 1997.

Smith, Barbara Herrnstein. *Poetic Closure: A Study of How Poems End*. Chicago: University of Chicago Press, 1968.

Spoto, Donald. *The Art of Alfred Hitchcock*. New York: Hopkinson and Blake, 1976.

———. *The Dark Side of Genius: The Life of Alfred Hitchcock*. New York: Ballantine, 1983.

Stam, Robert, and Roberta Pearson. "Hitchcock's *Rear Window:* Reflexivity and the Critique of Voyeurism." In *A Hitchcock Reader*. Ed. Marshall Deutelbaum and Leland Poague. Ames: Iowa State University Press, 1986. 193–206.

Tomasulo, Frank P. "The Intentionality of Consciousness: Subjectivity in *Last Year at Marienbad*." *Post Script* 7 (winter 1988): 58–71.

———. "Life Is Inconclusive: A Conversation with Michelangelo Antonioni." *On Film* 13 (fall 1984): 61–64.

———. "The Rhetoric of Anti-Closure: Michelangelo Antonioni and the Open Ending." *Purdue Film Studies Annual*, 1983. 133–39.

———. "The Sounds of Silence: Modernist Acting in Michelangelo Antonioni's *Blow-Up*." In *More than a Method: Trends and Traditions in Contemporary Screen Performance*. Ed. Cynthia Baron, Diane Carson, and Frank P. Tomasulo. Detroit: Wayne State University Press, 2004.

Tomlinson, Doug. "Performance in the Films of Robert Bresson: The Aesthetics of Denial." In *Making Visible the Invisible: An Anthology of Original Essays on Film Acting*. Ed. Carole Zucker. Metuchen, NJ: Scarecrow Press, 1990. 365–90.

Weis, Elisabeth. *The Silent Scream: Alfred Hitchcock's Sound Track*. Rutherford, NJ: Fairleigh Dickinson University Press, 1982.

Wood, Robin. *Hitchcock's Films Revisited*. New York: Columbia University Press, 1989.

Wyndham, Frances. "Antonioni's London," *London Sunday Times*, March 12, 1967, 13–15.

Zucker, Carole, ed. *Figures of Light: Actors and Directors Illuminate the Art of Film Acting*. New York: Plenum, 1995.

———. *Making Visible the Invisible: An Anthology of Original Essays on Film Acting*. Metuchen, NJ: Scarecrow Press, 1990.

Melo-Thriller

Hitchcock, Genre, and Nationalism in Pedro Almodóvar's *Women on the Verge of a Nervous Breakdown*

Ernesto R. Acevedo-Muñoz

Hitchcock's work is visually the richest in the history of the cinema.
— PEDRO ALMODÓVAR

Introduction: Almodóvar, Spanish Cinema, and Intertextuality

Pedro Almodóvar has been probably the most internationally prominent Spanish filmmaker since his breakthrough films of the 1980s, *The Law of Desire* (1987), and *Women on the Verge of a Nervous Breakdown* (1988). The critical and commercial success of some of his films in the United States (*Women on the Verge, Tie Me Up! Tie Me Down!* [1989], *High Heels* [1991], *Kika* [1994], and the Oscar-winning *All About My Mother* [1999]) has made his name synonymous with Spanish cinema in many circles. Almodóvar's films have been celebrated as irreverent, self-reflexive, and self-conscious explorations of Spanish national identity, sexuality, repression, and desire. His films are recognizably excessive, full of colorful characters, vertiginous plotlines, rich intergeneric allusions, and complex media intersections that include television commercials, billboard advertisements, popular songs, kitsch art, and the cinema.

Critics and historians of Spanish national cinema in general and Almodóvar in particular have pointed out how national identity in the cinema after 1980 has been reflexive of the crisis in which the country found itself after the end of General Francisco Franco's regime in 1975 and the beginning of redemocratization in the early 1980s. In the transitional period after forty years of the repression of many cultural practices that were not sanctioned by the state, Spanish popular art was reborn with a vengeance, appropriating and revising the past cultural markers of fascism (the reduction of Spanish cultural identity to the kitsch aesthetics of bullfighting, flamenco dancing, Catholic imagery), and reinvented itself as signifying change, tolerance, political and sexual liberation, and artistic freedom. Almodóvar emerged as an artist in the cusp of this transitional period, becoming representative in the cinema of this "new Spanish mentality" (Kinder 432; Yarza 117–22). Almodóvar's films (along with some other directors') celebrate "cultural anxiety" (Yarza 174), generic instability (Acevedo-Muñoz 25), "marginality" (Kinder 429–33), the revision of social and political institutions (D'Lugo 50), and eventually the return to a pastoral, country setting as a symbol of stability (Del Pino 170). These themes suggest the problematic transition into democracy and the reintegration into the European community as symptomatic of the nation's new identity, troubled but open, paradoxically stabilizing and unstable.

Among the signs and symptoms of Spain's and Spanish cinema's "new mentality" and reinvention as a site of the convergence of diverse cultural practices was the appropriation and adaptation to Spanish contexts of discursive and stylistic models from high, low, and popular culture from abroad, including Hollywood and European cinema. Almodóvar and some other directors (Vicente Aranda, Agustín Villaronga, Eloy de la Iglesia) managed to break through into "specialized" international film audiences, writes Marsha Kinder, and "Almodóvar was celebrated as a cross between Billy Wilder, Douglas Sirk, and David Lynch" (437). Almodóvar's films are full of cinematic allusions to and quotations from formative figures of international, Hollywood, and independent cinema including Luis Buñuel, Ingmar Bergman, Rainer Werner Fassbinder, Wilder, Sirk, Vincente Minnelli, Nicholas Ray, John Cassavettes, and Alfred Hitchcock. But said appropriations, allusions, intertextual references and citations serve to cement Almodóvar's own style as something in a constant state of transition and maturation, arguably analogous to Spain's own cultural heterogeneity after the end of Franco's regime. In reference to Almodóvar's most popular film of the 1990s, *All About My Mother,* I have argued elsewhere that the film finally settles into a definably melodramatic format, neutralizing the generic schizophrenia of earlier films (like the thriller/melodrama/musical *High Heels*) in what results in "an understanding of identity as something ambiguous (sexually, culturally) and problematic, yet ultimately functional" (Acevedo-Muñoz 27). Even earlier on, however, in *Women on the Verge of a Nervous Breakdown,* Almodóvar's use of Hitchcock's films as intertextual discourse was showing signs of a generically hybrid quality (in *Women on the Verge* between the thriller, screwball comedy, and melodrama). In *Women on the Verge,* his most popular film of the 1980s and the definitive breakthrough into American movie theaters, and later in *All About My Mother,* intertextuality is in itself signifying of the process of building and rebuilding, inventing and reinventing an identity that is occasionally defined by its own instability. More than any other outside text, acknowledged or otherwise, it is Hitchcock's work, "visually the richest in the history of the cinema" (*Almodóvar on Almodóvar* 147), that becomes more eloquent of a schizophrenic identity that paradoxically leads to a happy ending.

The presence of Hitchcock in Almodóvar's films often appears in the form of "appropriation" rather than homage. While allusions to Sirk, Minnelli, Bergman, and other directors are usually referential and frequently acknowledged (for example, among Almodóvar's *Patty Diphusa* writings there is a story in homage to Sirk entitled "Scrotum in the Wind," and in *High Heels* the two principal characters discuss how their lives mimic the relationship between Ingrid Bergman and Liv Ullmann in Bergman's *Autumn Sonata*), citations from Hitchcock's films are incorporated into the narrative and generic configurations with which the director plays. Hitchcock becomes Almodóvar's own discourse. Almodóvar's interest in Hitchcock as a visual stylist is well documented, as illustrated in the opening epigraph also cited above (*Almodóvar on Almodóvar* 147), but while some critics dismiss Almodóvar's generic and intertextual games as "ironic humor or pastiche" (Smith 112), they help to understand better Almodóvar's aesthetics as a discourse on crisis that aspires constantly to reinvent and "correct" itself.

This essay explores the meaning and contribution to Almodóvar's style and discourse of the Hitchcockian appropriations present in his most popular film, *Women on the Verge of a Nervous Breakdown.* Almodóvar has long been recognized as the defining, most important voice of Spanish cinema since the middle 1980s, and this essay analyzes the meaning and relevance of Hitchcockian texts to the work of Almodóvar and their contribution to the Spanish director's thematic interest in issues of identity and desire. Specifically I argue that Almodóvar's style, which is based in part in the instability of genre as a metaphor for sexual and national identity, draws from Hitchcockian themes and direct quotations of Hitchcock's oeuvre in order to signify.

The meaning of a dramatic moment in many of Almodóvar's films is often based on the recognition of its Hitchcockian allusion to make meaning. Below I analyze the dramatic and formal significance of direct citations and motifs from Hitchcock's *The Lady Vanishes* (1938), *Spellbound* (1945), *Rope* (1948), *Strangers on a Train* (1951), *Dial M for Murder* (1954), *Rear Window* (1956), *Vertigo* (1957), *Psycho* (1960), and *The Birds* (1963) in *Women on the Verge of a Nervous Breakdown.* Almodóvar's films exploit their generic "indefinition" for dramatic value, playing equally with conventions of melodrama, screwball comedy, and the thriller. Helping to hold the structure of *Women on the Verge* together are the Hitchcockian allusions that emerge in key moments of crisis and revelation. Almodóvar's intertextual experimentation is instrumental to the exploration of identity issues that characterizes his films. His reworking of Hitchcock in *Women on the Verge of a Nervous Breakdown* is particularly meaningful (as is his visit ten years later to Elia Kazan, Joseph L. Mankiewicz, and Tennessee Williams in *All About My Mother*), but not just because of its postmodernist irreverence. Its significance lies in the complexity of intertextuality and how it serves to deepen the meaning of what really is an emerging multicultural aesthetic that has helped Almodóvar redefine the meaning of national cinema. Almodóvar here appropriates Hitchcock and Hitchcock's meaning to make a statement on Spanish national and cultural identity in a moment of crisis.

Hitchcock and *Women*

Almodóvar's *Women on the Verge of a Nervous Breakdown* tells the story of television-commercial and voice-dubbing actress Pepa Marcos (Carmen Maura) and her attempts to communicate with her ex-lover Iván (Fernando Guillén). They have recently broken up, but Pepa has just learned that she is pregnant. That information serves as the MacGuffin, and the movie follows Pepa through her attempts over the course of two days to speak with Iván, tell him the news, and perhaps convince him to get back together with her. In the process she puts their apartment up for rent. Coincidentally, Iván's son, Carlos (Antonio Banderas), and his girlfriend, Marisa (Rossy de Palma), come to see the apartment for possible rental. Pepa's friend Candela (María Barranco) seeks out Pepa for help, as she discovers that her Shiite boyfriend is a terrorist planning to kidnap a plane bound for Stockholm, which Iván plans to take with his new girlfriend, the "feminist" lawyer Paulina Morales (Kiti Manver). Meanwhile, Iván's insane ex-wife, Lucía (Julieta Serrano) also tries to get to Pepa, with whom she assumes Iván plans to leave the country.

At face value, the movie is structured around the coincidences and "disphasure" or "bad timing" typical of the maternal subgenre of classic melodrama (Doane 91), following Pepa after the news of her pregnancy through a series of missed telephone connections and her search for Iván around the city. The complications of the plot insistently call attention to the self-reflexive and allusive content of the film (with the presence of film technology and different types of recording devices), to the city of Madrid itself, and to the frantic search for a vanishing gentleman, all of which build up to the "verge" of a nervous breakdown. The film's credit sequence is typical of Almodóvar, with pictures simulating magazine cutouts allusive to the film content and the different filmmaking tasks described in the credits, accompanied by a torrid love song ("I Am Unhappy" by Lola Beltrán) in the soundtrack. The sequence ends with a picture of a movie set serving as background to the words "screenplay and direction by Pedro Almodóvar." Then the film opens with a fade-in to a simulated conventional establishing shot of an apartment building at dusk. It is clearly revealed however, that the structure is only a scale model of Pepa's apartment building. Accompanied by music heavy on strings reminiscent of Bernard Herrmann's all-strings score for *Psycho,* the shot of the building refers to that Hitchcock movie first, and suggests the opening bird's-eye view of Phoenix and the hotel where Marion Crane and Sam Loomis have their sexual rendezvous. The *Psycho* reference is later confirmed with the revelation of Lucía's insanity and unhealthy relationship with her son Carlos. The shot of the apartment model is followed, incongruously in this apparently modern urban setting, by a shot of a duck, hens, and other birds in a pen, an assured reference to *The Birds.* The opening references to filmmaking, Bernard Herrmann (whose *Psycho* score Almodóvar directly used in *Kika*), *Psycho,* and *The Birds* establish Hitchcock as a formal point of reference from the beginning. As the film progresses, the themes of miscommunication and insanity and the terrorist plot extend the recurring formal references to Hitchcock's films into narrative ones.

The film's MacGuffin turns out to be the elusive meeting between Pepa and Iván operating, as in Hitchcock's films, as a narrative pretext to set off the protagonist on her search (Brill 7–8). In this film, one can argue, the search is for a "vanishing gentleman," posing an analogous reference to the disappearance of Miss Froy in *The Lady Vanishes* (1938). As Patrice Petro has argued, Miss Froy's disappearing act, and Iris's search for her, ultimately serve to call attention not only to the invisibility of the woman as that which refuses representation but also to bring under patriarchal control the searching woman's gaze, an argument familiar in feminist film theory after Laura Mulvey (Petro 128–29). In *Women on the Verge,* however, the search is for a "vanishing gentleman" and it is the image of the man that becomes visually difficult to represent. While Iván refuses to allow Pepa to see him, he does leave his voice recorded in numerous telephone messages and other voice recording devices; in Pepa's dreams he appears speaking through a microphone, and he even dubs Sterling Hayden's voice for a Spanish version of Nicholas Ray's *Johnny Guitar* (1954). In *Women on the Verge,* which, as most of Almodóvar's films, is populated by a largely female cast, the man's voice becomes a substitute for his image, and Pepa's search ultimately leads to the synchronization of the man's image and sound. Almodóvar's attention to Iván's voice also poses him as a sort of feminized leading man, his voice disembodied, which, as Amy Lawrence argues, is another way for classical cinema to repress women in the hierarchization of the visual (male) and sound (female) tracks (10).

I have detoured here into this discussion because the presence of Hitchcock in *Women on the Verge* is also a way for Almodóvar to revise Hitchcock as the subject of criticism itself. From Raymond Bellour to Laura Mulvey, Mary Ann Doane, Amy Lawrence, and Kaja Silverman, Hitchcock's films arguably appear more insistently than any other director's as case studies in feminist film theory and criticism. From *Blackmail* to *The Lady Vanishes*, from *Notorious* to *Vertigo*, *Psycho*, *The Birds*, and *Marnie*, what Hitchcock does to women is often taken as exemplary of the classical cinema's fixation with controlling, repressing, and occasionally even destroying troubled women. Almodóvar himself speaks of Hitchcock, and while acknowledging the latter's influence in his own style and narratives, he also discusses women as characters and actresses, and their two different relationships, as directors, with them:

> The way I deal with my heroines is less neurotic than Hitchcock's. His female characters are very neurotic, but behind them there's a man whose relationship with women [is] just as highly neurotic . . . Hitchcock used the scenes of his films as a way of relating to his actresses. His difficult relationships with women enriched his female characters and inspired the most memorable scenes of his films, even if they also end up giving a rather negative image of the men. I haven't such a complicated relationship with women; it's much more generous and limpid. (*Almodóvar on Almodóvar* 147)

Almodóvar's admiration for Hitchcock retains some echoes of the general critical perspective on Hitchcock and women. While Iván seems to be displaced into the position of Hitchcock's "women," Almodóvar's "women on the verge" can also be seen as reflections of some of Hitchcock's "men on the verge," from the neurotic Scottie Ferguson in *Vertigo* to the psychotic Norman Bates in *Psycho*, to the murderous Dr. Murchison and the amnesiac Dr. Edwardes in *Spellbound*. Unlike Hitchcock, however, Almodóvar allows his women the narrative agency (as it is Pepa's search for Iván that structures the plot), the power to liberate themselves from the neurotic men in their lives, and the chance to build a narrative in which men become neutralized or harmless, and, ultimately, to vanish.

Hitchcock "On the Verge"

Women on the Verge of a Nervous Breakdown thus begins with immediate self-reflexive attention to filmmaking, Hitchcock, and the reversal of the roles women and men assume in classical cinema, as exemplified by Hitchcock's films. As discussed above, Pepa's life in the two-day story time of the movie is organized around the need to find this vanishing gentleman so that she can give him the news of her pregnancy. The promise of an oedipal narrative is ultimately subverted, as Spanish cinema so often does, but in this case that happens by focusing on the organization of the narrative around the intertextual Hitchcock allusions, rather than the oedipal story itself. The movie's attention to the filmmaking process resumes early on in the film, when it is revealed that one of Pepa's (and Iván's) jobs is to dub Spanish dialogue for American movies. The choice scene for that revelation is from Nicholas Ray's *Johnny Guitar* (1954), in which Joan Crawford and Sterling Hayden are reunited after many years, and it is revealed that (in exact opposition to Pepa and Iván's situation) Joan Crawford is no longer romantically interested in the nominal hero. Iván shows up first at the EXA studios to do his recording, in the first of a series of missed encounters between him and Pepa (she has overslept due to her dependency on sleeping pills). Iván seductively moistens his lips in extreme close-up, almost touching the microphone, and we see Sterling Hayden's face speaking with Iván's voice. It's the famous "tell me some lies" dialogue in *Johnny Guitar,* and we see Joan Crawford's moving yet mute lips responding to Sterling Hayden's requests for lies ("Tell me you still love me as I love you"). The vanishing gentleman Iván always speaks in clichés and is always mediated by recording technology, whether a cinema soundtrack or an answering machine, telephones, or tape recorders. After his "out of synch" love confession, Iván quickly goes to a telephone booth and places a call to Pepa. She does not answer the telephone (out cold with sleeping pills), but he leaves a message on the recorder, which introduces the first reference to *Dial M for Murder*. A close-up shot of the telephone and answering machine not only paraphrases the shots of the ringing telephone in the 1954 Hitchcock film, but the choice of a wide-angle lens allows for a distorting effect and shot size that even suggests *Dial M*'s original stereoscopic (3-D) format. Then the wide-angle close-up of the telephone and answering machine is directly juxtaposed to a medium close-up shot of Iván in the phone booth: we see him through the right angle made by the two glass panes that make the booth, one red and one blue, precisely as if they were the two lenses of a pair of 3-D glasses. The motif of telephones is as insistent in *Women on the Verge* as it is in *Dial M for Murder*. Eventually the action in *Women on the Verge* is also temporarily confined to "real time," a single set, and somewhat theatrical space, as in *Dial M*. These two stylistic choices also refer to Hitchcock's other "single-set" films, *Lifeboat* (1944), *Rope* (1948), and *Rear Window*. Pepa spends most of the film calling Iván from her home, pay phones, and other people's telephones, or trying to retrieve her messages in the belief that Iván will eventually call. In *Women on the Verge,* as in *Dial M,* there is an implicit danger in answering the phone and a heightened sense of suspense about how difficult it becomes to actually have the conversation. While in *Dial M* answering the phone means death for Grace Kelly, in *Women on the Verge* for Pepa it means the misery of a relationship with a man that she considers as murderous, in a way, as Ray Milland in the Hitchcock film: later Pepa even refers to what Iván has done to her as "terrorism." Yet it also means "life" rather than death since Pepa's main intention is to give Iván the news of her pregnancy. In *Women on the Verge,* as in *Dial M,* there is no real telephone conversation, and yet the telephone miscommunication leads to a tragedy and to the arrival of the police on the scene to investigate a crime (due to an anonymous tip about the terrorist attack plotted by Candela's boyfriend).

Pepa eventually makes it to the studios to do her dubbing of Joan Crawford's voice in *Johnny Guitar*. The studio setting allows for more self-reflexive licenses on Almodóvar's part, beginning the sequence with a view of the recording studio from inside the projection booth. The shot shows the studio through the projector window. We then see the film leader running through the projector, the film loop inside the projector, and then the screen as the synch-sound mark bleeps when the leader hits "2." Besides the direct reference to the opening of Ingmar Bergman's *Persona* (1966), the close-up of Pepa in front of the microphone reveals her to be wearing glasses similar to those worn by several female characters in *Strangers on a Train* (Patricia Hitchcock and Laura Elliot, who plays "Miriam") which upset the murderer Bruno (Robert Walker) so much. Pepa recites Joan Crawford's lines in Spanish, paradoxically having the conversation she wishes to have, only with Iván's voice in the "projected" setting of the recording studio. Pepa's delivery is ironic in the sense that unlike Joan Crawford in that film, Pepa does mean the words she addresses to Iván: "I still love you . . ." At the end of the recording, overcome by heartbreak, emotion, and morning sickness, Pepa faints and collapses on the floor of the booth. The shot of Pepa on the floor is a direct citation of Miriam's death in *Strangers on a Train*. We see Pepa through her inverted glasses lying on the floor, the view distorted and mediated by the myopic lenses. In *Strangers on a Train* we see Miriam's murder reflected on and also distorted by her glasses, the image, as Robin Wood argues, "a sexual culmination for both killer and victim" (173). Unlike *Strangers on a Train,* where Bruno's sexual perversion and strange relationship with his mother is a theme linked to Hitchcock's "difficult" relationship with women and to which he returns in *Psycho:* in *Women on the Verge* it is precisely Pepa's dubbing director, standing in for Almodóvar, who enters the frame to rescue her. He bends over her body, picks her up, asks her if she's okay. In *Strangers on a Train* Bruno's "perverted sexuality" is emphasized by the distortion of the image as we see Miriam reflected on the glasses. Formally, Almodóvar's shot is different from Hitchcock's since we see Pepa not reflected, but *through* the glasses, so it appears as mediation rather than a cinematic reflection. The shot's meaning is revised as well, since ultimately she is rescued, not doomed, by the directorial presence. Pepa has her first hysterical crisis over a Hitchcockian moment, and yet the perversion of Bruno's (and Hitchcock's) action is here neutralized.

After her hysterical, symptomatic fainting, Pepa goes directly to the telephone again to call Iván's house. His ex-wife, Lucía, answers the telephone. Lucía's heavy makeup and nervous demeanor suggest her mental instability (which is later confirmed in conversation). Lucía is in the process of putting on her elaborate makeup and trying on wigs. In her insanity and instability Lucía is like Marnie or even Norman Bates, distanced from reality, in drag, and with a criminally psychotic disposition. After insulting and dismissing Pepa on the phone (again, a fruitless telephone conversation), Lucía's son, Carlos, enters the scene to question her. They stand in a two-shot, facing each other and both in sharp medium close-up profile, the shot a perfect facsimile of one of Marion Crane and Norman Bates in *Psycho,* when in the office parlor they have their first real conversation. The shot of Lucía and Carlos is completed in the background with a glass frame full of dissected butterflies. As in *Psycho* where Norman's stuffed owls and cravens in the background suggest Norman's mother's dead, stuffed state and foretell Marion's destiny, in *Women on the Verge* the butterflies help to frame the spectator's discovery of this mother/son relationship. The shot in perfect profile is always significant in Hitchcock's films and Almodóvar's use of it here (and later in *All About My Mother*) is equally important. In his book *Hitchcock: The Murderous Gaze,* William Rothman writes that Hitchcock characteristically used the profile shot to indicate a character's impenetrability, his or her "complete abstraction and absorption in an imagined scene to which we have no access" (22). Almodóvar uses the profile shot identically formatted, but to convey instead the knowledge of a character. We are introduced to Lucía and Carlos in the form of this succinct yet direct quotation from *Psycho,* including the dissected butterflies in lieu of the stuffed birds in the background (also suggestive of the wallpaper flowers reflected in the mirrors in Norman's office) and the nervously stuttering young man. Thus, the knowledge of their troubled relationship and her insanity is suggested a priori, before we are given that information in the narrative. For those of us who are able to identify the reference, this particular *Psycho* citation mediates our knowledge of these characters as they are introduced. We may remember other Hitchcock stuttering characters like Shaw Brandon (John Dahl) in *Rope* and Bruno (Robert Walker) in *Strangers on a Train* who, like Norman Bates and Carlos, have unresolved issues with their mothers (Rothman 271). With it, the theme of the troubled relationships between parents and children in Spanish cinema is practically condensed into a type of Hitchcock-inspired shorthand. So, as it is common in Almodóvar's intertextual appropriations of other directors' work (with the occasional yet logical exception of Luis Buñuel in *Kika* and *Live Flesh*), the reference needs to be adapted into something fitting to the cultural function of Spanish cinema in the 1980s, in this case the "troubled" past and the promise of recovery. While the stuffed birds are indicative of death, decay, and aggressiveness, the butterflies, although equally dead, are suggestive of change, grace, and some sign of hope (of recovery from the troubled Spanish national identity issues of the 1980s). This theme is symptomatic of Spanish cinema of the period as seen in movies by Almodóvar and other directors. In *Women on the Verge,* insanity mediates the relationship between Carlos and Mother (who, like Mother Bates, is also suspicious and jealous of his new "girlfriend"). The insane mother and nervous, stuttering son (like Norman) clearly have an unresolved, traumatic relationship. Furthermore, as in *Psycho,* Lucía has, like Norman's mother, neglected her son for the love of a man. It is revealed eventually that Lucía's insanity, which caused her institutionalization, resulted in Carlos being brought up by his grandparents. And her insistent pursuit of Iván after being released from the mental institution has led to a further estrangement from her son. Lucía and Carlos's traumatic relationship, and even the shot citation from *Psycho,* make a direct connection between the two films. Unlike *Psycho,* however, where Norman/Mother's troubled relationship is, as explained by the psychiatrist at the end of that film, the cause of Norman's psychosis and his murderous ways, Carlos's distance from his insane mother allows him to grow up somewhat normal (in spite of his Norman Bates–style

As in many Hitchcock films, Almodóvar's *Women on the Verge of a Nervous Breakdown* focuses on a problematic heroine.

symptomatic stuttering). Significantly, the revision and rearticulation of the oedipal narrative is a recurring theme in Spanish cinema of the last two decades (Kinder 198–200). In Almodóvar's films (especially *Labyrinth of Passion, Matador, The Law of Desire,* and *High Heels*) dysfunctional father/mother/son/daughter relationships are suggestive of the nation's traumatic track to recovery from the forty-year dictatorship. The nuclear family is reconstituted in a revision of the nation-as-family allegory exploited in Franco's days. Carlos in *Women on the Verge,* unlike Norman in *Psycho,* is saved by his estrangement from his mother, who is in this case the murderous one. As he does with the references to *Dial M for Murder* and *Strangers on a Train,* Almodóvar appropriates *Psycho* formally but revises its meaning to make it fit a Spanish national thematic specificity. In the process, Almodóvar links insanity and sexuality to the national cultural trauma and not to the customary Freudian/Lacanian connotations listed by Hitchcock critics (see for example, Bellour on *Psycho*).

After the failed new attempt at a telephone conversation with Iván, Pepa goes back to her apartment, which she now intends to put up for rent. The modern Madrid apartment setting is reminiscent of the use of similar mise-en-scène in *Rope.* First, the apartment windows allow us to see the day go by outside, with some indications of the passage of time, the way the set design (by Perry Ferguson) and the cinematography (by Joseph Valentine and William V. Skall) do in *Rope*. Also, the apartment serves an intimate, enclosing function, as mentioned before, similar to the way Hitchcock's other single-set films (*Lifeboat, Dial M,* and *Rear Window*) operate. Finally, there are two long, significant sequences in *Women on the Verge of a Nervous Breakdown* in Pepa's apartment that are staged and filmed to simulate "real time." These scenes do not pretend to give the impression of Hitchcock's celebrated series of sequence-shots in *Rope,* but they do imitate the integrity of the physical and temporal space, as Hitchcock did in 1948.

Once in the apartment, the first thing Pepa does is run to the telephone and play the messages on the answering machine. But the call she expects has not been received. Pepa then goes to the kitchen, where she prepares a tasty gazpacho (Iván's favorite) and dopes it with prescription barbiturates, so that when Iván comes she will be able to keep him there, even if it is against his will. The drugged gazpacho will return later, performing the same function as the glass of equally drugged milk offered to Gregory Peck's John Ballantine / Dr. Edwardes in *Spellbound*. While alone in her apartment, Pepa packs all of Iván's clothes in a suitcase and accidentally burns their bed with a box of matches. The remains of their relationship charred and stored, she goes back out into the street to look for Iván in his apartment. Another missed connection follows: this time Pepa leaves Iván a note which is intercepted and thrown in the garbage by Lucía on her way out of the apartment. Pepa returns to her apartment and the Madrid skyline begins to reveal itself in the background. As in *Rope,* the sight of the skyline in the background of the main set serves as an indication of the passage of time. Besides the *Rope*-inspired view from her apartment balcony containing a number of recognizable Madrid landmarks (like the Phoenix building dome at the corner of Gran Vía and Alcalá), Pepa's run through the city works, like Scottie's in *Vertigo,* as a veritable checklist of recognizable places. Unlike *Vertigo,* however, where Hitchcock exploits the city of San Francisco and its outskirts for their tourist value, Pepa's run through Madrid concentrates on real places that are of generally little interest to the outsider. Pepa's given home address, as well as Lucía's and Paulina Morales's (Iván's new lover) are all real places in the city. The neighborhood of "Cuatro Caminos" is mentioned by name as are the EXA sound-recording studios, and the sight of the famous Spanish television antenna also appears a number of times in the background. There is a sense of great familiarity with this city, unlike the somewhat uncanny quality of San Francisco in *Vertigo*. As Marvin D'Lugo has argued, the city of Madrid itself is symbolic in Almodóvar's films of the "radical reformulation of Spanish cultural values"

(49), of the cultural trajectory from Franco to freedom. In *Vertigo,* however, the city and the characters' trajectory round and about San Francisco are instead symptomatic of their helplessness and desperation. As Lesley Brill states, in *Vertigo* the characters tend to "wander," and their wandering is ultimately destructive (B200–201). In Almodóvar's film, Pepa's search has some structure to it, and her final intention, the recovery, reconstitution, and revision of the family, delivers the promise of reconstruction and further life.

In her wait for Iván, Pepa nervously and rhythmically paces her apartment. She watches the television, where one of her commercials, for the laundry powder "Ecce Homo," comes on. The character she plays in the detergent commercial could come from any number of Hitchcock's films: Pepa is "the murderer's mother" and she proudly displays her son's sparkling clean shirt, which she has washed after his latest crime. The policemen's complaint "no sign of blood or guts" seems a humorous revision of Norman's cleanup after "Mother's" murder of Marion in *Psycho.* While Pepa waits, her friend Candela arrives. Candela has been involved with a Shiite terrorist who plans to hijack a plane to Stockholm that evening. (In a purely melodramatic coincidence, it happens to be the same flight that Iván plans to take with his new girlfriend, Paulina, to escape from both Lucía and Pepa.) But Pepa leaves Candela alone and goes back out to stake out Iván in front of his apartment building.

Pepa sits on a street bench outside Iván's building and inspects the place with an inquisitive gaze. Her wait outside the apartment building leads to the most direct reference to *Rear Window.* Pepa examines some of the oblivious building dwellers through their windows and balconies. Through an open window, Pepa observes a young lady joyfully dancing in her black underwear for some (unseen) spectator in her apartment. The young lady first reminds us of the shapely dancer "Miss Torso," and of the sexually active newlyweds that L. B. Jefferies spies upon. Pepa also sees a lonely man on a balcony, a reference to the lonely music composer in *Rear Window.* The young man seems to be wiping some tears off his face, which connects him to the pathetic "Miss Lonelyheart" as well. Pepa soon discovers Marisa (Carlos's girlfriend) sitting outside the apartment inside a car. Former model and actress Rossy de Palma's striking features immediately catch Pepa's attention. Pepa's gaze finally settles in on Iván's wife and son, whom she can see through the window. They are having an argument (presumably about Carlos's plans to move out). Pepa's expression suggests that she, like L. B. Jefferies, is judgmental of the events she witnesses, her facial expression changing as do her feelings of amusement (at the sight of the dancing beauty), concern (for the crying loner), and curiosity (over Carlos and Lucía's argument). Pepa also serves a kind of mediating function since her activities are often seen or heard through some kind of representational apparatus (recordings, television, answering machines, telephones, voice dubbing). Unlike *Rear Window,* where L. B. Jefferies' voyeurism is symbolic, reflexive, and deconstructive of Hitchcock and his manipulation of the cinematic apparatus (Stam and Pearson 196–97), Pepa's situation positions her quickly within the projected diegesis of the apartment building (and not so much as a director or spectator). While Jefferies is initially passive and brought by chance and routine to spy on his neighbors, Pepa begins by going out in search of the story and becomes immediately and intrinsically involved. Jefferies' position as a "surrogate for the director" (Stam and Pearson 196) dictates his existence outside of the diegetic world (of his neighbors); he is an image-maker and cinematic speaking subject. Pepa retains the "directorial" control for a moment before choosing to enter the action and claim instead narrative agency, something Grace Kelly (as Lisa) is not allowed to do since she is "directed" by Jefferies to enter the action in Thorwald's apartment.

Pepa enters the action by going directly to the telephone booth outside the building, once again to check her messages in the chance that Iván may have called. Of course, he hasn't, but then the telephone booth shakes and rattles violently and noisily, startling Pepa inside the booth. Pepa turns around desperately seeking the reason for the booth's sudden violence, and the medium shot of her turning around in the booth, the noise, the shaking, and the rattling are clear references to Melanie Daniels (Tippi Hedren) in the phone booth in *The Birds.* It turns out that, angry at her son's apparent intention to move out, Lucía throws the suitcase he was packing out the window and it falls on top of the phone booth. Some articles fall out of the suitcase and Pepa comes out to help Carlos and Marisa pick them up. Pepa finds a photograph of Carlos and Iván together, thus discovering their relationship. The introduction of the *Birds* reference is significant since that film, like *Psycho,* which Almodóvar had already cited, also presents the problem of an unresolved mother/son oedipal conflict as the reason for the punishment of the heroine. In his conversation about *The Birds* with François Truffaut, Hitchcock stated that the film was supposed to be the story of "a possessive mother" and that "her love for her son dominated all of her other emotions" (Truffaut 291–92). Carlos in *Women on the Verge of a Nervous Breakdown* shows signs of anxiety (his insistent stuttering) and like Norman Bates in *Psycho* and Marnie Edgar in *Marnie,* his relationship with his mother provokes his symptoms. But Carlos's mother, Lucía, is also troubled, and like Mrs. Brenner (Jessica Tandy) in *The Birds* and Mrs. Edgar (Louise Latham) in *Marnie,* she loses control of her emotions with the threat of her child's departure, which leads to a "hysterical" reaction (Horwitz 279).

After the chance meeting with Carlos, with whom Pepa eventually develops a pseudomaternal bond, she returns home and again confronts the answering machine. But as always, the message she is expecting has not come in. Instead there are repeated calls from her friend Candela. Exasperated, Pepa yanks out the telephone and throws it out the window, mimicking Lucía's hysterical action. Candela arrives, desperately in need of Pepa's help, but Pepa goes out again to look for Iván on the street. Coincidentally, Iván's son, Carlos and his girlfriend Marisa arrive to look at the apartment, now for rent. Once the action is contained in the apartment set, Pepa returns from the street and Almodóvar stages the first of two interior sequences in Pepa's apartment that occur in real time, like Hitchcock's *Rope*. The editing structure in Almodóvar's sequence does not conform to the complexity and claustrophobia of Hitchcock's experiment. However, the single-set locale, real-time action, theatrical mise-en-scène, and eventually the presence of a "body," clearly imitate the spatial, temporal, and narrative continuity of *Rope*. In the two separate sequences inside Pepa's apartment, the visual and thematic references to *Rope, Vertigo,* and *Spellbound* follow each other and eventually converge as the story itself takes on the Hitchcockian quality of a thriller about a terrorist plot.

Initially, Candela, desperate to talk to Pepa but incapable of getting her attention now that Iván's son is present, goes out to the terrace and tries to jump off the balcony. Suddenly repentant, Candela holds on to the railing screaming for help. Certainly, the scene is reminiscent of Scottie at the beginning of *Vertigo* hanging from the ledge of the building. Candela is seen from above in a medium close-up that reveals her hands in the foreground, her face, and the depth and danger of the possible fall. As in *Vertigo*, Candela is the victim of a traumatic situation (with her terrorist boyfriend) that in this case leads to her momentary suicide attempt. After helping Candela climb back up with the help of Carlos and Marisa, Pepa listens to Candela's story about the terrorist, prescribes her own tranquilizers to Candela, and goes out to talk to a "feminist" lawyer about Candela's problem. Carlos and Marisa have become involved in the action when Marisa accidentally drinks some of Pepa's spiked gazpacho (which contains "twenty-five or thirty" sleeping pills) and passes out in a profound sleep. Marisa thus becomes the "corpse" of this *Rope* situation, and like the dead man in that film, her body remains in the background of the action until the plot is fully resolved.

While Pepa is away speaking with the lawyer, who is, unbeknownst to Pepa, Iván's new girlfriend Paulina Morales, Carlos and Candela at the apartment discuss the Shiite men's plot to kidnap the airplane leaving that night for Stockholm. Pepa's visit to Paulina allows for the only ellipsis in the time of the story between the two sequences. Meanwhile at the apartment, Carlos, who has fixed the telephone, makes an anonymous call to the police to report the terrorist plot. Soon Pepa returns after her failed attempt to get Paulina interested in Candela's "case." Angry about a new missed call from Iván, she yanks the telephone out again and throws it out the window, and the second "real-time" sequence in Pepa's apartment begins. The sequence retakes the *Rope* motif, and as time passes by the Madrid skyline in the background slightly changes its light pattern, from warm sunny gold to dusk-red to cool blues, indicating the passage of time and the arrival of the evening hours. Also, like the oblivious dinner guests in *Rope*, Lucía arrives at Pepa's apartment accompanied by two plainclothes policemen who have traced Carlos's call back to Pepa's. The party is completed when the telephone repairman, who had been called early in the morning, also arrives. An interrogation follows with Pepa, Lucía, the policemen, Carlos, and Candela discussing the telephone call. Pepa explains that the telephone has been reported broken since the morning, so the tip about the plane hijacking could not have come from there. The "guests" are all offered a glass of Pepa's gazpacho. Holding her glass carefully (knowing of its sedative properties), Pepa finally ties up the loose ends of the plot: she realizes that Iván is leaving for Stockholm with Paulina (having seen the plane tickets in the lawyer's office) and that the Shiites coincidentally plan to hijack the very same airplane. Like James Stewart in *Rope*, Pepa comes to a plot-solving epiphany.

The single set, real time, and Marisa's "corpse" in the background of the action emphasize the *Rope* reference, which is then intersected by *Spellbound*. The policemen, the repairman, Carlos, and Candela quickly react to the drugged gazpacho and begin to fall asleep, but neither Lucía nor Pepa drink. Lucía runs across the room and picks up the policemen's guns, and points them both at Pepa. Lucía confesses to her insanity, and to how she pretended to be cured in order to get out of the mental institution and kill Iván. Her glass in one hand, a gun in the other, Lucía says to Pepa, "Now, let's drink." She raises her glass and the gun. A shot of both objects shows the gun barrel in a tight close-up as at the end of *Spellbound* when the murderous psychiatrist, Dr. Murchison (Leo G. Carroll) points the gun at himself and shoots in a similarly composed shot. Here too, the topics are amnesia (which Lucía has also suffered), insanity, and criminality (Lucía's). Also like Dr. Edwardes (Gregory Peck) in *Spellbound,* Lucía pretends to be "cured" to escape the asylum. Almodóvar's shot contains the two gazpacho glasses, which take on the place of the similarly drugged milk glass in *Spellbound* that Professor Brulov (Michael Chekhov) offers to Gregory Peck. As in *Notorious* and *Spellbound,* a glass of some harmless liquid easily transforms into something else, something dangerous: poison or sedatives. In *Women on the Verge* Almodóvar even copies the shot of the glass of milk in extreme close-up (through which we see the intended "victim") substituting the blood-red gazpacho for the milk.

The significance of the *Spellbound, Rope, The Birds,* and *Vertigo* citations in this sequence condenses and explains the function Hitchcock serves in Almodóvar's cinema as a whole and in *Women on the Verge of a Nervous Breakdown* in particular. Almodóvar's films tend to revise and exploit the theme of traumatic relationships between men and women and between parents and children, because Spanish cinema after the 1970s practices a reversal of the oedipal scenario, classic in Hitchcock, to suggest the need to resolve the traumatic past of the nation, symbolized by the absence of a "strong" father and the presence of unstable mothers (Kinder 198–200). *Psycho* and *The Birds* give the characters in *Women on the Verge* a point of reference for signification that mediates the oedipal relationship through what is already a recognized cinematic allusion. *Rope* and *Vertigo* emphasize that link to Hitchcock with direct formal references (to lighting, composition, and temporal-spatial continuity). *Spellbound* emphasizes both the need for a psychiatric solution and the ineffectiveness of that very solution, since Lucía, like Dr. Edwardes, is a psychiatric "impostor" of sorts, and like Dr. Murchison, a potential murderer.

The gazpacho standoff between Lucía and Pepa ends when the former splashes the spicy drink on Pepa's face, blinding her momentarily, and then at gunpoint hijacks Pepa's biker neighbor to drive her to the airport. The film's climactic sequence is a frantic pursuit as Lucía rushes to the airport to kill Iván while Pepa follows her in a taxi to prevent it. The race is made even more dramatic by the formal retention of the real-time structure: it continues the sequence begun upon the reunion of Pepa, Candela, Marisa, and Carlos some thirty-two minutes before. We ride with them from Pepa's apartment on Montalbán Street to Madrid Barajas Airport. As in *Rope* and partly in *Psycho*—where the entirety of the acquaintanceship between Norman Bates and Marion Crane is contained within one temporary continuous sequence that is only briefly interrupted during Norman's drive to the pond with Marion's whole life stuffed in the trunk—the insistence on real time grants the entire sequence realism, intimacy, and a strong sense of identification. The most disturbing effect in *Psycho* is certainly Marion's death, not just because of its violence, but because of the time, effort, and formal elements invested in building identification with her before she is brutally and abruptly taken away. These strategies include her imagined scenario about the discovery of her crime (which we hear in voice-over as she drives) juxtaposed with the shots of the empty road, and the candid reactions that we see on her face (in direct close-up) as she drives to her "private island," or rather to the Bates Motel. To cement that sense of identification that will make Marion's death even more disorienting for the cinematic spectator, Hitchcock retains the "real time" of the entire Marion/Norman meeting. Although Hitchcock dismisses his formal experiment in *Rope* as "a stunt," the continuity of time and space in that movie also underscores the sense of danger, and, upon the arrival of James Stewart, the inevitability of its own resolution (Truffaut 179). Equally in *Psycho,* the temporal containment of Marion and Norman's entire meeting in a single thirty-two minute sequence has the effect of underscoring the sense of intimacy. In *Women on the Verge of a Nervous Breakdown,* Almodóvar's staging of Pepa's discovery and resolution of the "plots" (both Iván's and the Shiite terrorists') in "real time" equally allows for the character's trajectory to be completely rounded; we see Pepa go from the "verge" of insanity, from the frantic desperation of a jilted lover, into the role of a full-fledged heroine. Unlike the Hitchcock heroines Pepa resembles, Marion Crane or Judy/Madeleine (Kim Novak) in *Vertigo,* who, writes Lesley Brill, breakdown or "shatter . . . their personal coherence," becoming inarticulate as they swirl into their own "traps," Pepa's dramatic arc leads her from drug-induced incoherence, heartbreak, and desperation to redemption, regeneration, the assertion of her subjectivity and desire, and the satisfying closure of her unresolved narrative (227).

At the airport, as in many Hitchcock endings, a last-minute resolution seems less satisfying than the MacGuffin itself: the sequence involves a motorcycle/car chase, a crazy woman with two guns, and a thwarted terrorist plot. Pepa prevents Lucía from killing Iván, the crazy woman is quickly arrested after missing one shot, the flight to Stockholm is saved, and almost as an afterthought Pepa finally has the conversation with Iván that serves as the main narrative pretext. She informs him that she only wanted to speak to him, and that she now wants nothing to do with him, not even revealing that she is pregnant. Like in *Spellbound* and even *Rebecca,* the woman's love and partial sacrifice saves the troubled man from death or the law (and the "madness" of the ex-wife). But the climax turns out to be improbably elusive (we don't even learn the fate of the Shiite terrorists), and Pepa emerges from the "verge" to reconstitute herself, reconstruct her family, and rebuild her whole life.

In the end Pepa returns home, her apartment cluttered with the sleeping policemen, Carlos, Candela, Marisa, and the telephone repairman. In the background, the *Rope*-style skyline is now darkened, unrealistically compressing several Madrid landmarks. Pepa decides to keep the apartment, because she says she "loves the view," while we hear her birds, now a homey sound, in the background. Marisa, finally awakened from her drugged sleep, becomes the first person to hear Pepa's news about her pregnancy. The two women bond over the revelation, and Marisa confesses she had an erotic, orgasm-inducing dream during her sleep, which has made her a different woman. "I was a virgin when I walked through that door this morning, now I'm not sure I am," she announces. Maternity and sexuality are resolved in the epilogue. These two topics are initially the cause of the women's "troubles" and the mediating forces that repress Hitchcock's heroines (Marion Crane, Marnie Edgar, Melanie Daniels, Constance in *Spellbound,* and others), but in *Women on the Verge* they become ultimately liberating. The greatest revision of Hitchcock's themes in *Women on the Verge of a Nervous Breakdown* is that Almodóvar's heroine does not cross from the "verge" into full-blown hysteria, or dementia, or death, for that matter. Out of the chaos of her relationships and the shadow of her past, through a Hitchcockian crucible, Pepa emerges at the end as a well-adjusted, socially and psychologically functional woman.

By Way of Conclusion: "Curing the Disease of the Past"

We all go a little mad sometimes.

—NORMAN BATES

In his book *The Hitchcock Romance: Love and Irony in Hitchcock's Films,* Lesley Brill argues that many of Hitchcock's characters are victims of the "traps" of their own past (as Norman would say), inevitably and fatally paying for their own and their parents' crimes and sins. In reference to *Vertigo* and *Psycho* (but applicable to other characters), Brill writes that:

> The central figures [in Hitchcock's films] struggle to understand and resolve destructive personal histories . . . They fail. Their defeats reflect the unforgiving necessities of Hitchcockian tragic irony . . . Retribution replaces forgiveness. Confusion and ambiguity baffle resolution. [The] films give centrality to human illness and decay, not healing . . . [T]he disease of the past is incurable . . ." (200)

Pedro Almodóvar's films since 1980, as many critics and historians of Spanish cinema have argued in the last two decades, are centered on the trauma of

Spain's history since 1936, presenting a specifically Spanish strain of the "disease of the past." In Almodóvar's films, characters are forced to confront the nation's mistakes under Franco (1936–1975) that eventually led to the bumpy road into redemocratization in the 1980s. While Almodóvar's early films began as irreverent satires of Spanish national history, cultural definition, politics, and social and sexual relations (*Labyrinth of Passion, What Have I Done to Deserve This?,* and *Matador,* for example), his later films (beginning with *The Law of Desire* and *Women on the Verge*) rehearse more positive, optimistic views of the nation's psychological forecast without ignoring or trivializing its troubled origins. The trauma of the past, expressed as stressed, criminal, incestuous, or improbable relations between parents and children, mental patients, criminal nuns, or serial killers (in *Labyrinth of Passion* and *What Have I Done, Dark Habits,* and *Matador,* respectively) ultimately leads to emotional and, by extension, psychological "healing" in *Women on the Verge, Tie Me Up! Tie Me Down!, High Heels, The Flower of My Secret,* and *All About My Mother* (Del Pino 170, Acevedo-Muñoz 38). But most importantly, in Almodóvar's films "the disease of the past" is curable, and must be cured, because on its healing rests the stability and survival of the nation. Almodóvar's films, as Alejandro Yarza argues, are known for articulating Spanishness from a "camp" perspective, reappropriating cultural and historical symbols that had been adopted in Franco's Spain and "recycling" them in order to deconstruct, as a form of therapy, the mechanisms of cultural and religious repression.

In *Women on the Verge of a Nervous Breakdown* Almodóvar allegorically extends his treatment of the national trauma into the convergence of generic instability (in this case mainly between Hitchcock's thrillers and Sirk's melodramas) with the stabilizing presence of Hitchcock as intertext. Hitchcock citations in *Women on the Verge of a Nervous Breakdown* serve to underscore the typical excesses of melodrama. Similar to Almodóvar's adoption of Joseph L. Mankiewicz's *All About Eve,* Tennessee Williams' *A Streetcar Named Desire,* and Elia Kazan's film version of the Williams play in *All About My Mother,* the Hitchcock citations in *Women on the Verge* become symptomatic of the characters' emotional trajectory. Furthermore, Almodóvar adopts Hitchcock as part of his own nationalist discourse. As I have argued elsewhere, Almodóvar's use of generic instability can be seen as a way of referring to the nation's process of coming to terms with its own cultural complexity and self-recognition as a rich, multicultural, even transnational space. *All About My Mother* settles ultimately as melodrama, reconstituting the national family and offering the promise of a new, redefined and redeemed social and cultural construct. In *Women on the Verge* Almodóvar already attempts to build stability and consensus out of the film's chaos. In this case, however, even before treating the nation as a generic hybrid, Almodóvar goes directly to the characters' psychological traumas, and with the help of the multiple insistent yet revisionist Hitchcock citations, allusions, and references, he explores the nation's "disease of the past." Unlike the Hitchcock characters to whom they refer, however, Almodóvar's women remain "on the verge" of insanity. With the exception of the unstable "Mother" (a character Almodóvar explores in *Matador* and *High Heels* as well), Pepa and the others ultimately reach some emotional stability. Relationships between mothers and their children are a recurring motif in Hitchcock's films, but they point to "personal" problems of identity and sexuality. Almodóvar mediates the same themes through Hitchcock, but his attention to identity and the family is allegorical of the nation's process of reconstitution and recovery.

At the end of *Women on the Verge of a Nervous Breakdown* Lucía, the unstable mother, asks to be taken back to the mental hospital where she belongs, after her failed assassination attempt of her ex-husband. Unlike Norman Bates, for whom the idea of sending Mother "someplace" is a threat to everything his psychotic mind believes to be true, in *Women on the Verge*, it is acceptable to put the crazy woman, the one who is "beyond the verge," away so that maybe the others can recover from the effects of repression. In Almodóvar's case, of course, "repression" is as much political as it is sexual, and its resolution or containment is good for the individual and the collective mind. Hitchcock's contribution to Almodóvar's films, especially *Women on the Verge of a Nervous Breakdown* (but also *High Heels, Kika, Live Flesh, Talk to Her*), is that it allows for a kind of cinematic shorthand: every Hitchcock moment in *Women on the Verge* deals with the psychological and sexual traumas of desire and repression, and their conflict with the law. But Almodóvar's revision of those moments denies the fatal implications or the ironic distance of how those relations are presented and resolved (or unresolved) in Hitchcock's films. On the contrary, Almodóvar suggests that even though "we all go a little mad sometimes," the "disease of the past" can be cured, or at least neutralized by understanding that instability (formal, narrative, generic) can be, paradoxically, a redeeming force.

Works Cited

Acevedo-Muñoz, Ernesto R. "The Body and Spain: Pedro Almodóvar's *All About My Mother*." *Quarterly Review of Film and Video* 21, no. 1.

———. Review of Alejandro Yarza, *A Cannibal in Madrid: Camp Sensibility and the Recy-*

cling of History in the Films of Pedro Almodóvar (Madrid: Ediciones Libertarias, 1999) in *Anales de la literatura española contemporánea* 26, no. 2 (2001): 271–73.

Almodóvar, Pedro. *Almodóvar on Almodóvar*. Frédéric Strauss, ed. Yves Baignères, trans. London: Faber and Faber, 1996.

———. *Patty Diphusa and Other Writings*. London: Faber and Faber, 1992.

———. Interview with Annette Insdorf, January 10, 2000, Columbia Tri Star DVD, 2000.

Bellour, Raymond. "Psychosis, Neurosis, Perversion" in *A Hitchcock Reader*. Marshall Deutelbaum and Leland Poague, eds. Ames, IA: Iowa State University Press, 1986, 311–31.

Brill, Lesley. *The Hitchcock Romance*. Princeton, NJ: Princeton University Press, 1988.

Del Pino, José M. "La tradición permanente: apuntes sobre casticismo y europeísmo en los fines de siglo" in *Nuevas perspectivas sobre el '98*. John P. Gabrielle, ed. Madrid: Iberoamericana, 1999, 161–70.

D'Lugo, Marvin. "Almodóvar's City of Desire." *Quarterly Review of Film and Video* 13 (1991): 47–65.

Horwitz, Margaret M. "*The Birds:* A Mother's Love" in *A Hitchcock Reader*. Marshall Deutelbaum and Leland Poague, eds. Ames, IA: Iowa State University Press, 1986, 279–87.

Kinder, Marsha. *Blood Cinema: The Reconstruction of National Identity in Spain*. Berkeley: University of California Press, 1993.

Lawrence, Amy. *Echo and Narcissus: Women's Voices in Classical Hollywood Cinema*. Berkeley: University of California Press, 1991.

Petro, Patrice. "Rematerializing the Vanishing 'Lady': Feminism, Hitchcock and Interpretation," in *A Hitchcock Reader*. Marshall Deutelbaum and Leland Poague, eds. Ames, IA: Iowa State University Press, 1986, 122–33.

Rothman, William. *Hitchcock: The Murderous Gaze*. Cambridge: Harvard University Press, 1982.

Smith, Paul, J. *Desire Unlimited: The Cinema of Pedro Almodóvar*. London: Verso, 1999.

Stam, Robert, and Roberta Pearson. "Hitchcock's *Rear Window:* Reflexivity and the Critique of Voyeurism" in *A Hitchcock Reader*. Marshall Deutelbaum and Leland Poague, eds. Ames, IA: Iowa State University Press, 1986, 193–206.

Truffaut, François. *Hitchcock/Truffaut*. New York: Simon and Schuster, 1984.

Williams, Linda. *Figures of Desire: A Theory and Analysis of Surrealist Film*. Berkeley: University of California Press, 1992.

Wood, Robin. "*Strangers on a Train*" in *A Hitchcock Reader*. Marshall Deutelbaum and Leland Poague, eds. Ames, IA: Iowa State University Press, 1986, 170–81.

Yarza, Alejandro. *Un caníbal en Madrid: la sensibilidad camp y el reciclaje de la historia en el cine de Pedro Almodóvar*. Madrid: Ediciones Libertarias, 1999.

"Knowing Too Much" about Hitchcock
The Genesis of the Italian *Giallo*

Philippe Met

Enigmatic childhood trauma flashbacks; the fetishistic ritual of black gloved hands getting ready for the kill; point-of-view shots of a faceless murderer wearing a shiny trench coat; the flash of a blade in the dark (be it a knife, a razor, a meat cleaver, or a hatchet); scantily clad "scream queens" being stalked and subjected to shocking and sadistic acts of violence; a morally decadent and sexually deviant upper-class milieu; an inept local police force and an eye witness as impotent amateur sleuth; a deleterious atmosphere of rampant suspicion; an abundance of red herrings and twist endings (that not too infrequently lapse into non sequiturs); a baroque or mannerist use of lighting and color. Short of cohering into an elegant, formal definition, all of the above feature prominently amongst the quasi-formulaic trademarks of the *giallo*, a hybrid, horror-meets-crime (sub)genre that emerged in early 1960s Italy. "Giallo" is Italian for yellow, in reference to the distinctive color of the dust jackets used for a collection of lurid crime pulp novels that Mondadori started to publish in 1929. Not unlike the development of the *série noire* in post–World War II France, these page-turning whodunits were first translated and adapted from the English but increasingly penned by native authors.

Fast-forward to the late 1950s (and well into the 1970s): in its filmic avatar, the giallo can be regarded as an integral part of a certain golden age of Italian genre cinema. Alongside such subcategories as peplums (or sword-and-sandal epics), supernatural Gothic horror, spaghetti westerns, cannibal or zombie films, mondo movies or shockumentaries, nunsploitation and the like, it arguably helped delineate and consolidate the popular underside of Italian cinema: what its numerous detractors prefer to term its "sleazy" or "exploitative" underbelly; what one might qualify, more polemically, as the dark secret harbored behind a respectable art-house façade flaunting its officially sanctioned neorealism. In spite of the advent of DVD facilitating access to an ever increasing number of the actual films (hitherto available only on murky bootleg tapes for the most part) and spawning renewed interest in the genre at large (among fans, if not scholars), the "founding fathers" and major players of the giallo are still conspicuously absent from most of today's encyclopedias and dictionaries of Italian film, and the generic constellation itself does not appear to be worthy of an autonomous entry.

Admittedly, the issue is to a degree compounded by existing discrepancies of a semantic or taxonomic nature. It is for instance ironic to note that in the very country where it originated, the *all'italiana* specificity of the genre is more often than not subsumed by and diluted into a much broader understanding of the giallo designation as coextensive with crime cinema, thereby cutting across national boundaries and the typological spectrum (detection, suspense, noir, thriller, procedural, German *krimi,* French *polar,* etc).[1] Stateside, on the other hand, the giallo undeniably retains its original flavor, and whether one can viably and legitimately stretch it to create an "American giallo" label is a seriously, indeed hotly, debated issue, most notably in fannish circles. In that respect, Brian De Palma's *Dressed to Kill* (1980) and Paul Verhoeven's *Basic Instinct* (1992) are two of the usual suspects, both being equally in Alfred Hitchcock's debt as well; lesser-known candidates would include a low-budget chiller like Alfred Sole's *Alice, Sweet Alice* (aka *Communion,* 1976). This sort of immediate, visible connection is not, however, unaccompanied by a certain amount of denial or distraction at times. Sole, for one, recognizes only Hitchcock and Nicolas Roeg as direct models for the visual feel of his film.[2] Based on a short story by Daphne du Maurier—a regular source of inspiration for Hitchcock, from *Jamaica Inn* (1939) to *Rebecca* (1940) and *The Birds* (1963)—and set in Venice, Roeg's 1973 cult classic, *Don't Look Now,* is a brilliant hybridization of art and horror. As such, it clearly intersects with the giallo, and indeed went on to influence several later Italian thrillers.[3] Sole, however, claims he had never seen any of Dario Argento's films, for example, at the time, and curiously represses the unmistakable traits of the genre shared by a film that, to this day, is possibly the single most "gialloesque" American film (as well as a definite one-off for the filmmaker) as it uses most of the motifs in the repertoire, including a warped sense of humor and a less-than-flattering depiction of religion within the context of a Catholic community in New Jersey. In the case of De Palma, the all-too-obvious Hitchcockian overtones of his films might be hiding more covert giallo undertones which have rarely been considered by scholars of his oeuvre or by himself, in part, because of his difficult rapport with Argento, who is otherwise on friendly—and collaborative—terms with such American genre directors as George A. Romero, John Carpenter, and John Landis.

Just as for the varying definitional confines of the giallo, an ironic reversal in terms of film history is here perceptible concerning a national brand of genre cinema which has been much maligned in the past and remains largely discredited today for its exploitative tactics and derivative modi operandi. In all fairness, this sort of aspersion is not entirely unjustified. To mention but one glaring example, some gialli have tended to piggyback unscrupulously on successive box-office hits from across the Atlantic. *The Exorcist* (1973) thus became a notorious template for countless and increasingly cheap imitations. Irrespective of one's appreciation of William Friedkin's supernatural blockbuster, the distinction between innovation and formula is crucially important. Related issues would include: high art vs. commercial filmmaking, auteurism vs. opportunism, citational homage vs. crass plagiarism, creative genius vs. uninspired epigones, etc. Such a convenient construct of binary logic must of necessity be at the core of this essay (as it aims to simultaneously weave and untangle a possible intertextual web around Hitchcock and the giallo) while stretching far beyond its limits, especially if one considers that these presuppositions are regularly questioned, if not actively transgressed, by the overlapping of porous provinces of the world of cinema. This in turn is aligned with a tradition of genre hybridity in Italian popular cinema which has always strived to appeal to culturally and geographically diversified audiences: more urban and educated in the north, more rural and entertainment-oriented in the south, to fall back on somewhat schematic dichotomies. A couple of examples involving Mario Bava and Dario Argento, the two foremost giallo directors (not to mention, the historical founders of the genre), will suffice to give a more specific sense of such crisscrossing and/or cross-fertilization. After the fashion of the angry young men of the French New Wave, only about a decade later Argento started out as a film critic before graduating to screenwriting (his main achievement in that sole capacity is a collaboration with Bernardo Bertolucci and Sergio Leone on *Once Upon a Time in the West*, 1968) and, soon after, helming his first directorial effort, *The Bird with the Crystal Plumage* (*L'Uccello dalle piume di cristallo*, 1969), which initiated an ongoing concern throughout his career with combining genre trappings or peculiarities and art-house sensibilities or discourses. Similarly, Mario Bava's *Lisa and the Devil* (*Lisa e il diavolo*, 1972) is as much a surreal, oneiric art film as a Euro-horror opus. On a more anecdotal, albeit related, note, his *Blood and Black Lace* (*Sei Donne per l'assassino*, 1964), arguably the first cinematic giallo worthy of the name, was coproduced by Georges de Beauregard, better known for his long-standing involvement with auteur cinema, most notably that of the *nouvelle vague*. It is even less of a coincidence that Argento picked Luciano Tovoli, who had previously served as cinematographer on Antonioni's *The Passenger* (*Professione: Reporter,* 1975), to shoot his own masterpiece in the genre, *Deep Red* (*Profondo Rosso,* 1975), and David Hemmings, who had earlier achieved international stardom in *Blow-Up* (1966), to lead his cast. Part art film, part psychological thriller,[4] *Blow-Up* is a classic case of artistic miscegenation and revolves on visual hermeneutics, which profoundly innervated Argento's effort. The growing opacity and indecipherability of the blown-up photographic image in Antonioni's film, the ultimately elusive meaning of reality, give way to optical and spectatorial riddles, successfully solved *in fine* in Argento's gialli: telling the attacker and his/her victim apart in the visually ambiguous *tableau vivant* that opens *The Bird with the Crystal Plumage* as the protagonist, trapped behind the glass door of an art gallery, watches on helplessly; distinguishing a painted portrait from the reflection of the murderer's face in a wall mirror in *Deep Red*. Legend also has it that the viewing of *Blow-Up* prompted Hitchcock to remark, in a rare moment of apparent humbleness, that "the Italians [were] years ahead of [him]." Although it is highly doubtful that Sir Alfred ever saw Bava's 1964 *Blood and Black Lace,* could his words still be read as a prophetic pronouncement about the evolution of the giallo as a genre as well?

Equally at ease with opera and comics,[5] the art of statuary and fashion design, estheticism and sleaze, realistic violence and abstract stylization, the world of the giallo is, as we have just seen, a perfect illustration of the degree of arbitrariness, ambiguity, instability, or worse, fallacy, inherent in any given generic categorization, theoretical systematization, or notional definition. What are we then to make of much bandied appellations like "The Hitchcock of Cinecittà" or "The Italian Hitchcock" (to say nothing of the even more dubious honor received from denominations like "The Ravioli Hitchcock" and "The Italian Would-Be Hitchcock"),[6] indistinctly applied by many a critic to Mario Bava, the indisputable albeit neglected initiator of the giallo on celluloid, and Dario Argento, his putative spiritual heir and the most illustrious continuator (as well as enricher and diversifier) of the genre? Are we to dismiss them disdainfully as mere gimmicks—unabashedly commercial, grossly sensationalist, and largely gratuitous—or perhaps as the combined result of irresistible gravitation towards Hollywood-centric normativity and reverent gesturing (or is it mostly lip service?) toward an exclusive coterie of iconic yet entertaining, canonized yet "sellable" auteurs where Hitchcock has long enjoyed prime membership? Separated by a comparable generation gap but perhaps less clearly affiliated than Bava and Argento, French directors Henri-Georges Clouzot and Claude Chabrol have after all also been successively hailed as "The Gallic Hitchcock"—and not without some reason. Rumor has it that with *Diabolique* (*Les Diaboliques,* 1955) Clouzot beat Hitchcock to the copyrights of "Celle qui n'était plus," a detective story authored by partners-in-literary-crime Pierre Boileau and Thomas Narcejac. After finding out about Hitchcock's earlier intentions, the French duettists proceeded to write their next thriller in a similar vein and with the master of suspense in mind, and sure enough *D'entre les morts* became *Vertigo* (1958) on the silver screen.[7] As for Chabrol, he has always professed his profound admiration for Hitchcock (Fritz Lang being a close contender) and aspired to emulate him. It should therefore come as no surprise that he cowrote a groundbreaking book-length study of Hitchcock's oeuvre in 1957 with fellow *Cahiers du cinéma* critic Eric Rohmer, patterned his directorial debut, *Le Beau Serge* (1958) on *Shadow of a Doubt* (1953), and went on to work primarily, unlike the other founding figures of the New Wave movement, in the thriller vein throughout his career, liberally reusing such key Hitchcockian motifs as the transference of guilt and/or identity, shared secrets, coincidence, and suspicion, or voyeuristic identification.

Are we then to infer that, just as for time-honored, if time-worn, proverbs or adages, an ounce of truth and objectivity can be found in such seemingly artificial approximations and potentially reductive correlations, provided, however, that one does not read them too literally? Here again, the confines of this essay can hardly accommodate an in-depth analysis of what might constitute the definition of full-blown intertextuality, or the exact terms of established filiation, and therefore warrant a claim of legacy or influence: elective affinities, for instance, as opposed to fortuitous points of contact; recurring or quasi-systematic, long-term linkage (in terms of narrative, style, thematics or visuals), rather than discrete reminiscences, isolated allusions or tenuous touches; formal traces, explicit markers, or ostensible signs, more than just an impressionistic, nebulous cluster of potential clues. For illustrative purposes, one might observe that echoes of *Vertigo* in Rohmer's *Ma nuit chez Maud* (1969) (the detective tailing a mysterious woman) or Truffaut's *Une belle fille comme moi* (1972) (the clock tower murder) do not suffice to make those films or their directors Hitchcockian per se, regardless of the open fervor of the two Young Turks of the *nouvelle vague* for their older British counterpart. The dynamics of a "meaningful," lasting connection with a given model (here the Hitchcockian archetype), as well as the modalities of its inscription, therefore imply a recognizable or visible modicum of durability, consistency, and recurrence. In that respect, Mario Bava and Dario Argento are precisely two eloquent, if distinct, cases in point, as the rest of this essay will now try to demonstrate.

Mario Bava is sadly long dead, and courtesy of a supreme and final twist of irony in a notoriously ill-fated career, his passing away in 1980 was completely eclipsed by none other than Hitchcock's three days later! Not that the Italian people were on the verge of declaring a day of national mourning for their own maestro to begin with. Whether he would have continued to worship at the Hitchcock shrine remains an open question, especially in view of the fact that the bulk of his output was hardly along giallo lines in the last decade of his life. Indeed, within a predominantly Gothic corpus, the Hitchcockian inspiration is foregrounded in essentially two of his films: *La Ragazza che sapeva troppo* (*The Girl Who Knew Too Much*, aka *The Evil Eye*, 1962) and *Il Rosso segno della follia* (*A Hatchet for the Honeymoon*, 1969). Although virtually devoid of any thematic or narrative link with *The Man Who Knew Too Much* (1934; remade in 1956), short of the "American(s) Abroad" trope, Bava's 1962 film flaunts in its very title a transparent reference to Hitchcock which elicited varying responses from one side of the Atlantic to the other. American International Pictures (AIP), distributor of *La Ragazza* (not to mention a multitude of other low-budget chillers) in the United States, felt so strongly about it that they senselessly changed it (as was their wont) to *The Evil Eye*, not without first drastically cutting and rescoring the entire film, supposedly for the benefit of their young matinee audiences. In late 1950s Italy, however, the prevailing sentiment—indeed, the main source of frustration—amongst genre directors like Mario Bava, Riccardo Freda, or Antonio Margheriti was that local audiences appeared to be instinctively skeptical or incredulous of any filmic attempt at anchoring horror or detection in a specifically Italian context, as if sun-drenched locales were little conducive to ghastly or ghostly storylines, and hot-blooded temperament scarcely receptive to gloomy or noir atmospheres.

In Freda's eyes, for instance, only British or American filmmakers (Hitchcock in particular) could obtain a willing suspension of disbelief from his compatriots.[8] After the commercial failure of *I Vampiri* (*The Devil's Commandment*, 1956), the first Italian horror film of the sound era (which Bava had to complete after Freda walked off the set) with proto-giallo ingredients already thrown into the mix, he went on to adopt an English-sounding pseudonym, Anthony Dawson, for enhanced "credibility." Not only did many of his fellow *filone* directors follow suit, but cast and crew were oftentimes similarly anglicized in credit titles. From there it was only a short step to the actual inscription of Hitchcock's name, even if purposely misspelled for obvious legal reasons, in the title of a film, under the leadership of Freda: *L'Orribile segreto del dottor Hichcock* (*The Horrible Dr. Hichcock*, 1962) whose eponymous protagonist would soon return to the screen, although played by a different actor, in an ostensible, more giallo-inflected sequel, *Lo Spettro* (*The Ghost*, 1963) (sometimes short for *Lo Spettro de Dr. Hichcock*). Despite Freda's later deemphasizing of this not-so-subtle allusion as less a personal tribute than a purely commercial gimmick concocted by his producer,[9] echoes of Hitchcock's corpus abound throughout *The Horrible Dr. Hichcock*, thanks in large part to Ernesto Gastaldi's script: from *Suspicion* (1941), with the poisoned glass of milk, to *Under Capricorn* (1949), with the skull that Cynthia, the persecuted heroine, finds in her bed. The most central reference nonetheless remains *Rebecca* (1940): taking a leaf out of Mrs. Danvers' book, Martha, the sinister housekeeper, proves to be insanely devoted to her master's first wife, whose unnerving portrait is also prominently featured in the manor, and the film similarly ends in a cathartic conflagration. Not to mention more "serious" and profound connections of a thematic or symbolic order, such as a necrophiliac form of *amour fou* that is perhaps reminiscent of *Vertigo*, or a shared fascination with the workings of scopophilia.[10]

Can the same be said of Bava's film on the basis of its equally overdetermined title, notwithstanding the director's own comment—typically part self-deprecatory, part tongue-in-cheek: "I thought it [*La Ragazza*] was far too preposterous. Perhaps it could have worked with James Stewart and Kim Novak, whereas I had . . . oh, well, I don't even remember their names"[11]? Flash-in-the-pan actresses or "B picture" regulars (Leticia Roman in the title role and John Saxon as the male lead, respectively) in *The Girl Who Knew Too Much*, a fascinating horror icon like Barbara Steele in the influential Gothic chiller *Black Sunday* (*La Maschera del demonio*, 1960), or subpar, best-forgotten performers in much of the rest of his filmography,[12] as opposed to internationally renowned A-list Hollywood stars gracing Hitchcock's vintage films—this is just one of many disparities between two directors who could hardly be further apart in terms of working conditions and environment. Throughout his career the Italian maestro also had to make the best of threadbare scripts, tight shooting schedules, last-minute improvisations and shoestring budgets. As a point of comparison regarding the last item alone, at around $150,000 at the very most, the typical cost for a Bava project was but a fraction of even a Hitchcock film like *Psycho* which, to the dismay of studio executives, the Master insisted on shooting for under a million dollars in order to "emulate" the low-budget (and usually fairly successful) horror productions of the day. That being said, Freda and many other Italian genre directors obviously had to face the same cohort of constraints and restraints that Bava did, as well as generally precarious production circumstances. Because he belongs to a later generation and his father produced, or helped produce, most of his films until his death, Dario Argento, on the other hand, was affected to a much lesser degree, and just as uncharacteristic of the genre are his repeated efforts, more often than not to little avail, to cast Hitchcockian actors. Although he managed to use Austrian actor Neggie Nalder, who played the part of the assassin in the 1956 remake of *The Man Who Knew Too Much*, in a similar capacity for a pursuit sequence in *The Bird with the Crystal Plumage*, he was unsuccessful in securing *Vertigo*'s Madeleine, Kim Novak, for the role of Adriana, the avenging, "headhunting" mother of *Trauma* (1993), which went instead to Piper Laurie, once considered for *Psycho*'s Marion Crane. A looping of the loop would most certainly include a mention of Maximilian, the necrophiliac, homicidal mama's boy of Bava's *Lisa and the Devil*, as the tailor-made role said to have been originally offered to *Psycho* star Anthony Perkins, who naturally turned it down.

The specificity of *The Girl Who Knew Too Much*, however, is that it may be seen today as a swan song for the Anglo-Saxon whodunit archetype (both epitomized and popularized by Hitchcock) and a proto-giallo in the history of Italian genre cinema, thereby actuating a shift of paradigms. Causation between the two aspects (the decline of ratiocination and mystery precipitating the advent of spectacle and gore) is indeed hardly questionable. If this film still retains a fairly linear investigative approach and keeps graphic violence to a minimum, the mechanics of suspense and detection—the search for truth—will soon take a backseat to the creation of an atmosphere of frantic fear and the aestheticized representation of physical aggression and sadistic acts—no later, as a matter of fact, than *Blood and Black Lace* in 1964, and perhaps nowhere more exemplarily. This is achieved through a succession of gruesome murder set pieces that seem to take on a "life" of their own, and a disturbingly intense one at that. The conventional narrative structure is thus streamlined and turned on its head to such a degree that only the flimsiest of connective tissue remains: the film is no longer plot-driven, but simply *driven* in a primal and literal sense, powered by the murderous impulses of its protagonists, *Blood and Black Lace* is also a pictorial, if perversely brutal, study in color scheme. Anticipating the slasher craze in the United States by a full decade,[13] the darkly humorous and deliriously offbeat *Bay of Blood*, aka *Twitch of the Death Nerve* (*Antefatto/Ecologia del delitto*, 1971) is similarly (de)structured around a series of incongruous vignettes or tableaux—hallucinatory and realistic, ecstatic and grisly, connected and disconnected. Its working title, *Reazione a catena* (i.e., "chain reaction") is highly symbolic of this form of narrative and thematic concatenation. Despite a total of no less than thirteen killings in this one film, and many more, one might add, in the subsequent string of unsurprisingly inept body-count riffs in the hands of hack directors, this process is not a mere mechanical, or *by the numbers,* dumbed-down version of the classical murder scene. Rather, it partakes of a flamboyant shattering or dissemination of the Hitchcockian thriller formula and, as such, frequently includes an exacerbated or radicalized treatment of the famous "MacGuffin," resulting in such a vertiginous proliferation of red herrings that virtually every single character becomes a potential suspect and sometimes turns out to be an actual murderer (and victim) playing his/her part in a vicious circle of mutual violence. Loosely based on Agatha Christie's *Ten Little Indians,* Bava's *Five Dolls for an August Moon* (*Cinque bambole per la luna d'agosto,* 1969) is another spectacular example of this paroxysmic mode. The "cloning" device is at times more oblique and unexpected, as when the attendees at a boxing convention in Argento's *The Bird with the Crystal Plumage* turn out to be all dressed in the same garish yellow jacket as the hired killer the protagonist has been chasing through the city streets and into a hotel conference room. It almost seems as if the entire sequence, a stylish albeit drawn-out game of hide-and-seek, were devised for the sake of that final visual pun.[14]

Alluding to the Alphabet Killer of *The Girl Who Knew Too Much,* presumably modeled on Agatha Christie's *The ABC Murders,* Tim Lucas wittily ends his liner notes for the DVD release of the film (Image Entertainment, 2000) on the most direct of lineages: "Hitchcock, Bava, Argento—it's as clear a progression as . . . ABC." Although one should generally be wary of any type of ex post facto logic seeking to bring out or reconstruct a perfectly coherent, neatly chronological and necessary progression, one cannot but note that the age-old tension between *imitatio* and *inventio* was at work again for Bava. Things were no different for Argento: prior to using his predecessor's *Blood and Black Lace* as a point of departure and letting all giallo hell break loose in his sumptuous *Deep Red,* he experimented with new aesthetic possibilities and intensely personal obsessions within the more subdued context and standard narrative of his feature debut, *The Bird with the Crystal Plumage,* a film based on a more or less Hitchcockian murder-witness-in-peril premise. In fact, one gets the distinct impression that for these artists, a self-reflexive and parodic take on a generic model was an absolute prerequisite in order for the innovative process whereby a (sub)genre is radically redefined and irreversibly recodified to be initiated and brought to fruition. Hence the self-ironic frame of *The Girl Who Knew Too Much:* as a sort of ultimate rhetorical pirouette, the

MacGuffin of the opening sequence—a pack of cigarettes suspected of being marijuana joints after the arrest for drug trafficking of the man Nora Davis had accepted them from—reappears at the close of the film. It retrospectively suggests the possibility of perceptual distortion (since Nora had smoked one of these cigarettes) and, as a corollary, calls into question the reality of the events she has witnessed. The film, which so far has been a permanent blend of melodrama, comic relief, and cheap scares à la *Haunted Spooks* or *The Cat and the Canary,* now concludes on a comedic note, putting a final twist on what is evidently a self-de(con)structing narrative: the discarded pack is picked up by an unsuspecting priest passing by. Paramount, however, are the presentation, right from the outset, of the heroine as an avid reader of hard-boiled detective stories, and the fact that the rest of the film is punctuated by a male-voiced narration of her inner thoughts. This gendering is not insignificant as it is redolent of the archetypal noir figure of the private eye as narrator and therefore implies that Nora is possibly crafting her own crime thriller as she goes along, liberally peppering it with such clichéd, two-dime chestnuts such as "The threatening door with its invisible hinges. The door that was forever locked." An unusual cameo by the director, reportedly added at AIP's request, further contributes to this distancing, *mise-en-abîme* effect: the portrait of Nora's late uncle leering at her from the wall is actually a photograph of Mario Bava himself sporting a fake mustache à la Dali—which implicitly reiterates the connection between avant-garde art and pulp fiction, between the genre of the giallo and voyeurism.

Not that self-irony is in any way limited to the early stages of Bava's career. Seven years later, *A Hatchet for the Honeymoon* is equally replete with touches of macabre irony, cruel visual puns, and tongue-in-cheek self-citations. John Harrington, a psychopathic fashion designer, is seen at night incinerating the dead body of his latest model-victim in a furnace in his hothouse (a decadent locale par excellence with its exotic flowers and lush vegetation, and as such evocative of deviant sexuality), under the watchful, peaceful eye of a turtle dove. The spine-tingling implications of this lugubrious contrast are immediately and fiercely reinforced when the camera cuts from the smoke coming out of the incinerator to toast burning at the breakfast table the following morning. A genuinely Hitchcockian moment arises when Harrington next turns against his own wife, Mildred: his fateful deed barely accomplished, the police inspector (a precursor to Columbo) and the fiancé of the missing model come knocking on his door. The protagonist is thus forced to leave Mildred in the throes of death and make conversation in the lobby as blood is slowly dripping from the victim's hand sticking through the grand staircase posts above their heads. Here again, the irony of the situation is sustained throughout the scene when the two visitors proceed to inquire about a female scream they heard from outside the house. By way of explanation John simply points them in the direction of a television set where a shocker is playing: Mario Bava aficionados are sure to recognize a black-and-white clip from his classic horror anthology *Black Sabbath* (*I tre volti della paura*, 1963): the "Wurdalak" episode starring Boris Karloff, to be exact!

As earlier notations in the present essay suggest, be they contrapuntal or analogous in nature, an assessment of Argento's relation to Hitchcock and the thriller genre must necessarily differ to some extent from Bava's. If the latter embraced the generic ebullience and effervescence of a past era (indeed, pioneering some of its modalities), the former is still very active today as he continues to carry the torch of the giallo (and, more largely, of Italian horror) almost single-handedly, be it in a director or producer capacity—with widely erratic results. In fact, many, including those among his fan base, would contend that he has been past his creative prime since at least the early 1990s, with the much reviled *Il Fantasma dell'opera* (*The Phantom of the Opera*, 1998) as a particularly disastrous low point. However, his latest feature films, *Non ho sonno* (*Sleepless*, 2001) and *Il Cartaio* (*The Card Player*, 2004), are a clear, if arguably flawed, attempt to revive the style of his 1970s gialli and jumpstart his flagging career in the process. At the time of writing, Argento was also shooting a TV movie to be part of a series for RAI (Italian state television) titled *Ti piace Hitchcock?* (*Do You Like Hitchcock?*). Replete with "fiendish bargains, double-cross, MacGuffins, and mistaken identity culled from plot ideas and themes contained in the entire Hitchcock back catalogue",[15] the action will be centered around a film student cramming for an exam on Sir Alfred's oeuvre. This long-overdue homage comes at a point when Argento, now in his mid-sixties, is perhaps less eager to return to form (which most of his admirers would take to mean, however unrealistically, reworking the magic of *Deep Red*) than to go back to his innermost roots in an effort to both come full circle and tie up loose ends, as it were. This will hopefully include the supernatural horror facet of Argento's filmography as well, since he is scheduled to complete at long last the "Three Mothers" trilogy, inaugurated by *Suspiria* (1977) and continued by *Inferno* (1978) over a quarter of a century ago. Despite Argento's avowed discomfort with the perennial "Italian Hitchcock" label, the project of *Ti piace Hitchcock?* seems to have been conceived more specifically in belated acknowledgment of the extent of his personal admiration for—and artistic debt to—the British master. By virtue of the film being an explicit tribute, a primarily self-referential, ludic exercise, it seems to preemptively defuse any renewed charge of mediocre derivation. Not content with promising to pack his film with nods—and potentially deceptive or confusing ones with regard to the whodunit plot—to most of Hitchcock's classic thrillers, Argento furthermore said he would for the occasion forego his baroque idiosyncrasies and, instead, carefully strive to emulate his model in terms of style and technique. This should extend from presentation (he plans on introducing the film in person in the style of *Alfred Hitchcock Presents,* a role he already successfully essayed for a 1972 TV series consisting of four mini-gialli, *Door into Darkness*)[16] to sound (he has commissioned "a typical Bernard Herrmann score") and camera design ("I'm relying more on dolly and crane shots rather than Steadicam because I'm going for Hitchcock's classical simplicity").[17]

All of this, of course, stands in stark contrast with Argento's trademark signature in the areas concerned: a certain degree of self-effacement or camera-shyness—except for the above TV presentations, a cameo appearance in another director's film (John Landis's *Innocent Blood,* 1992), and the anonymous inclusion of his knife-wielding arm or black-gloved hand in most of the murder sequences of his own opuses; the pulsating prog-rock music of the Italian group Goblin in some of his most influential films—starting with *Deep Red* and *Suspiria;* the killer's point-of-view shots—a technique that Argento obviously did not invent but perfected with stunning results, using it as a systematic, highly stylized, and ritualized cue years before Carpenter's *Halloween* (1978) and countless copycat hacks thereafter; the creation of breathtakingly intricate and sophisticated visual fireworks through the innovative use of pre-CGI high-tech equipment such as the famed Louma crane sequence in the recursive *Tenebrae* (*Tenebre,* 1982) where the camera pans over an entire three-storied house, in and out of windows, before giving us a glimpse of the murderer sneaking in, all in one extended yet fluid and uninterrupted movement.[18] Not that Hitchcock, a consummate master of cinematic ingenuity, was ever averse to technical invention and audacity. Witness, for instance, the celebrated tour de force in his penultimate film, *Frenzy* (1972), when the camera, after following the necktie killer and his newest soon-to-be victim to his apartment, tracks back from the closed door, down a winding flight of stairs, out of the building and into the street, and through the constant, heterogeneous flow of Covent Garden hawkers, pedestrians, and cars. An impressively seamless shot, were it not for a barely perceptible jump cut as a worker carrying what looks like a sack of potatoes on his shoulder passes through the frame. After upping the ante on onscreen violence with the first murder-rape scene, remarkably protracted and brutal, Hitchcock now seems to frustrate the voyeuristic drive of his viewers deliberately, albeit ambiguously. After all, the camera is perhaps not so much recoiling in horror from the unseen crime scene as stealthily withdrawing as would a co-conspirator of sorts. Or is it making a statement about the unabated presence of depravity right in the midst of everyday life? And if so, what is the exact nature of that statement: Cynical? Misanthropic? Disillusioned? Realistic? Generally, however, Hitchcock's approach is subdued and low-tech, while remaining every bit as effective, as in the case of a lightbulb hidden inside a glass of milk to make the latter glow ominously in *Suspicion* (1941) and the dizzying track-out zoom-in shot in *Vertigo*, clearly referenced in the staircase sequence at the Villa Graps in Mario Bava's supernatural Gothic chiller, *Kill, Baby, Kill* (*Operazione paura*, 1966). Or take the acclaimed storyboarding and editing of the shower scene in *Psycho* (1960) which showed relatively little in the way of graphic violence and nudity, despite numerous spectators, including censors before the film could even be released, claiming they had seen the victim's bare breast, or the blade penetrating her flesh when each flash cut is meant to feel like a stab of the knife. In a sense, the Hitchcock touch might be situated somewhere between the superb craftsmanship of a Mario Bava, who would literally work wonders with bits and pieces (glass mattes, color gels, and sundry makeshift devices), and the operatic or grand guignol flourishes, at times verging on hysteria, of a Dario Argento.[19]

Needless to say, in the eyes of many, this would serve as an oblique definition of Hitchcockian classicism, more or less equally removed from the all-too basic tricks of the trade (the actual handcrafting of visual trickery, the nitty-gritty confection of special effects in low-budget productions predating the computer age) on the one hand, and the allegedly over-the-top, crass, sensationalistic gesturing and ultimately vacuous posturing of the giallo output on the other. Conversely, this binary construct cannot but raise a number of objections. Firstly, a symmetrical and much more "genre-friendly" perspective could detect a definite streak of Italian "baroquization" of Hitchcockian formalism in the cream of the giallo crop—among its Argentoesque avatars, most noticeably. Far from being gratuitous or extranarrative as is too often suggested, including by well-disposed scholars like Gallant who describes it, in a rather unconvincingly contrived and convoluted fashion, as "a *frivolous* piece of cinematic virtuosity" whose sole purpose is "to draw attention to the process of signification: the presence of the camera, and its involvement in producing either progression or stasis,"[20] the previously mentioned Louma sequence in *Tenebrae*, for instance, is after all not so dissimilar to the staircase shot in *Frenzy*—just more extreme in duration and visibility (or intricacy).

Within the dual context of highly sexualized, gender-bending murdering and self-referential (or dare we say "postmodern"?) genre-bending deconstructing, it serves a dilatory purpose, voyeuristic and fetishistic in nature, and as such perhaps is more stimulating than frustrating—not unlike a perverted variety of foreplay deferring the release in the form of bloodshed. Besides, this putative *visual* razzle-dazzle paradoxically leads to an *aural* play between non-diegetic and diegetic music when the adrenaline-pumping soundtrack that Argento has turned into an integral part of the impact of his cinematic horror-mongering ever since his teaming up with Goblin (shades of Hitchcock's fruitful and long-lasting collaboration with Herrmann) turns out to originate from one of the characters' record player.

Secondly, with its unusually gritty emphasis on explicit violence—in and of itself a sign of the times, if not a response to the increasingly savage tone set by Italian thrillers since the mid/late 1960s—Hitchcock's *Frenzy* certainly transgresses the bipolar configuration mentioned above. That some critics were prompt to lambaste it as an unwelcome departure from the preferred aesthetics of understatement and restraint therefore comes as no surprise. Interestingly, this type of axiological dichotomy has traditionally dominated the reception of horror cinema per se (suggestion and ellipsis vs. spectacularization and overstatement; off-screen action vs. shock tactics), at least until *Psycho,* which represented a critical watershed and, arguably, a point of no return in the history of the genre, if only because of the aura of legitimacy cast by an acknowledged *auteur* pushing the envelope in terms of the taboo-breaking depiction of not just violence (situating horror in the everyday context of the family unit, and monstrosity inside the human psyche), but the body and bodily functions (Janet Leigh in a brassiere on a lunch-break tryst in a seedy hotel room; the toilet being shown and then flushed at the Bates Motel, etc.). If *Psycho* is undeniably the *mother* (pun intended) of modern cinematic horror at large,[21] its impact on the development of the giallo was a fortiori pivotal, not least because of the marked oedipality of Hitchcock's film. To put it in psychoanalytic terms, for proponents and practitioners of the burgeoning subgenre in Italy, the film as a whole came to carry the emblematic weight of a veritable *childhood trauma*—a complex manifestly allegorized by the narrative of *Psycho,* but foregrounded as early as in *Spellbound* (1945) and later revisited in *Marnie* (1964), for instance[22]—and the shower sequence in particular to be hypostasized and fetishized as a form of *primal scene*. It might first appear unwise to predicate an entire genre on the mere expansion, or compulsive repetition, of such an iconic detail,[23] no matter how much *mise-en-abîme* one wishes to ascribe to it. Tying in with a noticeable scopic motif (e.g., Norman voyeuristically eyeing his future prey through a concealed peep-hole in the wall as she disrobes) which will become a staple of Italian horror and reach its apex with Argento's *Opera*,[24] the first murder sequence in *Psycho* famously ends on a dissolve from Marion Crane's lifeless eye to the plughole, as if the entire film was centripetally sucked into this—its own—center, not unlike a vortex draining water and blood, drawing the viewer's gaze in and replicating the mesmerizing effect produced by the geometric, oddly psyche-delic patterns in *Vertigo*'s title sequence. Self-reflexivity and recursiveness are patently at their peak here.

Argento's oeuvre literally teems with more or less direct, more or less com-plete echoes of this (self-)definitional motif: at the start of *Deep Red*, a close-up of water spiraling down a sink in an unexpectedly decrepit, albeit all white and minimalist, restroom (in contrast with the conference room bathed in glorious reds and golds) is followed, a couple of minutes later, by an extreme close-up of the murderer's eye being made up; the opening sequence of *Sus-piria* features a tight shot of torrential rainwater gushing into a storm drain; the first killing in *Tenebrae* includes a static shot of the victim's eye and her face slowly sliding to the side. That these instances occur early in each film and are only distant, partial approximations of the original is no coincidence: rather than offer endless variants of the shower scene montage, Italian horrific thrillers at their best tend to reinscribe, occasionally as a *mise-en-abîme* effect, the primacy, or "primalness," of this trauma. This can be achieved as early as the opening sequence or the front credits, the film thereby creating a virtu-ally unattainable or at least unsurpassable template for itself, much in the way *Psycho*'s shower scene may be held to be an inaccessible pinnacle by aspiring horror-meisters. The prime example in this instance has to be Dario Argento's *Deep Red*, as the theme music and minimal white credits against a black back-ground are abruptly suspended and replaced, via a black screen when the titles momentarily disappear, by a brief colorful vignette: in a 1950s-styled room a murder is being committed in silhouette to the haunting, wordless tune of a children's song whose creepiness is but enhanced by a piercing scream. A blood-smeared knife is then thrown onto the wooden floor and into frame as a child's pair of legs (in suitably non–gender specific white high socks and black patent shoes as a possible bichromatic echo of the titles) is seen approaching. Fade to black; credit titles and Goblin's signature tune resume, uninterrupted this time, until the screen goes black again and the music suddenly stops. Then, and only then, does the film truly "begin." With its reliance on styl-ized shadow play, this bracketed or inserted sequence points to a staging or mise-en-scène (in theatrical, cinematic, or phantasmatic terms) of a childhood trauma which will eventually prove to be a primal/murder scene: rather than observe, in actuality or in fantasy, parental sex and subsequently equate intercourse with aggression and violence (in accordance with the Freudian vulgate), the child has witnessed one parent brutally butchering the other. This unusual paratextual (or parafilmic) location, to borrow a term from narratology (i.e., its marginal or liminal positioning)[25] is therefore perfectly congruous with an obscure "prior," an originary crisis tragically left unresolved—the perfect vehicle for morbid repetition and compulsive reenactment. Later on in the film, the c(l)ue to each murder set piece will in fact be the exact same song (as a homicidal warm-up or self-conditioning ritual, so to speak) or fetishistic pans over items from a "perverted" childhood (marbles, dolls, violent drawings, and bloodstained switchblade knives) where the banal and the sinister are disturbingly juxtaposed in a filmic equivalent of stream of consciousness.

Six years earlier, Mario Bava's *A Hatchet for the Honeymoon* appeared to be even more explicitly in the sphere of influence of Hitchcock's horror masterpiece. More than just another retread of late 1960s Euro-horror, *Psycho*-based oedipal narratives,[26] however, Bava's opus is a decidedly ironic and hybrid take on its model. If the Italian maestro, just like Hitchcock before him, shifts gears halfway through his film, he does so in order to veer off into ghost-story-cum-black-comedy territory when Mildred, the protagonist's late wife, starts to make an invisible comeback. By the same token, Hitchcockian suspense is turned on its head: the hero is presented as a murderer compulsively targeting women in bridal gowns in the very first sequence and next introduces himself as a psychopath via a voice-over narration (as he meticulously shaves in front of his mirror and pampers himself): "My name is John Harrington. I'm thirty years old. I'm a paranoiac . . . Nobody suspects that I'm a madman, a dangerous murderer." Each murder bringing him one step closer to total recall, his desperate pursuit of the primal scene eventually comes full circle when he meets his childhood trauma head-on and in its entirety—in this case, the realization that he killed his mother (whom he did not want to remarry) and his future stepfather. Finally, not unlike Norman Bates this time except for the switch from parent to spouse (as well as inner voice to physical manifestation), John Harrington appears doomed to a life of torment with the ghostly Mildred forever by his side in the coda of the film: "At first you couldn't see me, and now nobody will see me except you," his shrewish wife prophesies. "And we'll always be together, first in the insane asylum and then in hell for eternity!" What evidently distinguishes Bava from Hitchcock here is *Hatchet*'s worldview, predicated as it is on an absurdist, fantastical, almost funereally fanciful humor à la Gogol. As a result, it allegorically reduces mankind to mannequins (not unlike the female dummies dressed up as virginal brides that the impotent hero secretly kisses, fondles, and embraces in a hideaway room),[27] human ashes used as fertilizer or carried around in a leather bag, or frail flies that can be casually fed to a parrot as an illustration of Harrington's quasi-entomological views on man's existence early in the film: "Life is a ridiculous and brief drama." The fly motif, recurrent in Bava's oeuvre,[28] might be read as a distant quote from the ending of *Psycho* when a fly settles on Norman Bates' hand and we hear Mother in a voice-over (right before the flash dissolve of Norman's smiling face into the skull of his mother): "I hope they are watching. They'll see. They'll see, and they'll know, and they'll say . . . 'Why, she wouldn't even harm a fly!'"

Not only is Bava's John Harrington a matricide and a psychopath following in Norman Bates' footsteps; hiding his insanity behind a stylish, cool front, he may also be regarded as a precursor to *American Psycho*'s (2000) demented yuppie, Patrick Bateman. More than just trivia or speculation, this type of linkage is ultimately a symptom of the subterranean dialogue between the giallo and American horror through the pivotal mediation of Hitchcock. As we have seen, the web of pregnant intersections between Sir Alfred and the two Italian maestri is particularly rich and complex, from a Freudian approach of criminal psychopathology (sometimes too glib in the case of Hitchcock, oftentimes ham-fisted in Bava's or Argento's thrillers) and alleged streaks of misogyny (epitomized by Argento's much vilified, and perhaps misunderstood, statement: "I like women, especially beautiful ones. If they have a good face and figure, I would much prefer to watch them being murdered than an ugly girl or man."),[29] to an insatiable fascination with voyeurism, violence, and the macabre. One might even argue that a film like Argento's *The Cat o' Nine Tails* (*Il gatto a nove code*, 1971)—at once an echo chamber vibrating with Hitchcockian moments (Carlo realizing that Anna Terzi may have poisoned the milk he is about to drink; the bravura finale recalling the opening and the ending of *Vertigo*; etc.) and a possible influence on Hitch's own *Frenzy* (strangulation murders, an unusual *modus operandi* for a giallo; the unappetizing recipes of a cop's wife; retrieving an important clue from a victim's body; etc.)—constitutes a unique interface showing inspiration to be an at least occasional two-way process. The fact remains nonetheless that Hitchcock's *Psycho*, however tame it may appear to today's jaded or desensitized audiences, probably had the most profound impact on the inventors and practitioners of the giallo, acting as a catalyst, if not for the onslaught of graphic violence, then at least for the hypostatization of elaborate or shocking murder set pieces, and the oedipal thrust of film narratives. In return, the Italian horrific thriller gave an indispensable and brand new impetus to American productions in genre cinema and beyond, not without a notable time lag however. Once again, Bava's seminal impact cannot be overstated, but it was not felt until the 1980s—that is, perhaps uncoincidentally, after his (and Hitchcock's) death. As already mentioned, the gory body-count slasher *Bay of Blood* went on to inspire the *Friday the 13th* franchise, and the atmospheric sci-fi/horror shocker *Planet of the Vampires* (*Terrore nello spazio*, 1965) the *Alien* series. To say nothing of Martin Scorsese's Bavaesque remake of *Cape Fear* (1991), David Lynch's reappropriation of a memorable scene from *Kill, Baby, Kill* (a man chasing his double through a time warp) for his cult TV series *Twin Peaks* (1990), or Quentin Tarantino's use of *Black Sabbath* as one of many sources of inspiration for *Pulp Fiction* (1994).

Hitchcock, the giallo, and modern American horror may not be "kindred spirits" in the truest, noblest sense of the phrase, but one would be hardpressed to come up with a more creatively fecund and inspiring genre genealogy for generations to come.

Notes

1. See, among many examples, Giancarlo Grossini, *Dizionario del cinema giallo*, Bari: edizioni Dedalo, 1985.

2. From the commentary track on the DVD release of *Alice* (Anchor Bay Entertainment).

3. A giallo like Aldo Lado's *Who Saw Her Die?* (*Chi l'ha vista morire?*, 1972) could also be viewed as a (coincidental?) precursor, rather than a followup, to Roeg's film.

4. As tangential evidence to be added to the art vs. genre case file, one might point out that before his films began enjoying commercial and critical success in the 1960s, Antonioni served as oftentimes uncredited second-unit director on several peplums.

5. See in particular Argento's *Opera* (1987) and *The Phantom of the Opera* (1998), on the one hand; Bava's *Diabolik* (1968), based on one of the most popular Italian *fumetti*, on the other.

6. At the same time, Argento's cinematic flamboyance and melodramatic excess have earned him another nickname, "The Visconti of Violence," perhaps also because of the latter's noir-inflected *Ossessione* (1943).

7. With *Les Diaboliques*, Clouzot also anticipated Hitchcock's famous publicity stunt for *Psycho* (1960) by a few years: journalists were denied access on the set during the shooting and when the film was theatrically released, audiences were not allowed in after the screenings had started. On a more personal note, both directors shared an intense fascination with the morbid and the macabre as well as an exhausting and uncompromising sense of perfectionism with their casts and themselves.

8. See Eric Poindron, *Riccardo Freda, un pirate à la caméra*, Paris: Institut Lumière/Actes Sud, 1996.

9. While disowning it, Freda did however acknowledge directing his last film, *L'Ossessione che uccide* (*Murder Obsession*, 1980), in the spirit of Hitchcock. See Poindron, op. cit.

10. See Phil Hardy (ed.), *The Aurum Film Encyclopedia. Horror*, London: Aurum Press,

1985/1996. "Alfred's 'horrible' secret—his uncanny knack for constructing a cinema that traces the contours of the desire for sexual looking that underpins cinephilia—also animates Freda's fantasy" (149). In addition, the same entry interestingly surmises that the face of Barbara Steele, a "figure of beauty as the sublimated appearance of death," is "probably how Norman Bates remembers his mother in *Psycho.*"

11. In Luigi Cozzi, "Operazione Paura," *Horror*, no. 13, 1971, p. 47. Qtd. in Troy Howarth, *The Haunted World of Mario Bava,* Guildford: Fab Press, 2002, p. 324.

12. Italian genre films of the period are generally panned for the thespian abilities, or lack thereof, of too many of their actors—an issue that is usually further compounded by incompetent dubbing. Criticism is also periodically levied at Bava, Freda, Argento et al. for their inadequacies as directors of actors.

13. The *Friday the 13th* franchise, in particular, did not hesitate to crib several scenes from Bava's film quite literally, including the infamous one involving a teenage couple being caught and impaled in the coital act.

14. Earlier in the film a presumably cutting-edge computer analysis of clues had produced a profile of the wanted criminal that ended up fitting about 150,000 individuals!

15. http://www.darkdreams.org/darkdreams.html. Entirely devoted to Dario Argento, this website is apparently the largest of its kind.

16. This program (*La Porta sul buio*) was instrumental in solidifying Argento's cult status, as Roberto Curti explains: "It allowed him to become an icon, a trademark, a household name—his painfully skinny appearance providing a vivid, startling contrast with Hitch's paunchy silhouette." In Chris Gallant (ed.), *Art of Darkness. The Cinema of Dario Argento,* Guildford: Fab Press, 2001, p. 253. In the late 1980s, Argento went on to participate in a TV show called *Giallo* where he presented his "Nightmares" (*Gli Incubi di Dario Argento*), a series of nine short films, including a two-minute remake of *Rear Window* (ibid., p. 256)!

17. Again, the information regarding *Ti piace Hitchcock?* is based on an interview for the darkdreams.org site.

18. Other prominent examples would include the use of a "snorkel," or endoscopic camera, going down a victim's throat in *The Bird with the Crystal Plumage;* the Pentazet, a special industrial camera, imported from East Germany and capable of shooting thousands of frames per second, for the ultra-slow-motion decapitation of the villainess in the finale of *Quattro Mosche di Velutto grigio* (*Four Flies on Grey Velvet,* 1972); or the aerial shots reproducing the perspective and swooping arabesques of an invisible evil spirit or a raven in *Suspiria* and *Opera,* respectively. As a counterpoint, one might add that regarding this last film, by his own admission, Argento essentially followed the example of Hitchcock's *The Birds* (1963) in using mostly live avian subjects rather than mechanical models.

19. See also the corrosively chiasmatic statement purportedly made by Lucio Fulci, who directed numerous gialli and horror films (including zombie outings), and whose rapport with Argento was often difficult, if not downright conflictual: "Argento is a great journeyman who likes to think of himself as an artist, while Hitchcock is a great artist who considers himself a journeyman."

20. Op. cit., p. 79 (my emphasis).

21. See for example Paul Wells (in *The Horror Genre: From Beelzebub to Blair Witch,* London: Wallflower, 2000, p. 76): "Arguably, *Psycho* inspires the two dominant paradigms of the horror film in the late twentieth century. Firstly, in identifying, implicitly summating and definitively expressing the core meanings of the horror genre: psychosexual and psychosomatic angst, non-socialized violent imperatives, the instability and inappropriate nature of established socio-cultural structures and the oppressive omnipresence of 'death,' *Psycho* 'ends' the horror movie, and ushers in the *postmodern* era in the genre. . . . The second model may be viewed as *ambivalent realism,* and is predicated on locating horror in a realist context but playing out an essentially amoral agenda or determining a scenario where moral or ethical certainty is unattainable."

22. Extraneous roots of a biographical order might also be considered here: as a child, Hitch was briefly locked up in a police cell as per his father's instructions, presumably for educational purposes. The experience instilled instead an indelible fear of the police into the future filmmaker. Tellingly, it is on this traumatic anecdote that François Truffaut, a shrewd judge of character, opens his *Entretiens* with the Master (*Hitchcock/Truffaut*, New York: Simon & Schuster, 1984, p. 25).

23. See, however, Serge Chauvin's suggestive article: "Furore italienne ou le film qui en savait trop: du thriller au *giallo*, notes autour de Bava," in Véronique Campan and Gilles Menegaldo (eds.), *Du maniérisme au cinéma*, Poitiers: Faculté des lettres et des langues de l'Université de Poitiers, 2003, pp. 145–49.

24. Regarding scopophilia as dual locus (source and target) of erotic and homicidal urges (Eros and Thanatos), the equally seminal influence of Michael Powell's *Peeping Tom*, released the same year as *Psycho* but to diametrically opposed critical reviews and box-office results, should not be overlooked.

25. See also, in an otherwise mediocre giallo, the precredits sequence (titled "Prologue") of Lucio Fulci's *Voices from Beyond* (*Voci dal profondo*, 1990) where a couple engaged in passionate lovemaking is interrupted by their unseen child calling out "Mommy!" The infuriated father gets up, picks up a dagger, goes to his son's room, and stabs him in the chest. The camera next cuts to the mother waking up from a nightmare and finding out her little boy is peacefully asleep in his own bed after all, then segues into the credit titles to the musical accompaniment of a children's choir and against a background of children's drawings. The story proper finally starts with a scene fading in from black: in an ironic reversal, several members of the family are now gathered around the father who is unexpectedly dying in a hospital bed.

26. *The Third Eye* (*Il terzo occhio*, 1966), a largely unsavory giallo by Mino Guerrini (who coscripted Bava's *The Girl Who Knew Too Much*), is a fairly representative example. One of Mario Bava's most embittering career mishaps was when his personal project, *Lisa and the Devil*, performed poorly at the box office and was later drastically re-cut as a demonic possession flick and retitled *The House of Exorcism* (*La Casa dell'exorcismo*, 1975) in an attempt to capitalize on an even more phenomenal success than *Psycho*—William Friedkin's *The Exorcist* (1973).

27. The sequence that first makes us privy to this hidden lair and private ritual ends with the camera panning across mannequin heads and seamlessly onto the motionless faces of a group of séance attendees, including John Harrington himself. In a sense, Bava enthusiasts are here referred back to the credit sequence of *Blood and Black Lace* where each cast member is introduced striking a pose next to a dummy—a clear foreshadowing of the systematic reification of most of the characters as sacrificial victims throughout the film.

28. See the "A Drop of Water" ("La Goccia d'acqua") segment of his *Black Sabbath* in particular.

29. This is after all but an (admittedly coarse and somewhat provocative) explication or adaptation of a famous aphorism in Edgar Allan Poe's *The Philosophy of Composition:* "The death of a beautiful woman is, unquestionably, the most poetic subject in the world." Argento regularly quotes the American initiator of modern forms of detection and horror in literature as one of his greatest and earliest admirations.

PART V: THEORETICALLY HITCHCOCKIAN

If Hitchcock's influence on other filmmakers has been immense, his influence on critics and theorists has arguably been even greater. In fact, over the past two decades, he has come to occupy a position in the academic discipline of film studies not unlike that of Shakespeare in literary studies, in the sense that it is in reference to his work that critical questions are almost inevitably defined and theoretical positions most frequently (and often belligerently) assumed. Theorists have been particularly persistent in choosing Hitchcock's films as the textual terrain on which to wage battle over the interrelated issues of spectator identification and the social effects of screen violence. Robert Sklar chronicles this ongoing conflict and examines the role which the particular nature of the films has played in shaping the debate. On these issues as on others, Hitchcock's films often seem, paradoxically, to both invite and resist appropriation to a range of theoretical positions. As John Belton demonstrates, this is at least in part because the films are themselves so "theoretical," most particularly so in the problematical way in which they position themselves in relation to the dominant paradigm of classical narrative film generally.

In the 1970s, especially in *Frenzy,* Hitchcock took advantage of newly relaxed censorship rules to offer a more explicit and horrific treatment of sexual violence.

Death at Work

Hitchcock's Violence and Spectator Identification

Robert Sklar

Writing the first extensive critique on *Psycho* in English, Robin Wood in 1965 described the "showerbath murder" as "probably the most horrific incident in any fiction film." He devoted much of his subsequent analysis to the impact on spectators of this gruesome scene and its aftereffects. Having been drawn in by the filmmaker to experience Marion's emotional turmoil as our own—"Hitchcock uses every means to enforce audience identification," Wood declared—"we" have been shattered almost beyond recovery: "Never . . . has identification been broken off so brutally." Yet, within moments of Marion's blood swirling down the drain, we shift our sympathies to her killer, Norman Bates, for "Hitchcock uses all the resources of identification technique to make us 'become' Norman." Ultimately, after considerable further exploration of the director's methods of shaping viewers' complicity in the desires and dilemmas of screen characters, Wood asserted, "We have been led to accept Norman Bates as a potential extension of ourselves."[1]

In later decades, as the rise of academic cinema studies produced a vast effusion of critical work on Hitchcock, much of it drawing energy from psychoanalytically oriented theories of spectator identification, Wood found himself in a conundrum. Wishing to reject the "constricting and reductive" concepts of identification that he found in some of the most widely influential scholarship on the director, he nevertheless did not choose to abandon his own continuing use of the term or reconsider the value of its deployment in his earlier work on *Psycho* and other Hitchcock films. He allowed only that the term was "problematic" and elaborated on the breadth and multiplicity of its meanings so extensively that its usefulness as a tool of critical analysis appeared to wane.[2] Wood's fallback position left him vulnerable to the stance of critics and theorists who completely refuted the notion of spectators' identification with characters. Then there was the wily director himself: when François Truffaut raised the issue of audience reaction to *Psycho*'s characters in a remarkably similar way to Wood, Hitchcock replied, "I doubt whether the identification is that close."[3]

If identification is a term that is unlikely to prove entirely satisfactory, nevertheless it is also not likely to disappear. While its utilization in film theory and Hitchcock criticism extends to the full range of techniques for producing spectator involvement, it also has a more limited but also potentially more socially potent meaning when it comes to acts of screen violence. Is it truly the case that we have been brought by Hitchcock at the end of *Psycho* to recognize that we, too, are capable of committing the same crimes as Norman Bates? One doubts that Wood intended his identification formula literally. His further words, indeed, suggested a vague universality, in which "we all share in a common guilt" that sounds as much theological as psychological.[4] But in other branches of film theory the questions raised by analysis of spectator identification with screen violence may intersect more closely with social policy. Can Hitchcock's "resources of identification technique," in making us "'become'" Norman, as Wood wrote, increase the propensity to commit violent acts in some of us—all of us? Or perhaps they evoke a form of recognition that deters rather than impels.

Can the critical and theoretical studies on identification in Hitchcock, or on the actual scenes of violence in his films, throw light on the director's effect on spectators or his influence on later cinematic violence? "The vast corpus of critical work on Alfred Hitchcock," wrote J. David Slocum in his introduction to the anthology *Violence in American Cinema*, "consistently addresses film violence."[5] *Consistently* in this sense may be rephrased as regularly, or more often than not. It does not imply agreement, harmony, or compatibility. More precisely, the vast corpus of critical work on Alfred Hitchcock *in*consistently addresses film violence. If the critical scrutiny of Hitchcock's violence has been persistent, at least over the past several decades, it has also been highly discordant. The range of response has been remarkably personal, running the gamut from enthusiasm to abhorrence, and it has also deployed a wide array of approaches, from reductive biographical explanation to recondite theoretical speculation—sometimes simultaneously. Where the critical discourse on Hitchcock's violence almost invariably stops short is at a point where the relation between spectator identification and the actual commission

of violence—the question of the social effects of screen violence—becomes
an issue.

One

Two general perspectives orient an approach to Hitchcock's violence. The
first is that, no matter how many deaths by murder occurred in Hitchcock's
dozens of films from the 1920s through the 1950s, the critical writing on the
director during those years hardly addressed film violence at all. The second is
that Hitchcock began to rearticulate his ideas and strategies concerning film
violence at a late point in his career, at a time of changing values both in media
culture and in society at large.

"By God, I am typed . . ." Hitchcock wrote to Sidney Bernstein in 1953,
"what with the label 'thriller' and the search for 'suspense,' " and indeed it was
as a maker of suspense-thrillers that he was largely known up to and through
that period.[6] Victims and perpetrators of fatal violence certainly formed basic
elements of plot and characterization in his films and in the genres in which he
worked, as well as in such other genres as the detective film and the Western.
Yet in part because of code restrictions and actual and threatened censorship,
how violence was represented, or how spectators responded to it, was little discussed. "Violence seemed facile, factitious, and unreal," director Sam Peckinpah
later remarked of this era in cinema. "People die without suffering and violence provokes no pain."[7]

If Hitchcock was associated with violence during those years, it was more
likely to be through his public pose as a blasé, sophisticated joker on the subject. This popular persona was honed in the droll prologues and epilogues he
delivered to open and close episodes of the *Alfred Hitchcock Presents* television series beginning in 1955.[8] A print version of this performance appeared in
a 1961 photo spread under his byline in the men's magazine *Esquire* entitled,
fortuitously for this inquiry, "Violence." The putative author appears in a full
body picture on the article's title page, with his nose superciliously uplifted,
as he points to the word "Violence" printed as if it were an instructor's aid
projected on a portable screen. The subtitle read, "An Ever-Handy Reference
Manual to the Selection, Dispatchment and Disposal, with Taste, of a Likely
Victim." In the first of several brief captions to the comically posed photographs, on "Selection of a Victim," he advised not to murder "out of spite or
from a sense of irony," but for "amusement" or "whimsey [*sic*]."[9] In
vision monologues and in occasional journalistic forays such as this
figured as a subject for urbane humor.

These publicity mannerisms aside, Hitchcock clearly began thinking in new ways about cinematic violence during the early 1960s. An unusual instance of public rumination on the subject was the dialogue he conducted with the psychiatrist Fredric Wertham for a 1963 issue of the woman's magazine *Redbook*. A well-known figure at that time, Wertham gained fame in the 1950s for his critique of mass media's influence on children, in particular what he regarded as the excessive violence and sadism in comic books aimed at the young. One of the psychiatrist's themes in the conversation with the filmmaker was that "an atmosphere of needing and wanting violence which exists in our society at present" influenced Hitchcock to make his representations of violence "stronger" than in the past, notably in the *Psycho* shower murder scene. Remarkably, however, Wertham admitted up front that he had not seen *Psycho*.[10]

In response, Hitchcock simultaneously affirmed and demurred. He agreed that the shower scene was more violent than were murders in his past films. He also described it as "very violent," but added after that the word "impressionistic," explaining, "It was montaged by little pieces of film giving the impression of a knife stabbing a victim." It was, he said, a tactical devise to instill apprehension in the audience and thus "reduce and practically eliminate all further violence . . . Violence for the sake of violence I don't think has any effect. I don't think the audience is moved by it. It's so obvious." After this, the conversation swiftly lost focus, but the psychiatrist returned to his central concern in getting in the last word: "Violence, guns, killing, they are all around us. And you know, Mr. Hitchcock, this affects your audience. All this exposure to violence desensitizes them. They want stronger and stronger stuff."[11]

Sidney Gottlieb regards Hitchcock as clearly the master of this debate, calling his interlocutor "glib," "pompous," "philistine," "literal," and "simplistic."[12] Invariably attuned to audience taste and psychology, however, Hitchcock was listening as well as parrying. While rejecting Wertham's implication that the shower murder catered to an increased appetite for violence, he conceded that he was thinking of "young people today" in "making the lovemaking scenes a little more risqué than I normally would, only because I felt that modern manners had changed, to some extent."[13] That he continued to ponder the evolving youth audience is evident from his November 1965 telegram to Bernard Herrmann concerning the music the composer was to write for *Torn Curtain* (1966): "This audience is very different from the one to which we used to cater. It is young, vigorous, and demanding. It is this fact that has been recognized by almost all of the European film makers where they have sought to introduce a beat and a rhythm that is more in tune with the requirements of the aforesaid audience." [14]

Hitchcock's analysis of this new audience's tastes plainly involved an appetite that the psychiatrist had identified, for "stronger and stronger" violence. Discussing *Torn Curtain* with the director, Truffaut declared, "The strongest scene, of course, is Gromek's killing on the farm; it's the one that grips the audience the most. Since it is played without music, it is very realistic and also very savage." Hitchcock responded, "In doing the long killing scene, my first thought was to avoid the cliché. In every picture somebody gets killed and it goes very quickly. They are stabbed or shot, and the killer never even stops to look and see whether the victim is really dead or not. And I thought it was time to show that it was very difficult, very painful, and it takes a very long time to kill a man." [15]

Hitchcock biographer Donald Spoto characteristically ascribed the idea— but not the savagery—to someone else: the film's screenwriter, novelist Brian Moore. Drawing on his experience as a volunteer during the German air raids on London in World War II, according to Spoto, Moore advised Hitchcock that people do not die "easily and cleanly" the way they do in movies. "On this point he really went to town developing the murder scene," the biographer quoted the screenwriter. "He went further than I think he should have in that case." [16] To be sure, the death in question is also in a manner of speaking a wartime death, in a Cold War context. The victim is a Soviet agent, Gromek, who has been assigned as a bodyguard to an American atomic scientist (played by Paul Newman) who has apparently defected to East Germany. When Gromek correctly suspects that the scientist is functioning as a spy, a woman, whom the American is meeting at a farmhouse, attacks the Soviet. She hits him in the head with a milk jar, stabs him (the knife breaks off and lodges in his chest), and strikes his legs with a shovel. Still he fights back, until the woman and the scientist force his head into a gas oven. A high-angle shot shows his hands twitching and then finally going limp.

It was time to show the savagery, as Hitchcock later told Truffaut. "Resulting from the industry's efforts to connect with a young, contemporary audience and the period in which that audience lived," Stephen Prince wrote in his introduction to the anthology *Screening Violence*, "motion picture violence began its remarkable escalation in 1967." [17] To what extent does the Gromek murder deserve a (dis)honorable place as a precursor or even an instigating intertext for the growth of late-1960s screen violence? Compared to controversial 1967 films such as *Bonnie and Clyde* and *The Dirty Dozen*, and the multiple social and industrial causes that Prince noted—including urban riots, the Vietnam War, political assassinations, and the demise in 1966 of the Motion Picture Production Code—perhaps not all that much. Yet Peckinpah, master of screen violence in films such as *The Wild Bunch* (1969), and, less acknowledged, a figure who gave considerable thought to its meaning and effects, did notice. In the 1974 interview cited earlier, he said of *Torn Curtain,* "this is one of the rare films in which one can really see death at work. Hitchcock, with all of his immense talent, shows us that it is not easy to kill a man and that the human body has an extraordinary power of resistance to physical aggression." [18]

As Prince by implication reminded us, the Gromek murder in *Torn Curtain* was still filmed under the surveillance of the old Production Code. "It was not until *Frenzy* [1972] that he had the opportunity to take advantage of the new climate of freedom in American cinema," Prince wrote of Hitchcock. And what he brought forth was "easily the most grotesque and graphic act of violence in all of [his] films." [19] This is the ten-minute sequence in which the "Necktie Murderer" Bob Rusk enters the office of Brenda Blaney, rapes and strangles her, and then casually departs. "Ten years ago we wouldn't have been able to show that scene in the same detail," the director was quoted in *Newsweek* magazine, "and something very crucial would have been lost: You would never have seen the killer at work." [20] Hitchcock's brief remark implied that his interest centered on the perpetrator. It's significant that Peckinpah, instead, viewed this sequence through a focus on the victim. "The murder . . . in *Frenzy* is just as remarkable because Hitchcock really causes us to feel the intensity of the suffering of a person who decomposes under our very eyes," Peckinpah went on to say in the 1974 interview. "I am not a Hitchcock fanatic, but all the same one has to admit that he knows how to render tangible . . . human suffering." [21]

If the rape-murder in *Frenzy* marked the culmination of Hitchcock's decade-long transformation of his modes of representing violence, it was also embedded in a narrative that allowed contemporary critics to type him generically as of old. "[*Frenzy*] is a cause for jubilation among those who admire suspense-thrillers," Albert Johnson wrote in *Film Quarterly.* Johnson regarded this "one graphic sequence of mayhem" as a "testament to the demands of today's horror film genre." He compared the techniques employed to a pretend-strangling in a party scene of *Strangers on a Train* (1951), although he acknowledged the realism in this case of "the excruciating, gurgling descent into death that evokes astonishment and dismay on the part of an audience." [22] Vincent Canby's rave review in the *New York Times* took pleasure in the film's humor, its mastery of style and technique, and the presence of the storyteller's "mock woe." The rape-murder is noted with reference to locations where the Necktie Murderer's victims are found, "even sitting at their office desks, understandably somewhat disheveled."[23]

Two

Robin Wood's pioneering early analysis of *Psycho* examined Hitchcock's "means to enforce audience identification" but did not consider that such techniques might be utilized to establish an ambiguous and perhaps ultimately illusory form of identification with the director himself. Yet as Hitchcock's violence became a subject for scholarly inquiry in later years, a notion of self-reflexivity has been intrinsic to nearly every critical commentary. An exemplary instance is one of the first academic studies on *Frenzy,* by Dennis Turner. "Hitchcock's movies have always provided rare examples in commercial moviemaking of the subjective narrative, in which incidents are presented filtered through the foregrounded consciousness of the auteur," Turner wrote. "Thus audiences always watched Hitchcock's movies with a strong awareness of the presence of the filmmaker . . ." Turner argued that critics who had been disappointed with Hitchcock's late films—among whom he includes such luminous explicators of the director's work as Andrew Sarris, Raymond Bellour, and the aforementioned Wood—underestimated the significance of self-consciousness in these works. He proposed to read *Frenzy* as a film that "challenges its viewer to participate in its production." However, this test plays a trick on spectators. In Turner's metaphor, the director is a spider, and the film "weaves a . . . web . . . for ensnaring" the audience.[24]

His argument culminated in a reading of the film's closing sequence, in which Richard Blaney, having been falsely convicted as the Necktie Murderer, has escaped and returned to wreak vengeance on the actual rapist-murderer, his erstwhile friend Bob Rusk. Carrying a tire iron, Blaney enters Rusk's flat, sees a still prone figure that he takes to be Rusk, and repeatedly strikes at it with his weapon. "Blaney has already crossed into real perversion when he smashes the tire iron into what he believes to be a sleeping human being," Turner wrote. Yet the audience "welcomes" the revelation that the figure in the bed is Rusk's latest female victim, already dead, "because that lets Blaney keep his 'innocence' . . . we are glad to have a strangled, naked woman turn up." Where Wood postulated that spectators might gain a generalized sense of guilt and acknowledge in themselves an abstract potential for murder as outcomes of Hitchcock's identification techniques, Turner argued that the director has self-consciously structured a situation that makes spectators actively pleased that another rape-murder has been committed. Thus Hitchcock has forced the audience to recognize "that it shares those very values he is attacking," namely, the values of "a repressive social and sexual organization." For Turner, *Frenzy* is a film in which Hitchcock "engages in the eminently moral art of satire."[25]

When such terms as "subjective narrative," "foregrounded consciousness of the auteur," and "presence of the filmmaker" are invoked, however, the door is opened to interpreting not only screen images but also the character, psychology, life experience, and motivation of their principal creator. If Turner managed to discover moral intent in Hitchcock's violence, someone else might unearth sublimated criminal cravings. Discussing *Frenzy*, biographer Spoto found Hitchcock's fundamental life story revealed in the 1972 film. "*Frenzy* was at once a concession to modern audiences' expectations and a more personal self-disclosure of the director's angriest and most violent desires," he wrote. The rape-murder of Brenda Blaney marks the end point to which "the director's life work had tended" since his 1926 silent film, *The Lodger*, in which blonde women are serially murdered. "Now at last—encouraged by the new freedom in movies—his imagination of this sordid crime could be more fully shown in all its horror," Spoto continued. "But this would not exorcise the desire; it followed him as an obsession right to the end of his life."[26]

Spoto's characterization of Hitchcock's entire body of work as personal documents of perverse lust both drew on, and fueled, a feminist critique of the filmmaker. A feminist viewpoint on Hitchcock's violence was launched in response to Vincent Canby's amused and lighthearted review of *Frenzy* in the *New York Times*. Several weeks after the review appeared, the newspaper published an opinion piece by an English professor, Victoria Sullivan, with the title, "Does *Frenzy* Degrade Women?" Among Sullivan's points is the argument "that it is quite possible a certain percentage of the movie audience is really titillated by the loving camera treatment of the murder, the lingering focus on the slowly expiring victim, the flashback strangulation, the frequent shots of nude dead female bodies."[27] Whether or not such pleasurable agitation at screen violence constitutes spectator identification in the sense that film critics and theorists use the term, Sullivan made a basic distinction that frequently eludes Hitchcock's interpreters: individual readings are not necessarily universal experiences, and the director's "technique of audience participation" (again, Wood's term) does not invariably operate in a uniform way on a collective "us."

Feminist film scholars began to explore the subject of violence against women in Hitchcock's films during the 1980s, offering analyses of works such as *Blackmail* (1929), *Shadow of a Doubt* (1943), *The Birds* (1963), and *Marnie* (1964).[28] Jeanne Thomas Allen reopened the case of *Frenzy* in a 1985 *Film Quarterly* article. She critiqued the rape-murder sequence in considerable detail,[29] postulating the director's misogyny, and also by extension that of the film, in order to raise questions concerning spectator response. Although she drew on Spoto's views on Hitchcock's personal psychology, she faulted the biographer for ignoring "the director's skill in implicating the spectator in morally questionable behavior through filmic techniques of identification." Allen's language here echoed both Robin Wood and Dennis Turner: Does identification enlighten the spectator, as Wood might have it, or lead him or her into a compromised moral position, as Turner intimated? "Whether Hitchcock's narration induces a self-critical reflection in the spectator . . . or simply gratifies the desire to victimize women," she conceded, "is difficult to determine."[30]

Following this cautionary note, Allen nevertheless sought to arrive at some form of determination. Invoking terminology that was widely utilized—although not uncontested—in current film theory at the time of her essay, she generalized the specificity of the rape-murder sequence outward toward broader concepts of the "male gaze" and the camera "eye." Photographic realism and narrative action combine to create a tangible, persuasive form of social representation that objectifies "a particularly pathological but culturally logical male subjectivity in patriarchy," she wrote. "The film spectator, male or female, is unambiguously forced to share it." Once again she acknowledged the Turner position, the argument that what Hitchcock forces a spectator to share is a "textbook lesson . . . on his/her own voyeurism." But she cautioned against too readily accepting this "ethical" stance on the grounds of Hitchcock's "systematic ambiguity." How can one know whether the filmmaker is criticizing the killer's actions or spectators' voyeuristic participation through viewing them? It may be just as likely that he is "affirming the pleasure" of watching a rape-murder, or leaving it up to the spectator's moral values to render judgment on the scene. Even though, as she argued earlier, the spectator is forced to "share" in the film's pathological misogynistic violence, it may be possible for those spectators who possess "an ability to shift perspectives and a stance critical of dominance-submission structures of interpersonal relations" to feel discomfited by what they witness.[31]

Allen's article thoroughly considered various possibilities both of directorial intention and spectator response. Her conclusion was that Hitchcock "has us participate in this exercise in detachment and objectification far more than he comments reflexively on the implications of our ability and perhaps desire to do so." Female spectators no less than male are compelled to go along. As a curious note, however, she appealed in her final paragraph to Victoria Sullivan's 1972 *New York Times* commentary on *Frenzy* for a confirmatory view. "Th[e] process which enables women's consciousness to be 'colonized,' is, I think, what Victoria Sullivan found so objectionable about *Frenzy*," Allen wrote, "that here it was insinuated into our consciousness in a more sophisticated and therefore more subversive manner, more difficult to defend against than ordinary daily misogyny."[32] This was not Sullivan's point. Her complaint about *Frenzy* had nothing to do with "our consciousness" but with the film's presumed capacity to stimulate the "neurotic" male spectator, "the man who regularly fantasizes rape."[33] As a woman spectator, Sullivan did not describe herself as drawn to a position of identification with rape/murder, but rather as one who identified with the film's women victims, feeling both anger and impotence at their suffering.

"I could not disagree more strongly with Jeanne Thomas Allen," declared Tania Modleski in her 1988 study *The Women Who Knew Too Much: Hitchcock and Feminist Theory*.[34] Modleski's specific disagreement concerned differences in interpreting a detail of Brenda Blaney's behavior in the face of the rapist/murderer's attack, but it was also part of a larger critique central to her book as a whole. "While it is not at all accurate to say that I wanted to 'save Hitchcock,'" she wrote, "I did indeed aim to save his female viewers from annihilation at the hands not only of traditional male critics but of those feminist critics who see women's repression in patriarchal cinema as total, women's 'liking' for these films as nothing but masochism." Modleski's overall project situated *Frenzy* as the last of seven Hitchcock films she analyzed through the lens of feminist psychoanalytic theory, in which the film's possible meanings for female spectators were expounded in lieu of speculation about how some collective "we"—gendered or not—is forced to respond. She alluded only once to the director's putative powers of manipulation in *Frenzy*, in which "Hitchcock makes rather extensive use of point of view shots and in so doing it might be said that he forces the spectator into symbolically sharing" or identifying with a character's behavior. However, the specific reference for this observation is not the rape-murder sequence, but rather the police inspector's repulsion at the meals his wife serves him.[35]

To summarize her complex theoretical approach to *Frenzy* for the purposes of this discussion, Modleski argued that the film illuminates the psychological roots of male violence—that is, it provides knowledge of such behavior to the female spectator—as much as it may seem to revel in the representation of male violence in action. Situating *Frenzy* historically, she regarded the extremity of its graphic violence less as a product of the new freedom from censorship constraints and more "as a cultural response to women's demands for sexual and social liberation, demands that were, after all, at their height in 1972 when *Frenzy* was made." In this sense, however heinous patriarchal power may appear in the film, what it reveals is patriarchy in crisis. "It is not because male dominance is so firmly entrenched that ideas about women such as those found in *Frenzy* are held," she wrote, "but rather because it *isn't*."[36]

In this light, Modleski took issue with Donald Spoto's castigation of the explicit scenes of sexual violence in *Frenzy*. "One might ask why," she wrote, "if a sordid crime like rape/murder is to be depicted at all, it should *not* be shown 'in all its horror.'" Contrasting *Frenzy* with the shower scene in *Psycho*, she suggested that the graphic details of Brenda Blaney's rape-murder and Hitchcock's refusal "to eroticize the proceedings" make "the crime more difficult for the spectator to assimilate—more 'repellant,' in Spoto's word." The disturbing nature of the violence, to paraphrase her view, reduces the possibility that spectators predisposed to such scenes—or even those who in other circumstances, against their better judgment, may have been excited by violence or sexually titillated—could get a voyeuristic thrill out of it.[37]

Against what some critics have regarded as Hitchcock's ambiguity, or uncertainty of meaning, Modleski postulated the director's ambivalence—his opposed or conflicted feelings on a subject, in this case, in her word, femininity. "Hitchcock's fear and loathing of women is accompanied by a lucid understanding of—and even sympathy for—women's problems in patriarchy," she wrote, and this duality reaches an extreme form for her in *Frenzy*. Despite the rape-murder sequence and grotesque scenes of other female corpses, "woman is never completely destroyed . . . There are always elements resistant to her destruction and assimilation." For one thing, in *Frenzy* as opposed to other Hitchcock works, "the film links the sexual violence it depicts to a system of male dominance rather than confining it to the inexplicable behavior of one lone psychopath." Modleski found in *Frenzy*'s violence, as in Hitchcock's films more generally, "reason to hope that [women] will be able to survive patriarchy's attacks."[38]

Three

The debate over *Frenzy*'s violence occurred within the boundaries of Hitchcock studies, where the director's personality and motivation, his representa-

tional strategies and their effects, consumed scholars' interest. Even though
shortly after *Frenzy*'s 1972 release date ever-increasing graphic violence became
a staple of the horror film and elsewhere in genre cinema, *Frenzy* seems rarely if
ever to have been acknowledged as precursor. (Peckinpah's insightful remarks
on the violence in *Torn Curtain* and *Frenzy*, for example, were published in
a Quebec French-language newspaper and only became available to English-
language readers some years later, when scholars unearthed a translated transcript in the director's papers.) Where Hitchcock's influence is detected on the
post-1970 movement toward what Stephen Prince calls "ultraviolent movies,"
the work cited is almost invariably *Psycho*.

The most detailed exploration of "the *Psycho* template" for later horror
movies appeared in Carol J. Clover's studies on the slasher film, inaugurated
with her 1987 essay "Her Body, Himself: Gender in the Slasher Film." She
enumerated the familiar elements on which the genre drew: the killer; the
victim; the location; the weapon; the attack. What made *Psycho* so central
were its popular success and "above all the sexualization of both motive and
action," she wrote. "The spiritual debt of all the post-1974 slasher films to *Psycho* is clear, and it is a rare example that does not pay a visual tribute . . . to the
ancestor." In a note she added, "The shower sequence in *Psycho* is probably
the most echoed scene in all of film history."[39]

Clover's primary purpose, to be sure, was to elaborate on the differences
between *Psycho* and its successors, particularly the emergence in the latter of
what she calls the Final Girl and this figure's implications for both gender
representation and spectator identification. Other key aspects of difference
include the slasher films' multiplication of female victims and, of course, the
extraordinary new explicitness in the representation of graphic violence. By
valorizing *Psycho* and its "oblique rendition of physical violence," Clover situated Hitchcock at the end of an old style of cinematic reticence in rendering
violence, rather than, for example, assessing *Frenzy*'s rape-murder as a beginning of the new graphic candor.[40]

As Clover pursued the questions of the Final Girl, the role of her gender
in horror narrative, and what she means to male and female spectators, she
asserted that Hitchcock intended the shower scene to be an attack on the
audience as well as on the victim. "Not just the body of Marion is to be rup-
tured, but also the body on the other side of the film and screen: our witnessing body," she wrote. "As Marion is to Norman, the audience of *Psycho* is to
Hitchcock . . . Hitchcock's 'torture the women' then means, simply, torture
the audience."[41] Later, she described this linkage of victim and audience as

a "brand of spectator experience that Hitchcock designated as 'feminine' in 1960."[42] It seems incumbent to point out that, in seeking to construct Hitchcock as a precursor figure in relation to her otherwise compelling argument concerning male spectators and the Final Girl in the slasher genre, Clover appears to have placed her own formulations in quotation marks—"torture the women" and "feminine" in the previous two sentences—in a manner that allows the reader to infer that they are Hitchcock's words.

Four

The trajectory of film criticism and theory relating to Hitchcock's violence and spectator identification—if the latter term has managed to retain any of the tenuous meanings it may once have held—has moved through three major phases. In Robin Wood's early formulation, audience identification with the filmmaker's violent characters such as Norman Bates deepened an understanding of human nature, of one's capacity of acting for good or evil. Later academic studies retained Wood's emphasis on identification as enlightenment, but shifted its meaning. They proposed that Hitchcock's technique of audience participation, as Wood had named it, was a trick that forced spectators, whether male or female, to recognize their complicity in patriarchal violence. (Tania Modleski offered the hope that such recognition could be an aid to resistance.) A third stage, drawing in part on biographical interpretations of Hitchcock as a pathological sadist obsessed with violence against women, asserted that the director's intended target of screen violence was the audience, we spectators ourselves: the outcome of our identification was not enlightenment or recognition, but fear and abasement.

Before Carol Clover briefly deployed this third position, William Rothman had presented it with considerably greater hyperbolic force in his 1982 book, *Hitchcock: The Murderous Gaze*. In his analysis of the appearance of the knife-wielding murderer in *Psycho*'s shower scene, Rothman expanded the horror of spectator identification almost sentence by sentence. At first, he wrote, the moment provokes "the nightmarish fantasy that we are the murderer's intended victim. We are face to face with our own murderer, confronting the imminent prospect of our own death." A few sentences later, reality supercedes fantasy: "It has to be clear that this figure stands in for Hitchcock," who "confronts us with his unfulfilled appetite and his wish to avenge himself on us." And then the final twist: "Yet . . . it is also no creature of flesh and blood but a projection from within ourselves that appears before us. We are confronting ourselves."[43]

Perhaps it's a consolation that, for all the alarming rhetoric, what Rothman was doing was squaring the circle, returning the argument to Robin Wood's assertion, "We have been led to accept Norman Bates as a potential extension of ourselves."

Slavoj Žižek's contribution to the discourse on Hitchcock's violence and spectator identification focused on an instance upon which few other critics have dwelled: the murder of Gromek in *Torn Curtain*. For the purpose of his analysis, it's significant that, in comparison to the more frequently debated murders of women in *Psycho* and *Frenzy*, this murder of a man—the killing of an enemy in the midst of (cold) war conflict—in conventional narrative terms may be regarded as necessary and even desirable. Drawing on concepts from a work by Jacques Lacan, "Kant avec Sade," Žižek bridged the second and third phases described above: Hitchcock the trickster not as satirist, as Dennis Turner phrased it with reference to *Frenzy*, but as "'sadist' playing with the viewer" in the *Torn Curtain* murder scene. "First, he sets a trap of sadistic identification for the viewer by way of arousing in him/her the desire to crush the bad guy . . ." Then the filmmaker "closes the trap by simply realizing the viewer's desire: in having his/her desire fully realized, the viewer obtains more than he/she asked for . . ." Although Žižek did not describe the murder, he alluded to its "nauseous *presence*." [44] What's central to the argument is that this is not an "oblique rendition of physical violence," as Clover characterized the shower murder in *Psycho:* it is, as Peckinpah described, one "in which one can really see death at work."

In acquiescing to Hitchcock's manipulation, Žižek continued, the viewer confronts "the contradictory, divided nature of his/her desire (s/he wants the bad guy to be crushed without mercy, yet at the same time s/he is not prepared to pay the full price for it: as soon as s/he sees his/her desire realized, s/he draws back in shame)." [45] But with that recognition, in Žižek's analysis of Hitchcock's strategy through the prism of Lacanian psychoanalytic theory, also comes a diminution of abashment. The Gromek murder, after all, is socially sanctioned: as Žižek emphasized, "one is so to speak allowed to break the Law in the name of the Law itself." With rapid-fire leaps across historical and ideological territory—touching on such subjects as the Ku Klux Klan and Nazi Germany—Žižek has moved from the spectator's mortification to something closer to pleasure in an approved form of "transgression of the Law." [46]

From *Torn Curtain*, Žižek turned to the more familiar instance of Hitchcock's violence in *Psycho*, and, inevitably, to Robin Wood's inaugurating conceptions of spectator identification with the film's characters. Žižek accepted half of Wood's formulation—the spectator's identification with Marion—but rejected Wood's account of Hitchcock's tactical maneuver to switch identification to Norman Bates. "After the murder of Marion," he wrote, "identification with the personality who dominates the diegetic space becomes impossible." [47] In an endnote directly citing Wood, he added, "What eludes [Wood] is the *structural impossibility* of identifying with Norman." [48] The distinction Žižek sought to draw was between Marion's familiar forms of desire, with which spectators could identify, and Norman's "psychotic drive," identification with which the author so implacably denied. [49] Did this difference relieve the spectator of the culpability and "common guilt" that Wood had postulated as the acknowledgments that spectators owed to their identification with Norman? No. Rather, it forces "him/her to *identify with the abyss beyond identification*." [50] This Lacanian concept, in broad paraphrase, unveils not identification with Norman but with our own all-encompassing murderous desires, different from Norman's drive but nevertheless activated by Hitchcock's narrative strategies. It is an abyss of abjection to which nearly all of the critical writing on Hitchcock's violence and spectatorship, with few exceptions, tends.

Scholarly theorists have avoided many of the flaws that Sidney Gottlieb found in the psychiatrist Fredric Wertham's approach to Hitchcock's violence: if they are occasionally glib and pompous, they are rarely philistine, literal, or simplistic. One sometimes wonders if the latter characteristics might not at times prove beneficial to the discourse. Hitchcock's complexity and ambiguity, and his apparent mastery over spectator response, clearly offer important clues to the way audiences may be thrilled or repulsed by screen violence. The director, so his critics say, leads us all to recognize the murderer within ourselves. The next step for interpreters of Hitchcock's violence would be to help us understand how and why we act on that knowledge.

Notes

Thanks to Rahul Hamid for research assistance, and to Adrienne Harris and Susan Coates for their comments and suggestions on earlier drafts.

1. Robin Wood, *Hitchcock's Films Revisited* (New York: Columbia University Press, 1989; original publication, 1965), pp. 144–48.

2. See *Hitchcock's Films Revisited*, pp. 303–310, 362–64; quotation from p. 303. A further analysis of identification in Hitchcock and *Psycho* based on psychoanalytic theories appears in Peter Benson, "Identification and Slaughter," *CinéAction!*, No. 12 (Spring 1988), pp. 12–18.

3. François Truffaut, with the collaboration of Helen G. Scott, *Hitchcock* (New York: Simon and Schuster, 1967), p. 272. For a refutation of character identification, see Noël Carroll, *The Philosophy of Horror* (New York and London: Routledge, 1990), pp. 88–96.

4. *Hitchcock's Films Revisited*, p. 148.

5. J. David Slocum, "Violence and American Cinema: Notes for an Investigation," in *Violence in American Cinema*, ed. J. David Slocum (Routledge: New York and London, 2001), note 24, p. 27.

6. Letter, Hitchcock to Sidney Bernstein, n.d. [1953], in Dan Auiler, *Hitchcock's Notebooks: An Authorized and Illustrated Look Inside the Creative Mind of Alfred Hitchcock* (New York: Avon; London: Bloomsbury, 1999), p. 162. The British title is *Hitchcock's Secret Notebooks*.

7. English-language transcript of a 1974 interview published in the Quebec newspaper *Le Devoir*, cited in Stephen Prince, *Savage Cinema: Sam Peckinpah and the Rise of Ultraviolent Movies* (Austin: University of Texas Press, 1998), p. 221. See also note 89, p. 258.

8. See Donald Spoto, *The Dark Side of Genius: The Life of Alfred Hitchcock* (New York: Little, Brown, 1983; Ballantine edition), p. 397 ff.

9. Alfred Hitchcock, "Violence: An Ever-handy Reference Manual to the Selection, Dispatchment and Disposal, with Taste, of a Likely Victim," *Esquire* 56 (July 1961), pp. 107–112.

10. "A *Redbook* Dialogue: Alfred Hitchcock and Dr. Fredric Wertham," *Redbook* 120 (April 1963), pp. 71, 108, 110–12, reprinted in *Hitchcock on Hitchcock: Selected Writings and Interviews*, ed. Sidney Gottlieb (Berkeley and Los Angeles: University of California Press, 1995), pp. 146–54. Quotations from pp. 146–47. Wertham's ideas and influence in the 1950s are discussed in James Gilbert, *A Cycle of Outrage: America's Reaction to the Juvenile Delinquent in the 1950s* (New York: Oxford University Press, 1986). Hitchcock repeated several of the anecdotes and examples concerning violence that he used in the Wertham dialogue several years later in remarks following a screening of *Rear Window* at the Academy of Motion Picture Arts and Sciences. See Alfred Hitchcock, "*Rear Window*," *Take One* 2, no. 2 (1968), pp. 18–20.

11. "A *Redbook* Dialogue," in Gottlieb, *Hitchcock on Hitchcock*, pp. 146–47, 154.

12. Gottlieb, *Hitchcock on Hitchcock*, p. 105.

13. Gottlieb, *Hitchcock on Hitchcock*, p. 147.

14. Telegram, Hitchcock to Herrmann, November 4, 1965, in Auiler, *Hitchcock's Notebooks*, pp. 525–26. Ultimately, Hitchcock was dissatisfied with Herrmann's score and replaced him on the picture.

15. Truffaut, *Hitchcock*, p. 234.

16. Spoto, *The Dark Side of Genius*, pp. 517–18.

17. Stephen Prince, "Graphic Violence in the Cinema: Origins, Aesthetic Design, and Social Effects," in *Screening Violence*, ed. Prince (New Brunswick, NJ: Rutgers University Press, 2000), p. 9.

18. Prince, *Savage Cinema*, p. 222. I first raised some of the themes of this essay in an omnibus review that included Prince's impressive book, Auiler's *Hitchcock's [Secret] Notebooks*, and several others works, in the *Times Literary Supplement* (London); see Robert Sklar, "Will Blood Have Blood?" October 1, 1999, pp. 18–19.

19. Prince, *Savage Cinema*, p. 222.

20. *Newsweek*, June 26, 1972, quoted in Spoto, *The Dark Side of Genius*, pp. 551–52.

21. Prince, *Savage Cinema*, p. 223.

22. Albert Johnson, review of *Frenzy*, *Film Quarterly* 26 (Fall, 1972), pp. 58–60, quotes from p. 59.

23. Vincent Canby, "*Frenzy*, Hitchcock in Dazzling Form," *The New York Times*, June 22, 1972, p. 48.

24. Dennis Turner, "Hitchcock's Moral *Frenzy* in the Declining Years," *Film/Psychology Review* 4, no. 1 (Winter-Spring 1980), pp. 59–69. Quotes from pp. 60, 61, 69.

25. Turner, "Hitchcock's Moral *Frenzy*" pp. 68–69.

26. Spoto, *The Dark Side of Genius*, p. 545.

27. Victoria Sullivan, "Does *Frenzy* Degrade Women?" *The New York Times,* July 30, 1972, Section II, p. 9.

28. See Rebecca Bailin, "Feminist Readership, Violence, and *Marnie,*" *Film Reader* 5 (1982), pp. 24–36, and Kay Sloan, "Three Hitchcock Heroines: The Domestication of Violence," *New Orleans Review* 12, no. 4 (Winter 1985), pp. 91–95.

29. The most extensive shot-by-shot description of the rape-murder sequence in *Frenzy,* as well as of the entire film, appears in Stefan Sharff, *Alfred Hitchcock's High Vernacular: Theory and Practice* (New York: Columbia University Press, 1991), pp. 167–233.

30. Jeanne Thomas Allen, "The Representation of Violence to Women: Hitchcock's *Frenzy,*" *Film Quarterly* 38, no. 3 (Spring 1985), pp. 30–38. Quotes from pp. 31–32.

31. Allen, "The Representation of Violence," pp. 35–36.

32. Allen, "The Representation of Violence," pp. 37–38.

33. Sullivan, "Does *Frenzy* Degrade Women?"

34. Tania Modleski, *The Women Who Knew Too Much: Hitchcock and Feminist Theory* (New York and London: Methuen, 1988), note 17, p. 137.

35. Modleski, *The Women Who Knew Too Much,* pp. 120, 109–110.

36. Modleski, *The Women Who Knew Too Much,* p. 111. Italics in original.

37. Modleski, *The Women Who Knew Too Much,* p. 113. Italics in original. In her comparison of *Psycho* to *Frenzy,* Modleski nodded to the director's universal powers of control over the spectator. In the former film, she wrote, Hitchcock is "teasing viewers with shots of Janet Leigh in her brassiere and Janet Leigh stripping so that even while she is being stabbed to death we *irresistibly* wonder if we'll get a glimpse of her naked breasts" (italics added).

38. Modleski, *The Women Who Knew Too Much,* pp. 112, 121. Published in the same year as Modleski's book, Leslie Brill's *The Hitchcock Romance: Love and Irony in Hitchcock's Films* (Princeton, NJ: Princeton University Press, 1988) discusses *Frenzy* predominantly in terms of the book's subtitle, noticing violence chiefly through a remark that the rape/murder is a "ghastly sequence." See pp. 125–44. Quote from p. 138.

39. Carol J. Clover, "Her Body, Himself: Gender in the Slasher Film," in *Screening Violence,* ed. Prince, pp. 125–74. Quotes from note 29, pp. 132, 134, 171. Originally published in *Representations* 20 (Fall 1987), pp. 187–228. Other works that discuss the influence of *Psycho* on slasher films, the horror genre, and other filmmakers include Robert E. Kapsis, *Hitchcock: The Making of a Reputation* (Chicago: University of Chicago Press, 1992) and Stephen Rebello, *Alfred Hitchcock and the Making of* Psycho (New York: Dembner Books, 1990).

40. Clover, "Her Body, Himself," p. 149.

41. Clover, "Her Body, Himself," p. 159. Clover's endnote citations are unhelpful in providing documentation for her argument that "at least one director, Hitchcock, explicitly located thrill in the equation victim = audience." She provided a Hitchcock quotation as support following this sentence, and ended the quoted passage with endnote 56. But the information given in endnote 56, p. 173, made no reference to the passage quoted in the text. (In the original journal publication, the endnote in question is no. 57; as incorporated in Clover's book, *Men, Women, and Chain Saws: Gender in the Modern Horror Film* [Princeton, NJ: Princeton University Press, 1992], the sentence above and the subsequent quotation are on p. 52, along with footnote no. 46, which cites a page number in a source text where the quoted passage does not appear.)

42. Clover, "Her Body, Himself," p. 164.

43. William Rothman, *Hitchcock: The Murderous Gaze* (Cambridge, MA: Harvard University Press, 1982), p. 299.

44. Slavoj Žižek, "'In His Bold Gaze My Ruin Is Writ Large,'" in *Everything You Always Wanted to Know About Lacan (But Were Afraid to Ask Hitchcock),* ed. Žižek (London and New York: Verso, 1992), p. 222.

45. Žižek, "'In His Bold Gaze,'" p. 223.

46. Žižek, "'In His Bold Gaze,'" p. 225. The quoted words appear in italics in the text.
47. Žižek, "'In His Bold Gaze,'" p. 227.
48. Žižek, "'In His Bold Gaze,'" p. 266, note 25. Italics in original.
49. Žižek, "'In His Bold Gaze,'" p. 229.
50. Žižek, "'In His Bold Gaze,'" p. 226. Italics in original.

Hitchcock and the Classical Paradigm

John Belton

Modernism

Alfred Hitchcock's interest in the cinema has always had a theoretical bent. His notions about the cinema were shaped, in part, by the theoretical agendas of British film culture in the 1920s. His apprenticeship as a filmmaker included screenings of German, Soviet, and other modernist films at the London Film Society.[1] The Film Society drew its membership from a broad spectrum of the film community, ranging from critics such as Iris Barry, Ivor Montagu, and Walter Mycroft, to directors and writers such as Anthony Asquith, Adrian Brunel, George Bernard Shaw, and H. G. Wells, to producers such as Sidney Bernstein, with whom Hitchcock would form a partnership in 1946.

Starting with *The Lodger* (1926), Hitchcock's own filmmaking began to reveal the influence of German Expressionism and Soviet Constructivism.[2] In fact, it was at this point in his career that Hitchcock began to collaborate with Ivor Montagu, a founding member of the Film Society who was quite well-versed in Soviet film theory, having translated theoretical essays by Pudovkin and Eisenstein into English.[3] Montagu was assigned to edit *The Lodger* (1926) and continued to work as Hitchcock's editor on *Downhill* (1927) and *Easy Virtue* (1927). After his sojourn with Eisenstein in Hollywood, Montagu returned to England where he served as associate producer on Hitch's major projects of the mid-1930s: *The Man Who Knew Too Much* (1934), *The 39 Steps* (1935), *The Secret Agent* (1936), and *Sabotage* (1936).

Hitchcock never wrote theoretical essays on the cinema, as Eisenstein, Vertov, and other filmmakers did. Nor did he refer to theoretical writings in his numerous interviews, though in his interview with Truffaut he spoke of what he called "pure cinema," and made references to Pudovkin and Kuleshov.[4] Here, Hitch cited Kuleshov's editing experiments to explain his own POV/ reaction-shot trope. But even if he rarely spoke of theory, Hitchcock's film practice regularly explored theoretical issues.

Theoretical Film Practice

While "criticism" properly concerns itself with the meaning of individual works, the focus of "theory" involves the nature of the medium itself. Hitchcock's theory of film practice has served as a fundamental ground for his explorations of the nature of narrative cinema, often in the form of "experiments" which he has conducted in individual films. He set himself arbitrary temporal and spatial restrictions in films like *Lifeboat* (1944), *Rope* (1948), *Under Capricorn* (1949), *Dial M for Murder* (1954), and *Rear Window* (1954), testing his abilities to tell stories with little or no editing and within confined spaces.[5] At the same time, Hitchcock investigated the nature of spectatorship, ranging from isolated experiments with untrustworthy narration (*Stage Fright*, 1950) to sustained studies of voyeurism, identification, and fabula construction (*Rear Window, Vertigo* [1958]).[6]

As Raymond Williams suggests, theory is "a scheme of ideas which explains practice."[7] But for Hitchcock the opposite is equally true: his film practice "explains" film theory. That is, it thinks through theoretical issues in response to specific challenges. Technological innovation provides one area in which practice constitutes a form of response to theoretical questions about the nature of the medium. With the coming of sound, for example, Hitchcock implemented his own version of Eisenstein, Pudovkin, and Alexandrov's theory of asynchronous sound, coupled with expressionist experiments in the distortion of sound. Films such as *Blackmail* (1929), *Murder* (1930), and *The Secret Agent* (1936) call into question common associations of the coming of sound with notions of greater realism. In a similar way, Hitchcock's expressionist manipulation of color, found in his use of red suffusions in *Rear Window* and *Marnie* (1964), extends the role of color in the cinema beyond simple verisimilitude to the sort of *Materialtheorie* championed by Rudolf Arnheim.[8] The point is not so much the director's fascination with technology and technique but his larger project of creating a film practice that was truly "cinematic"; i.e., that was grounded in an understanding of the nature of the medium, an understanding of how images and sounds worked.

Narrative Presence

Hitchcock's experiments with the conventional narrative and formal practices of classical Hollywood cinema put him at its boundaries. Though he is not as transgressive of the classical Hollywood paradigm as art-cinema directors such as Jean-Luc Godard, his work does exhibit a narrative and formal self-consciousness which surfaces most obviously in the foregrounding of his presence as narrator—in what critics might refer to as "Hitchcockian touches." Audiences understand these "touches" as features of a narrative persona, characterized by the director's macabre sensibility, wry wit, and intrusive presence as a storyteller.

As I argued elsewhere,

> Hitchcock's visibility as a narrator has become part of his "contractual" relationship with his audiences. Viewers expect a Hitchcock film to be "Hitchcockian"—that is, to have a certain kind of narrative sensibility, much as they expect Hitchcock's own cameo appearances within the films themselves . . . By means of this sort of visibility, Hitchcock violates the norms of classical Hollywood cinema; he winks, as it were, at the audience and conspires with them in constructing the illusion of the fiction: he thus acknowledges that the film *is* a construction and that he has constructed it.[9]

Hitchcock's visibility as a narrative presence is not unique within the classical paradigm. Lubitsch, Ford, and a host of other directors have established themselves as narrative brand names. What makes Hitchcock unique as a visible narrative presence is his penchant for acknowledging the hide-and-seek game he is playing as narrator with his audience. Thomas M. Leitch has devoted an entire book to this aspect of Hitchcock as narrator—*Find the Director and Other Hitchcock Games* (Athens: University of Georgia Press, 1991).

One must surely admire the exemplary nature of the director's film practice whereby he functions as paradigmatic of classical Hollywood cinema in general while, at the same time, distancing himself from the paradigm through his critical scrutiny of it. But Hitchcock's visibility tends to function in a somewhat paradoxical fashion. It undermines the invisibility of the classical paradigm while harnessing his own authorial visibility as a dominant feature of the narrative experience, as that which makes it "Hitchcockian." The ultimate effect of this destabilization is a restabilization of the audience that occupies a position of knowing participation in the game Hitchcock plays with the classical narrative paradigm.

1970s Film Theory

Hitchcock's relationship to the classical paradigm is clearly complex. Since his mastery of film technique is virtually flawless, he has often been used as a source of examples for illustrating basic features of classical Hollywood cinema. No other director can execute the POV/reaction shot or shot/reverse shot tropes as elegantly.[10] With the possible exception of D. W. Griffith, only Hitchcock understood and mastered the basic principles of suspense editing, i.e., cutting away in midaction.

Hitchcock's skill as an editor led to his appropriation by contemporary theory as a paradigm for classical cinema's ability to manipulate visual pleasure. Laura Mulvey, for example, cites both Hitchcock and Sternberg as examples of patterns of looking within patriarchal cinema. Hitchcock demonstrates the sadistic side of voyeuristic scopophilia while Sternberg displays its fetishistic side.[11] If Hitchcock's films exemplify the male gaze (including fetishistic scopophilia), they also resist paradigmatic reductionism. As Tania Modleski argues in her critique of Mulvey on *Vertigo*, the gaze of Hitchcock's male hero cannot be reduced to simple sadism (or fetishism). In fact, the gaze of Hitchcock's dizzy detective is identificatory; Scottie identifies with Madeleine and is feminized in the process.[12]

One might note as well that although Scottie is a representative of the Law, his association with it is so weak that he is unable to implement it. Instead, he is used by the villain, Gavin Elster, to violate the law, to commit a near-perfect crime. Scottie's look does not exemplify that of the typical male in patriarchy, but, in fact, undermines that look.

More often than not, Hitchcock provides contemporary theory with examples that *expose* the operations of the classical paradigm, the formal equivalent to Category E (Five) in Jean-Louis Comolli and Jean Narboni's discussion of the degree to which classical cinema transmits the dominant ideology. These are films which "throw up obstacles in the way of ideology, causing it to swerve and get off course."[13]

In the parlance of the Russian Formalists, Hitchcock's editing "lays bare the device."[14] Victor Shklovsky concludes his discussion of the ways in which Sterne's *Tristram Shandy*'s narration foregrounds the very act of narration with a remark that might apply equally well to a work by Hitchcock: "*Tristram Shandy* is the most typical novel in world literature."[15] Hitchcock's editing is "the most typical in world cinema," yet it is grounded in an awareness of itself, in a "laying bare of its own devices" that is uncannily Constructivist and Modernist in nature. It makes visible the techniques and strategies of its own construction in ways that conventional cinema does not.

The visible invisibility of Hitchcock's editing techniques provides the basis for Kaja Silverman's discussion of the operations of suture in Hitchcock. She examines several instances of shot/reverse-shot editing in *Psycho* and the disjunctive editing of the film's famous shower sequence to illustrate how the film "exposes the negations on which filmic plenitude is predicated."[16] Her conclusion: "The film terrorizes the viewing subject, refusing ever to let it off the hook. That hook is the system of suture, which is held up to our scrutiny even as we find ourselves thoroughly ensnared in it." In other words, Hitchcock's editing constantly threatens to disrupt the pleasures of plenitude inherent in the suture process, but that threat of disruption does not disrupt the process; it enhances it. "What *Psycho* obliges us to understand is that we want suture so badly that we'll take it at any price—even with the fullest knowledge of what it entails . . ."[17]

Stephen Heath's use of Hitchcock in his discussion of "narrative space" reveals a similar portrait of Hitchcock's problematic relation to the classical paradigm. In his discussion of a scene in which two policemen visit Lina, the heroine in *Suspicion* (1943), Heath notes how the classical depiction of space briefly "goes askew" and how a centered space momentarily decentered (by one policeman's gaze at an offscreen painting) introduces an "interruption [into] the homogeneity of the narrative economy."[18] It is this sort of modernist eccentricity that prompts Heath to link Hitchcock to Stan Brakhage, Ken Jacobs, and American independent cinema.[19]

Žižek

These appropriations of Hitchcock by contemporary theory as a modernist manipulator of the classical paradigm provide some insight into the unique nature of his narrative presence, but these discussions remain frustratingly limited, restricted by the very nature of the arguments themselves which "instrumentalize" Hitchcock, relegating him to the status of an example that is designed to illustrate a more general, theoretical point. Perhaps the most egregious "instrumentalization" of Hitchcock takes place in Slavoj Žižek's introduction to *Everything You Always Wanted to Know About Lacan (But Were Afraid to Ask Hitchcock)* (New York: Verso, 1992).

Žižek is relevant to this discussion in that he, like Silverman and Heath, recognizes the complex relation Hitchcock has with the classical paradigm (or what Žižek refers to as "realism"). For Žižek, "Hitchcock is of special interest precisely in so far as he dwells on the borders of [the] classificatory triad" of "realism-modernism-postmodernism." Arguing that Hitchcock is "realist, modernist, and postmodernist" at the same time, Žižek suggests that he cannot possibly be contained within the realist paradigm of classical Hollywood.[20] Žižek then uses the three categories of "realism," "modernism," and "postmodernism" to break Hitchcock's oeuvre down into five historical periods, using Hitchcock's career to illustrate his (and Fredric Jameson's) periodization of the history of the cinema. Hitchcock's first and second periods belong to the director's work in England. These films (e.g., *The 39 Steps*) feature a "classic narrative, centered on the oedipal story of the couple's initiatory journey."[21] The Selznick period (*Rebecca* to *Under Capricorn*) finds Hitchcock as a modernist; it is "thematically centered on the female heroine, traumatized by an ambiguous (evil, impotent, obscene, broken . . .) paternal figure."[22]

After the "modernist" phase comes the "postmodernist Hitchcock," which covers a fourth and fifth period. The fourth period consists of the 1950s films (e.g., *Rear Window, North by Northwest, Psycho*), which are "thematically centered on the perspective of the male hero, to whom the maternal superego blocks access to a normal sexual relation."[23] The films from *Marnie* onward constitute the "post-films"—these works are not described in terms of the heterosexual couple, the female heroine, or the male hero; nor do they share a specific narrative pattern; they are, quite vaguely, "films of disintegration."

Žižek's triad of "realism-modernism-postmodernism," as illustrated in his discussion of narrative periodization, seems somewhat idiosyncratic in relation to conventional definitions of "realism," "modernism" or "postmodernism." Following Barthes, film studies (via Colin MacCabe) has tended to conflate classical Hollywood cinema with the classic realist text.[24] But Žižek's notion of a modernist text ("the irruption of a trauma which undermines the complacency of our daily routine and resists being integrated into the symbolic universe of the prevailing ideology")[25] tends to ignore the element of self-reflexivity crucial to works of modernist art. Modernist works, including Hitchcock's borderline classic realist texts, draw attention to their own methods of construction and to the processes by which meaning is constructed. "Shock" and "trauma" may be terms that are applicable to Hitchcock, but they convey little about his stylistic (i.e., formal) practices. Žižek describes postmodernism as "the mess we are in today," which is perhaps not a bad definition of a term that resists easy definition.

This is perhaps not the time or the place to attempt to define postmodernism. For Jameson, postmodernism reflects the cultural logic of late capitalism, a world of alienation compounded by social fragmentation and the inner fragmentation of the individual subject. Aesthetic practices within postmodernism include "pastiche" and the recycling of aesthetic codes (such as those of film noir) that simulate a historical past that is no longer accessible. Aesthetic creation occurs within a world in which there is no distinction between high and low popular art and where artists recognize their inability to say anything that has not already been said.

Jameson connects this inability to be original—what he calls "the failure of the new"—with nostalgia and a retreat from the fragmentation and incoherence of the present to the coherence of the past, where the self was whole and the individual was part of a larger, unified community (see *American Graffiti,* 1971). However, this representation of the past is not "real," but merely a simulation of "pastness." Postmodern works reflect the schizophrenic breakdown of the normal experience of the world as a continuous, coherent, and meaningful phenomenon. These works consist of a series of "isolated, disconnected, discontinuous material signifiers which fail to link up into a coherent sequence." Postmodern artists thus convey the incoherence that informs the social and cultural reality of contemporary existence.

For Žižek, Hitchcock is postmodern "from *Marnie* on." *Marnie* (1964), *Torn Curtain* (1966), *Frenzy* (1972), and *Family Plot* (1976) are "films of disintegration" where "the breaking apart of Hitchcock's universe into its particular ingredients . . . enable[s] us to isolate these ingredients and grasp them clearly."[26] To argue, as I instinctively feel obliged to do, that Hitchcock is *not* a postmodernist is to play Žižek's game on his own turf. It makes little sense to quibble over which slot to shove Hitchcock's final films into, especially since Žižek provides no compelling evidence to support his argument or textual readings for anyone to refute. Rather than arguing with Žižek, a paraphrase of Bela Lugosi's famous line in *The Black Cat* might suffice. Hitchcock? Modernist, perhaps; postmodernist, perhaps not. For my money, Hitchcock is the "original." It is De Palma who is the postmodernist.

Though the realism-modernism-postmodernism triad may be Jamesonian, its application to the narrative typologies outlined mixes Marx with Freud. Žižek's narrative typology would seem to be more or less psychoanalytic, but then he quickly shifts to social-economic notions of subjectivity, arguing that "the dominant type of subjectivity in each of the three central periods" coincides with "the three stages of capitalism (liberal capitalism, imperialist state capitalism, and 'post-industrial' late capitalism."[27]

Žižek's argument is grounded in contradiction: first he insists that Hitch-

Hitchcock's fascination with doubleness and duplicity in *Frenzy* centers on the morally ambiguous main character, who is proven a "wrong man" only in the film's closing sequence.

cock is all three (realist, modernist, postmodernist) at the same time. Then he insists that realism, modernism, and postmodernism constitute three successive periods in Hitchcock's oeuvre. But Žižek is notorious for the contradictions which structure his arguments: contradiction, for Žižek, becomes a vantage point on the fluid surface of a dialectical stream-of-consciousness argument from which to direct quasi-ephemeral insights that briefly light up various nodal points in his own thought.

More problematically, Žižek uses Hitchcock as a "field" on which to demonstrate the supposed viability of certain theoretical paradigms. At one moment, Žižek views the work through the grid of Jameson's three stages of capitalism and at another through that of Lacanian psychoanalysis. In both instances, his goal is not the production of knowledge about Hitchcock's films, but the QED confirmation of his theoretical paradigms. In the hands of certain critics, theory can easily dissolve away the object of its study, replacing it with a simulation of that object that is designed to reproduce the object in its (theory's) own image.

Bellour

Theoretically, the same could also be said of Raymond Bellour's work on Hitchcock. It is ultimately directed toward the illustration of the basic elements which drive classical narration, but Bellour's work actually problematizes its own agenda, acknowledging, at the very outset, the essential "unattainability" of the text, the impossibility of describing a film in words.[28] For Bellour, detailed analysis constitutes a "murder" of the object being analyzed.[29] In an attempt to "protect" the film, Bellour describes it in precise detail. Recast in the form of still-frame enlargements and written description, the film is no longer the object with which the analyst began. But it has not entirely vanished either; it exists in the form of a "quote." For Bellour, film analysis "constantly mimics, evokes, describes; in a kind of principled despair it can but try frantically to compete with the object it is attempting to understand."[30] Bellour, like all critics, necessarily rewrites the film he is analyzing to reveal or make clear its operations. For the original text, he substitutes, out of necessity, his engagement with the text and this becomes the subject of his analysis. Though clearly re-presented, the original presence of the object is reflected in the analysis upon which it has left its trace.

Žižek's discussion of Hitchcock's relation to the classical paradigm cites Bellour, "for whom [Hitchcock's] films vary the oedipal trajectory and are as such 'both an eccentric and exemplary version' of the classic Hollywood narrative."[31] In other words, Hitchcock is paradigmatic of all classical Hollywood cinema in that his narratives, like classical cinema's, are grounded in an oedipal struggle which concludes with a reconciliation between desire and the law. But at the same time, Hitchcock routinely "contravenes the classical model of narrative . . . not in order to elude the system but rather . . . to determine its regimes."[32] In other words, Hitchcock's transgressions of the classical paradigm invoke—and thus depend upon—that paradigm at the moment of its violation. Each instance of rupture, substitution, or displacement achieves its expressive power against the background of the regularity of its shadow, the absent (yet present) classical paradigm.

Bellour's larger project is to identify and describe the oedipal structures which underlie classical Hollywood narrative cinema; Hitchcock's films function as his primary texts. Bellour sees in classical American cinema the same preoccupation he found in his study of eighteenth- and nineteenth-century literature: the use of "Oedipus and castration to organize conflict and sexual difference around the restricted scene of the nuclear family."[33] Hitchcock's films exemplify the oedipal nature of narrative through their implementation of what Bellour refers to as "symbolic blockage."[34] By this he means that the films move through a "series of constraints" in which desire is gradually reconciled with the law. This movement occurs on a variety of levels. It can be seen narratively in terms of the hero's oedipalization, a process that is most elaborately worked out in the journey narrative of *North by Northwest*. But it can also be seen stylistically in the movement from shot to shot and from scene to scene—a movement which plays on difference, repetition, violations of expectation, variation, alternation, symmetry, and dissymmetry.

Bellour's oedipal reading of Thornhill's journey in *North by Northwest* is grounded in the hero's overly close relationship with his mother and his quest for a more suitable love object, Eve Kendall. It is Thornhill's desire to send a telegram to his mother (and his misrecognition as Kaplan) that initiates his oedipal itinerary. Bellour is surely joking when he speculates that the play that Thornhill and his mother were to see that night at the Winter Garden was *Oedipus the King,* but the action that follows lends itself to Bellour's suggestion that the film's narrative reworks the drama of the play that Thornhill wanted to see and missed. Even if the reluctant reader remains wary of Bellour's insistence on viewing slain United Nations diplomat Townsend as a father figure for Thornhill, Thornhill's oedipal triangle with Eve and Vandamm gives solid geometric form to the scenario Bellour seeks to spin. The heart of Bellour's analysis is a seventy-page segmentation of the crop duster sequence which, like his reading of a segment from *The Birds,* relies extensively on alternating patterns of seeing/being seen and the significance of variations in those patterns. Thus Bellour segues from an alternating pattern between Thornhill and what he sees to delineate two axes of movement (the highway extends in two directions; perpendicular to this are the two fields on either side of the highway). A car pulls out of one field, answering the movement of the bus on the highway that dropped Thornhill off. The departure of another bus, headed along one axis in the opposite direction to Thornhill's bus is then answered by the attack of the crop duster, which flies along the other axis from the field on the opposite side of the highway (and in the opposite direction of the car that came out of the cornfield). Out of these perpendicular axes, opposing movements, mirroring, alternations, and echoes, Bellour traces a logic of vehicles of locomotion and movement that links the first shot (Thornhill's arrival by bus) and answering shots (the arrival of the crop duster) to the final shots (the crash of the plane into a gas tanker; Thornhill's flight in a farmer's truck). In Bellour's hands, the logic of the decoupage achieves absolute clarity. The scene becomes a perfect example of the dramatic powers of Hitchcock's manipulation of the classical paradigm.

It displays the insistence of an order, determined by a set of formal operations, singular and general at once (alternations, ruptures of alternation, condensations, displacements, oppositions, similarities, differences, repetitions, resolutions, etc.), borne along by figurative, narrative, and representational options.[35]

What is remarkable about Bellour's work is his ability to read the relation of shots to one another and to communicate the intricacy of the operations of displacement, condensation, alternation, symmetry, and dissymmetry that occur over the span of a segment that consists of 133 shots in *North by Northwest* (or of 84 in *The Birds*). But, unlike other close readings, his microscopic analyses in no way *reduce* the text to its fundamental elements, nor do they leave it like an autopsied cadaver in the morgue. They actually bring the text to life, lovingly animating its various pieces and revealing the intellectual and emotional force—what Bellour calls "the desire of the film"—that drives the film itself.

At any rate, Bellour invokes the classical paradigm not so much to illustrate it through examples from Hitchcock as to use it as a tool for *reading* Hitchcock. The classical paradigm is nothing more than the sum total of classical film practice. It's not a system that should be imposed, top down, on texts to measure their exemplarity of the system; rather, it is a *structure* erected out of films themselves that *shadows* individual films, providing a background against which unique expression can take place. Bellour's work is additionally productive in that he does not focus exclusively on Hitchcock; he deals with Griffith, Lang, Hawks, Minnelli, and others, as well. Each emerges as a unique idiolect within a larger, common semiotic practice. The classical paradigm functions to foreground individual and unique articulations of it. Hitchcock, however, remains especially interesting in this context in that his films are, at once, "both an eccentric and exemplary version" of the classical paradigm, which is not the case for other filmmakers. And Hitchcock's filmic practice defines itself, more than others do, through a self-reflexive relation with this paradigm.

This brief review of Hitchcock's relationship with the classical paradigm suggests that critical analysis needs to instrumentalize theory, not texts. Theory should have as its goal the explanation of phenomena, not the use of phenomena to legitimize itself. Theory's relationship to practice is long and complex. Though often opposed in the form of contemplation vs. action, theory and practice are necessarily interrelated. There is no theory without a specific practice on which it is based; no practice devoid of a theory which informs it. This is more or less what Hitchcock understood. He used "theory" to make films. His films engage us on the level of film practice with their characters, stories, and stylistic techniques, but they also provide theoretical appeal, encouraging us to view that practice in terms of a discourse about the nature of the cinema itself. In this sense, Hitchcock's films constitute a body of theoretical practice that go a long way in explaining his appropriation by film theory as a paradigm for classical cinema. His interest in the cinema *as cinema* so informs his film practice that it becomes impossible to see him simply as an example of what is normative about it. He remains unique in his exemplariness of the system he exemplifies.

Notes

1. Donald Spoto notes that Hitchcock frequented the Film Society, which screened a number of German films, including *The Cabinet of Dr. Caligari* (Weine, 1919), *The Golem* (Wegener, 1920), and *Dr. Mabuse* (Lang, 1922). See *The Dark Side of Genius: The Life of Alfred Hitchcock* (New York: Ballantine, 1983): 80. Rachel Low reports that *Mother* (Pudovkin, 1926), The *End of St. Petersburg* (Pudovkin, 1927), *Battleship Potemkin* (Eisenstein, 1925), and other films were screened at the London Film Society in the 1920s. See *The History of the British Film, 1918–1929* (London: George Allen & Unwin, 1971): 65.

2. In an interview published in *Screen* (Vol. 12, No. 3 or 4) in the Autumn of 1971, Ivor Montagu acknowledged that "*The Lodger* was made directly under the influence of the German films. You see, Hitch was working in Munich on the previous two and he'd seen the pictures of the Film Society and it was made directly under the influence of the German films . . ." (88).

3. Montagu translated Pudovkin's *Film Technique* (1933) and a series of essays by Eisenstein, including "The Cinematographic Principle and Japanese Culture" (1930), "The Principles of Film Form" (1931), and "Film Form, 1935: New Problems" (1935); he accompanied Eisenstein on his visits to Berlin, Paris, London, and Hollywood in 1929–1930, eventually writing a book about the latter experience, *With Eisenstein in Hollywood* (1968).

4. François Truffaut, *Hitchcock* (New York: Simon and Schuster, 1967): 159.

5. In 1937, Hitchcock stated his preference for editing bits of film together over long takes by confessing that he always felt he was losing his grip on a scene, "from a cinematic point of view," when he filmed action in long takes. "Direction," in *Hitchcock on Hitchcock: Selected Writings and Interviews*, ed. Sidney Gottlieb (Berkeley: University of California Press, 1995): 255. The fact that Hitchcock could abandon editing for long takes ten years later provides powerful evidence of his interest in testing the boundaries of cinematic expression and suggests the theoretical implications of his "experiments."

6. The term "fabula construction" refers to the spectator's construction of story information out of data presented by a narrative film's images and sounds. See David Bordwell, "Classical Hollywood Cinema: Narrational Principles and Procedures," in *Narrative, Apparatus, Ideology: A Film theory Reader*, ed. Philip Rosen (New York: Columbia University Press, 1986): 19.

7. *Keywords* (New York: Oxford, 1976): 267.

8. *Film as Art* (Berkeley: University of California, 1957): 2. Arnheim, of course, viewed sound and color as elements that brought greater realism to the cinema and that thus

threatened its potential status as an art form. But Hitchcock's nonillusionist uses of sound and color effectively suggest ways in which these technologies might enhance the aesthetic capabilities of the cinema and could extend Arnheim's argument on film as art from the silent, black-and-white cinema to a cinema in sound and color.

9. *Alfred Hitchcock's* Rear Window, ed. John Belton (New York: Cambridge, 2000): 10–11.

10. See, for example, Tim Hunter's discussion of Hitchcock's editing in "Alfred Hitchcock: The Mechanics of Clarity," in *The Harvard Crimson* (June 12, 1968).

11. Laura Mulvey, "Visual Pleasure and Narrative Cinema," in Rosen, 207.

12. Tania Modleski, *The Women Who Knew Too Much: Hitchcock and Feminist Theory* (New York: Methuen, 1988): 92.

13. "Cinema/Ideology/Criticism (1)," trans. Susan Bennett in *Screen Reader 1: Cinema/Ideology/Politics* (London: SEFT, 1977): 7.

14. Victor Shklovsky, "Sterne's *Tristram Shandy,*" in *Russian Formalist Criticism: Four Essays,* ed. Lee T. Lemon and Marion J. Reis (Lincoln: University of Nebraska Press, 1965): 26, 30.

15. Shklovsky, 57.

16. *The Subject of Semiotics* (New York: Oxford University Press, 1983): 206.

17. Silverman, 212.

18. "Narrative Space" in his *Questions of Cinema* (Bloomington, IN: Indiana University Press, 1981): 24.

19. Heath, 57.

20. *Everything You Always Wanted to Know About Lacan (But Were Afraid to Ask Hitchcock),* ed. Slavoj Žižek (New York: Verso, 1992): 2.

21. Žižek, "Introduction: Alfred Hitchcock, or, The Form and its Historical Mediation," 3.

22. Žižek, 4.

23. Žižek, 5.

24. Colin MacCabe, "Realism and the Cinema," *Screen* 15, No. 2 (1974).

25. Žižek, 1.

26. Žižek, 5.

27. Žižek, 5.

28. Raymond Bellour, *The Analysis of Film,* ed. Constance Penley (Bloomington, IN: Indiana University Press, 2000): 21–27.

29. Bellour, 2.

30. Bellour, 26.

31. Žižek, 2–3.

32. Bellour, 238.

33. Bellour, 12.

34. Bellour, 12.

35. Bellour, 14.

PART VI: MODUS OPERANDI

Any consideration of Hitchcock's influence eventually has to confront the curious case of Hitchcock's most indefatigable imitator, Brian De Palma. But where most critics have been content to catalogue and either celebrate or (more frequently) denounce De Palma's countless Hitchcockian allusions, reworkings, and outright thefts, Thomas M. Leitch instead examines the uses to which they are put and the purposes they are made to serve, carefully discriminating, for instance, among the very different implications of the reworkings of the shower scene from *Psycho* in *Carrie, Dressed to Kill,* and *Blow Out.* Approaching De Palma as an exemplary case, rather than an exceptional one, Leitch undertakes a comprehensive reconsideration of the poetics of cinematic intertextuality, revisiting and rethinking those fundamental questions about imitation and influence, authorship and originality, which have recurred throughout this volume.

The doubled strangers, just acquainted, in De Palma's *Body Double* share a Hitch-cockian interest in the pleasures of voyeurism.

How to Steal from Hitchcock

Thomas M. Leitch

No filmmaker has ever produced a more extended meditation on the work of another filmmaker than Brian De Palma. Nor has any filmmaker taken more critical drubbings than De Palma has for his borrowings from Hitchcock. On the strength especially of a small but provocative minority of his films—*Sisters* (1973), *Obsession* (1975), *Carrie* (1976), *Dressed to Kill* (1980), *Blow Out* (1981), *Body Double* (1984), and *Raising Cain* (1992)—De Palma has been variously characterized as a Hitchcock imitator, a creator of Hitchcock homages, an acolyte, an heir apparent, a parasite, a scavenger, and a thief. In reviewing *Blow Out,* Richard Corliss went so far as to argue that "there are three Brian De Palmas"—the horror-smitten child of *Psycho,* the black humorist who echoes *The Trouble with Harry* in *Phantom of the Paradise* (1974) and *Home Movies* (1979), and the passionate dramatist of *Vertigo*'s obsessive love—and they are "all the grinning, scheming sons of Alfred Hitchcock."[1]

De Palma has reacted to these charges with predictable ambivalence. In essays, interviews, and the obligatory featurettes that stud the DVD releases of his older films, he has repeatedly acknowledged his profound debt to the "master of suspense," which he has taken pains to deepen in film after film. Yet he has long been impatient at being typecast as a Hitchcock wannabe. Asked on the release of *Body Double* why he kept reprising the shower scene from *Psycho,* he replied blandly: "If I'm attracted to something I shouldn't refuse to use it just because Hitchcock was attracted to it too."[2] Six years later, on the release of *The Bonfire of the Vanities* (1990) when questioned why he was so often accused of being derivative of Hitchcock, his response was snappier: "When you're writing a story about Brian De Palma, that's the spin. I could make Disney pictures from now on, and they'd still be talking about the shower scene I'd stolen from *Psycho*."[3]

Whatever its accuracy, this latter remark is interesting for two reasons. One is De Palma's assumption that if he weren't making Hitchcock movies, he'd be making Disney movies—that is, films in a conventional mode closely associated with another specific filmmaker. The other is his obvious hurt over being typecast on the basis of having borrowed a single scene. Yet the charge he is recalling is not exactly captious, since De Palma has pressed Hitchcock's most famous scene into service at least eight times. The first big scene in *Carrie* is a shower scene, and *Dressed to Kill* and *Blow Out* both begin and end with shower scenes. But De Palma seems to delight as well in smuggling shower scenes into films where they don't seem to belong. *Phantom of the Paradise* reprises the scene as farce, with a plumber's helper standing in for Mother Bates' carving knife. *Body Double* runs its end credits over the shooting of a film-within-the-film in which a showering woman is attacked by a vampire. Even *Scarface* (1983) sets its memorable chainsaw dismemberment in a shower.

Although De Palma has largely emerged from Hitchcock's shadow in more recent years, the question that continues to rage over his early homages, from *Sisters* to *Body Double*, is how they compare to the films of his great predecessor, and the consensus is inevitably to De Palma's disadvantage. *Sisters* is a "modest horror exercise out of Hitchcock."[4] *Obsession* is "no more than an exercise in style."[5] *Dressed to Kill* is "a shamefully straight steal from *Psycho*, among other things."[6] *Body Double* is "desperately derivative" of Hitchcockian models from *Rear Window* to *Vertigo*.[7] For their part, De Palma's leading advocates—Robin Wood, Michael Bliss, Susan Dworkin, Laurent Bouzereau, and Kenneth MacKinnon—have adopted a distinctly defensive posture in objecting to the characterization of De Palma as "an inferior plagiarist" or "the bastard son of Alfred Hitchcock" and his work as "a rip-off" filled with "merely gratuitous additions" by someone who "can do nothing but produce imitations."[8]

Satisfying as it would be to enter into this fray as a partisan of either Hitchcock or De Palma, I would like in this essay to waive questions of relative value in order to focus more directly on the nature of De Palma's borrowings from Hitchcock and on the questions they raise about the nature of film authorship. Of all De Palma's commentators, MacKinnon has consistently been the best, not at purging value judgments from his analysis, but at keeping the judgments from substituting for an analysis of De Palma as enunciator. I hope in this essay to maintain an equally analytical focus in the service of quite a different premise. Conceding, for the sake of argument, the harshest claims of De Palma's detractors—that he steals his most characteristic effects from Hitchcock—I'd like to consider De Palma's thefts as exemplary, not only of certain tendencies among Hitchcock imitators or De Palma's film-school generation of directors, but of commercial cinema generally. What exactly do De Palma's blatant and repeated thefts from the master, treated as positive prescriptions, have to teach about how to steal, and what it means to steal, from Hitchcock?

Steal Everything That Isn't Nailed Down

Since De Palma's work habits, which emphasize visual ideas over dialogue and involve storyboarding each shot in advance, already echo Hitchcock's, it is not surprising that he borrows from Hitchcock in so many other ways as well. From the amusingly botched attempt of Jon Rubin (Robert De Niro) in *Hi, Mom!* (1970) to take a leaf from *Rear Window* by using his movie camera to record his seduction of Judy Bishop (Jennifer Salt), the neighbor he has been spying on across his courtyard, De Palma steals from Hitchcock at every level. He obsessively quotes favorite moments like the shower scene from *Psycho* and the 360-degree pan from *Vertigo* in which Scottie Ferguson embraces Judy transformed into Madeleine, even in non-Hitchcockian contexts like the table around which the four title characters are sitting in *The Untouchables* (1987). He transforms the body-in-a-chest MacGuffin of *Rope* into the body-in-a-sofa MacGuffin in *Sisters*. He liberally borrows elements of Hitchcockian grammar and mise-en-scène, which he has identified as a "cinematic vocabulary."[9] His use of mirrors to double the characters throughout *Dressed to Kill, Blow Out,* and *Body Double* (in which a particularly audacious theft introduces Holly Body [Melanie Griffith] reflected in a mirror from behind which Jake Scully [Craig T. Wasson] is peering at her, exactly as Scottie had spied on Madeleine mirrored in the florist shop in *Vertigo*) hearkens back to Hitchcock's fascination with mirrors in *Vertigo, North by Northwest,* and *Psycho*. Recalling Hitchcock's fondness for setting scenes on staircases, De Palma provides a virtual anthology of staircase sequences in *Obsession,* and he turns the celebrated track-in/zoom-out that elongates *Vertigo*'s staircase on its side to show Jake's nightmare view of the tunnel in which his claustrophobia traps him in *Body Double*.

More unexpectedly, De Palma gilds his large-scale homages to Hitchcock films with small-scale thefts from other Hitchcock films. When Danielle Breton (Margot Kidder) appears on the set of the television show *Peeping Toms* in *Sisters,* a reaction shot of the audience instantly isolates one spectator, soon identified as her estranged husband Emile (William Finley), as the only one not smiling and looking at her, in an allusion to Bruno Anthony watching Guy Haines play tennis in *Strangers on a Train*. The slide show of the romance of Michael and Elizabeth Courtland (Cliff Robertson and Genevieve Bujold) that opens *Obsession* is based on the home movies of the de Winters' honeymoon in *Rebecca;* the sequence in which Sandra Portinari (Bujold again) gets the key to Elizabeth's locked bedroom recalls Alicia's search for the closet keys in *Notorious;* and the film's hints of incest echo those scattered throughout *Shadow of a Doubt*. The escape of Dr. Robert Elliott (Michael Caine) from Bellevue at the end of *Dressed to Kill* is cheered on by dozens of fellow inmates, borrowing liberally from Richard Blaney's escape from the prison hospital in *Frenzy*. *Blow Out* takes from *Psycho* not only its framing joke about screaming in the shower but an overhead camera setup that turns an innocuous washroom in Philadelphia's 30th Street Station into a mirrored trap. Having borrowed the lethal scissors from *Dial M for Murder* for the death of Bob La Salle (John Lithgow) in *Obsession*, De Palma thriftily returns to the scene of the same crime to appropriate its other leading elements—a woman's slow strangulation by an intruder in her apartment—for the death of Gloria Revelle (Deborah Shelton) in *Body Double*.

Perhaps De Palma's most recognizable borrowings are the large-scale elements from Hitchcock screenplays he uses to structure *Sisters* (*Psycho* with conjoined twins substituting for a mother and son), *Obsession* (*Vertigo* with the addition of the incestuous overtones of a father so besotted with his late wife's apparent reincarnation that he almost marries his own daughter), *Dressed to Kill* (a transvestite killer out of *Psycho* moves from the stylized trap of a motel shower to the even more stylized trap of an apartment-building elevator to punish a straying heroine before being tracked to his lair by a second heroine and her unlikely male partner), and *Body Double* (an amalgam in which *Rear Window*'s voyeuristic spectacles are staged deliberately to hook the voyeur, and Scottie Ferguson's acrophobia in *Vertigo* is transformed into claustrophobia). De Palma's devotion to his Hitchcockian sources can lead him to reprise even such problematic scenes as the psychiatrist's explanation of Norman Bates' psychosis, pressed into service to explain Dr. Elliott's transsexuality in *Dressed to Kill*.

Such familiar stories demand familiar characters, and De Palma casts his Hitchcock homages as if from a Hitchcock stock company, knowing that fans will expect to find such familiar character types as the unwisely romantic idealist (Michael Courtland in *Obsession* and perhaps Jack Terry [John Travolta] in *Blow Out*), and the damaged child either growing into fragile adulthood (Danielle Breton in *Sisters,* Carter Nix [John Lithgow] in *Raising Cain*) or failing to grow, like the heroine of *Carrie* and the voyeuristic hero: "I like to watch," Jake tells Holly in the pornographic film-within-a-film in *Body Double*, summarizing the vocations of the eyewitnesses, spies, and surveillance experts who throng *Sisters, Dressed to Kill,* and *Blow Out.* The heroine is demonized because of her sexuality: Danielle fatally separated from her twin Dominique in *Sisters* because her physician-husband wanted a normal sex life; the budding Carrie White [Sissy Spacek] spurned by her fanatic mother; Kate Miller [Angie Dickinson] slashed to death in *Dressed to Kill* on the way back to the apartment of her pickup to retrieve her engagement ring. Rounding out this cast of characters are the unhappy wife (Gloria Revelle impersonated by porn actress Holly Body in *Body Double*). The cops in *Sisters, Dressed to Kill, Blow Out,* and *Body Double* are unreasonably antipathetic. When De Palma wants a distinctive look for the cross-dressing killer of *Dressed to Kill,* he copies the disguise the kidnapper Fran assumes—blond wig, dark glasses, and trench coat—for the first ransom pickup in *Family Plot.*

In addition to recycling these Hitchcock stereotypes, De Palma has established occasional family connections outside the fictional frame, casting Tippi Hedren's daughter Melanie Griffith when Janet Leigh's daughter Jamie Lee Curtis declined the role of Holly Body in *Body Double* (and using Griffith again in *The Bonfire of the Vanities*) and hiring Hitchcock's longstanding collaborator Bernard Herrmann to write the scores for *Sisters* and *Obsession.* Indeed, De Palma's first collaboration with Herrmann almost foundered at the outset when the famously short-tempered composer found that the idolatrous director had pre-scored key scenes in *Sisters* with Herrmann's music from *Vertigo, Psycho,* and *Marnie.* Herrmann's synthesizer-inflected score for *Sisters* does not sound especially derivative of his earlier work. His score for *Obsession,* however, echoes that of *Vertigo* at any number of points. Michael's nightmarish ransom drop-off aboard a New Orleans paddle wheeler is scored to a reminiscence of Scottie's nightmare. His grieving at the monument he has erected in Pontchartrain Memorial Park is backed up by *Vertigo*'s signature falling motif. The organ music and string chords inside the Florentine church re-create the ethereal auditory ambience of the Mission Dolores. And in the denouement at the airport, the delirious 360-degree pan from *Vertigo* is accompanied by the carnival version of the love theme that accompanied it back in the Empire Hotel. When Herrmann's death made it impossible for him to score *Carrie,* the commission was given to Pino Donaggio, who, in the first of his six collaborations with De Palma, signaled each of the heroine's telekinetic outbursts of rage with repetitions of Herrmann's stabbing chord from *Psycho.*

More generally, De Palma, sharing Hitchcock's fascination with doubles—

a fascination literalized in *Sisters* but present metaphorically throughout his work—trades on several related themes. The seductive transition between watching and killing is reflected by the sequences shot from the killers' point of view in *Dressed to Kill* and *Blow Out,* echoing the voyeurism of so many of De Palma's heroes. The bonds that watching forges between the subject and the object of the gaze are revealed when the reporter Grace Collier (Jennifer Salt) comes to share the dream space of the murderous Danielle Breton in *Sisters,* when witnessing Kate Miller's murder makes Liz Blake (Nancy Allen) the killer's next victim in *Dressed to Kill,* and when Jake is forced to watch the murderous assault on the woman he has been spying on in *Body Double.* Sex is associated with violence, as so often in Hitchcock, in Carrie White's horror when she gets her first period in the girls' shower room in *Carrie* and in the masturbation scenes of Kate in *Dressed to Kill* and Gloria in *Body Double* as preludes to their slaughter. The ambivalent role of avenging kidnap victim Sandra Portinari in *Obsession,* the dying Kate's agonized reaching out to call-girl witness Liz in *Dressed to Kill,* and Gloria's rescue of her claustrophobic would-be rescuer Jake from the tunnel in *Body Double* all show the intimacy between victims and avengers. And the even more radical confusion between assailants and victims is dramatized by Danielle's terrified murder of Philip Woode (Lisle Wilson) in *Sisters,* Carrie's self-defensive crucifixion of her murderous mother (Piper Laurie) in *Carrie,* Liz Blake's persistent mistaking of her police guardian, Betty Luce (Susanna Clemm), with her razor-wielding double Bobbi in *Dressed to Kill,* and Sally's bashing of her cohort Manny Karp (Dennis Franz) when he forces himself on her in his red-and-green hotel room, with a vertical neon sign outside showing only the letters "HOT"—a reference both to the Empire Hotel sign that casts a lurid green light over Judy's transformation to Madeleine in *Vertigo* and to the Hotel Europe sign in *Foreign Correspondent* that Huntley Haverstock's flight transforms to "HOT EUROPE."

Why does De Palma compound his offense by stealing so much more than he can comfortably carry? Partly, as Robin Wood, has pointed out, to construct "a complex dialectic of affinity and difference" with his Hitchcockian model;[10] partly to overload his films with contradictory meanings drawn from an allegedly monolithic source in order to explode that source's coherence; partly to set his work apart from the endless recycling of figures and motifs typical of Hollywood at its most banal; and partly to provide a model of intertextuality richer and more challenging than the more-of-the-same model the industry seems to prescribe. The relations among these rationales are best illuminated by the more specific rules De Palma's thefts observe.

Make Sure Your Thefts from Hitchcock Take
Precedence Over All Your Other Thefts

Apart from their explicitly acknowledged literary sources (Stephen King's novel *Carrie*, John Farris's *The Fury*, Edwin Torres's *Carlito's Way* and *After Hours*, even Tom Wolfe's *The Bonfire of the Vanities*) and their inspirations in popular culture (*Mission: Impossible*, 1996), De Palma's films borrow from a wide range of materials. *Carrie*'s presentation of high-school culture owes a good deal to *American Graffiti*, and the elaborate forward-moving Steadicam shots that follow Dr. Waldheim (Frances Sternhagen) on her meandering way through the corridors of *Raising Cain* and take Rick Santoro (Nicolas Cage) through the backstage maze of the Atlantic City boxing arena in *Snake Eyes* (1998) are modeled on the tour de force of Henry Hill's entrance to the Copacabana in *GoodFellas*. The railroad-station shootouts of *Carlito's Way* (1993) and especially *The Untouchables* include brazen homages to the Odessa Steps sequence in *Potemkin*. De Palma himself identified Buñuel as a more pervasive influence on *Dressed to Kill* than Hitchcock, and even critics who disagreed noted the debt the film's deceptive opening dream owed to *Belle de jour*. *Scarface* is an update of the 1932 gangster film Ben Hecht wrote for Howard Hawks, though De Palma's credits mention Hecht and Hawks only in its closing dedication. *Blow Out*, with its echoes of Watergate, Chappaquiddick, and the JFK assassination, owes a more obvious debt to *Blow-Up*, *The Conversation*, *The Parallax View*, and *Winter Kills* than to any Hitchcockian models. And the single most decisive influence on *Raising Cain* is *Peeping Tom*, Michael Powell's creepy essay on the catastrophic things fathers do to their sons. Other films reviewers have cited as sources for De Palma include *Halloween*, *The Texas Chainsaw Massacre*, *The Godfather*, *The Silence of the Lambs*, *Echoes of Silence*, *David Holtzman's Diary*, and *Alice Doesn't Live Here Anymore*.

On its own terms this list of sources and influences is unremarkable. What is remarkable is that although he has often been accused of stealing, De Palma has never been accused of stealing from Tom Wolfe or Luis Buñuel or Howard Hawks. Quite the contrary: reviewers have been virtually unanimous in distancing him from all his other sources, dismissing his claim that *Dressed to Kill* owed any significant debt to Buñuel's peerlessly naughty sexual surrealism, that he had succeeded in shoehorning Tom Wolfe's sprawling novel into two hours, or that his update of the Depression-era gangster was worthy to stand alongside Hawks' model. The reason why is presumably that some thefts are so inevitable or laudable that they escape the name *thefts*. Adaptations of novels are expected to steal their material as faithfully as possible: for most reviewers, that's the whole point of adaptation. And eye-level two-shots are such an obvious and idiomatic device for shooting dialogue scenes that no filmmaker who depends on them is likely to be accused of stealing from Hawks. But borrowing Hitchcock's trick of dispensing with dialogue for long scenes in *Obsession*, *Body Double*, and especially *Dressed to Kill;* bringing Hitchcock's favorite composer back to Hollywood after a long absence; staging one violent tableau after another inside a shower . . . Such devices are so gratuitous that they efface all subsidiary thefts, reinforcing a line indispensable to critical orthodoxy between thefts that count as thefts and thefts that don't, or between bad thefts and good.

Flaunt Your Thefts

De Palma may be a copycat, but he is no plagiarist. Though he has grumbled about being too easily tagged as a Hitchcock wannabe, the texts of his films tell a different story, since they take extraordinary pains to emphasize every point at which his material is stolen from Hitchcock. Indeed a distinctive pleasure to be had from De Palma's most brazen thefts is identifying their relation to their sources. De Palma's thefts are so often gratuitous that viewers are left gaping, for instance, at the farcical shower interlude in *Phantom of the Paradise* or at the *Potemkin*-inspired sequence in *The Untouchables* in which the baby carriage glides in surrealistic slow motion down a flight of stairs on which a gun battle is imminent. In this regard, De Palma's thefts go beyond derivations, beyond even allusions, and become directorial signatures comparable to Bernardo Bertolucci's dance sequences, Hawks' recycling of dialogue tags like "It [kissing] is even better when you help," and Hitchcock's own cameo appearances.

It is ironic that so many of the same reviewers who complained for years about De Palma's freely and brazenly acknowledged thefts from Hitchcock also complained about De Palma's baroque, mannerist style. David Ansen spoke for many of them in remarking that "De Palma hasn't crafted his story with the same care that goes into his shots" in *Blow Out*.[11] By the time of *Raising Cain*, contended Jonathan Romney, the "flauntings of signature [that] jeopardised the narrative or stylistic coherence" of *The Untouchables* and *Casualties of War* (1989) had overwhelmed the film, which "jettisons coherence from the start; it is an extended hysterical assertion of De Palma trademarks."[12] The truism that De Palma was a pictorialist rather than a storyteller, coupled with the observation that he was always ready to sacrifice narrative coherence for the sake of a great image, took root early.

There are several ironies here. The most obvious is the tacit but universal preference for a realistic, self-effacing style that emphasizes narrative coherence over visual manner, as if the first were self-evidently more important than the second. Scarcely less obvious is the damned-if-you-don't argument that condemns De Palma for the brazen gratuitousness of his Hitchcock thefts, even though it would condemn him even more strongly if he sought to conceal those thefts—unless, of course, he concealed them by assimilating them into what Sarris in another connection has called a personal style [q.v.], in which case they would no longer be thefts. A more piquant irony is that Ansen and Romney are condemning De Palma in contrast to Hitchcock for precisely the same sins for which so many early reviewers castigated Hitchcock. Graham Greene's review of *The Secret Agent,* for example, complains that Hitchcock's films consist of "a series of small 'amusing' melodramatic situations . . . Very perfunctorily he builds up to these tricky situations (paying no attention on the way to inconsistencies, loose ends, psychological absurdities) and then drops them; they mean nothing; they lead to nothing." [13]

By the time De Palma's career began, of course, Hitchcock's stylistic excesses, widely criticized by studio bosses like C. M. Woolf as well as early reviewers like Greene, had largely been converted in the popular imagination into a classic balance of expressive signatures with narrative equipoise. But this conversion cannot have been motivated simply by the fact that Hitchcock's films became more realistic, since virtually all the reviewers of his American films agreed that, for better or worse, they were even less realistic than his British films. *Secret Agent* is surely a manneristic film, but it is no more obviously an exercise in style than *Foreign Correspondent, Lifeboat, Rope, Rear Window, Vertigo,* or *Frenzy.* It seems likely Hitchcock became eligible for canonization not because he toned down the expressiveness so many of his earlier viewers found disruptive or trivializing, but because his once-bristling stylistic expressiveness entered the Hollywood mainstream through his own half-century example, his influence on a generation of filmmakers, the long tenure of the more proletarian expressiveness of film noir, and the bracing counterexample of even more mannerist epigones like De Palma.

But there are still more ironies to be mined from critical revulsion to De Palma's mannerism. In reviewing *Dressed to Kill,* Andrew Sarris rejected De Palma's equation of himself with Buñuel on the grounds that, "from the beginning, Buñuel's style has been disconcertingly direct and uncluttered, in contrast to De Palma's ego-enhancing mannerist flourishes," [14] and J. Hoberman expressed a corresponding reservation in his generally favorable interview: "What's disturbing is not that De Palma uses Hitchcock so much as the

flaming mannerism with which he does so."[15] Richard Combs noted on the
same occasion that "because De Palma's suspense mechanisms are so free of
emotional content, they become enjoyable simply as absurd conceits, more
dada than Hitchcock."[16] There is a good deal of truth in all these assertions,
especially the last—even though it overlooks the extent to which contemporary reviewers of Hitchcock up through *Vertigo* considered his films more
dada than Hitchcock as well. What they overlook in their equation of mannerism with ego-enhancement is the peculiar nature of De Palma's Hitchcock
thefts as directorial signatures. Because they reveal De Palma's directorial presence by referring more directly to some other director, typically Hitchcock,
they are in a peculiar way more modest than their analogues in Bertolucci or
Hawks, certainly more self-effacing than their Hitchcockian models. As Kenneth MacKinnon announced in reviewing *Dressed to Kill:* "De Palma's work
increasingly demands assessment on a broadly authorial basis as, paradoxically,
it seems increasingly to borrow from, or embroider on, Hitchcock."[17] De
Palma, in other words, is the auteur whose authorship is secured precisely by
his thefts; the meaning of each of his thefts is inseparable from the fact that it
is expected to be recognized as a theft. This paradox can be resolved only by
the deeper paradox of another rule.

Earn Your Thefts by Making Them Yours

At first this prescription seems like nonsense. How can you earn a theft, which
by definition is stolen rather than earned? And how can you make a theft
yours when whatever you've stolen belongs to someone else? The economy
of film authorship as it has traditionally been conceived dictates two mutually
exclusive intertextual positions. Assuming they make no attempt to invent a
wholly new cinematic grammar that would likely baffle and repel audiences,
aspiring filmmakers are left with two possibilities: either plagiarize from particular filmmakers you admire and hope you don't get caught, or restrict your
borrowings to conventions so widely used (shot-reversals, eyeline matches,
crosscutting, overdetermined musical cues, and so on) that they have entered
the public domain.

De Palma's work is a scandal to establishment cinema because it suggests
a third practice that indicates the impossibility of rationalizing either of the
other two. Whether because of its ontology (the photographic specificity of the
film medium), its economics (the capital intensiveness that has concentrated
mainstream filmmaking in the hands of a small number of corporations), or its
legal status (films and sequences can be copyrighted, but camera setups and

lighting effects cannot), cinema has never made the sharp distinction between plagiarism and fair-use copying, or copying material in the public domain, that publishing has. After a certain number of years, copyrighted films pass into the public domain, but even before they do, they are hardly impervious to theft. Apart from frequent lawsuits tellingly alleging theft from an earlier screenplay and more occasional suits involving the literal replication of original footage or sound, has any filmmaker ever successfully been prosecuted for copying, imitating, or borrowing from another film? Just as it would be impossible for even the most high-minded filmmaker to shoot a feature without recourse to the example of earlier filmmakers, the vulnerability of movies to imitation, homage, parody, and theft makes it as impossible to protect a classic film from imitators as it is for the imitators to conceal their thefts, and Hitchcock's films have been directly quoted in extenso not only by De Palma but by filmmakers as different as François Truffaut, Claude Chabrol, and Mel Brooks.

Most of these references pass either unnoticed (because they are so generalized or understated) or unreproved (because their contexts imply such officially sanctioned categories as parody, homage, or quotation). De Palma's case is scandalous because his Hitchcock borrowings are so frequent, literal, and obsessively focused that he forces what would otherwise be the silence greeting the implicitly sanctioned inevitability of intertextual reference to yield to uncomfortable questions of intertextual theft—questions that get tougher as his borrowings become more baroque.

Take the most notorious of De Palma's Hitchcock thefts: the shower scene from *Psycho*. Avoiding any direct reference to the scene in the *Psycho*-esque *Sisters* (which does, however, include an important scene set in an antiseptically white bathroom when Philip inadvertently brushes what turns out to be Danielle's antipsychotic medication down the drain), De Palma introduces it as a stand-alone parody in *Phantom of the Paradise,* obeying the unwritten rules for approved borrowing. When he returns to the shower for the opening of *Carrie* to show his teenaged heroine, kept in ignorance of her own sexuality by her minatory evangelist mother, it is both more and less like its model in *Psycho*. More, because it is not a joke but part of an elaborate pattern that links blood (now the menstrual blood a horrified Carrie finds between her legs) to forbidden sex, invoking not only *Psycho* but *Marnie* through the puritanical condemnations of the alienated heroine's formerly promiscuous mother; less, because it is not set up as a scary scene—the location, the girls' shower room in a public-school gym, could hardly be more public or reassuringly peopled, and the flute music is deceptively gentle—and because the murderous aftermath, when it does come in the form of dozens of hostile fellow students responding to Carrie's uncomprehending pleas for help by hurling tampons at her and shouting "plug it up!", is symbolic rather than literal. Yet even these differences depend for their effectiveness on the analogy to *Psycho,* which allows the audience to appreciate the way in which this is indeed a scary scene focusing on Carrie's horror of her own body and her symbolic murder at the outset of her story, a point viewers would be much less likely to appreciate if they did not recognize the allusion to Hitchcock.

The shower scenes that bracket *Dressed to Kill* are far more literal echoes of *Psycho* in both tone and import. Once again, however, the differences are critical. Kate Miller's languorous masturbation fantasy that opens the film combines the activities of the two principals in Hitchcock's scene—Marion, eager for a purifying escape from her troubles, and Norman, presumably masturbating to the sight of her in the next room. De Palma not only places both male and female performers in the same space but changes both the dynamic between them (the shaving husband is now ignoring his wife's pleading face and seductive gyrations, even when she is assaulted by another man who magically appears in the shower behind her) and the dramatic proportions of the sequence (which now, even allowing for the differences in contemporary cinematic representations of sexuality, includes more sexual byplay and less violence). The emphasis of sex over violence—an emphasis absent from the De Palma's first version of the scene, in which a naked man shaving ended up castrating himself with his razor[18]—is logical because this sequence is only a prelude to the film's shocking central set piece, the elevator murder that alludes more obliquely but terrifyingly to the shower sequence and emphasizes violence to the virtual exclusion of sex. In the final scene, as Bobbi, escaped from Bellevue, stalks Liz in Kate's shower, De Palma retains Hitchcock's mise-en-scène while reversing its dramatic valence. By this point, not even audiences who had never seen *Psycho* could possibly take the shower as a place of safe refuge for Liz, especially since De Palma intercuts Liz's shower with teasing shots of Bobbi's feet in the white shoes she stole from the nurse she strangled. To use Hitchcock's distinction, this final sequence is a suspense murder rather than a surprise murder: instead of soaping herself, placid and unwitting, until she is killed in a flurry of quick cuts, Liz hears Bobbi breaking in, turns off the shower, and, in an excruciatingly prolonged sequence, tiptoes toward the medicine cabinet and the razor inside as Bobbi's feet wait in obliging immobility until the fatal moment when Liz sees Bobbi's face reflected in the mirror—capping two hours of fatal mirror images, from Dr. Elliott's smiling glance at his own mirrored face as he deflects Kate's question of why he doesn't sleep with her to the cab driver's avid readjustment of his rearview

mirror reflecting Kate and her pickup having sex in his backseat to Liz's traumatic sight of Bobbi's face reflected in the elevator mirror to the cab driver's
glimpse of the policewoman he thinks is Bobbi in his outside rearview mirror
to Elliott's face reflected once more in the mirror on his desk as he responds
to Liz's come-on by smiling and loosening his necktie. Bobbi cannot kill Liz
until Liz sees her in the mirror because the sight of her face completes the
pattern. In every case, the mirror allows the person reflected to return the
watcher's gaze, breaking down the barrier voyeurs build to protect themselves
from identification with the people they are watching. De Palma's most outra-
geously mannerist, ritualized use of Hitchcock's signature scene literalizes its
sexual charge and slows its pace to the point of parody in order to make not
Hitchcock's point—we are as others see us—but his own: we are what we see,
we are what we dream.

The dreamiest of all De Palma's shower scenes, of course, comes at the beginning of *Blow Out,* in the sophomoric parody of the film-within-a-film *Coed
Frenzy,* which borrows from *Halloween* the killer's point of view for a series
of gliding Steadicam shots through a dormitory whose tenants evidently do
nothing but dance topless, party, make love, and of course shower as a knife-
wielding hand closes in on them. The victim's comically inadequate scream
not only kicks off the plot, as sound recordist Jack Terry's slimeball boss Sam
(Peter Boyden) orders him to find a better scream and Jack responds by taking his rifle-shaped mike and recording rig to the Wissahocken Creek Bridge,
where he will end up recording the sounds of Governor George McRyan's
fatal car crash, but also lays the groundwork for its epilogue. In the sickest joke
of his career, De Palma cuts from Jack's apartment, where the dazed recordist
is listening to his tape of the final moments before McRyan's companion Sally
(Nancy Allen), whom Jack had wired so that he could follow her, was killed
by the soldier-of-fortune Burke (John Lithgow) to a screening room where
Coed Frenzy is being shown again, now with Sally's death scream dubbed in.
Reviewers of *Blow Out* were quick to point out that this final scene "trashes
[Jack's] character completely."[19] Why would he volunteer this tape for a job
for he's held in contempt from the beginning, especially since he's already
changed from someone "physically revolted by [Sally's] unsavory past" to an
idealistic hero distraught with grief at her death?[20] What critics overlooked
or ignored was the fact that the film has from its opening sequence consistently subordinated any psychological interest in the characters to the logic of
dreams, nightmares, wishes, fantasies, quotations, allusions, and sick jokes.

Blow Out represents the culmination of De Palma's tendency to displace
psychology by a logic of overdetermined intertextuality in which relations

among the fictional characters, as in Hitchcock's late films for Universal, are always less important than the relation between filmmaker and audience, a relation which is mediated primarily by intertexts outside the frame rather than fictional characters within. This tendency is intensified still further by the shower scene in *Body Double,* a throwaway epilogue in which Jake, having proved by overcoming his claustrophobia and rescuing Holly from the open grave the villain has dug for them his worthiness to work in the porn industry to which Holly has introduced him, poses as a lustful vampire in a shower with a porn starlet who is replaced just after the establishing shot by a body double whose breasts Jake can fondle in close-ups. The reference, as De Palma has acknowledged, is only incidentally to *Psycho;* the scene's true inspiration is the opening scene in *Dressed to Kill,* in which Angie Dickinson, like Janet Leigh before her, was replaced for all but facial close-ups and head-and-shoulders shots by a body double. As in the sick framing joke of *Blow Out,* De Palma is imitating himself imitating Hitchcock, and each new remove adds new ironies.

But are these ironies really earned? This question has been the crux of De Palma commentary, with Andrew Sarris arguing on one hand that De Palma "steals Hitchcock's most privileged moments without performing the drudgery of building up to these moments as thoroughly earned climaxes,"[21] and Robin Wood on the other hand citing *Blow Out*'s notoriously overblown climax, which sets the deaths of Sally and Burke against Philadelphia's deafening, witless celebration of Liberty Day: "The excess, the flamboyance, the cinematic rhetoric, are here entirely earned by the context."[22] The disagreement is compounded by different notions of context (Sarris's is psychological and narrative, Wood's political, sexual, and thematic) and earning (Sarris's privileged moments must be earned textually, but Wood's may be earned intertextually). An even more fundamental disagreement, however, surrounds the words *privileged* and *rhetoric.*

In defending De Palma against the charge of "inert" imitation, Wood asserts that Hollywood recognizes originality, in a debased version of the relatively recent rise of originality as an aesthetic criterion in Romantic art and criticism, "either if the viewer is ignorant of [a film's] sources or if it imitates a (generally European) model of critically ratified 'genius.'"[23] Tendentious as this argument may seem, it would be even stronger if it were pushed further, since the attack on De Palma's lack of originality for failing to earn his borrowings from Hitchcock waives the whole question of how original Hitchcock's privileged moments were, and what precisely he had done to earn them in the first place. In a medium whose syntax is helplessly empirical and derivative, and whose every individual image is literally copied from life, what does it mean to be original?

Aestheticians as far back as Rudolf Arnheim have been wrestling with this question, but De Palma suggests an answer everybody but the theorists already knows: Movies are never original. De Palma's shower scenes clearly refer to the shower scene in *Psycho*, but what makes Hitchcock's scene a privileged moment is not its originality but its prodigious influence. Its authority stems not from its being the first movie scene set in a shower, or the first to stage a murder in a shower, but from its success in using both this pivotal scene and its immediate context (the banality of the world Marion Crane seeks to escape, her surprising affinities with her murderer, Lila Crane's tour of the Bates house as a demystification of the Bates family, the consistent tone of black comedy) to effect a powerful reconfiguration of the horror film, lodging its alien monster, as Wood has often remarked, in the heart of the American family, and using Hitchcock's commercial and critical prestige to bring that new vision into the mainstream of American cinema. Neither *Psycho*'s story nor its mise-en-scène was Hitchcock's invention; both were adapted, along with many other signature touches, from Robert Bloch's 1958 pulp novel. Hitchcock can be said to earn the shower scene most obviously by paying Bloch for the adaptation rights, and to make the scene his own by the details he adds (the much more elaborate buildup of Marion's theft, interior and exterior iconography juxtaposing a banal American commercial landscape with the conventions of Hollywood Gothic, staging Marion's murder in much more brutal detail than Bloch) and changes (making Norman younger and more wholesome-seeming, encouraging viewers to share Marion's point of view rather than Norman's until the doubly shocking moment when she is attacked). Despite initially mixed reviews, the film's box-office success, coupled with the concurrent rise of Hitchcock's stock as the exemplary Hollywood auteur, encouraged critics to take it more seriously, valorizing it rather than Bloch's novel, Hitchcock's earlier bathroom scenes, or any of the hundreds of previous films that had encouraged their viewers to identify closely with an imperiled or transgressive heroine as significant. But this respectful attention arose from a confluence of many circumstances, not simply from the unquestioned textual brilliance of the film itself.

More generally, although a few of the Hitchcock signatures to which De Palma keeps returning—the shower scene, the 360-degree pan—are uniquely associated with Hitchcock (despite, for example, Jean-Luc Godard's use of an even more stylized 360-degree pan in the Action Musicale segment of *Weekend*), many others—the obsession with voyeurism, the persistent doubling of

characters with their nominal opposites, the fondness for sexual double enten-
dres and black humor—are the province of a much wider array of filmmakers.
It is clear not only from De Palma's own interviews but from the violence they
visit upon women that De Palma's shower scenes refer specifically to *Psycho*.
But why is it so certain that his even more numerous 360-degree pans refer to
Scottie and Judy's embrace in *Vertigo* rather than Godard's shot, or for that
matter the 360-degree swish-pan that indicates the heroine's fainting in 1934's
The Man Who Knew Too Much?

This question can be partly answered by considering the textual and thematic features De Palma's 360-degree pans share with the shot from *Vertigo*.
The pan that takes Michael Courtland from 1959 to 1975 in *Obsession* invokes
not Scottie's dazed exaltation at having re-created his lost love but his initial
grief at having lost her, just as the delirious final reunion of Michael with the
disappearing fiancée he has determined to kill show him changing his mind
and acknowledging her as his daughter rather than refusing to accept her
as she is. The 360-degree pan in between that introduces Sandra to her late
mother's locked bedroom recalls both the keys Alicia Huberman has acquired
in *Notorious* and Lila's investigation of the Bates house in *Psycho*. The prom
climax of *Carrie* quotes Hitchcock's *Vertigo* shot much more literally, showing Carrie and Tommy Ross (William Katt) spinning in a surrealistically dance
as the camera circles them, but this time the context itself is ironic, since De
Palma has broadly hinted that Carrie's dreams of teen romance, themselves a
far cry from the romantic obsession of *Vertigo* and *Obsession,* are about to be
shattered. The 360-degree pans in *Blow Out*—one circling Jack in his apartment as he realizes all his tapes have been erased, another heightening his
panic as he listens to Sally and Burke on his live feed and struggles to find a
clue where they are going—isolate Jack from Sally, emphasizing his dedication to his work, his paramount determination to protect his videotape rather
than her. And the 360-degree pans in *Scarface* (Tony Montana [Al Pacino]
passing through immigration) and *The Untouchables* (the title characters cel-
ebrating their first big success) are even more thematically remote from their
stylistic inspiration. Only the corresponding shot in *Body Double* in which
Jake embraces Gloria outside the tunnel from which she has rescued him,
showing the background madly spinning from the brilliant colors of the beach
to the stylized drawing of sailboats on the wall to the grim tunnel interior as
Jake repeatedly confuses the Gloria he is groping with the nude performer—
actually Holly Body—who first captured his interest, recycles all the leading
elements of Hitchcock's shot, and even this shot flattens Hitchcock's romantic
obsession by making Jake's attraction to Gloria much more explicitly sexual.

All the others, like De Palma's shower scenes, quote Hitchcock expressly in order to mark De Palma's distance from him. Instead of naturalizing his inevitable stylistic borrowings by assimilating them into the unmarked rhetoric of Hollywood cinema, De Palma heightens their status as allusions by making them ever more ironic, more gratuitous, more stylized, more mannerist. Such a development can have only one logical conclusion.

Start by Stealing from Hitchcock, End by Stealing from Yourself

Several of the reviewers who recoiled from the intertextual maze of *Blow Out* argued that De Palma was now more interested in recycling "the more outrageous of his own past practices"[24] than anything from Hitchcock (a suggestion that had first surfaced the year before when *Dressed to Kill*'s climactic dream sequence so closely echoed the epilogue of *Carrie*). Generally speaking, this tendency toward self-quotation caps a distinct trajectory in the career of De Palma's thefts. They begin as the detachable jokes and parodies of *Hi, Mom!* and *Phantom of the Paradise;* they proceed to press Hitchcockian motifs into unexpected contexts in *Carrie* or into the unofficial remakes of *Sisters, Obsession,* and *Dressed to Kill* that use Hitchcock's signature techniques to reopen Hitchcock's signature thematic questions; and they broaden into self-quotation and self-parody in *Blow Out, Dressed to Kill,* and *Raising Cain.*

Whatever one thinks of these last three films and of De Palma's tendency to substitute self-quotation for quotation from Hitchcock, there can be no doubt that the results are thoroughly characteristic of De Palma as the auteur without portfolio, the filmmaker whose closest approach to self-definition is that he is clamorously not Alfred Hitchcock. De Palma's frequent references to Hitchcock as the filmmaker who best incarnates the zero degree of Hollywood style obscures the fact that Hitchcock is often willfully as mannerist and prone to self-quotation as De Palma, and that De Palma's latest films are his most mannerist of all. In turning from quoting Hitchcock to quoting himself, De Palma is simply following Hitchcock's own formula for defining an individual style. Even more characteristic of his work than the shower scenes, 360-degree pans, and wordless set pieces extrapolated from Scottie's pursuit of Madeleine in *Vertigo,* for example, are two devices associated much more closely with De Palma. The first is the slow-motion sequences favored as well by Sam Peckinpah to inflate and prolong big dramatic moments, from *Carrie* to *Raising Cain.* The second, even more idiosyncratic, is split-screen sequences that owe less to the moment in *Marnie* that shows the thieving heroine robbing the Rutland safe on one side of the screen while an oblivious cleaning woman toils in the next office on the other side than to De Palma's film version of *Dionysus in '69* (1969), presented in triptych with the stage show sandwiched between continuous reaction shots of the audience. Pressed into service to literalize the doublings of *Sisters, Dressed to Kill, Blow Out,* and *Snake Eyes* and suggested more subtly by many *Marnie*-esque setups in *Obsession,* the device has ironically earned De Palma at least one negative criticism, in John McCarty's review of *Sisters,* for departing too licentiously from his Hitchcockian model by using a technique Hitchcock never employed.[25]

It might seem that De Palma is asking too much of slow-motion and split-screen, which are inadequate in themselves to constitute a recognizable style. But surely they are integrated in his case into a larger system of signatures, though one at key points very different from Hitchcock's: an essentially scenic and visual imagination, a fascination with set pieces, a sovereign disdain for character, a surprising sympathy for the problems of women, an inveterately dark sense of humor, a determination to push the envelope of censorship, a keen eye for color, a fondness for parody and self-parody, an attachment to scruffy character actors like William Finley and Dennis Franz rather than stalwart romantic heroes like James Stewart and Cary Grant, and a romantic yearning to hold the pivotal moments in his films for as long as possible (as if he were a Hitchcock who had never learned the lessons of *Rope* and *Under Capricorn*). The sensibility these ingredients imply would be highly unlikely to develop a visual style as integrated, not to say as inescapable, as Hitchcock's. De Palma may not be the ironist his defenders consider him, but his echoes of the establishment icon Hitchcock do nothing to hide De Palma the iconoclast, the director whose authority comes from his thefts.

Honor Hitchcock as You Honor Yourself

Galling as it may have been for De Palma to find himself recast from "the heir to Hitchcock's throne" to "the scavenger of his vaults,"[26] there can be no doubt that De Palma's High Hitchcock period—roughly the ten years from *Sisters* to *Body Double*—was, if not his most commercially successful, certainly his most critically distinctive. Before gravitating to the Hitchcockian models of *Rear Window, Vertigo,* and *Psycho,* De Palma had enjoyed only modest success as one of a score of promising independent filmmakers, and neither the counterculture testaments of *Greetings* (1968) and *Hi, Mom!,* now best remembered as showcases for the young Robert De Niro, nor the calculated commercialism of *Get to Know Your Rabbit* (1972), his biggest-budget project before *Sisters,* had given him a more distinctive profile. It was through his

Hitchcock homages that De Palma found his own voice—a voice that began to fade as early as *Scarface* and was almost completely buried under the high gloss of *Mission: Impossible* and *Mission to Mars* (2000). De Palma before and after his Hitchcock phase has been a minor filmmaker. His Hitchcock thefts have honored him not only with lively critical controversy and commercial success but with his greatest influence over a generation of horror films whose highly allusive throwaway black humor owes a great deal more to De Palma than to Hitchcock.

In the end, however, Hitchcock owes as much to De Palma as De Palma does to Hitchcock. If the master of suspense declined to profit from whatever filmmaking lessons *Sisters* and *Obsession* might have offered him, his legacy from his most ardent disciple was vastly more important. By ripping off the shower scene, De Palma established that scene as a locus classicus of commercial cinema. Obsessively recycling a single 360-degree pan from *Vertigo,* he valorized the shot, its film, and the sensibility that had left reviewers cold in 1958—a sensibility the corresponding reviewers were only too ready to dismiss him for having missed in 1975. *Psycho* had been called many things before De Palma—disgusting, shocking, disappointing, influential—but De Palma's devotion to it finally made it necessary to call it original in order to mark his failure to duplicate it. In short, the classic status commentators have claimed for Hitchcock in order to proclaim his superiority to De Palma is not so much a cause of De Palma's devotion to his master as an effect of it. By establishing himself as the anti-Hitchcock, De Palma has helped make it possible for a generation of filmgoers to invest Hitchcock as a classic.

Notes

1. Richard Corliss, "Bad Crash," *Time* 118 (27 July 1981): 62.
2. Marcia Palley, "'Double' Trouble," *Film Comment* 20: 5 (September-October 1984): 17.
3. Julie Salamon, *The Devil's Candy: The Bonfire of the Vanities Goes to Hollywood* (Boston: Houghton Mifflin, 1991), p. 397.
4. Jonathan Baumbach, "Show-Offs," *Partisan Review* 41 (1974): 276.
5. Pauline Kael, *When the Lights Go Down* (New York: Holt, Rinehart & Winston, 1980), p. 209.
6. Andrew Sarris, "De Palma: Derivative," *Village Voice* 25: 30 (23–29 July 1980): 42.
7. Sheila Benson, "Elevating Voyeurism to New Lows," *Los Angeles Times,* 26 October 1984, Calendar, p. 20.
8. Kenneth MacKinnon, *Misogyny in the Movies: The De Palma Question* (Newark: University of Delaware Press, 1990); Laurent Bouzereau, *The De Palma Cut: The Films of America's Most Controversial Director* (New York: Dembner, 1988), p. 13; Susan Dworkin, *Double De Palma: A Film Study with Brian De Palma* (New York: Newmarket, 1984), p. 10; Michael

Bliss, *Brian De Palma* [*Filmmakers,* no. 6] (Metuchen, NJ: Scarecrow, 1983), p. xiii; Robin Wood, "Brian De Palma: The Politics of Castration," in *Hollywood from Vietnam to Reagan* (New York: Columbia University Press, 1986), p. 139.

9. Dworkin, p. 10.

10. Wood, p. 140.

11. David Ansen, "The Sound of Murder," *Newsweek* 98 (27 July 1981): 74.

12. Jonathan Romney, "*Raising Cain,*" *Sight and Sound* 2: 8 (December 1992): 46.

13. Graham Greene, *Graham Greene on Film: Collected Film Criticism, 1935–1939* (New York: Simon and Schuster, 1972), p. 75.

14. Andrew Sarris, "Dreck to Kill," *Village Voice* 25: 38 (17–23 September 1980): 44.

15. J. Hoberman, "De Palma: Dazzling," *Village Voice* 25:30 (23–29 July 1980): 44.

16. Richard Combs, "*Dressed to Kill,*" *Monthly Film Bulletin* (November 1980): 213.

17. Kenneth MacKinnon, "*Dressed to Kill,*" *Film Quarterly* 35: 1 (Fall 1981): 42.

18. Bouzereau reprints the screenplay for the original opening scene in *The De Palma Cut,* pp. 11–12.

19. Sheila Benson, "Movies: Slinky Spy, Suspicious Sound Man," *Los Angeles Times,* 24 July 1981, Calendar, p. 10.

20. Andrew Sarris, "Needle in the Haystack," *Village Voice* 26: 31 (29 July–4 August 1981): 35.

21. Sarris, "Dreck to Kill," p. 44.

22. Wood, p. 160.

23. Wood, p. 140.

24. John Coleman, "Films: *Blow Out* and *Endless Love,*" *New Statesman* 102, no. 2640 (23 October 1981): 27.

25. John McCarty, "*Sisters,*" *Cinefantastique* 3 (Fall 1973): 28.

26. Richard Corliss, "Knife of Brian," *Time* 116 (28 July 1980): 66.

Notes on Contributors

Ernesto R. Acevedo-Muñoz is Associate Professor of Film Studies, Comparative Literature, and Humanities, and Associate Director of the Film Studies Program at the University of Colorado at Boulder. He is the author of *Buñuel and Mexico: The Crisis of National Cinema* (California, 2003) and of several articles published in *Quarterly Review of Film and Video, Film and History, Lit: Literature Interpretation Theory,* and various anthologies. He is currently writing a book on Pedro Almodóvar.

John Belton is a professor of English at Rutgers University, where he teaches courses in American cinema and film theory. Belton is the author of many journal articles and book chapters devoted to various aspects of American film history and film theory. His books on the cinema include *Widescreen Cinema* (Harvard, 1992), the textbook *American Cinema/American Culture* (McGraw-Hill Humanities, 1993; second edition 2004), and *Alfred Hitchcock's Rear Window* (Cambridge, 1999).

David Boyd is research associate in English and film at the University of Newcastle in Australia. He is the author of *Film and the Interpretive Process* (Peter Lang, 1989), editor of *Perspectives on Alfred Hitchcock* (G. K. Hall, 1995), and coeditor of *Re-Reading Frye: The Published and Unpublished Works* (University of Toronto Press, 1999).

Lesley Brill is professor of English at Wayne State University, where he teaches courses in Alfred Hitchcock and introduction to film. Brill's film criticism has appeared widely in academic journals and as book chapters. He has also published *The Hitchcock Romance* (Princeton, 1988) and *John Huston's Film-making* (Cambridge, 1997).

Ina Rae Hark is professor of English and film studies at the University of South Carolina. She is an editor of *Screening the Male, The Road Movie Book, Exhibition: The Film Reader,* and the forthcoming volume on the 1930s in the *Screen Decades* series. Her essays on a broad spectrum of American film and television have appeared in over thirty different venues, including *Cinema Journal, Film History, QRFV, Literature/Film Quarterly, Journal of Popular Film, Hitchcock's Rereleased Films, Alfred Hitchcock Centenary Essays,* and *Film and Television After 9/11.*

Adam Knee is assistant professor in the School of Film at Ohio University and has previously taught at universities in Thailand, Taiwan, and Australia. His writing on film has appeared in a variety of academic journals, as well as in such anthologies as *Horror International* (ed. Steven Jay Schneider and Tony Williams, Wayne State, 2005); *Moving Pictures, Migrating Identities: Exile and Migration in Cinema* (ed. Eva Rueschmann, Mississippi, 2003), and *Soundtrack Available: Essays on Film and Pop Music* (ed. Pamela Wojcik and Arthur Knight, Duke, 2001).

Thomas M. Leitch is professor of English at the University of Delaware. He has a special interest in such popular narrative modes as detective stories and Hollywood genre films (Westerns, musicals, gangster films, and comedies of all sorts). Since 1989 he has reviewed mystery and suspense fiction for *Kirkus Reviews,* where he is Senior Editor. Leitch is the author of *What Stories Are: Narrative Theory and Interpretation* (Penn State, 1986), *Find the Director and Other Hitchcock Games* (Georgia, 1991), *Crime Films* (Cambridge, 2002), and *The Encyclopedia of Alfred Hitchcock* (Checkmark, 2002).

Philippe Met is associate professor of French at the University of Pennsylvania. A specialist in modern poetry and the fantastic, he has published *Formules de la poésie* (PUF, 1999) and is editing a collection of critical essays on the poetry of André du Bouchet and writing a book on the subversion of signs in fantastic literature. His interests in film studies include international horror cinema and French film noir. A current book project is an examination of the figure of the child and other representations of childhood in films.

Walter Metz teaches the history, theory, and criticism of film, television, and theater at Montana State University. He is a specialist in intertextual film theory, having just published his first monograph, *Engaging Film Criticism: Film History and Contemporary American Cinema* (Peter Lang, 2004). He is the author of numerous academic journal articles and book chapters on film adaptation, genre, and authorship. Metz was a 2003–2004 Fulbright Guest Professor at the John F. Kennedy Institute at the Free University in Berlin.

Richard Neupert is professor of film studies at the University of Georgia. His books include *A History of the French New Wave* (Wisconsin, 2002) and *The End: Narration and Closure in the Cinema* (Wayne State, 1995), as well as a translation from the French of Michel Marie's *The French New Wave: An Artistic School* (Blackwell, 2002) and Jacques Aumont et al., *Aesthetics of Film* (Texas, 1992).

R. Barton Palmer is Calhoun Lemon Professor of Literature and director of the film studies program at Clemson University. He is the author of *Joel and Ethan Coen* (Illinois, 2004) and *Hollywood's Dark Cinema: The American Film Noir* (second revised and expanded edition, Illinois, forthcoming) and has recently edited two volumes on film adaptations of literature for Cambridge University Press, *Nineteenth* and *Twentieth Century American Fiction on Screen* (2006). With Robert Bray, he wrote *Hollywood's Tennessee: Tennessee Williams on Screen* (forthcoming from University of Texas Press). With Linda Badley, Palmer serves as general editor of the *Traditions in World Cinema* series for the Edinburgh University Press; Badley and Palmer edited the flagship contributory volume for the series (2006) and are also writing a future entrant, *Contemporary American Commercial/Independent Film*. Palmer is the author of the forthcoming *David Cronenberg* (Illinois).

Robert Sklar is a professor of cinema studies at New York University, with major interests in screen studies, radio, gender, sport, and cultural policy and theory. Among his many books on film are *City Boys: Cagney, Bogart, Garfield, Performance and Politics in the Movies* (Princeton, 1992), *Prime-Time America: Life on and Behind the Television Screen* (Oxford, 1993), and *Movie-Made America: A Cultural History of American Movies* (Random House, 1994), which won the Theatre Library Association Award in 1975 for best book on motion pictures and television.

Frank P. Tomasulo is professor of film and director of the BFA Program at the Florida State University Film School in Tallahassee. Tomasulo has previously taught cinema history and theory, as well as film production and screenwriting, at Ithaca College, the University of California–Santa Cruz, Georgia

State University, and Southern Methodist University. The author of over sixty scholarly articles and essays, and 150 other academic papers, Tomasulo has also served as Editor of *Journal of Film and Video* (1991–1996) and *Cinema Journal* (1997–2002). His anthology on screen acting, *More than a Method: Trends and Traditions in Contemporary Film Performance* (2004), coedited with Cynthia Baron and Diane Carson, was published by Wayne State University Press.

Constantine Verevis teaches in the School of English, Communications and Performance Studies at Monash University, Melbourne. He has published widely in the area of film studies and is the author of *Film Remakes* (Edinburgh University Press, 2005).

Index